DATE DUE

DEC - 8 1995	

This book focuses on the behavior of the ruling families of Brescia, a rich and strategically vital city under Venetian rule, during the late sixteenth and early seventeenth centuries.

The first part of the book conceptualizes the civic leadership of Brescia, with a profile of its origins and a brief history of the process of aristocratization. Further, it examines the relationship between family structure and the local socio-political structures. Size, wealth, education, and marriage ties were all pivotal factors which helped determine the family's position in public life. Its strength rested ultimately on its continuity over time. Women and women's property are given careful attention. The second part places the Brescian elite within the Venetian state. Besides controlling urban political institutions, the Brescians held strong economic links with the surrounding countryside, the basis of their power, and they enjoyed ample authority in the rural communities subject to the city. This section of the book examines the different ways in which these families sought to preserve their control over local resources. It also analyzes the Brescian civic leadership's weight in public life, in relation to that of Venetian authorities, illuminating some of the important ways in which the Venetian state was knit together.

CAMBRIDGE STUDIES IN ITALIAN HISTORY AND CULTURE

FAMILY AND PUBLIC LIFE IN BRESCIA, 1580–1650

CAMBRIDGE STUDIES IN ITALIAN HISTORY AND CULTURE

Edited by GIORGIO CHITTOLINI, Università degli Studi, Milan
CESARE MOZZARELLI, Università Cattolica del Sacro Cuore, Milan
ROBERT ORESKO, Institute of Historical Research, University of London
and GEOFFREY SYMCOX, University of California, Los Angeles

This series comprises monographs and a variety of collaborative volumes, including translated works, which will concentrate on the period of Italian history from late medieval times up to the Risorgimento. The editors aim to stimulate scholarly debate over a range of issues which have not hitherto received, in English, the attention they deserve. As it develops the series will emphasize the interest and vigor of current international debates on this central period of Italian history and the persistent influence of Italian culture on the rest of Europe.

FAMILY AND PUBLIC LIFE
IN BRESCIA, 1580–1650

THE FOUNDATIONS OF POWER
IN THE VENETIAN STATE

JOANNE M. FERRARO

San Diego State University

CAMBRIDGE
UNIVERSITY PRESS

Published by Press Syndicate of the University of Cambridge
The Pitt Building, Trumpington Street, Cambridge CB2 1RP
40 West 20th Street, New York, NY 10011-4211, USA
10 Stamford Road, Oakleigh, Victoria 3166, Australia

© Cambridge University Press 1993

First published 1993

Printed in Great Britain at the University Press, Cambridge

A catalogue record for this book is available from the British Library

Library of Congress cataloguing in publication data

Ferraro, Joanne Marie
Family and public life in Brescia, 1580–1650 / Joanne M. Ferraro. p. cm.–(Cambridge studies in
Italian history and culture)
Includes bibliographical references (p.   ) and index. ISBN 0 521 41953 0 (hc)
1. Political leadership – Italy – Brescia – History. 2. Elite (Social sciences) – Italy – Brescia –
History. 3. Family – Italy – Brescia – History. 4. Brescia (Italy) – Politics and government. 5.
Brescia (Italy) – Economic conditions. I. Title. II. Series. JS5925.B742F47 1992
306.2′0945′26 – dc20 91–47167 CIP

ISBN 0 521 41953 0 hardback

FOR JENNIE FERRARO AND
IN MEMORY OF CORRADO FERRARO

CONTENTS

ILLUSTRATIONS

TABLES

ACKNOWLEDGMENTS

It is a pleasure to express my appreciation for the support and assistance I have received throughout the course of this project. The Gladys Krieble Delmas Foundation; the American Council of Learned Societies; the National Endowment for the Humanities; the College of Arts and Letters, the Graduate Division, and the Office of Faculty Affairs at San Diego State University generously funded my research in Venice and Brescia. The National Endowment for the Humanities also provided a one-year fellowship which released me from teaching in order to write this manuscript. My colleagues in the History Department at San Diego State University supported the year's leave as well.

I was fortunate to have the courteous help of the staffs at the State Archives in Venice and Brescia, at the Archivio Storico Comunale and Biblioteca Queriniana in Brescia, and at the Biblioteca Nazionale Marciana and Biblioteca of the Museo Correr in Venice. I especially thank archivists Michela Dal Borgo and Sandra Sambo for their valuable assistance with the collections in the State Archives in Venice; and Leonardo Mazzoldi and Roberto Navarrini for directing me to the catalogue of family papers in the *Hospedale Maggiore* at the State Archives in Brescia.

I owe a special debt to the scholars who have very generously given me the benefits of their professional expertise. My teacher Geoffrey Symcox sparked my interest in the field of early modern Italy and gave critical direction to my study of Brescia. He has followed all phases of my research and writing, offering valuable criticisms and advice. Any errors in the manuscript, of course, remain my sole responsibility. I am grateful to Marilyn J. Boxer for her scholarly insights and critical advice throughout the preparation of this manuscript and for her constant encouragement of my professional development as a mentor as well as a friend. Edward Muir and Guido Ruggiero have also been strong sources of encouragement; I gratefully acknowledge their professional guidance and scholarly support. I thank Marino Berengo for giving valuable direction to the early stages of my archival research. Finally, I appreciate all the helpful advice my colleagues have given me through the years. Debbie Wilson helped with the final editing of the manuscript.

I extend my appreciation to family and friends. My own family was patient and understanding of my extended sojourns abroad. In Venice I enjoyed the warmth and comforts of family as well. Elsa Dalla Venezia deserves special recognition for giving me the invaluable experience of a home on the lagoon where I could participate fully in Venetian life and learn Venetian ways. Edda and Ezio Crosara also joined in providing friendship in a family atmosphere during my research trips. Friends and colleagues Giulio Bergamasco, Giovanni Caniato, Linda Carroll, Stanley Chojnacki, Gigi Corrazol, Renzo DeRosas, Rebecca Edwards, Laura Gianetti, Rona Goffen, Michael Knapton, Marian Leathers Kuntz, Peter Laven, John Martin, Dennis Romano, Kris Ruggiero, and Anne Jacobson Schutte made research in the archives intellectually stimulating and life in Venice a true delight.

ABBREVIATIONS

Archives

ASB   Archivio di Stato di Brescia
ASCB   Archivio Storico Comunale di Brescia
ASV   Archivio di Stato di Venezia

Libraries

BMCV Biblioteca del Museo Correr di Venezia
BNMV Biblioteca Nazionale Marciana di Venezia
BQ   Biblioteca Queriniana di Brescia
BQSV   Biblioteca Querini Stampaglia di Venezia

Periodicals and miscellaneous

CAB   *Commentari dell'Ateneo di Brescia*
RA   *Rivista del Collegio Araldico*
RSI   *Rivista Storica Italiana*
RV   *Relazioni dei rettori veneti in Terraferma*
SS   *Studi Storici*

Archival and manuscript citations

Consiglio dei Dieci. LCRB   Lettere ai Capi del Consiglio dei Dieci dai Rettori di Brescia

Senato. APRB Archivio proprio dei rettori di Brescia
Senato. DRB Dispacci dei rettori di Brescia

HM. AEP Hospedale Maggiore. Atti di Eredità e Processi

F   *filza*
B   *busta*
f   *foglio*
fasc.   *fascicolo*
u.d.   unfoliated document
n.d.   no date

MONEY

Brescian monies were based upon the Lombard system of *lire imperiali*. One *lira imperiale* was equivalent to 1.1066 *lire italiane*. Each gold ducat, of Phillip II in 1579 and of Phillip IV in 1641, was equivalent to 10.46 *lire italiane*. (A. Martini, *Manuale di metrologia ossia misure, pesi e monete* [Turin, 1883], pp. 101; 354; 356. According to Martini's figures, there should be 9.45 *lire imperiali* in each ducat. Contemporary sources, however, furnish an exchange rate of three *lire planet* per ducat. For example, ASB, *HM.AEP, Famiglia Ugone*, F. 1, No. 75 [u.d.], Testament of Giulia Omi Ugone, June 16, 1640.)

WEIGHTS AND MEASURES

Land
1 *piò* (100 *tavole*) = 0.32553938 hectares
1 *tavola* (4 *pertiche*) = 0.00325539 hectares

Weights
1 *somma* (12 *quarte*) = 145.92 liters
1 *peso* = 8.02 kilograms
(Taken from Martini, *Manuale di metrologia*, p. 101.)

INTRODUCTION

THE HISTORIOGRAPHICAL BACKGROUND

THE ITALIAN REGIONAL STATE

Two central questions have left their imprint on the literature of Italian regional states over the nineteenth and twentieth centuries: did their formation in the fifteenth century mark the beginning of political decline, or did this development signal the dawn of the modern state?[1] Both queries were tied to the broader task of comparing the Italian peninsula's political development to that of the western European states in general. The move, in starts and stops, of the northwest monarchies in the direction of centralization has served as a model for historians attempting to chart the course of the Italian regional states through the fifteenth to eighteenth centuries.

One view, launched with Sismondi in the nineteenth century, proclaimed the decline of communal power and the rise of lordships in the fifteenth-century Italian cities as the beginning of (political and moral) decadence.[2] At the twilight of the nineteenth century Volpe

[1] E. Fasano Guarini, "Gli stati dell'Italia centro-settentrionale tra quattro e cinquecento: continuità e trasformazioni," *Società e Storia* 21 (1983): 626. I am indebted to the following sources for this historiographical essay: M. Berengo, "Il Cinquecento," in *La storiografia italiana negli ultimi vent'anni* (Milan: Marzorati, 1970), vol. 1, pp. 483–518; G. Chittolini, "Alcune considerazioni sulla storia politico-istituzionale del tardo medioevo: alle origini degli 'stati regionali,'" *Annali dell'Istituto Storico Italo-germanico in Trento* 2 (1976): 401–419; Fasano Guarini, "Stati," pp. 617–640; E. Fasano Guarini (ed.), "Introduzione," *Potere e società negli stati regionali italiani del '500 e '600* (Bologna: Il Mulino, 1978), pp. 20–45; J. S. Grubb, "When Myths Lose Power: Four Decades of Venetian Historiography," *Journal of Modern History* 58 (1986): 60–86; J. S. Grubb, *Firstborn of Venice. Vicenza in the Early Renaissance State* (Baltimore and London: The Johns Hopkins University Press, 1988), pp. ix–xvi.

[2] Sismondi's work, *Storia delle repubbliche italiane dei secoli di mezzo* (Capolago: Tipografia E. Libreria Elvetica, 1844–1846) is reviewed in Fasano Guarini, "Stati," pp. 617–619.

and Salvemini reiterated this pronouncement, linking the origins of decline with the arrest of bourgeois development, a stance that has also attracted the sympathy of twentieth-century historians studying failed transitions.[3] Aristocratization, refeudalization, a weak bourgeoisie – common themes in Italian historiography into the 1970s – all obstructed state growth.[4] When compared to northwest Europe, the Italian regional state experienced delays and failures.

Another view emerged by the second decade of the twentieth century that challenged the assumptions underlying the decline argument. It raised doubts about the notion of communal liberty. Questioned as well was the use of the urban venue as a primary index of progress or regression in the Peninsula's history. The focus of this line of thought, the internal structure and functions of the postcommunal polity, was broader; and the aim was not to illuminate decline but rather to discover the antecedents of the modern state. Forerunners of this approach, Anzilotti (1910) and Ercole (1914) argued that the rise of lordships in fifteenth-century Italy was a step in the direction of more progressive forms of government.[5] It was Federico Chabod, however, who determined the methodological course this line of inquiry would take when he set out to test for modernity with an examination of the bureaucratization of the sixteenth-century Milanese state.[6] Chabod's aim was to illuminate centralizing tendencies, an objective that was in full synchronization with post Second World War debates on the strides and limits of state development in western Europe. It was also in harmony with currents in post Second World War Italian historiography attempting to locate the origins of unification during the Risorgimento.

Not every Italian regional state, however, lent itself to Chabod's test for modernity. Unlike Milan or Florence,[7] some Italian regional states

---

[3]   See Fasano Guarini, "Stati," pp. 618–619.
[4]   See M. Berengo, *La società veneta alla fine del Settecento* (Florence: G. C. Sansoni, 1956); A. Ventura, *Nobiltà e popolo nella società veneta del '400 e '500* (Bari: Laterza, 1964); R. Romano, "La storia economica. Dal secolo XIV al Settecento," in *Storia d'Italia* (Turin: Giulio Einaudi, 1974), vol II, pp. 1,813–1,931; R. Romano, *Tra due crisi: l'Italia del Rinascimento* (Turin: Giulio Einaudi, 1971).
[5]   Fasano Guarini, "Stati," p. 620.
[6]   *Ibid.*, pp. 619; 622–624. See F. Chabod, *Lo stato di Milano nell'impero di Carlo V* (Milan: Tuminelli, 1934); F. Chabod, "Ya-t-il un État de la Renaissance?," in F. Chabod, *Scritti sul Rinascimento* (Turin: Einaudi, 1967), pp. 593–604; F. Chabod, "Usi ed abusi nell'amministrazione dello stato di Milano a mezzo il '500," in *Potere e società*, ed. E. Fasano Guarini.
[7]   Litchfield advances our knowledge of the legacy the Florentine ducal bureaucracy of the sixteenth to eighteenth centuries bequeathed to state-builders of the Risorgimento. R. Burr Litchfield, *Emergence of a Bureaucracy. The Florentine Patricians, 1530–1790* (Princeton: Princeton University Press, 1986), pp. 6–8.

did not establish bureaucracies. Moreover, even those that did had to contend with local forces in peripheral areas. Thus Marino Berengo's study of the eighteenth-century Venetian state served as a case study not of modernization but of decadence.[8] *La società veneta alla fine del Settecento*, published in 1956, was a watershed for Venetian studies as the historical landscape shifted for the first time away from the islands of the lagoon to that of the territorial dominion.[9] Berengo established a new field of inquiry, one that was in synchronization with the broader interest in the workings of the postcommunal polity. He described the Venetian Republic as a "fragmentary" and "disorganic state,"[10] without executive structures or a bureaucracy in the provinces, where feudal privilege and a backward, landed economy prevailed. There were deep fissures between the Venetian ruling class and the mainland aristocracies, who were excluded from central government and hostile to Venetian intrusion in the affairs of city councils; and between the provincial aristocracies, allowed ample local authority, and the disenfranchised. The Venetian ruling class failed to repair the gaps between capital city and provinces, between privileged and non-privileged groups, between Venetian economic interests and those of the provinces, a failure that prevented unification and modernization.

Elsewhere Berengo, while acknowledging Chabod's contributions to the study of state development, also found his methodological focus rather limited. He drew attention to this in 1967 with an important essay on Italian historiography since the Second World War.[11] It was insufficient to study the centralization of Spanish governors, Berengo noted, for there was a plurality of powers in the Milanese (and, by implication, Italian) regional state. More attention should be devoted to investigating the centrifugal forces that opposed centralization: fiefs, groups, provinces, cities.[12] In this context, the process of aristocratization in the Italian cities was a fundamental line of inquiry, and a number of significant studies on the subject had already begun to be published, particularly for the Veneto and for Tuscany. Many more would emerge in the following decade both for these regions and for Lombardy, the Papal States, and Liguria as well.[13] Berengo's own path-breaking examination of aristocratization in sixteenth-century

[8] See Grubb, "Myths," pp. 70–71; 74–76; Grubb, *Firstborn*, p. xiii.
[9] Berengo, *La società veneta*.
[10] *Ibid.*, chs. 1 and 2.
[11] Berengo, "Il Cinquecento," pp. 483–518.
[12] Fasano Guarini, "Stati," p. 625.
[13] For a review of the literature, see C. Mozzarelli, "Stato, patriziato e organizzazione della società nell'Italia moderna," *Annali dell'Istituto Storico Italo-germanico in Trento* 2 (1976): 421–512.

Lucca was among the first,[14] together with Angelo Ventura's *Nobiltà e popolo nella società veneta del '400 e '500*, a pioneering study of the inner workings of the Venetian territorial state.[15] Though several of Ventura's arguments have subsequently been adjusted and others continue to be controversial,[16] *Nobiltà e popolo* remains a standard work in the field.

Ventura, largely in sympathy with Berengo's characterization of the eighteenth-century Venetian state, traced the process of aristocratization in the Venetian mainland cities back to the fifteenth and sixteenth centuries. Particularly after 1509, Venice endorsed aristocratic rule, which was largely corrupt, at the expense of the popular classes. Yet at the same time, Ventura maintained, state intervention progressively reduced local freedoms. Themes of decline and of an incapacity to build a modern state again colored the literature. Decadence was linked in Ventura's case to aristocratization; in Berengo's Lucca to the extinction of free republics and a crisis of liberty. Berengo concluded in his 1967 review essay that power constricted throughout the Peninsula during the sixteenth century, and within some regional states more flexible political forms declined as the state pushed for more control. Though local freedoms were eroded, however, centralization did not take place.[17] Hence the historiographical problem remained that of locating power within the Italian regional state and, more broadly, of reconstructing the sociopolitical structure of the ancien régime in Italy. This is an area of inquiry not just for Italian historiography but for that of Europe as a whole. It has already been widely established that many South German, Spanish, French, Swiss, and Dutch cities moved, whether from feudalism or from communalism, towards oligarchy by the sixteenth century. Yet their differing relationships with princes, monarchs, and dominant cities and their own individual systems of power require further exploration and comparison.

For the Italian peninsula, historians throughout the 1970s and 1980s have been researching the plurality of powers within the regional states. Peripheral areas have attracted major attention.[18] Studies have focused on ruling orders, on the workings of provincial magistracies, and on the

---

[14] M. Berengo, *Nobili e mercanti nella Lucca del '500* (Turin: Giulio Einaudi (Toso), 1965).
[15] Ventura, *Nobiltà e popolo*.
[16] For reviews of Ventura, see C. Clough in *Studi Veneziani* 8 (1966): 526–544; G. Cozzi in *Critica Storica* 5 (1966): 126–130; A. Tenenti in *SS* 4 (1966): 401–408; and, more recently, D. Hay and J. Law, *Italy in the Age of the Renaissance, 1380–1530* (London: Longmans, 1989), pp. 113–116; Grubb, "Myths," pp. 76–78; Grubb, *Firstborn*, pp. xiii–xiv.
[17] Berengo, "Il Cinquecento," pp. 491–492.
[18] Fasano Guarini, "Stati,"p. 625.

relationship of rural institutions with those of both urban centers and the state. The result has been to produce some new conceptualizations of the study of the regional state. Ornaghi, for example, has emphasized that the state did not control all political power and that politics was not necessarily synonymous with the state.[19] Thus we find a shift in focus as historians attempt to locate centers of power and politics throughout the regional state. Of note, the work of Giorgio Chittolini investigates how powers outside urban centers affected the evolution of political institutions.[20]

The paths of investigation charted by Berengo, Ventura, and Chittolini and pursued by a number of recent scholars have all given direction to my study of the Brescian ruling class, an attempt to illuminate the systems of power in an important area of the Venetian territorial state. The issues Stuart Woolf raised about representation in the Italian, and more specifically Venetian, state also helped put this study of Brescia on the drawing board. How did Republics behave towards peripheral areas? To what degree were the latter integrated into the state? What institutional dependence was left at the local level? How far were various social classes able to make their voices heard? Were there pressure groups in the capital city? To what extent did the central government use local representation for justice, taxes, and defense? What were the limits of state authority? How far were local rivalries encouraged to redress local authority?[21] In much of Europe, urban centers had to defend their political and economic privileges either before the newly rising aristocratic monarchies or before great princes. On the Italian peninsula, by 1559 Milan, Naples, Sicily, and Sardinia had become Spanish viceroyalties. Even independent Papal Rome was at times under the weight of Spain. Other centers, such as Genoa, Antwerp, Augsburg, Holland, Strasbourg, and Ulm resisted absorption but at the same time linked their economic fortunes to the more

---

[19] L. Ornaghi, "'Crisi' del centro statale e 'disseminazione' di centri politici. Note su un indice di trasformazione dello Stato moderno," *Quaderni sardi di storia* 4 (July 1983–June 1984): 49–50.

[20] Chittolini, "Considerazioni," p. 407; G. Chittolini, "Le terre separate nel Ducato di Milano in età Sforzesca," in *Milano nell'età di Ludovico il Moro. Atti del convegno internazionale 28 febbraio-4 marzo 1983* (Milan: Biblioteca Trivulziana del Comune di Milano, 1983), vol. I, pp. 115–128. In this last article Chittolini draws attention to the importance of territories that became detached administratively from urban centers during the Visconti and Sforza lordships.

[21] S. Woolf, "The Problem of Representation in the Post-Renaissance Venetian State," in *Liber Memorialis Antonio Era. Studies presented to the International Commission for the History of Representative and Parliamentary Institutions*, vol. XXVI, New York: Unesco, 1961 and 1963, pp. 67; 80–82.

powerful monarchies.[22] Venice remained one of the rare European examples of an independent city republic. It is hoped the study of its relations with its subject territories will contribute to our understanding of its unique position. At the same time it will provide a case study for comparative history with other Italian and western European states.

Currently, models of political decline or modernity are giving way to alternative conceptualizations of the Italian regional state. Waquet, for example, points to the necessity of disengaging political history from a completely linear perspective. There were interruptions and developments that went in indefinite directions. In this context the sixteenth and seventeenth centuries in Italy may be viewed as centuries of transformation but not necessarily as ones of progress or decline.[23] Chittolini's paradigm for the Visconti and Sforza states is finding broad acceptance: the regional state was neither medieval nor modern nor centralized. Rather, it was rife with local particularism.[24] Ornaghi also emphasizes that political history cannot simply be tied to the central state, as there were other centers of socioeconomic power.[25] In this general framework we can assess intentions and attempts to strengthen state structures while at the same time recognizing the survival of a plurality of powers.[26] Applied to the Venetian state, this conceptualization revises the bipolar approach of center and periphery, creating a broader picture of the centers and systems of power. It is important to note, for example, that the Venetians relied to a considerable degree on the provincial aristocracies to govern local society. Thus Venetian patricians and provincial aristocracies were not necessarily antithetical forces but at times complementary in their functions.[27]

Release from ideological themes such as decline or modernity enables historians to focus instead on the dynamic changes that took place in the systems of power from the fifteenth to the eighteenth centuries. The behavior of ruling classes such as the one in Brescia is critical to acquiring a better understanding of the causes of change in the period between the Renaissance and the Risorgimento.

---

[22] T. Brady, *Turning Swiss: Cities and Empire, 1440–1550* (Cambridge: Cambridge University Press, 1985), pp. 224–227.

[23] J. Waquet, *Le Grande-Duché de Toscane sous les derniers Médicis* (Rome: Ecole Française de Rome, 1990), pp. 48–50.

[24] Grubb, *Firstborn*, p. xiv.

[25] Ornaghi, "'Crisi' del centro statale," pp. 49–54.

[26] Fasano Guarini, "Stati," p. 629.

[27] *Ibid.*, p. 628.

ARISTOCRATIZATION

The problem of how to characterize the ruling elites of north and central Italy has sparked intense monographic study since the Second World War, and particularly over the last three decades. As I have noted, Ventura has produced the standard work on the process of aristocratization in the Venetian territorial state, though there is still disagreement over the question of Venetian intentions.[28] Subsequently, Marino Berengo, reviewing Giorgio Borelli's data on Veronese elites, opened new discussion by placing the lifestyles, culture, patrimonial strategies, and political behavior of these families into two distinct categories, patriciate and nobility.[29] The problem Berengo presented was not nominalistic but conceptual. His finely nuanced observations of the diverse lifestyles and traditions of Verona's ruling families prompted historians to move beyond studies of aristocratic closure to analyze more acutely the realities of aristocratization. That is the primary intent of this study. It will focus principally on the behavior of the families who participated in the government of sixteenth- and seventeenth-century Brescia.

The book begins by placing Brescia within the context of the Venetian state. A geopolitical and economic survey underlines both the strategic and fiscal importance of this province for the Venetian Republic. Brescia and the Bresciano were among Venice's most prized subjects. The next part of the book conceptualizes the civic leadership, with a profile of its origins and a brief history of the process of aristocratization. Brescian councillors, like their Veronese neighbors, were a hybrid class of nobles and non-nobles that underwent a considerable degree of amalgamation. By the sixteenth century their identity was significantly tied to such professions as law and the notarial arts, professions that were fundamental to the system of municipal power. Part II also examines the relationship between family structure and the local sociopolitical structures. Size, wealth, professional study, and marriage ties were all pivotal factors that helped determine the family's position in public life. Its strength ultimately rested on its continuity over time. What emerges from part II is a picture of an elite which not only distinguished itself from the disenfranchised but also consolidated its own ranks over the course of the sixteenth century. The workings of the family are the prime *modus operandi* behind this

[28] J. E. Law has rejected the notion that aristocratic closure was due to Venetian policy. "Venice and the 'Closing' of the Veronese Constitution in 1405," *Studi Veneziani*, N.S. 1 (1977): 69–103.

[29] M. Berengo, "Patriziato e nobiltà: il caso veronese," *RSI* 87 (1975): 493–517.

constriction of political power, and those workings are most visible in the behavior of the lineage or the even smaller unit of the household.

The third part of the book situates Brescia's ruling families within the Venetian state. Besides controlling urban political institutions, they held strong economic links with the surrounding countryside, the basis of their power, and they enjoyed ample authority in the rural communities subject to Brescia. As such Brescian councillors – and kinsmen whose lifestyles revolved more around the rural hinterland – held substantive political weight over a rich and strategically vital portion of Venetian territory. Part III examines the different ways these families sought to preserve their control over local resources in the specific economic context of the late sixteenth and early seventeenth centuries. The time frame 1580 to 1650 was chosen with specific criteria in mind: the period witnessed important transformations in the economy that played some role in shaping the behavior of Brescia's – and the Peninsula's – ruling orders. In particular, catastrophic mortality in 1630 seriously destabilized all economic sectors. Brescia's ruling families sought to maximize their income from land, credit operations, and the benefits of office. Their governing methods reflected the symbiotic relationship between family and municipal government. The latter was shaped to a considerable degree by the family's economic exigencies.

Part III also aims to shed light on the relationship between Brescia's ruling families and the Venetian state. Again the time frame 1580 to 1650 was chosen with specific criteria in mind. Historians of early modern and modern Italy have been preoccupied with the role aristocratization played in state formation. Were civic offices less important than rural jurisdictions and country estates? Did urban councils lose their political significance, making way for the growth of state authority? The answers to these questions will vary from place to place. In Brescia the interests of the rural nobility and the citizen elite converged in the communal age and continued to find political, social, and cultural expression in the city during the sixteenth and seventeenth centuries. The Venetians relied to a significant degree on Brescian councillors to govern local society. Thus, an analysis of the Brescian civic leadership's weight in public life, relative to that of Venetian authorities, illumines ways in which this important Italian regional state was knit together. Again the family and its thick web of kinsmen and allies constitute the real protagonists of urban history. Venetian statesmen's efforts to govern Brescia required not simply skills of administration but also an acute ability to work through the local social arrangements formed by kinship, clientage, and patronage networks.

The approach of this study is comparative, with urban centers in western Europe and on the Italian peninsula in general and with the Venetian state in specifics. The latter now affords a rich historiographical literature to which this author is in debt for its instructive and comparative value. For the Venetian state more work recently has been done on the fifteenth and sixteenth centuries than on that of the seventeenth and eighteenth centuries, and the Lombard provinces have been studied less than those of the Veneto. While that literature provides an indispensable foundation for an investigation of Venetian relations with the Bresciano, the variety of experiences that emerges from studies of different areas, particularly in other historical periods, cautions against generalization. Gaetano Cozzi's work on the legal systems of Venice and its subject cities illuminates some of these differences.[30] The Venetian territorial state was vast, incorporating peoples with different histories and cultural traditions. Venetian Lombardy, far from the capital city and with a clear view of the Milanese horizon, did not witness the same kind of state penetration as the subject cities nearest the capital. Significantly, Venetian patricians did not buy real estate in the Bresciano, as they did in the territories nearest their own urban center, because of an ancient statute which prohibited the alienation of Brescian properties to foreigners. Moreover the physical and psychological distance separating Venice and subjects *al di là del Mincio* prior to modernity, a distance of approximately 160 kilometers that crossed innumerable cultural divides – not the least of which was linguistic – significantly modulated their relationships.[31] Thus it is important to highlight the unique features of the Brescian case in order to appreciate the variety of experiences within this Italian regional state.

[30] G. Cozzi, "La politica del diritto nella Repubblica di Venezia," in *Stato, società e giustizia nella repubblica veneta (secoli XV–XVIII)* (Rome: Jouvence, 1981), vol. I, pp. 79–121.

[31] See G. Cozzi, "Ambiente veneziano, ambiente veneto. Governanti e governati di qua dal Mincio nei secoli XV–XVIII," in *Storia della cultura veneta. Vol IV/II: Il Seicento* (Vicenza: Neri Pozza, 1984), p. 497.

PART I

THE STRUCTURAL FRAMEWORK

CHAPTER I

DEFINING BOUNDARIES

CONSTRUCTING THE POLITY: VENICE AND THE TERRITORIAL DOMINION[1]

Venetian absorption of northeast Italy began with the conquests of Treviso and Conegliano, in 1339 and 1344 respectively. Rivalries with the great landed dynasties, the Scaligeri, the Carrara, and the Visconti, triggered further expansion in the following century, the most decisive period for the establishment of the Venetian territorial dominion. Vicenza, shunning Carrara dominance, placed itself under Venetian rule in 1404. Asiago, Feltre, and Belluno followed shortly thereafter. In 1405 Venice seized Padua from the Carrara, while Verona joined itself to the Republic, and the following year the Duke of Ferrara ceded Rovigo. Then in the second decade of the fifteenth century Venice pushed farther north and west. The Republic conquered the Patria del Friuli, with the mountainous territory of Carnia, in 1420. The Lombard wars against Filippo Maria Visconti followed, bringing Brescia (1426) and then Bergamo (1428) into the Republic. Visconti attempts to recover their Lombard possessions between 1438 and 1440 failed. Thus by 1438 the entire territory from the Friuli to the Bergamasco and from Cadore to Polesine acknowledged the Lion of St. Mark as the symbol of Venetian dominion.

The assemblage of the Venetian territorial state was not the product

---

[1] Much has been written on the organization of the Venetian territorial state. This synthesis is based on the following sources: Ventura, *Nobiltà e popolo*; G. Cozzi and M. Knapton, *Storia della repubblica di Venezia. Dalla guerra di Chioggia alla reconquista della terraferma* (Turin: UTET, 1986), pp. 205–348; Hay and Law, *Italy in the Age of the Renaissance*, pp. 112–123; A. Ventura, "Il dominio di Venezia nel Quattrocento," in *Florence and Venice: Comparisons and Relations*, vol. I: *Il Quattrocento* (Florence: La Nuova Italia, 1979), pp. 167–90; M. Knapton, "Il Territorio vicentino nello stato veneto del '500 e primo '600: nuovi equilibri politici e fiscali," in *Dentro lo "stado italico." Venezia e la Terraferma fra Quattro e Seicento* ed. G. Cracco and M. Knapton (Trent: Gruppo Culturale Civis, 1984), pp. 43–67; Grubb, *Firstborn*, pp. 165–181.

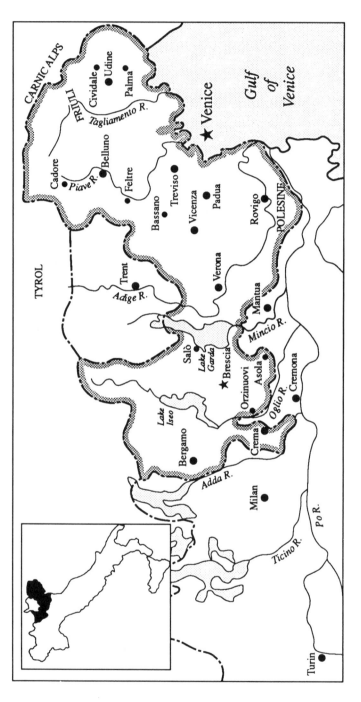

1. The Venetian mainland. (A. Brook, Graphics, SDSU.)

of any grand architectural design, but rather of contingent assertion. Above all, control of the hinterland safeguarded Venetian independence. Beyond the marshy lagoons extensive plains and rolling hills stood between the new capital and the Milanese state to the west, while to the north a labyrinth of deep valleys and mountain ranges acted as a buffer against the Dukes of Austria. Control of the Po and Adige Rivers was strategically vital too, both for commercial enterprise and for defense. At the same time the lands of the Terraferma (Venetian mainland) promised foodstuffs, raw materials, new commercial outlets, opportunities for landed investment, and the possibility for Venetian patricians to hold important ecclesiastical positions within the state. A final factor drawing Venice to the mainland was the need to secure the landed routes to western and central European markets. Though some members of the Venetian ruling class had doubted the wisdom of open expansionist policies and of extending Venetian energies so far west of the capital, the Lombard territories were a critical stepping-stone to France and to the Rhineland. The Venetians could not depend on Visconti benevolence for passage through this region.[2]

Venice maintained a skeletal governmental apparatus on the mainland during the early years of its rule. Supervision of the subject cities went to rectors, Venetian patricians elected from the Greater Council, who rotated through the mainland as part of their *cursus honorum*. The larger cities, such as Brescia, Padua, and Verona, had two rectors: a podestà, who supervised civil and judicial affairs; and a capitano, in charge of military affairs and finance. Medium-size cities were simply assigned one rector. Commissions to the more important urban centers went to the Venetian patricians with preponderant political and financial weight. Many of the most illustrious patrician names served in Brescia, considered one of the Republic's most important dominions because of its strategic and economic importance, and because it was ruled by families that vaunted long histories of social, economic, and political success. A rectorship in Brescia required substantial private wealth to meet the social and political demands of the office. Each subject city also had chamberlains (camerlenghi) to run the Camera Ducale, the financial office of the subject city and its hinterland. The chamberlains supervised the collection of indirect taxes (*dazi, imposte*), which were farmed out, and paid salaries to state representatives and the military. Government of the rural districts outside the respective subject cities varied. Those nearest Venice, in the Marca Trevigiana,

---

[2] F. Lane, *Venice. A Maritime Republic* (Baltimore: The Johns Hopkins University Press, 1973), pp. 228–230.

Padovano, and Polesine, were under the rectors' jurisdiction. In contrast Venice delegated the government of small urban centers in the Vicentine, the Veronese, and Lombardy to vicariates and minor podestarie, elected from the ranks of the respective urban councils. The exception was the Friuli, where the municipalities had little control over the countryside, and the rural districts remained largely the domain of feudatories.[3]

Venetian relations with its subjects were contractual in nature. In general, the municipalities that came under the Republic in the fifteenth century had been allowed to surrender and present petitions that protected or enhanced their liberties.[4] Early government was oriented around these *patti alla dedica*. Venice respected local statutes and worked through local administrative structures. Milan, in contrast to Venice, was less sensitive to the cities under its jurisdiction, for their powers threatened those of the dukes. The Milanese overlords tended to curry the favor of feudatories, giving them immunities and favorable jurisdictions.[5] The Florentine state, on the other hand, attempted to impose more control over its subjects from the outset than either Venice or Milan. Even Venice, however, eventually ignored or forgot prerogatives and privileges.[6] Moreover, as Venice became more dependent upon the fiscal resources of the Terraferma, local statutes were overridden by Venetian practice and legislation.[7]

Venice did not construct executive structures in the provinces, a critical limitation of the powers at the center. Many important governmental structures remained local and as a result were marked by local peculiarities: the collection of indirect taxes; the distribution and collection of direct taxes; courts and procedures of law, though Venetian rectors presided over criminal justice as well as some of the more important civil disputes;[8] grain provisioning; the institutions of charity; the granting of local citizenship; the establishment of municipal law and ordinances. Venice delegated the majority of these competencies to the members of the urban councils on the mainland. Venetian patricians could not participate in these municipal governments, nor

---

3 For the administration of justice see C. Povolo, "Aspetti e problemi dell'amministrazione della giustizia penale nella Repubblica di Venezia. Secoli XVI–XVIII," in *Stato, società e giustizia*, ed. Cozzi, vol. I, pp. 179–190.

4 Hay and Law, *Italy in the Age of the Renaissance*, p. 114. For the Vicentine case, Grubb, *Firstborn*, pp. 9–13.

5 Ventura, "Il dominio," p. 177.

6 See Ventura, *Nobiltà e popolo*, pp. 41–49.

7 Hay and Law, *Italy in the Age of the Renaissance*, p. 116.

8 For the differences in the municipalities' judicial systems, see Povolo, "Aspetti e problemi," pp. 181–192.

could mainland elites take part in the legislative and executive decisions which emanated from the center. Only in 1646 did the Venetian constitutional elite open its council membership to parvenus who could pay the stiff entrance fee of 100,000 ducats, a desperate move to repair finances during the burdensome war with Candia. Also, citizenship in Venice and in the mainland cities was mutually exclusive, save for *de intus* citizenship, an agreement which essentially conferred mutual trading rights (e.g. Brescian citizens would have the same trading rights as Venetians in the *Dominante* [capital city] and vice versa).

Though the Greater Council represented the overall sovereignty of Venetian authority, government was actually executed by smaller deliberating bodies. Decisions at the center emanated from the Venetian Senate or its executive members, collectively referred to as the Collegio; and the Council of Ten. Over the course of the fifteenth and sixteenth centuries, Venetian institutions evolved to adapt to the new territorial state. The power of the Council of Ten grew during this period, particularly in the areas of defense and expenditure, and it began to intervene increasingly in mainland affairs. Venetian magistracies were not commanded by unanimous decision, however, often competing with one another. On the mainland, for example, the rectors complained about the Avogadori and the Auditori, appeals tribunals in Venice that overrode their decisions. They complained as well when superior magistrates (provveditori) from Venice intervened in Terraferma affairs with extraordinary powers.[9] In the capital, the expanding power of the Ten was challenged and formally checked in 1582. The Young Party, a group of patricians out of power that was attempting to break oligarchic rule within the governing class, was able to limit the Ten's jurisdictions to justice and matters that affected state security, while the Senate took charge of finance and defense.

The late sixteenth and seventeenth centuries witnessed a turning point in Venetian relations with the mainland territories. The change corresponded with the shift in Venetian economic orientation from commercial to landed activities. As the Maritime Republic lost its hegemony on the seas and industrial output declined, income from the lands of the Terraferma became increasingly important. The growth of absolute monarchies, particularly those of the Hapsburg princes, whose lands neighbored the Venetian state, also loomed on the horizon, making it necessary to fortify the structures and resources of the state. The rising costs of maintaining an efficient army and navy stimulated the development of more institutions at center to deal with mainland

---

[9] *Ibid.*, p. 191.

affairs. In particular, Venice made more strenuous efforts to control the systems of justice and the fisc. There was an expansion of specialized magistracies (provveditori) to deal with specific problems: water, fiefs, sanitation, grain, forests, mines, common lands in the rural districts, borders, fortresses, artillery. Moreover, sindaci and inquisitori intervened increasingly in the systems of justice and the fisc, attempting to correct administrative abuse and to maintain order and stability.

State efforts of the late sixteenth and early seventeenth centuries, however, did not seriously check local authority. The experience of Agnadello in 1509, when the Republic temporarily lost its mainland possessions in the European wars, had already underlined the distances between Venice and its subjects. Brescia, for example, fell to the French between 1509 and 1512, and to the Spanish between 1512 and 1516. During this period the Brescian nobility split, several families supporting Venice, others finding the promises of foreign powers more inviting. Those loyal to Venice played a strategic role in helping the Republic reconquer its lost possessions. The lesson of this political crisis was clear: without executive structures and a state bureaucracy on the mainland, Venetian rule could only rest on collaboration with local powers. While in principle the Republic supported aristocratic rule throughout its dominions, it faced the difficult and complicated task of balancing the interests of urban elites, historically privileged groups, with those of other Venetian subjects. In the Bresciano, for example, besides the great family dynasties there were also multiple corps: the city, the Territorio, the clergy, the Valcamonica, the Valsabbia, the Val Trompia, and a few separate territories under private jurisdictions. Brescia and, after 1530, the Territorio, which represented rural interests, sent representatives (nunzi) and ambassadors to the capital city to voice their concerns and defend their interests. There they found nunzi from other provinces, with whom they sometimes collaborated to apply pressure on the capital. At the same time the more powerful families of the province availed themselves of informal channels to communicate with Venetian statesmen. While the priorities of Brescia were often privileged over those of the other corps, Venice could not and did not ignore the pressures that came from outside the subject city. Venetian response to such pressure was generally empirical: state action was designed to fit the circumstances of the moment. It sometimes opted to deal with more than one subject at a time, playing conflicting interests off against one another. Venice did not always intervene in local affairs, unless they directly affected its economic interests or its security. The state also acted as a mediator in local conflicts, at times involuntarily. Invitation by subjects to arbitrate

disputes, however, helped strengthen Venetian influence on the mainland, where local elites still wielded power.

A tour of the city[10]

It is the walls that ultimately define the urban space of a pre-modern
European city. Brescia's were rebuilt several times between the thirteenth and seventeenth centuries, to accommodate expanding numbers
but also with a view towards defense and security. It was the enclosing
structures of the fourth decade of the thirteenth century, however, that
defined the city's physical space for the following 600 years: a rectangle,
save for a small protruding triangle at the southeast corner, which
enclosed approximately 200 hectares measuring 1,700 by 1,300
meters.[11] A small area under Brescia's jurisdiction, the Chiusure,
spilled into the countryside for two or three kilometers. New walls
designed by the engineer Agostino Castelli went up in the sixteenth
century to accommodate an expanding population.[12]

Brescia was divided into four quarters (quadri). Five city gates – Porta
delle Pille, San Nazaro, San Giovanni, Sant' Alessandro, and Torlonga
– functioned as axes for the main streets. The northeast section, called
Cittadella, was the oldest and perhaps most prestigious part of the city.
It was divided into old and new districts at the point where the Roman
city and the first medieval expansion intersected. Containing the
vestiges of an ancient forum, Vespasian's Capitoline Temple and an
imposing castle rebuilt by the Visconti in the fourteenth century,
Cittadella occupied one-fourth of the enclosed space. The remainder of
the city was divided into three islands: San Faustino to the northwest;
San Alessandro and San Giovanni to the southeast and southwest,
respectively. The quarters were further divided into districts. Cittadella
and San Alessandro each had two; San Giovanni had six; and San
Faustino had seven, eight including Mompiano. While Cittadella held a
preponderant number of aristocratic dwellings, primarily medieval in
origins, from the sixteenth century onwards the upper orders chose to
build in all of the districts. Unlike Florence or Verona, in Brescia there

[10] C. Carozzi, "Brescia," in Storia d'Italia, vol. VI: Atlante (Turin: Einaudi, 1976), pp.
363–366; A. Macadam, Blue Guide. Northern Italy From the Alps to Rome (London:
A. & C. Black and New York: W. W. Norton, 1985), pp. 198–204. G. Da Lezze,
Il catastico bresciano di Giovanni Da Lezze (1609-10), ed. C. Pasero, vol. I (Brescia:
F. Apollonio, 1969).
[11] Carozzi, "Brescia," pp. 363–366.   [12] Ibid., p. 363.

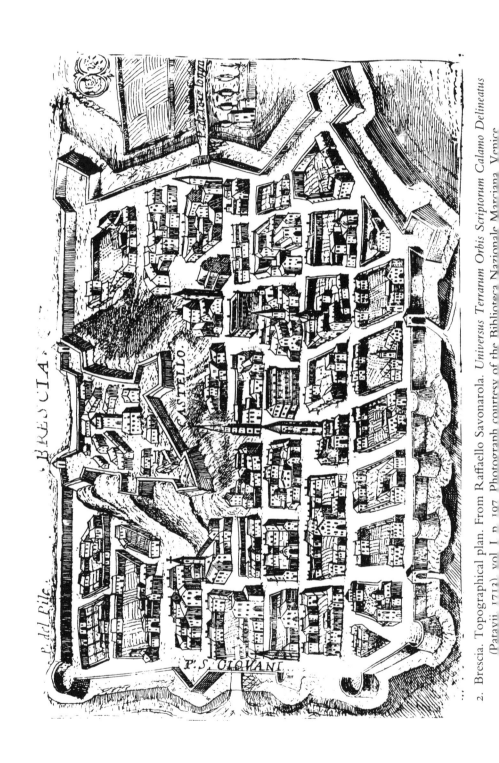

2. Brescia. Topographical plan. From Raffaello Savonarola. *Universus Terrarum Orbis Scriptorum Calamo Delineatus* (Patavii, 1713), vol. I, p. 197. Photograph courtesy of the Biblioteca Nazionale Marciana, Venice.

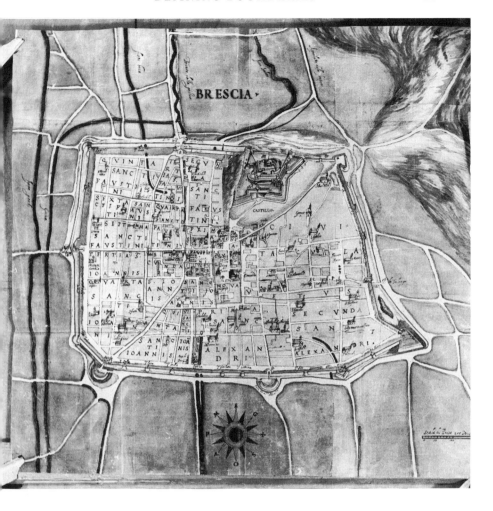

3. Brescia. Town plan. From Il catastico bresciano di Giovanni Da
Lezze (1609–10). ASV, *Sindaci ed Inquisitori in Terraferma*, Busta 64.
Photograph courtesy of the photographic department, State Archives,
Venice. Authorization No. 27/1991.

was no correlation between political representation in the city council
and residence in these districts. However, each district did elect its own
anziano, a neighborhood crier who would transmit new ordinances as

well as the announcements of the Venetian podestà and Brescia's
executive council.[13]

Venetian annexation of Brescia made an impact on the architectural
forms of the city during the fifteenth and sixteenth centuries. Piazza
della Loggia (1433–1550?), located in Cittadella Nuova, exhibited the
principal symbols of Venetian government: the podestà's palace and
government offices and the exquisite Renaissance Loggia (1492–1574)
for public meetings. The graceful Monte Vecchio (1484–1489) on the
south side of the square and the Torre dell'Orologio on the east side,
opposite the Loggia, recalled Venetian architectural forms.

The southwest quarter, San Giovanni, served as Brescia's commercial center. The first district was filled with market places for linen, fish,
wine, and meat. There were also sword manufacturers and a host of
other craft shops. The second district was the home of the Palazzo della
Mercantia, the merchants' guild. There were specialized conglomer-
ations of commercial and craft activity, however, throughout the city.
Of note, the iron merchants concentrated in the fifth district of San
Giovanni, while gold merchants, arms manufacturers, and cloth
weavers congregated in the first, fourth, and fifth districts of San
Faustino, respectively.

Also among Brescia's defining features were its religious buildings,
especially those of the Renaissance and Reformation eras. They
included churches, sacred places, the meeting grounds of devotional
associations, tabernacles, and the private chapels of preeminent families.
The Podestà Paolo Correr counted thirteen parishes with seventy-three
churches, eighteen monasteries, and sixteen convents in 1562. Giovanni
Da Lezze listed twelve parishes in 1609 to 1610, five in Cittadella
Vecchia alone.[14] The center of religious power was in Cittadella
Nuova, in the vicinity of the civic center. Beneath the Torre dell'Orologio at the northeast corner of Piazza della Loggia, a passageway leads
southeast to the Piazza del Duomo, the site of a Romanesque rotunda
(called the Duomo Vecchio), and the Duomo Nuovo, which was
begun in 1604 by the architect G. B. Lantana. To the left of these
religious edifices lies the Broletto (1187–1230), or town hall, fashioned
in Lombard style and flanked by an eleventh-century Torre del
Popolo.

Roman, Lombard, and Venetian art forms have all left their imprint
on Brescia's topography: classical ruins, graceful Renaissance civic and

---

[13] The fifteen anziani were also responsible for denouncing perpetrators of crime, for
sanitation and for burying the dead. C. Pasero, "Introduzione," Il catastico Da Lezze,
vol. I, p. 16, n. 30.
[14] Da Lezze, Il catastico Da Lezze, vol. I, pp. 63; 174.

4. Brescia. Town Hall (Il Broletto). Photograph courtesy of Alinari/Art Resource, New York, No. 32352.

religious architecture, noble palaces, and hundreds of fountains embellish the urban space. The defining features of the historic center now stand amidst constructs of the modern, industrial age. Impressive reminders of Brescia's rich and ancient past, they still win our appreciation.

Provincial borders

The position of the Bresciano was vital to the defense and security of the Venetian Republic. Approximately 160 kilometers northwest of the capital, at the outer limits of the state, the province shared borders with several powers beyond Venetian jurisdiction. To the west only the narrow stretch of Venetian territory that linked the Bergamasco with the Cremasco, an important passage way for imperial troops,[15] separated the Bresciano from the Milanese state, Venice's long-standing territorial rival. The southwest perimeter of the Bresciano followed the Oglio River, a natural barrier for defense, and bordered Cremona, which was also linked to the Milanese capital. By the third decade of the sixteenth century the Milanese territories would become Spanish Hapsburg possessions. To safeguard the plains, a gateway to Lombardy and to northwest Europe, the Republic fortified four towns in the Bresciano: Orzinuovi, Asola, Anfo, and Pontevico.[16] (Brescia, too, was fortified.) At the same time some areas of the Po plain continued to remain privileged and autonomous by Venetian concession: the Gambara family held sway over Verola Alghisi, Pralboino, and Milzano; the Martinengo over Urago d'Oglio, Gabbiano, Padernello, Pavone, Orzivecchi, and Barco; the Avogadro over Polaveno and Lumezzane.[17] The strength of these families, relative to that of the Venetian government and to that of Brescia itself, still needs to be explored. Nonetheless, it was particularly important for Venice to hold the loyalty of this subject nobility, whose castles stood preeminently on hill tops and along the rivers that flowed southeast into the Po. The southeast corner of the province bordered the Duchy of Mantua. The northern boundaries of the Bresciano, far from the capital city and characterized by less penetrable, mountainous terrain, were contiguous with Trento and the lands of the Lodrone counts to the east and with those of the Grisons to the west. Finally, an imaginary line down Lake Garda separated the Bresciano from another important Venetian territory, the Veronese.

[15] P. Lanaro Sartori, "Introduzione," *Podestaria e Capitanato di Crema, Provveditorato di Orzinuovi, Provveditorato di Asola*, vol. XIII of *RV*, ed. A. Tagliaferri (Milan: Giuffrè, 1979), p. xix.

[16] M. E. Mallett and J. R. Hale, *The Military Organization of the Renaissance State* (London and New York: Cambridge University Press, 1984), p. 416.

[17] C. Pasero, "Il dominio veneto fino all'incendio della loggia (1426–1575)," in *Storia di Brescia*, ed. G. Treccani degli Alfieri (Brescia: Morcelliana, 1963), vol. II, p. 127.

THE ECONOMIC SETTING

Natural resources

Brescia sits below the final crests of the Lombard Pre-Alps, where a crown of rolling hills meets the expansive fields of the Po Plain. The city rests at the threshold of a large furrow, the Val Trompia, into which the Mella and Garza Rivers descend.[18] At this junction the commercial highways of three Pre-Alpine valleys and the plains converged to make the urban center and its territories one of the Venetian Republic's richest and most prized possessions. "One could truly say it's a small kingdom," wrote the Venetian Captain Domenico Priuli in 1572.[19] In 1628 Alvise Valaresso, another Venetian captain, named the Brescian Territorio the Republic's "golden ass"; the castle which stands over the city a column of the Venetian state; and the Venetian Camera Ducale for Brescia, which sustained one-fourth of the mainland's fiscal responsibilities to Venice, the Republic's most opulent purse.[20] With a surface area of approximately 4,761 square kilometers, the province (circa 55 percent mountains, 16 percent hills, and 29 percent plains) had a relatively high population density in the period between 1579 and 1645, ranging from 62 to 92 persons per square kilometer.[21] The vastest province in Lombardy, the Bresciano stretched from the Adamello mountain group in the north to the lower Po plains in the south. Its three geographical zones were generously endowed with natural resources: minerals, forest, and pasture in the Alpine region; chestnuts, olives, and grapevines in the foothills; cereal, linen, and mulberries in the plains. Moreover, three lakes – the Iseo, Idro, and Garda – and several rivers served as important sources of energy and irrigation as well as vital arteries for transportation. Thus, from a mercantilist point

---

[18] R. Almagià, *Le regioni d'Italia* (Turin: UTET, 1960), vol. II, p. 503.

[19] "qual si può veramente dir, che sij un picciol Regno," report of Domenico Priuli, 1572, in *RV*, ed. A. Tagliaferri, vol. XI: *Podestaria e capitanato di Brescia* (Milan: Giuffrè, 1978), p. 116.

[20] Report of Alvise Valaresso, Capitano, January 26, 1628 in *RV*, ed. Tagliaferri, vol. XI, p. 305. Venetian income from Brescia and Salò in 1633 amounted to 205,858 ducats, which was approximately 22 percent of the revenues the Republic collected for the entire Terraferma. In 1641 the figure rose to 231,498 ducats, nearly 23 percent. F. Besta, ed., *Bilanci generali della Republica di Venezia*, 2nd series, vol. I, t. 1 (Venice: Grafico Vicentini, 1912), pp. 490; 566.

[21] This is a crude estimate. The surface area is taken from a modern census: *Annuario generale dei comuni e delle frazioni d'Italia*, Touring Club Italiano (Milan: Garzante Editore, 1980–1985), p. 167. The population figures are from the years 1579 (296,403) and 1610 (440,160). See table 1 in text. Population numbers in 1630 were no doubt lower than 1579, but the data are not available.

5. The Northern Bresciano. From Vincenzo Coronelli. *Corso geografico universale* (Venice, 1689), pp. 180–181. Photograph courtesy of the Biblioteca Nazionale Marciana, Venice.

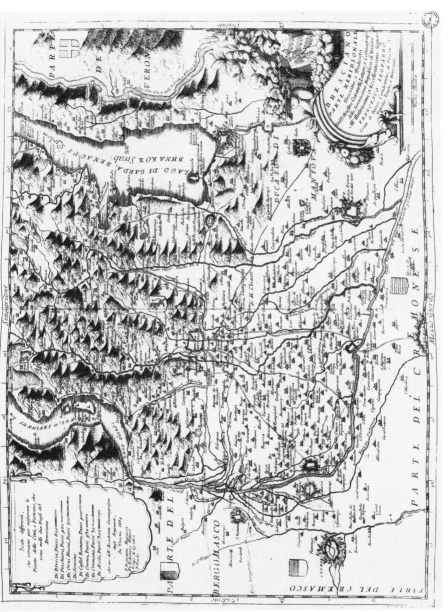

6. The Southern Bresciano. From Vincenzo Coronelli. *Corso geografico universale* (Venice, 1689), pp. 178–179. Photograph courtesy of the Biblioteca Nazionale Marciana, Venice.

of view the Bresciano was a rich garden from which the Venetian state could potentially reap many fruits.

Venetian statesmen and visitors alike lauded the natural wealth at Brescia's disposal by virtue of its geopolitical position. On his travels through Lombardy in the last years of the sixteenth century, Giovanni Botero ranked the magnitude of Brescia's domain second only to Milan,

> Not for its size, nor for a multitude of inhabitants (because it does not reach 50,000), but for the size of its jurisdiction, which embraces many, and large lands, and important valleys, which are populous. Among the lands subject to the city, Brescia boasts Asola, and Salò with Lake Garda; among the valleys, the Valcamonica, fifty miles long, with plenty of iron mines and men. The Iseo and Idri Lakes are part of Brescia's *contado*.[22]

The Republic entrusted the government of many of these lands to the Brescian Council. Twenty-one podestà and vicariates with civil and often criminal jurisdictions oversaw provincial administration: there were four major podestà for the Valcamonica, Salò, Asola, and Orzinuovi, respectively; three minor podestà for Chiari, Lonato, and Palazzolo; seven major vicariates for Iseo, Montichiari, Rovato, Gottolengo, Calvisano, Quinzano, and Pontevico; and seven minor vicariates for Gavardo, Manerbio, Ghedi, Gambara, Pontoglio, Castrezzato, and Pompiano.[23] At the same time Venetian representatives were stationed in the strategic locations of Salò, Lonato, Anfo, Asola, Orzinuovi, and Pontevico.

The city was in a fortunate position for landed proprietors, heavily represented on the city council, to market the goods that derived from their investments outside the urban center. As a consumer of raw materials, and as a center of some manufactures, Brescia linked the economies of three Pre-Alpine valleys with that of the plains. In the Valcamonica to the northwest, the soil was only marginally cultivable. While the population supplemented its grain needs with chestnuts, there was scarcely food for half the year. The circumscribed agrarian economy forced part of the valley's labor force to migrate to Brescia, to the plains, or to the Lombard and Venetian capitals in search of seasonal

[22] "La seconda città di Lombardia, è Brescia, non per giro di muraglia, ò per moltitudine di habitanti (perche non arriva a cinquanta mila huomini) ma per la grandezza della giurisdittione, che abbraccia molte, e grosse terre, e valli importanti, e popolose. Tra le terre a lei soggette, portano il vanto Asola, e Salò sul Lago di Garda; tra le valli, Valcamonica, lunga 50 miglia, piena di miniere di ferro, e d'huomini. Appartengono al suo contado i laghi d'Iseo, e d'Idri." G. Botero, *Delle relationi universali di Giovanni Botero* (Vicenza: Giorgio Angelieri, 1596), pp. 50–51.

[23] Report of Paolo Correr, Podestà, in *RV*, ed. Tagliaferri, vol. XI, pp. 69–71.

employment.[24] The Val Trompia and the Valsabbia (north and north-east of Brescia, respectively) also depended heavily on cereal imports. Brescia, on the other hand, held vital connections with the plains, the province's major grain producer. Moreover, the hills above the city, terraced with grapevines since pre-Roman times, were given over to viticulture.[25] Citizens who held preponderant land holdings in these areas had the option of exchange with the valleys. Brescia compensated the Val Trompia's basic alimentary deficiencies, grain and wine, in exchange for meat and dairy products. At the same time it acquired two important sources of energy from the valley, wood and charcoal. Merchants had worked out a similar commercial arrangement with the Valsabbia, supplying cereals in exchange for wood.[26] Further, Brescia availed itself of an abundance of raw materials from the province. The city enjoyed a natural advantage in that two of the Pre-Alpine valleys within its reach, the Valcamonica and the Val Trompia, were rich in iron and minerals, and supplied thousands with employment in the mining and metalworking industries. Brescian manufacturers also relied on raw materials from these valleys for the production of a variety of goods.[27] For example, the Valsabbia supplied raw wool, a primary product that sustained a segment of the city's weaving industry.[28]

South of the urban center lay the cradle of Brescian wealth, the densely settled, rich and vast Po Plains, divided topographically into high and low sections. The former – arid, more difficult to cultivate, and yielding smaller returns – were characterized by small farms that specialized in cereal production and viticulture.[29] In contrast, the well-irrigated low plains, which large landed proprietors divided into orderly fields lined with trees and shrubs, provided the city in normal times with wheat, rye, barley, millet, broad beans, and (in the seventeenth century) maize.[30] Some of this land was also given over to pasturage, which not only supplied Brescia with meat and dairy products but also furnished

---

[24] Pasero, "Introduzione," *Il catastico Da Lezze*, p. 65.

[25] E. Turri, "La fascia prealpina," in *I paesaggi umani*, ed. Touring Club Italiano (Milan: Touring Club Italiano, 1977), p. 40.

[26] Report of Paolo Correr, Podestà, April 1562, in *RV*, ed. Tagliaferri, vol. XI, pp. 77–80.

[27] Merchants in Brescia owned some of the richest mines in the Val Trompia. U. Tucci, "L'industria del ferro nel Settecento. La Val Trompia," in *Ricerche storiche ed economiche in memoria di Corrado Barbagallo*, ed. L. de Rosa (Naples: Edizioni scientifiche italiane, 1970), vol. II, pp. 422; 448.

[28] Da Lezze, *Il catastico Da Lezze*, vol. I, pp. 391–392; 397–398.

[29] C. Saibene, "La Padania," in *I paesaggi umani*, ed. Touring Club Italiano (Milan: Touring Club Italiano, 1977), p. 56.

[30] Pasero, "Introduzione," *Il catastico Da Lezze*, p. 66; A. De Maddalena, "Il mondo rurale italiano nel Cinque e nel Seicento," *RSI* 76 (1964): 359–360; 380, n. 73; 401.

the raw materials for the city's stamped leather and shoe industries,[31] products which were in demand both in the Bresciano and in neighboring regions throughout the first half of the seventeenth century.[32] Finally, the production of raw linen and silk were also vital activities that linked the economy of the southeastern plains, controlled to a large degree by wealthy citizens, to that of the city.[33] The prosperity of Brescian citizens thus rested upon supplying the city and outlying markets with a wide variety of alimentary products as well as the primary materials necessary to sustain the manufacture and exchange of goods. Thus the choice of landed investments over other sectors of the economy, given geographical position and natural resources, appears to be logical.

Human resources

Brescia's population (table 1) during the late sixteenth and early seventeenth centuries rose and fell in synchronization with that of the Italian peninsula. To the end of the sixteenth century, demographic numbers climbed, pressing heavily on the natural resources of the countryside. A visitation of the plague in 1575 to 1577 interrupted the steady cycle of demographic expansion, taking 10,000 lives in Brescia and the Chiusure, the rural area within a three-mile radius of the city.[34] Recovery, however, was fairly rapid: the population climbed from 31,403 in 1579 to 51,767 in 1610. In the city, Da Lezze registered 11,296 wage earners and 31,780 women, children, and aged in 1609 to 1610 (table 2).

Then the tide began to change. Agriculture reached the limits of its expansion in the 1590s,[35] no longer able to accommodate the exploding numbers of people. The population fell subject to periodic subsistence crises,[36] which inevitably weighed on rates of mortality and fertility. Economic conditions were particularly precarious during this decade. With a swollen population and smaller agricultural yields, grain prices

[31] Da Lezze, *Il catastico Da Lezze*, vol. I, p. 475.
[32] Leather was also exported to Venice and Bolzano. Pasero, "Introduzione," in *ibid.*, p. 69.
[33] Da Lezze, in *ibid.*, p. 398; De Maddalena, "Mondo rurale," p. 401.
[34] Losses in the province, excluding the city, totaled 12,000. C. Pasero, "Dati statistici e notizie intorno al movimento della popolazione bresciana durante il dominio veneto (1426–1797)," *Archivio Storico Lombardo* 9 (1961): 90.
[35] Romano, "La storia economica," p. 1,907.
[36] F. Braudel, *The Mediterranean and the Mediterranean World in the Age of Philip II* (translated by Sian Reynolds, New York: Harper & Row, 1972), pp. 427; 599–605.

Table 1. *The population of Brescia, the*
Chiusure, and the Province (1561–1658)

	Year	Brescia	Chiusure	Province
1.	1561	—	41,168	—
2.	1579	—	31,403	265,000
3.	1610	43,076	51,767	—
4.	1633	19,821	—	—
5.	1645	28,000	—	280,000
6.	1650	28,000	—	164,690
7.	1658	34,870	40,220	313,167

Sources: 1 and 2: K. J. Beloch, "Bevölkerungsgeschichte der Republik Venedig," *Jahrbuchern*
für National Ökonomie und Statistik (Jena: G.
Fischer, 1899), p. 20.
3: Report of Podestà G. Da Lezze in *RV*, ed.
Tagliaferri, vol. 11, p. 199.
4 and 7: C. Pasero, "Dati statistici e notizie
intorno al movimento della popolazione bresciana durante il dominio veneto (1426–1797),"
Archivio Storico Lombardo, series 9, 1 (1961): 94.
5: Report of Podestà B. Renier in *RV*, ed.
Tagliaferri, vol. 11, p. 443; 447.
6: Report of Capitano Andrea Dolfin, in *ibid.*,
pp. 468–469.

soared.[37] The period witnessed a temporary boom for landed investors, but after 1600 prices slowly stagnated save for the famines of 1610,
1620 to 1621, and 1628. Finally, the pandemic of 1630 proved to be a
watershed, relieving pressure in the countryside and destabilizing
conditions on the home market. Population figures dropped dramatically and only slowly recovered. The city of Brescia registered severe
losses: contemporaries claim as high as 61 percent, from 36,000 in 1630
to 14,000 in 1631.[38] Immediately afterwards urban numbers rose
abruptly, due to immigration, and then leveled off at 19,821 in 1633.[39]
Mortality rates were serious elsewhere, too: about 50 percent in Milan,

---

[37] For Venice, see B. Pullan, "Introduction," in *Crisis and Change in the Venetian
Economy*, ed. B. Pullan (London: Methuen and Co. Ltd., 1968), p. 13.

[38] ASV, *Senato. DRB*, F. 33, March 5, 1631, letter of Alvise Mocenigo, Capitano. On
the plague in Brescia and the Bresciano, P. Ulvioni, *Il gran castigo di Dio. Carestia ed
epidemie a Venezia e nella Terraferma, 1628–1632* (Milan: Franco Angeli, 1989), pp.
141–176, and on conflicting reports of urban mortality, p. 150.

[39] Pasero, "Dati statistici," p. 94.

Table 2. *The distribution of the urban population in 1610*

District	Utili[a]	Inutili[b]	Total number of a) people; b) households	
			a	b
Cittadella Vecchia				
Duomo	350	750	1,100	?
San Clemente	310	850	1,160	?
San Zanino	46	120	166	?
San Zeno	200	460	660	?
Santa Maria Calchera	500	1,500	2,000	800
Cittadella Nuova				
Duomo	500	1,600	2,100	400
San Giovanni				
First section	1,000	3,050	4,050	1,000
Second	500	2,000	2,500	400
Third	550	1,500	2,050	800
Fourth	800	2,100	2,900	2,000
Fifth	600	1,500	2,100	450
Sixth	400	1,200	1,600	350
San Faustino				
First section	300	1,300	1,600	120
Second	420	1,400	1,820	370
Third	400	1,250	1,650	345
Fourth	700	2,400	3,100	420
Fifth	500	1,400	1,900	800
Sixth	300	1,200	1,500	1,000
Seventh	550	1,700	2,250	700
Mompiano (Eighth)	1,350	?	1,350	213
Sant' Alessandro				
First Section	620	2,500	3,120	630
Second	400	2,000	2,400	700
Total	11,296	31,780	43,076	11,498

Notes: [a]Men.
[b]Women, children, the aged.
? = Statistics not furnished.
Source: G. Da Lezze, *Il catastico bresciano di Giovanni Da Lezze* (1609–1610), ed. C. Pasero (Brescia: F. Apollonio, 1964), vol. I, pp. 175, 182, 197, 205, 210, 216, 221, 224, 230, 236, 241, 247, 250, 255, 259, 262, 268, 272.

40 percent in Pavia, 30 percent in Como,[40] and about 40 percent in Venice and the mainland.[41]

[40] D. Sella, *L'economia lombarda durante la dominazione spagnola* (Bologna: Il Mulino, 1982), p. 96.
[41] S. J. Woolf, "Venice and the Terraferma: Problems of the Change from Commercial to Landed Activities," in *Crisis and Change*, ed. Pullan, p. 177. For Vicenza's

While Brescia gradually filled in the gaps in human resources, reaching 28,000 in 1645 and 34,870 in 1658, the growing numbers in the city cannot necessarily be interpreted as a sign of economic vigor. The drastic mortality rate of 1630 undercut economic stability.[42] Grain, for example, exceeded demand, reducing its market value. To urban investors who relied on agricultural income that fall potentially meant less revenue unless the cereal market could be manipulated. It also meant relying more on other investment outlets: loans, for example, or for city councillors the benefits of office. Falling grain prices affected the rural population as well.[43] Reduced purchasing power on the local market ultimately affected the city's ability to sell its goods. In sum, all sectors of the Brescian economy underwent a difficult period of adjustment after the demographic reversals of 1630, creating social problems which challenged the abilities of Venetian statesmen and Brescian councillors alike. The tax census (*estimo*) of 1641 offers us an approximate index of wealth distribution after the plague: one-third of the urban population fell into the category of *miserabili*, that is, too poor to sustain direct taxes to Venice (table 3). Whatever the imperfections of the census and whatever contemporary perceptions of *miserabile* actually meant, these figures suggest at the least that there was not necessarily any correlation between population density and fiscal capacity.

Demographic recovery in Brescia after the plague might be partially explained by rising natality. Catastrophic mortality opened new doors for survivors, bringing youth earlier inheritances, encouraging earlier first marriages and the union of widows and widowers and, as a consequence, reproduction.[44] That would mean, however, that a

population figures during this period see A. Tagliaferri, "Introduzione," *Podestaria e capitanato di Vicenza*, vol. VII of *RV*, ed. A. Tagliaferri (Milan: Giuffrè, 1976), p. xvi; for Verona: G. Borelli, "Introduzione,"*Podestaria e capitanato di Verona*, vol. IX of *RV*, ed. A. Tagliaferri (Milan: Giuffrè, 1977), p. xxxv; for Salò: C. Povolo, "L'evoluzione demografica di un centro urbano del Garda in età moderna: Salò," in *Un lago, una civiltà: il Garda* (Verona: Banca Popolare di Verona, 1983), p. 246.

[42] ASV, *DRB*, F. 33, letter of Alvise Mocenigo, Capitano, March 5, 1631. The letter offers a summary of the status of urban industries. Mocenigo dwells on the burden of *dazi*.

[43] For grain prices, Romano, "La storia economica," pp. 1,828; 1,832. See also Sella, *L'economia lombarda*, pp. 55; 72; 94–95; 123–124; For Desenzano, G. Zalin, "Il mercato granario in Desenzano nei secoli XVI e XVII. Problemi alimentari e politica annonaria nel territorio benacense," *in Atti del convegno su Camillo Tarello e la storia dell'agricoltura bresciana al tempo della Repubblica veneta* (Brescia: Geroldi, 1980), p. 34.

[44] Povolo finds that nuptial rates in Salò increased after the epidemic of 1630–1631 ("Evoluzione demografica," p. 246). This was true of Venice as well. D. Beltrami, *Storia della popolazione di Venezia dalle fine del secolo XVI alla caduta della Repubblica* (Padua: A. Milani, 1954), p. 124.

Table 3. *Brescia: The distribution of taxable households in 1641*

| District | Taxable households | Miserabili | | Total number of households in district |
		Number	Percentage of district	
Cittadella Vecchia	695	289[a]	29.3	984
Cittadella Nuova	199	110[a]	35.5	309
San Faustino				
First	159	71	30.8	230
Second	226	93	29.1	319
Third	257	177	40.7	434
Fourth	287	177	38.1	464
Fifth	210	121	36.5	331
Sixth	142	52	26.8	194
Seventh	243	108	30.8	351
Mompiano (Eighth)	97	59	37.8	156
San Giovanni				
First	383	177	31.6	560
Second	307	102	24.9	409
Third	287	173	37.6	460
Fourth	553	330	37.3	883
Fifth	287	135	31.9	422
Sixth	163	64	28.1	227
Sant' Alessandro				
First	461	262	36.2	723
Second	343	200	36.6	546
Total	5,299	2,700		8,002

Note: [a] The register does not specify *miserabili* for these two sections, but the format of the register suggests that this was simply an omission.
Source: ASCB, *Reg.* 188, "Estimo della sola città," a partially foliated document, which is best to consult by section and by number.

significant portion of the population was young, falling into the ranks of consumers rather than producers. Demographic recovery in Brescia can also be readily explained by immigration. The drastic mortality rate created space for rural inhabitants who wished to leave the countryside. This included a number of landless poor, in flight from worse conditions, who sought refuge in the city. Pre-industrial cities collected the indigent, especially during cycles of conjunctural crises: the poor in Cremona totaled 15 percent of the population in 1610; in Modena they totaled 11 percent in 1621; in 1629, a severe famine year in northern Italy, Milan received 9,715 paupers;[45] Naples was constantly swelled by immigrants from the countryside. A troubled agrarian economy in the 1630s, coupled with rising fiscal pressures and a fall in agricultural

[45] *Ibid.*, pp. 27–28

income, no doubt contributed to Brescia's quota of the indigent.[46] At the same time, the more favorable fiscal climate of the city, relative to that of the countryside, may have worked to promote the immigration of more prosperous members of the rural communities to the urban center as well. Finally, a loss of craftsmen and other workers in Brescia compelled city councillors, who controlled guild statutes, to replenish these corporations by encouraging immigration.[47] Following the plague in 1631, the Venetian Senate encouraged craftsmen to immigrate to Brescia, ordering the city's guilds and corporations (*paratici*, *scuole*, *arti*, and *mariegole*) to waive their entrance requirements for three years, and in 1632 the guilds' regulatory commission (correttori agli paratici) made such provisions.[48] In sum, there appears to have been an increase in mobility in Brescia after the pandemic of 1630, which helps explain the gradual rise in population figures. It does not, however, give us any indication of the level of productivity in the city. For this we must consult other sources.

Industrial activity

It is difficult to determine how active manufacturing in Brescia was during the late sixteenth and early seventeenth centuries primarily because we lack the empirical evidence with which to gauge this. The historical literature on this subject to date has largely relied on the reports of Venetian officials or the supplications for tax relief from the local ruling class,[49] sources that conflict, that represent particular bias, and thus that present serious methodological limitations. There is no detailed profile of Brescian manufactures based upon guild records. Therefore it is not within the limits of this chapter to provide an economic history of Brescia, but rather to place a study of the political behavior of Venetian statesmen and Brescian councillors within a general economic setting. The descriptive accounts of Brescian

---

[46] For fiscal conditions in the countryside, see J. Ferraro, "Proprietà terriera e potere nello Stato veneto: la nobiltà bresciana del '400–'500," in *Dentro lo "stado italico." Venezia e la Terraferma fra Quattro e Seicento*, eds. G. Cracco and M. Knapton (Trent: Gruppo Culturale Civis, 1984), pp: 159–182; on immigration, see Pasero, "Dati statistici," p. 93.

[47] In November 1630 the city council furnished a vivid description of the detrimental effects of the plague in Brescia. Commerce had virtually come to a standstill. ASB, *Cancelleria Prefettizia Inferiore*, Reg. 11, ff. 120v–121r, November 14, 1630.

[48] ASCB, *Statuti paratici*, vol. 1058, f. 247r, March 4, 1632.

[49] Compare Da Lezze, *Il catastico Da Lezze* with BQ, MS. F. II.11. f. 80, ff. 80r–85r, "Rappresentanza fatta l'anno 1619 al principe dagli ambasciatori della città. Averoldi, Baitelli e Ugoni," MS. F. II.11, ff. 94v–100r, L. Baitelli, "Supplica della città fatta l'anno 1648 per sollievo di gravezze."

and Venetian contemporaries will be evaluated in the context of what we already know about the northern Italian economy from modern empirical studies.

Historians have given us a detailed picture of commercial and industrial trends in the northern Italian cities during the late sixteenth and early seventeenth centuries. Large cities such as Venice and Milan witnessed an "Indian Summer" until 1619 to 1620, while in the four decades that followed the volume of trade and manufacture markedly slowed down.[50] Smaller urban centers, on the other hand, may have fared much better, while in some areas, such as Spanish Lombardy, the economic axis shifted to the countryside. Research since the Second World War has produced a number of explanations for this dramatic transformation, still the subject of debate. To summarize briefly, Sella and Cipolla have attributed transformations in the Italian economy to British and Dutch success: manufactures in Italy's urban centers collapsed when faced with competition from these rising commercial powers because of their antiquated systems, inflexible guilds, and high production costs.[51] Cipolla and others have also advanced the theory that the Italian economy was sustained principally by exports. When these fell in the 1620s, the economy collapsed. Both foreign and home demand for manufactures dropped, and this had a tendency to reduce the price of goods. Moreover, since the price of manufactures fell significantly lower than that of agricultural products, investment was diverted from industry into the land.[52] Yet another thesis, advanced by Romano, places the commercial and industrial decline within the context of collapsed purchasing power on the home market.[53] Finally, in a more recent study, Sella, setting the perimeters for further discussion, proposed that the home market be studied more closely. Focusing on Brescia's neighbors in Spanish Lombardy, the author found that in the seventeenth century a number of urban manufacturers shifted their activities to the countryside, where they were better able to survive the mid-century economic crisis.[54]

---

[50] R. Romano, "Tra XVI e XVII secolo. Una crisi economica, 1619–1622," *RSI* 74 (1962): 480–531.

[51] C. Cipolla, "The Economic Decline of Italy," in *Crisis and Change*, ed. Pullan, pp. 143–144. See also Romano, "Storia economica," p. 1,888. The thesis has more recently been criticized in P. Malanima, "Città e campagne nell'economia lombarda del Seicento. Qualche considerazione," *Società e Storia* 16(1982): 362.

[52] Cipolla, "Economic Decline of Italy," pp. 142–143.

[53] Romano, "La storia economica," p. 1,920.

[54] Sella, *L'economia lombarda*, pp. 181–225; see also the reviews of Sella's thesis in G. Politi, "I dubbi dello sviluppo. Rilevanza e ruolo del mondo rurale in alcune opere

While the causes are far from clear, there is some agreement that Italy's international network of commercial relations, based upon the activities of large urban centers, was reduced by the third decade of the seventeenth century to that of a regional market where rural industries achieved central importance. Unfortunately the economy of seventeenth-century Venetian Lombardy still awaits specialized research, where the rich legacy of hypotheses that economic historians have given us could be tested with fruitful results. It is particularly important to test Sella's model in the rural areas east of the Adda, which enjoyed a wealth of natural resources, particularly iron, minerals, and medium- and low-quality wools. As for Brescia, contemporary evidence strongly suggests that its industries experienced serious strains in the middle decades of the seventeenth century, not the least of which was the dramatic reversal of the ratio of supply and demand in 1630. The reports of Venetian rectors during these decades are void of the kind of optimism Da Lezze expressed in his survey of the city in 1609 to 1610. Moreover, demographic evidence also suggests that the balance of economic activities had shifted to the countryside: the ratio of rural inhabitants exceeded that of the urban center, and the industries that survived the mid-century tempest – textiles and iron – had their center of gravity outside Brescia.

On balance, and this tentative hypothesis must be confirmed with specialized study, it appears that certain activities in Brescia fit the picture given us by economic historians, perhaps with slightly different life cycles, while others survived the adverse conditions that character-ized the middle decades of the seventeenth century. The overall economy slowed down by the 1630s – the urban economy in particular atrophied – but the crisis was not definitive. Decline in some areas of the economy was offset by recovery and growth in others, particularly rural manufactures.

Among the areas in decline, the production of high-quality wool cloth stands out. Pasero's research dates the fall in production of this industry to the mid sixteenth century.[55] This is largely corroborated in Da Lezze's census (*catastico*) of 1609 to 1610 and the Brescian Councillor Lorenzo Averoldi's report to the Venetian Senate in 1619. The Venetian Podestà Da Lezze noted that Brescia produced 14,000 to 15,000 fine cloths for Levantine markets prior to 1580; by 1610 the city

recenti (secoli XV e XVII)," *Società e Storia* 16 (1982): 367–389; Malanima, "Città e campagne," in *Società e Storia* 16 (1982): 351–365.

[55] Pasero, "Il dominio veneto," p. 336; Pasero, "Introduzione," *Il catastico Da Lezze*, p. 71; See also D. Sella, "The Rise and Fall of the Venetian Woollen Industry," in *Crisis and Change*, ed. Pullan, p. 113.

was producing no more than twelve or thirteen cloths per year.[56] Closer to the middle of the century, Lodovico Baitelli, another Brescian councillor, described this activity as near extinction.[57] What accounts for the contraction of high-grade wool manufacture? Contemporaries placed the blame on governmental restrictions and excessive taxation. In 1517 Venice prohibited the importation of raw wool that did not come from its own reserves, and in 1543 the Republic imposed an extraordinary *dazio* on this product.[58] Both Averoldi and Baitelli argued before the Venetian Senate that eventually the woolen industry could not sustain the expense of indirect taxes in addition to that of transport, of labor, and of the requirement to buy raw materials from the capital city.[59]

No doubt the Venetian *dazi* reduced the profit margins of Brescian wool weavers. Rapp has found that between 1588 and 1630 the average price for one piece of wool cloth in Venice was 79 ducats. Forty-two percent of that figure went to the fisc.[60] While we have no such breakdown for Brescian wools, it is clear that the subject city's industries did not enjoy any fiscal advantages over those of the capital.[61] Certainly had the tax burden been alleviated Brescian wools would have been relatively more competitive. Nonetheless, if excessive taxation was the primary obstacle preventing the wool weavers from making a profit, craftsmen probably would have transferred their activities to a more favorable fiscal climate. Apparently there was little incentive to do this because the problem went farther than simply Venetian protectionism. Giovanni Da Lezze identified some of the Brescian wool weavers' other difficulties:

> The cause of this decline and lack of the cloth-making craft is because the merchants, who are in good number, know that it is to their advantage to buy cloths in Milan, and other foreign lands, in Modena, London, German territories, Flanders, and elsewhere. [The cloths] are of very poor quality. In particular the black ones are full of vitriol, and in four

[56] Da Lezze, *Il catastico Da Lezze*, vol. I, p. 390.
[57] Baitelli's report is reprinted in A. Zanelli, *Delle condizioni interne di Brescia del 1426 al 1644 e del moto della borghesia contro la nobiltà nel 1644* (Brescia: Tipografia Editrice, 1898), pp. 254–258.
[58] Pasero, "Il dominio veneto," p. 336.
[59] BQ, MS. F. 11, 11, f. 80, ff. 80r–85r.
[60] R. Rapp, *Industry and Economic Decline in Seventeenth Century Venice* (Cambridge, MA: Harvard University Press, 1976), p. 140.
[61] In order to protect its own industries, especially glass, printing, and textiles, the Republic had permitted its own producers to sell on the Brescian markets without limits in volume. Moreover, Brescian products were subject to costly taxes designed to protect Venetian interests. Pasero, "Il dominio veneto," p. 332.

months the fur falls off. [The merchants] calculate that making cloth in Brescia, which requires a year's time, great expense and interest, would mean not putting capital to work for that period, whereas buying it in other places is much more expedient. Local wool is good, but not as perfect as it should be given the pastureland, as compared to Flanders, England, Spain, and the Levant.[62]

Thus, the industry's primary problem was its inability to compete either in price or in quality with other producers, notably England and the Low Countries, as the podestà pointed out. Moreover, the wool industry was subject to market fluctuations that were beyond its control, such as the contraction of the demand for high quality cloth in the Levant after 1602.[63] Da Lezze offered a solution to the problem:

> The best remedy would be to prohibit the import of any kind of foreign cloth, with the exception of Venetian cloth. Thus the merchants who live in this city and territory, who are many and for the most part very rich, would be constrained to manufacture cloth in the city and territory and would provide poor persons with employment in the arts of spinning and weaving.[64]

Da Lezze did not mention that Brescia also had serious local competitors. Bergamo's woolen industry thrived in the seventeenth century, causing serious damage to Venetian activity because of its low-cost production. At the beginning of the eighteenth century this Venetian subject city still produced 10,000 to 15,000 fine cloths,[65]

[62] "La causa di questa declinatione, et mancamento dell'arte di fabricar pani procede perche le mercanti che sono in buon numero, conoscendo il loro avantaggio vano a comprar li pani a Milan, et in altre terre aliene a Modena, a Londra, Terra Tedesca, Fiandra, et simili, che sono anco pani disgratiati, et pessimi, et in particolar i negri che sono carichi di vedriol, che in quattro mesi casca il pello, facendo i loro conti, che fabricandoli in Bressa, se ricerca un tempo de un anno a redurle in perfettione ed gravissime loro spese, et interessi, rimanendo il danaro morto per quel tempo, che comprandoli in altri paesi come è detto le cose lore, e mercantie, passano piu espedite.
  Le lane del Paese sono ben buone, ma non sono in quella perfettione, che doverebbe esser rispetto alli pascoli, et come sono quelle di Fiandra, Inghiltera, Spagna, et Levantine." Da Lezze, *Il catastico Da Lezze*, vol. I, pp. 390–391.

[63] Sella, "Rise and Fall," p. 117.

[64] "Il rimedio ottimo sarebbe il prohibire, che non potessero venir in questo stato panine forestiere di alcuna sorte, salvo che Venetiane, perche di questa maniera li mercanti habitanti in questa città et paese che sono molti, et richissimi per la maggior parte, sarebbero necessitati di farne fabricar nella città et territorio, et darebbero occasione alle povere persone di viver con quest'arte filando, et tessendo essi panni, come di sopra." Da Lezze, *Il catastico Da Lezze*, vol. I, pp. 390–392.

[65] Rapp, *Industry and Economic Decline*, p. 161. See also Cipolla, "Economic Decline of Italy," p. 132.

which were reputedly cheaper than Brescian ones.[66] Bergamo was not Brescia's only competitor: Soncino and Mantua were able to cut their production costs because raw wool was not subject to indirect taxes. Pasero maintains that Cremona was also a competitor, though eventually the industry flagged in this urban center as well. The Cremonesi infiltrated Brescian markets, distributing raw wool to weavers in the countryside and then clandestinely selling the finished product at competitive prices.[67]

Wool weavers in Brescia also suffered because local merchants, concerned with keeping high profit margins and earning quick returns, preferred to import finished products rather than invest both the time and capital in a local weaving industry. Though direct evidence for guild inertia is not available, Da Lezze's descriptions make it plausible that the weavers' guild subjected production to strict quality control that was costly, time-consuming, and therefore uncompetitive. This corporation, however, was no match for that of the wool merchants,[68] who appear to have cut the local weavers out of the market. The choice was not simply left to the merchants, however. It is important to note that city councillors shared the government of both the wool guild and the merchants' guild with members of these corporations.

The fate of high-quality wool cloth in Brescia seems to mirror the experience of textile production in several other Italian cities of the late sixteenth and early seventeenth centuries.[69] Milan's woolen industry showed signs of fatigue in 1580[70] and entered into serious difficulties by the third and fourth decades of the seventeenth century. Cremona and Como's industries had collapsed by 1650. Meanwhile in Venice wool production fell by a dramatic 50 percent between 1600 and 1650. Sella finds that in these cities the Italian woolen industry was forced to bow to international competitors largely because inflexible guilds did not adapt to changing market conditions.[71] As to whether the wool weavers' guild in Brescia was "inflexible," the sources are silent, but this is a viable possibility. It appears, however, that the wool merchants had made the decisive choice, independent of the wool weavers: given market conditions, particularly Bergamasc success, it was more profitable to import finished products. Significantly, however, Brescian

[66] Pasero, "Il dominio veneto," p. 336.
[67] Ibid., p. 337.   [68] Ibid, p. 338.
[69] Romano, "Storia economica," pp. 1,887; 1,908–1,909; Sella, "Rise and Fall," p. 117.
[70] Sella, L'economia lombarda, p. 101.
[71] Sella, L'economia lombarda, pp. 141–143; Sella, "Rise and Fall," pp. 120–124; See also Cipolla, "Economic Decline of Italy," pp. 143–144.

wool weavers *did* adjust, finding it more worthwhile to concentrate on the production of medium- and low-grade cloth for local consumption, an industry which survived, though not without significant losses, into the seventeenth century. Production figures reached about 18,000 cloths per annum in the late sixteenth century,[72] dropping to 12,000 to 13,000 cloths in 1610.[73]

Another craft in Brescia that was clearly in difficulty by the early seventeenth century was the gun-barrel industry. The flight of Brescian armsmakers to neighboring states is a theme which appears in the rectors' reports to the Venetian Senate by the second decade of the seventeenth century. The Venetian Captain Stefano Viario reported only twelve workshops in the entire city in 1613.[74] Six years later the Brescian councillor Lorenzo Averoldi lamented that there were only two or three; in 1632 Angelo Contarini reported that the city's arms industry had expired, perhaps as a result of the plague; and in 1648 Lodovico Baitelli counted two or three shops that were barely active. Unlike the manufacture of high-quality wools, the contraction of arms production in Brescia was not the casualty of a shrinking market, especially in an era when warfare was endemic. Enjoying an international reputation, Brescian arms (and therefore armsmakers) were much in demand throughout the Italian peninsula and abroad.[75] According to Gaibi, technological know-how in this industry reached its apogee in the seventeenth century. Gun-barrel production declined in Brescia in good part because of Venetian protectionism but also because other Italian and European states offered craftsmen more attractive employment opportunities.

The arms masters, reported Angelo Contarini in 1632, are in the Milanese, the Genovese, the Parmigiano, and Rome.[76] Contemporar-

---

[72] Pasero, "Il dominio veneto," p. 337.

[73] Da Lezze, *Il catastico Da Lezze*, vol. I, pp. 72; 390. Production figures for Brescia are notably higher than those for Milan during this period: 4,500 in 1580 and 3,000 in 1640. Sella, *L'economia lombarda*, p. 101, n. 1. The art of making wool blankets grew in Brescia during this period. In 1622 the public deputies and the correttori placed the blanket-makers in the wool weavers' guild. ASCB, *Statuti paratici*, vol. 1058, ff. 40r–40v, May 10, 1622.

[74] Report of Stefano Viario, May 13, 1613, in *RV*, ed. Tagliaferri, vol. XI, p. 229.

[75] A. Gaibi, "Le armi da fuoco," in *Storia di Brescia*, ed. Trecani degli Alfieri (Brescia: Morcelliana, 1964), vol. III, pp. 848; 851–854. See also Sella, *L'economia lombarda*, p. 106; D. Sella, "Le industrie europee (1500–1700)," in *Storia economica d'Europa*, ed. C. Cipolla (Turin: UTET, 1979–1980), vol. II, p. 314; Rapp, *Industry and Economic Decline*, pp. 159–160.

[76] In *RV*, ed. Tagliaferri, vol. XI, p. 362. See also report of Lorenzo Capello, Capitano, May 7, 1621, in *ibid.*, p. 256; report of Nicolò Donato, September 22, 1640, in *ibid.*, p. 408.

ies continually complained that master craftsmen had abandoned the city because of Venetian protectionism and intense fiscal pressure. This was not simply a Brescian polemic but was widely proclaimed by Venetian rectors as well, particularly when they surveyed the contraction of gun-barrel production at Gardone.[77] Da Lezze reported that the fixed prices and fixed volume the Republic had imposed on this industry, irrespective of market conditions, was the primary reason behind the emigration of its master craftsmen.[78] The city council's spokesman, Lorenzo Averoldi, on the other hand, dwelt heavily on the detrimental effects of the Venetian *dazi*, transit and customs taxes on the import and export of raw materials. The figures he supplied are probably an exaggeration. Averoldi reported in 1619 that Brescia had approximately 200 arms factories at the end of the fifteenth century, providing work for 50,000 individuals and yielding an income of 200,000 ducats annually. In 1520, however, raw materials such as the iron used in gun barrels were made subject to costly government licenses. Venice introduced the double *gabelle*: primary materials had to be sent to the capital city, where they were subject to indirect, transit, and customs taxes (*dazi, dogane, balzelli,* or *pedaggi*) before they were transported to the mainland.[79] As a result, many arms masters fled to Carinthia, the Garfagnana, Genoa, Piedmont, Parma, Milan, Tuscany, France, and Spain. The Venetians revoked their order in 1533, but the number of workshops had dropped by then to sixty-seven. Subsequently, in 1577, the Venetians levied a transit tax (*dazio di sottovento*). It too had such damaging effects that it was revoked in 1581, but not before many craftsmen had left the province.[80] Finally in 1606 and 1609 the Venetians imposed a *dazio* on the manufacture of arquebus barrels. This tax, Averoldi argued, destroyed the arms industry.

Though we must read Averoldi's calamitous report, designed to win

---

[77] See reports of Antonio Mocenigo, December 14, 1619 in *RV*, ed. Tagliaferri, vol. XI, p. 242; Andrea Da Lezze, September 19, 1626, in *ibid.*, p. 285; and Angelo Contarini, September 23, 1654, in *ibid.*, p. 479.

[78] Da Lezze, *Il catastico Da Lezze*, vol. I, pp. 413–417. See also A. Alberti and R. Cessi, *La politica mineraria della Repubblica Veneta* (Rome: Provveditori generali dello stato, 1927), p. 141. In 1610 the Republic only allowed the sale of hunting guns and wheellocks, leaving craftsmen with warehouses full of products for which there was little demand. Pasero, "Introduzione," *Il catastico Da Lezze*, p. 86.

[79] *Ibid* p. 53.

[80] The Brescian city council complained of the damaging effects of *dazi*, sending a letter to their nunzio in Venice to present their complaints over the transit tax. ASCB, *Provvisioni*, vol. 556, ff. 33r–34r, February 28, 1581. In 1595 the city council also protested a new *dazio* of one *soldo* per *lira* on all the *dazi*, again mentioning the difficulties of the city's armsmaking industry. *Ibid.*, vol. 563, ff. 52r–54r, November 29, 1595.

fiscal relief, with extreme caution, his arguments, together with those of the Venetian rectors, are not without substance. To begin, Venice was both interested in assuring its own supply of military weapons[81] (the manufacture of private handguns, in contrast, enjoyed more freedom[82]) and in controlling those furnished to neighboring states. Thus in the middle of the sixteenth century the state prohibited the export of semi-finished and finished arms for warfare. The measure provoked an uninterrupted migration of masters. Later the problem grew worse when the state blocked the export of raw materials necessary for the production of war arms.[83] Then in 1606 the Republic made provisions for the establishment of two foundries for its own exclusive use, one in Brescia and the other in Gardone. The Venetian Captain Giovanni Paolo Gradenigo brought eight master craftsmen from Milan to Brescia in 1607, boosting the number of shops in activity to twenty-six.[84] But in 1613 the foundry closed, and in 1626 the number of armsmakers' shops in the city had fallen to twelve, which the Podestà Andrea Da Lezze described as *mezze disfatte*. This rector also took measures to encourage immigration, successfully expanding the number of shops to twenty-seven.[85] Nonetheless by 1639 there were no more than seven masters of this craft left in Brescia.[86] The efforts of the Venetian rectors appear to have failed because the state prohibited free enterprise, causing an exodus of craftsmen to neighboring states that offered higher profits and an unrestricted market.[87]

Further assessing Averoldi's report, we must take into account that state policies were indeed largely shaped by financial necessity during this period. The costs of warfare, coupled with the contraction of the commercial and industrial sectors of the Venetian economy after 1620, overrode any long-range projections assessing the consequences of taxation on Brescian industries. Venice came to rely heavily on the fiscal resources of the Terraferma, especially those deriving from indirect taxes. It was difficult for the Republic to avoid the fiscal exploitation of mainland industries when indirect taxes (*dazi*)

---

[81] See Mallett and Hale, *The Military Organization*, p. 397.

[82] See Gaibi, "Le armi da fuoco," pp. 871–872.

[83] Alberti and Cessi, *Politica mineraria*, pp. 142–143.

[84] January 13, 1607, in *RV*, ed. Tagliaferri, vol. XI, p. 172.

[85] September 19, 1626, in *RV*, ed. Tagliaferri, vol. XI, p. 285.

[86] ASV, *Senato. DRB*, F. 46, copy of mandate of June 12, 1639, attached to letter of Domenico Tiepolo, April 6, 1644. The sindico of the armsmakers' guild asked permission from the Venetian Senate to take on a contract from Germany for 800 guns, which would allow armsmakers to maintain activity in the city. *Ibid.*, letter of April 7, 1644.

[87] Alberti and Cessi, *Politica mineraria*, p. 141.

accounted for a major portion of the state's revenue.[88] The extraction
of *dazi* in Brescia increased four or five times between 1535 and 1648.[89]
Demography, inflation, smuggling, tax evasion, and faulty administration all played a part in this tax rise. There were added costs, tied to
inflation, as well.[90] While in 1572 the Venetian Captain Domenico
Priuli reported that the Camera Ducale collected 95,000 ducats in *dazi*,
including that of grain grinding (*macina*, which was 38 percent of the
Camera's revenues), by 1642 the Brescian Camera brought in 160,000
ducats in *dazi* (61.5 percent of the total revenues the Camera
collected).[91]

Indirect taxes, Brescian councillors and Venetian representatives
argued, weighed on industrial output because the costs they added to
goods rendered them less competitive. But the fact that many other
sectors of the iron industry, including the manufacture of gun cases and
arms made for purposes other than warfare, remained intact during this
period, giving work to thousands, belies contemporary arguments that
the *dazi* actually arrested industrial activity. This is not to say that
manufactures did not suffer the setbacks resulting from *dazi*. However,
the demand for certain basic necessities remained. Both local and
neighboring markets called for wrought iron, nails, horseshoes, tools,
muskets,[92] swords, corselets, and andirons, among other products.

When weighing contemporaries' grievances over fiscal burdens it
should also be noted that tax administration was far from flawless.

---

[88] Rapp, *Industry and Economic Decline*, pp. 142; 159.

[89] Baitelli, in Zanelli, *Delle condizioni*, p. 255. Cf. Knapton, "Territorio vicentino," pp.
      68–70.

[90] A 35–40 percent surcharge which tax farmers and chamberlains demanded in order
      to compensate for debased currency (Pasero, "Introduzione," *Il catastico Da Lezze*,
      pp. 45–46); a surcharge (*addizionali*) on indirect taxes (*dazi*) to confront the
      progressive devaluation of *moneta corrente* and to ensure a stable income for the state
      coffers. A detailed discussion of the *addizionali* is provided in Tagliaferri, "Introdu-
      zione," *RV*, ed. Tagliaferri, vol. XI, pp. xl–xliii. Besta noted that the *dazi* rose 91
      percent in the Terraferma between 1572 and 1706 because of the *addizionali*. *Bilanci
      generali*, 2nd series, vol. I, t. 1, pp. xxvii–liii. See also G. Gullino, "Considerazioni
      sull'evoluzione del sistema fiscale veneto tra il XVI e il XVIII secolo," in *Il sistema
      fiscale veneto*, eds. G. Borelli, P. Lanaro, and F. Vecchiato (Verona: Libreria
      Universitario Editrice, 1982), pp. 66–67. Another surcharge (*aggi*) protected indirect
      taxes (*dazi*) from inflation. In 1572 it was one *grosso* of gold per ducat for payments
      made in *moneta corrente* and in 1635 a fixed premium of 20 percent was added to the
      payment, whether in *moneta corrente* or in *buona valuta*.

[91] Report of Domenico Priuli, Capitano, 1572, in *RV*, ed. Tagliaferri, vol. XI, p. 123;
      report of Girolamo Foscarini, Capitano, July 7, 1643, *ibid.*, p. 426.

[92] At least 500 people were involved in making cases for muskets in 1644. ASV, *Senato.
      DRB*, F. 46, letter of Giovanni Antonio Bione, attached to the letter of Domenico
      Tiepolo, Capitano, April 16, 1644.

Evasion was a universal problem throughout the Venetian Terraferma during the late sixteenth and seventeenth centuries.[93] The decline in yields from the silk *dazio* in the Bresciano between 1619 and 1627, just after Venice had tripled the tax over a five-year span,[94] is instructive. Venetian rectors attributed the reduction in part to the inefficiency of the tax farmers, but they also complained that many individuals (nobles in particular) had refused to pay the tax.[95] In 1644 Venetian rectors again reported that yields from the silk *dazio* were declining when they should be rising, and again complained of tax evasion, especially by the powerful.[96] Were mulberry producers (e.g., nobles and other investors), craftsmen, and merchants unable or *unwilling* to meet their fiscal obligations? Indeed the reports of Venetian rectors make clear that the *dazi* were ill-tolerated throughout the first half of the seventeenth century.[97] The Venetian Captain Andrea Dolfin reported in 1650 that it was difficult to recruit tax farmers because they were targets of violence.[98] Moreover, evasion and smuggling raise the question of immeasurable productivity and cash flow, unknown variables which could revise the picture of economic activity furnished in bureaucratic reports.

It is not possible to ascertain the degree to which Venetian *dazi* made arms production uncompetitive. The flight of the Brescian armsmakers, however, is a sign that state regulation of exports decisively quashed incentive by confining production to the local market, when in fact there was infinitely wider demand, and by reducing the profit margins of merchants and craftsmen. Because Brescian armsmakers possessed a highly marketable skill, they had the opportunity to transfer their activities elsewhere.

[93] Gullino, "Considerazioni," pp. 69–72.

[94] A. Zanelli, "Le condizioni economiche di Brescia nei primi anni del seicento. A proposito di due recenti pubblicazioni," *Archivio Storico Lombardo*, N. S. 15 (1937): 248. The silk tax rose in Brescia, the Chiusure, and the Territorio from 1,439 ducats in 1612 to 5,256 ducats in 1617. ASV, *Senato. DRB*, F. 17, letter of Francesco Diedo, Capitano, May 31, 1617.

[95] ASV, *Senato. DRB*, F. 28, letter of Giovanni Capello, Podestà and Antonio Vallaresso, Capitano, March 17, 1627; letter of Zaccaria Bondumier (?), April 24, 1627; *Senato. Terra*, Reg. 99, ff. 20r and 20v, March 26, 1627. The Venetians also had trouble collecting the silk *dazio* in the Veronese. The tax was ill tolerated by the producers of raw silk. Borelli, *RV*, ed. Tagliaferri, vol. IX, pp. lxvi–lxviii.

[96] ASV, *Senato DRB*, F. 46, letter of Bernardino Renier, Podestà and Domenico Tiepolo, Capitano, April 22 and May 19, 1644; report of Domenico Tiepolo, Capitano, July 6, 1644, in *RV*, ed. Tagliaferri, vol. XI, p. 439.

[97] Part of the problem with collecting them is that many claimed exemptions. Report of Giovanni Paolo Gradenigo, Capitano, January 13, 1607, in *ibid.*, p. 171; report of Angelo Bragadin, Capitano, June 28, 1608, in *ibid.*, p. 188.

[98] Report of Andrea Dolfin, Capitano, December 3, 1650, in *ibid.*, p. 466.

To conclude, the city's industrial activity appears to have atrophied during the middle decades of the seventeenth century, and Brescia functioned more as a center of consumption than of production. Merchants appear to have fared much better than urban artisans, especially those merchants who had diversified their activities by investing in land. Aside from global trends in the economy, factors which weighed into the equation were heightened fiscal pressure, exacerbated by outbreaks of warfare in 1615–1617, 1630, and 1645; protectionism; and the disruption resulting from catastrophic mortality in 1630, including reduced purchasing power on the home market and a consequent fall in demand for manufactures. On balance, however, a number of manufactures hibernated during this tempest, and in better times would satisfy a market which reached beyond home demand. Among them, the multi-faceted iron industry; the lute and organ industries, which music historians tell us enjoyed an international reputation during the seventeenth century;[99] and gold work, in demand by the Counter-Reformation church.[100] Moreover, not all textiles fell into disarray. Silk thread and the manufacture of silk buttons and stockings were growing industries that would attain importance later on, in the eighteenth century.[101] The linen industry also thrived. Domenico Priuli wrote to the Senate in 1572 that linen was Brescia's second most important industry, next to iron. The plains produced 225,000 *pesi*, of which the province consumed about 30,000 to 40,000 *pesi*. The rest was exported to other Venetian territories or abroad in equal portions.[102] In 1621 the Venetian Rector Lorenzo Capello claimed that no other activity brought more capital into the Bresciano than linen. The nature of textile manufactures, however, based on the putting-out system, meant that their center of gravity was in the countryside.[103]

It appears that the real hub of economic activity by the third decade of the seventeenth century was not in Brescia itself but rather in the

---

[99] E. Meli, "Liutai e organari," in *Storia di Brescia*, vol. III, p. 898.

[100] G. Vezzoli, "L'oreficeria dei secoli XVII e XVIII," in *ibid.*, pp. 762–772. The demand for this art was apparently greater than Brescia's supply of craftsmen after the plague of 1630. In 1638 the correttori agli statuti di paratici waived the entrance fees of the gold workers in order to encourage new enrollments. ASCB, *Statuti paratici*, vol. 1058, ff. 247r–247v, March 4, 1632 and February 10, 1638.

[101] Da Lezze, *Il catastico Da Lezze*, vol. I, pp. 469; 472–473; Pasero, "Il dominio veneto," pp. 344–345. In contrast, silk weaving had fallen prey to foreign competition, notably the French, in Brescia and elsewhere. The silk industry in Milan declined by 1635, while in Venice production dropped 60 percent between 1600 and 1660. Sella, *L'economia lombarda*, pp. 101–102.

[102] Report of Domenico Priuli, 1572, in *RV*, ed. Tagliaferri, vol.XI, p. 122.

[103] Report of May 7, 1621, in *ibid.*, p. 256.

rural centers of the province, the home of small entrepreneurs and artisans. Perhaps this was because rural centers of production were less restricted than those in Brescia; the question merits the kind of specialized research that has been conducted for Spanish Lombardy. Moreover, while the Bresciano was richly endowed with the natural resources that sustained industrial activity, land still constituted the primary basis of subsistence and wealth for the majority of the population. The city remained, for the most part, a political and cultural center.

The shift of the economic and demographic axes from city to countryside, most apparent after 1630, provided the backdrop for interaction among Venetian statesmen, Brescian councillors, representatives of the rural communities subject to Brescia, and the disenfranchised in Brescia itself. These changes gave rise to the most important challenges that Venetian statesmen faced, which we will examine in chapters to come: how to maintain order and stability during periods of conjunctural crisis; how to ensure efficient administration of the city's charities; how to organize the cereal market and regulate grain prices; how to tap fiscal resources efficiently in city and countryside, and linked to this, how to oblige the city to live up to its fiscal responsibilities. Brescia's ruling families aimed to keep a firm grip on the landed resources of the countryside, the economic basis of their power, and to protect them from the fisc with the privileged status that citizenship and membership in the city council conferred. This brief survey of the Brescian economy, thus, is fundamental to an understanding of the governing tasks of Venetian statesmen, the logic behind the political behavior of city councillors, and the impact of that behavior on society at large.

PART II

CONSOLIDATION OF THE RULING CLASS

CHAPTER 2

THE EVOLUTION OF THE URBAN RULING CLASS: PROFILE OF A COMPOSITE ELITE

In 1426 the Republic of Venice waged war against the Milanese overlord Filippo Maria Visconti. Statesmen on the lagoon envisioned Lombard territories such as Brescia as a "fertile garden" from which they could reap provisions and secure lucrative trade routes. Counterbalancing Visconti expansion and establishing a strong territorial base were also state imperatives. Though the Doge Tomaso Mocenigo cautioned against war, which would drain resources and energies, in the end the proposal for more aggressive political action by Francesco Foscari, who would be the future Doge, won decisive ground.[1] With the aid of the skilled *condottiere* Carmagnola, the Venetians victoriously pushed west of the Mincio to capture the strategically vital city of Brescia. In October the seventy-two members of the Brescian Council, with the company of other citizens, swore their loyalty to the Venetian Republic.[2]

The history of Venice's new subject city was rooted in the ancient past. During pre-Roman times Ligurians and Celts had settled at the mouth of the Val Trompia. The Romans made Brescia, called Brixia, part of Cisalpine Gaul. Their first settlement, still visible today, was established around the hill that towers over the city. When Roman power waned, Brescia became a Lombard duchy (569–774). The Lombard's most famous king, Desiderius, was born in the vicinity. The Carolingians took Brescia in 774, and for the next 400 years the city was linked to transalpine powers. During this period several local families received imperial titles and firmly established their presence in the city and its *contado* (hinterland). Brescia liberated itself from the imperial designs of the Holy Roman Emperor Frederick Barbarossa in 1180, together with the other northern Italian communes. Then from the

---

[1]   Lane, *Venice*, pp. 228–230.
[2]   Pasero, "Il dominio veneto," p. 16.

middle of the thirteenth century until Venetian annexation local dynasties held sway: Ezzelino da Romano (1257–1259), Uberto Palla-vicino (1259–1265) and the Torriani (1266–1269), the della Scala (1332–1337), the Visconti (1337–1403), Pandolfo Malatesta (1403–1404), and Filippo Maria Visconti (1421–1426).[3]

Brescia thus had been under the tutelage of prominent families for generations when it came under Venetian rule. This included the despots on one hand and the local Brescian elites on the other. The Republic drove the despots out. However, it did not eviscerate the power of the local elite families at the time of annexation. Instead the political configurations of the medieval commune remained firmly imprinted on municipal life. In theory, power was in the hands of the sovereign, the closed, hereditary Venetian ruling class; in practice, however, Venice monitored urban affairs but generously delegated authority to the Brescian Council. Membership in this civic institution and power were not necessarily synonymous. There were Brescian families who demonstrated little interest in civic government, yet their special jurisdictions, recognized by the Venetian Republic, endowed them with ample powers over local society. At the same time there were families in the council who enjoyed little or no authority. Within limits, then, the members of the Brescian Council may be described as a ruling class. The term, however, is still laden with problems of definition, making descriptive terminology difficult and controversial.[4] One problem is that the composition of the council was not fixed over time, though there was some continuity in its membership. Families became extinct and new ones entered, while admission standards changed over the fifteenth and sixteenth centuries, reflecting transformations in the social and political consciousness of the Penin-sula's upper orders. The Brescian Council underwent a process of aristocratization, reflecting prevalent trends in the Venetian state, in north central Italy and in Europe as a whole.[5] As a result of these changes, it was never socially homogeneous. It is not possible, then, to

[3] A. Cappelli, *Cronología, cronografía e calendario perpetuo*, 4th edn (Milan: Ulríco Hoeplí, 1978), pp. 340–341.

[4] For the Veneto, compare Berengo, "Patriziato e nobiltà," pp. 493–517; A. Smith, "Il successo sociale e culturale di una famiglia veronese del '500," in *Dentro lo "stado italico." Venezia e la Terraferma fra Quattro e Seicento*, eds. G. Cracco and M. Knapton (Trent: Gruppo Culturale Civis, 1984), pp. 139–157, and especially pp. 140–143; see also Grubb, *Firstborn*, pp. 86–88; for Florence and Piedmont, compare E. Stumpo, "I ceti dirigenti in Italia nell'età moderna. Due modelli diversi: nobiltà piemontese e patriziato toscano," in *I ceti dirigenti in Italia in età moderna e contemporanea*, ed. A. Tagliaferri (Udine: Del Bianco, 1984), pp. 152–154.

[5] For the Venetian territories, Ventura, *Nobiltà e popolo*.

refer to city councillors as nobles, for not all of them derived from noble lineages. What is more, unlike a nobility, such as the one in Piedmont, they were not an open social order created by a sovereign.[6] The Venetians hardly intervened in the admissions process, which was largely a system of cooptation. Though the term patriciate could be used to describe city councillors, it is not entirely satisfactory, for patriciate is a structurally ambiguous term that has been used to define a variety of situations. In Milan, for example, "noble" was a generic term, while "patrician" was someone who held or was eligible to hold office.[7] Brescian councillors did not make these distinctions, nor did they refer to themselves as patricians. Like their neighbors in Verona,[8] the families that comprised the Brescian Council constituted a hybrid class that employed an aristocratic scheme to identify itself. Nobles with comital titles and outside jurisdictions as well as non–nobles played important roles in this civic institution. A second problem is that the way city councillors distinguished themselves from the rest of Brescian society was not fixed in time, nor was it established by law. In theory the council was not entirely closed; in practice, after 1488 its member-ship was an exclusive, hereditary elite. A brief history of how it acquired these attributes is the subject of this chapter.

COUNCIL MEMBERSHIP PRIOR TO 1488

The urban elite which comprised the council of the late sixteenth and early seventeenth centuries was the product of a slow crystalization between the late twelfth and fifteenth centuries. A great deal of the power and status of the families who enjoyed hegemony harked back to earlier political configurations.[9] Relatively few new families entered the Council after 1488. By then those responsible for urban adminis-tration during the years of Venetian domination had become associated with this municipal institution. This process of consolidation may be described in four phases, or regroupings, of the leading families:[10]

---

[6] See the definition of nobility in M. Cortelazzo and P. Zolli, *Dizionario etimologico della lingua italiana* (Bologna: Zanichelli, 1979), vol. III, p. 806.

[7] G. Vismara, "Il patriziato milanese nel Cinque-Seicento," in *Potere e società negli stati regionali italiani del '500 e '600*, ed. E. Fasano Guarini (Bologna: Il Mulino, 1978), pp. 156–157.

[8] G. Borelli, *Un patriziato della Terraferma veneta tra XVII e XVIII secolo* (Milan: Giuffrè, 1974), p. 388.

[9] See Ventura, *Nobiltà e popolo*, p. 108.

[10] F. Bettoni-Cazzago, "La nobiltà bresciana," in *Brixia* (Brescia, 1882), pp. 91–113, divides the history of Brescian councillors into two phases: the medieval period, which lasted until 1426, and the modern period, spanning from 1426 to 1797.

nobiles (nobles) and *cives veteres* (citizens of long standing), 1190 to 1331; signorial appointments, 1332 to 1425; *benemeriti*, 1426 to 1438; and the council provisions of 1488.

The first constituents of the Brescian Council, *nobiles* and *cives veteres*, coalesced at the end of the twelfth century, during the communal period that followed the city's breach with the Emperor Frederick I. The *nobiles* were divided into the *nobiltà palatina* and the *nobiltà rurale*. The first had been associated with comital and episcopal courts.[11] These families held sway over extensive lands, which included fiefs and monasteries. Among them were the Avogadro, who were in charge of the financial administration of a wide network of episcopal fiefs; and the Gastaldi, who held jurisdiction over the courts (*corti* or *curie*).[12] In addition to their properties in the Brescian hinterland, the *nobiltà palatina* established residences in the city, near the bishop's palace. From the twelfth century, then, the social and political orientation of these families was clearly urban, even though they maintained intimate ties with the countryside.[13] This was also true of the *nobiles rurales*, whose origins were secular. They were the descendants of the medieval counts, captains, and minor vavasors who had emigrated from the countryside to the city, taking their surnames from their fiefs (Calini from Calino; Sala from Sale; Caprioli from Capriolo; Gambara; Martinengo; Rodengo; Concesio; etc.). Several of these families, including the Fisogni, the Palazzi, and the Offlaga, constructed towers in the area of the old Roman walls, their property lines delineating the armed zones of family clans (*consorterie*).[14] On the other hand the *cives veteres* were the commune's first citizens during the early stages of urbanization. These families, most notably the Bocca, the Bona, the Borgondi, the Feroldi, the Luzzaghi, and the Medici, played an instrumental role in communal government during the eleventh and twelfth centuries. The free commune was governed by two councils, the 300 anziani (elders) and the 1,000 popolani.[15]

11 C. Manaresi, "I nobili della Bresciana descritti nel Codice Malatestiano 42 di Fano," *CAB* 129 (1930): 271–421.
12 A. A. Monti della Corte, "Il registro veneto dei nobili estimati nel territorio bresciano tra il 1426 e il 1498," *CAB* 159 (1960): 165–274; see also E. Von Schullern-Schrattenhofen, "La nobile famiglia Caprioli di Brescia," *RA* 26 (1928): 3–8.
13 For the characteristics of urban elites in Italy as a whole during this period, see P. Jones, "Economia e società nell'Italia medioevale: la leggenda della borghesia," *Storia d'Italia. Annali I. Dal feudalesimo al capitalismo* (Turin: Giulio Einaudi, 1978), pp. 230–231.
14 G. Panazza, "Il volto storico di Brescia fino al secolo XIX," in *Storia di Brescia*, vol. III, pp. 1,071–1,072.
15 A. Bosisio, "Il comune," in *Storia di Brescia*, ed. G. Treccani degli Alfieri (Brescia: Morcelliana, 1961), vol. I, pp. 706–707.

In the late twelfth century, the *nobiles* described above immigrated to the city and vied with the *cives veteres* for political hegemony. Gradually this struggle for power resulted in a fusion of the two social orders, who were then simply called *cives*.[16] The power of this composite class rested upon both its political hegemony in the city – the *cives* enjoyed equal juridical rights under the commune, made laws and money, and imposed taxes under the protection of the Holy Roman Empire – and its jurisdictions in the countryside. These connections would have an important impact on the evolution of Brescian institutions and, later, on relations between Venice and the local ruling orders.

While in the early thirteenth century the leading *cives* in Brescia began to guard their coveted status in the political life of the city through the exclusion of new men from civic government,[17] in following periods, under the rule of the *signori*, the council witnessed an infusion of new blood. Particularly under the tutelage of the della Scala in 1332, and the Malatesta and Visconti between 1404 and 1421, the social composition of the urban ruling class became more complex. The *signori* liquidated a part of the old feudal nobility and expanded the urban ruling class with immigrants from Como, Milan, and Bergamo.[18] Symbolically, many of the towers of the nobility disappeared

---

[16] Manaresi writes that the *cives* "erano innanzi i discendenti di quelle famiglie che nelle città partecipavano al potere, sia che fossero simultaneamente detentrici di potere feudale e perciò signorili, sia che appartenessero a quel ceto di cittadini abbienti non feudali, che ottenero verso la metà del secolo XI, di farsi rappresentare nel governo della città e che perciò, rese compartecipi del potere giurisdizionale esercitato dalla città, divennero esse pure signorili, cioè nobili di una nobiltà cittadina," in "I nobili della Bresciana," p. 273. The urbanization of feudal families in Italy by 1200, writes Jones, obfuscated the divisions between rural and urban nobility. "Economia e società," p. 236.

[17] G. Maresca, "La nobiltà bresciana," *RA* 30 (1932): 221–229.

[18] P. Guerrini, *La nobiltà bresciana nel periodo delle signorie e la famiglia Cavaleri* (Brescia: F. Apollonio, 1942); on the Luzzago, P. Guerrini, "I Luzzago," *RA* 28 (1930): 198–205; 297–304; 341–348; on the Martinengo, P. Guerrini, *Una celebre famiglia lombarda. I Conti di Martinengo. Studi e ricerche genealogiche* (Brescia: Geroldi, 1929); on the Bona, P. Guerrini, "I Conti di Bona di Brescia," *RA* 27 (1929): 227–229; on the Bornati, P. Guerrini, "La nobile famiglia Bornati di Brescia," *RA* 22 (1924): 281–287; 337–340; on the Gambara, P. Guerrini, "Per la storia dei Conti Gambara di Brescia," *RA* 23 (1925): 307; on the Maggi, E. Von Schullern-Schrattenhofen, "Cenni sulla nobile famiglia Maggi di Brescia," *RA* 26 (1928): 241–249; on the Calini, E. Von Schullern-Schrattenhofen, "La nobile famiglia bresciana Calini di Calino," *RA* 25 (1927): 243–257. For the organization of the commune under the *signorie* see F. Bettoni-Cazzago, *Storia di Brescia narrata al popolo* (Brescia: F. Apollonio, 1909), pp. 200–280; Guerrini, *La nobiltà bresciana nel periodo delle signorie*; Manaresi, "I nobili della Bresciana," p. 273.

during this period as well. Urban planning reflected the changes. Brescia's prominent families – the Galdaldi, the Malvezzi, the Calzaveglia, the Calini, the Avogadro, and the Martinengo – continued to build enclaves around the old Roman center, Cittadella, while the area west of the Roman ruins, Cittadella Nuova, became the center of government, housing the *signore*'s vicars and podestà as well as communal magistracies.[19]

Expansion of the Brescian ruling class continued during the first five decades of Venetian rule, between 1426 and 1473.[20] First, new families of industrial, artisan, and commercial origins were accorded civic responsibilities as municipal pride, inspired by the Brescian victory against Niccolò Piccinino in 1440, opened the ranks of the city council by making citizens who had participated in the historic siege eligible for membership.[21] Between 1438 and 1488, urban and provincial magistrates were mandated to *benemeriti cittadini*, that is, to all those citizens who were thirty years of age or older and were listed in the registers of the urban *estimo* (tax census) since at least 1438, who had paid taxes to the city since at least the same date, who had resided in the city for at least ten years (to the year 1454, when the residency requirement was raised to a minimum of twenty-five years), and who had aided in the defense of the city. Further, following Venetian annexation, the selection of city councillors was no longer the council's exclusive prerogative. Beginning in 1427, Venetian rectors helped determine the criteria of eligibility and drew up a list of all worthy candidates.[22] The names of nominees were written on slips of paper and put into a bag. Each year seventy-two names were drawn from the sack for the annual council, and from these twelve people were selected every semester to make up the Special Council. The latter convened together with the public deputies, the executive power within the city council.[23] Finally, council membership in the middle decades of the fifteenth century was given a wider social base, although the older families still predominated.

[19] Panazza, "Il volto storico," pp. 1,096–1,100.
[20] See Ventura, *Nobiltà e popolo*, pp. 106–112.
[21] Pasero, "Il dominio veneto," pp. 112–113.
[22] Venetian representatives intervened in Brescia in 1427 upon the invitation of city councillors. A. Menniti Ippolito, "La dedizione di Brescia a Milano (1421) e a Venezia (1427): Città suddite e distretto nello stato regionale," in *Stato, società e giustizia nella Repubblica veneta (secoli xv–xviii)*, ed. G. Cozzi (Rome: Jouvence, 1985), vol. II, pp. 49–54.
[23] Zanelli, *Delle condizioni*, p. 18.

All citizens, save those who bore arms or wore the cloth, were eligible to apply for membership, provided that they met the conditions listed above.[24] Hence, a number of families from Brescia's intermediate orders entered the council between 1427 and 1473, again making its social composition more complex.[25]

By 1473 the leading families in the council began to tighten their hold on political power by restricting the governing body's admission requirements.[26] The Venetians do not appear to have interfered with this development. Nor do they seem to have intervened in the selection of new councillors in Verona in 1405, Cividale di Belluno in 1423, or fifteenth-century Vicenza and Feltre.[27] Here the contrast is with the

---

[24] Pasero, "Il dominio veneto," p. 113.

[25] Maresca, "La nobiltà bresciana," p. 223. The Peace of Lodi was a decisive cut-off date, when the city council first began to restrict admission to inhabitants of the city who were twenty-five or older. Zanelli, *Delle condizioni*, pp. 18–24.

[26] J. Ferraro, "Oligarchs, Protesters, and the Republic of Venice: The 'Revolution of the Discontents' in Brescia, 1644–45," *Journal of Modern History* 60 (1988): 636–639. (I wish to thank the editors of the *Journal of Modern History* [copyright 1988 by the University of Chicago, 0022–2801/88/6004–0001] for permission to republish parts of my article, with some revision, in this chapter as well as in chapter 7.) In 1454 the Brescian Council raised the citizenship requirement from ten to twenty-five years. Zanelli, *Delle condizioni*, pp. 18–24. On the consolidation of power in Italian municipalities between the '300 and '400 see G. Chittolini's introduction to *La crisi degli ordinamenti comunali e le origini dello stato del Rinascimento*, ed. G. Chittolini (Bologna: Il Mulino, 1979), pp. 17; 24–26; and G. Chittolini, "La crisi delle libertà comunali e le origini dello stato territoriale," *RSI* 82 (1970): 115–116.

[27] For Verona in 1405 see Law, "Venice and the 'Closing,'" p. 94; cf. G. M. Varanini, "Note sui consigli civici veronese (secoli XIV–XV). In margine ad uno studio di J. E. Law," *Archivio Veneto*, 5th series, 112 (1979): 24. Varanini underlines the continuity of the Veronese civic leadership during the periods of Visconti and Venetian rule. Similarly, in Cividale di Belluno there was a fundamental continuity between the Rotuli, the families that ruled the town prior to 1423, and the new Consiglio dei Nobili established in 1423. C. Caro Lopez, "La formazione del ceto dirigente a Cividale di Belluno," *Archivio Storico di Belluno, Feltre e Cadore* 221 (1977): 179. The same kind of continuity must have existed in Vicenza, where the city council was closed prior to Venetian rule. J. S. Grubb, "Patriciate and Estimo in the Vicentine Quattrocento," in *Il sistema fiscale veneto*, eds. Borelli, Lanaro, and Vecchiato, p. 149. In fifteenth-century Feltre the members of the municipal ruling body clearly controlled its membership, although the Venetian rector had the option of proposing a family of popular origins to the city council. G. Corazzol, "Una fallita riforma del Consiglio di Feltre nel '500," *Rivista Bellunese* 3 (1975): 287. On the other hand, the Venetians did interfere in the Veronese constitution in 1462 out of concern for whether subjects loyal to Venice were being appointed to the Council of Fifty. Law, "Venice and the 'Closing,'" pp. 96–102. Moreover, they intervened in Brescia in 1427 upon the invitation of city councillors. Menniti Ippolito, "La dedizione di Brescia," pp. 49–54.

Florentine state, where the Medici restricted the action of oligarchies, even to the point of affecting their composition.[28]

Between 1473 and 1488 the Brescian Council was able to institute the restrictive norms that would consolidate its power as a ruling class. The critical years of this political development were 1465 to 1473, when fifteen members of the Brescian Council, with the approval of the Venetian Senate, reformed the *Statuto Potestatis*. This body of laws, originally promulgated in 1427, defined the authority of the Venetian podestà as well as the competencies and procedures of Brescia's citizen magistracies. Statutes 36–38, 41, 72, and 77 of the *Statuto Potestatis*, for example, stipulated how many citizens should be in the General Council (general deliberating body, consisting of seventy-two members), the Annual Council, and the Special Council; the attributes of these councils; when they should convene; and how they should register deliberations.[29] It was the revision of Statute 36,[30] the law dealing with citizenship requisites and nominating procedures for membership in the city council, that made this municipal institution more exclusive. First, the committee raised the minimum citizenship requirement from twenty-five to thirty years. Second, it modified the nominating procedures for admission to the city council. Prior to 1473, the Venetian rectors would designate nominees for council membership, and then the names were extracted at random from a sack (*bussola*). In 1473 the nominating procedures came more under the jurisdiction of the city council. Henceforward nominees would not simply be designated by the rectors but also by members of the General Council. Moreover, the nominees would only be voted upon after a special committee, the deputati alla civiltà, screened them. This may

---

[28] E. Fasano Guarini, "Principe ed oligarchie nella Toscana del '500," *Forme e techniche del potere nella città (secoli XIV–XVII)*, in *Materia e Storia* 4 (1979–80): 115–116. While in Renaissance Pescia the basis of government narrowed, the Medici exerted some control over the dominion town's ruling families through ties of patronage. J. Brown, *In the Shadow of Florence. Provincial Society in Renaissance Pescia* (New York and Oxford: Oxford University Press, 1982), pp. 184–186.

[29] *Statuta Civitatis Brixiae* (Brescia, 1557), pp. 11–14; 22. The revisions are treated in Zanelli, *Delle condizioni*, pp. 22–30; 182–186.

[30] Statute 36, *De Consilio Generali bonorum civium brix & electione eorum* stated "quod per dominos rectores cum consilio generali omnium civium imbursatorum ad consilia finita imbursatione, facta de omnibus & singulis civibus ad consilia imbursatis, inherendo ordini consuetudini hactenus observatae in ipso consilio, ad clarum omnium intelligentiam lecto libro extimi totius ambitus civitatus brix. ad petitionem cuiuslibet consiliarii, ballotari debeant illi cives omnes, qui ballotari debere nominabuntur dummodo ipsi cives ballotadi, sustinuerint onera & factiones cum communi brix. per triginta annos continuos, & etiam annorum triginta excesserint." *Statuta Civitatis Brixiae*, pp. 11–12.

have been, above all, a constitutional or institutional revision, making clear that final control of the selection of new councillors was in the hands of the civic leadership. Whether Venetian intervention in selection procedures between 1427 and 1473 had made a radical difference in the composition of the city council still needs to be explored.[31] Nonetheless, the revision of Statute 36 appears to have given Brescian councillors greater latitude in the selection of new members.[32] The council instituted another change in 1475 when it abolished the original Council of Seventy-Two. Instead, all those whose names were extracted from a sack were thenceforward members of the city council.

Subsequently, in 1488 the Brescian ruling class instituted further restrictions for entry into the council, though in this case the amendments were not written into the city statutes but rather remained provisions of the city council. Again the council revised the citizenship requirement, which was clearly critical to the process of aristocratization in Brescia.[33] The provisions of 1488 stipulated that a candidate applying for membership in the council had to be a legitimate descendant of either an original citizen whose family had been inscribed in the urban *estimo* since at least 1426,[34] or a *cittadino benemerito*, listed in the *estimo* from 1438.[35] Shortly thereafter the council modified this

[31] There is some evidence of continuity in the Brescian civic leadership both before and during the Venetian domination. See Bettoni-Cazzago, "La nobiltà bresciana," pp. 91–113; G. Bonfiglio Dosio, "La condizione giuridica del civis e le concessioni di cittadinanza negli statuti bresciani del XIII e XIV secolo," *Atti dell'Istituto Veneto di Scienze, Lettere ed Arti. Classe di scienze morali, lettere ed arti* 137 (1978–79): 530–531.

[32] Zanelli, *Delle condizioni*, pp. 22; 183–184.

[33] On the nature and importance of citizenship in Venice and the Veneto see J. Kirshner, "Between Nature and Culture: An Opinion of Baldus of Perugia on Venetian Citizenship as Second Nature," *The Journal of Medieval and Renaissance Studies* 9 (1979): 179–208; for Padua: A. Pino Branca, "Il comune di Padova sotto la Dominante nel secolo XV (rapporti amministrativi e finanziari)," *Atti dell'Istituto Veneto* 93 (1933–1934): 372–386; for Brescia: Bonfiglio-Dosio, "La condizione giuridica del civis," pp. 523–532; for Verona: J. Law, "*Super differentiis agitatis Venetiis inter districtuales et civitatem*: Venezia, Verona e il contado nel '400," *Archivio Veneto*, 5th series, 116 (1981): 5–32; for Vicenza: J. Grubb, "Alla ricerca delle prerogative locali: la cittadinanza a Vicenza, 1404–1509," in *Dentro lo "stado italico"*, eds. Cracco and Knapton, pp. 17–31 and p. 18 for additional bibliography.

[34] Giovanni Da Lezze, writing in 1609 to 1610, maintained that the cut-off date was the *estimo* of 1430, *Il catastico Da Lezze*, vol. I, p. 283. The original citizens of the Italian cities held some of the most jealously guarded offices and prerogatives of political citizenship. See Pino Branca, "Il comune di Padova," p. 375, n. 1; J. Kirshner, "*Civitas sibi faciat civem*: Bartolus of Sassoferrato's Doctrine on the Making of a Citizen," *Speculum* 48 (1973): 706; J. Kirshner, "Between Nature and Culture," pp. 182–183.

[35] On the *benemeriti*, Pasero, "Il dominio veneto," p. 75, n. 5.

provision to include also candidates who were not original citizens or *benemeriti* but whose families had resided in the city for fifty years and who could attest to the domicile of their ancestors.[36] Thus in theory at least council membership was not entirely closed, though the citizen- ship requirement made it less likely that new families without kinship ties in the council would be able to meet the qualifications for membership. The provisions of 1488 also stipulated that only those families that descended from houses listed either in the urban *estimo* of 1426 or in Cristoforo Soldo's book of *Custodie Notturne* of 1438 would retain hereditary rights to council membership.[37] In contrast, those who had acquired a place in the council after the siege of 1438 were denied the privilege of transmitting their places to male offspring. This restriction, in fact, was designed to prevent the fusion of old city councillors with new ones from more modest social backgrounds who had acquired membership during the fifty-year period between 1438 and 1488. It was not amended until 1517, when the council made hereditary rights the prerogative of all the families enrolled in the council, provided they met a legitimacy requirement instituted in 1494.[38] The importance of legitimacy, tied to the notion of gentility, emerged again in 1640, when the council ruled that the grandfathers as well as fathers of council applicants must be of legitimate birth.

Following the provisions of 1488, Brescian city councillors became a self-defined governing class that began to express an aristocratic con- sciousness, stressing first and foremost the importance of ancestry.[39] Family chronicles and genealogies became very important in the sixteenth century. All candidates for the city council were compelled to prove themselves legitimate descendants of a family inscribed in the Book of Gold, a book of the official civic nobility, similar to that of the Venetians, which was drawn up in 1509. They assembled meticulous dossiers called *processi di nobiltà*, substantiating titles, genealogy, and fiscal contributions which they submitted to the committee of public deputies charged with scrutinizing the material. Only when this

---

[36] Ventura, *Nobiltà e popolo*, pp. 110–111. Da Lezze makes no mention of this provision in the *catastico* of 1609–1610. *Il catastico Da Lezze*, vol. I, p. 283. Perhaps it was not closely followed in the seventeenth century.

[37] Ventura, *Nobiltà e popolo*, p. 111. The *libri delle custodie* contain the names of those citizens who had contributed towards communal expenses since at least 1438 and could attest to their genealogies.

[38] Zanelli, *Delle condizioni*, pp. 30–31; 39–40.

[39] See P. Guerrini, "Il 'libro d'oro' della nobiltà bresciana nel '500," *RA* 17 (1919): 196–201; 231–237; 272–276; 319–322; BQ, MS. Fe 9m 3a, "Elenco delle famiglie nobili di Brescia iscritto nel Gran Consiglio fino al 1796," ff. 143–284; ASCB, vol. 1426 1/2 A–C, "Estimi di ciascun nobile e geneologia antica (1400–1600)."

committee had confirmed a candidate's qualifications was his name submitted to the general deliberating body for approval, a procedure which in effect left the decision-making process almost entirely in the hands of the executive committee. The candidate then underwent an inquest into his civic merits. This was carried out in the Special Council and then confirmed by secret vote in the General Council. The applicant needed the approval of at least 50 percent of the membership for that biannual term. Once admitted, the new councillor became *in nobiltà confermato*, signifying that to hold council membership in Brescia was synonymous with being noble. The importance of citizenship was intimately linked to city councillors' conception of civic nobility: the title *nobile* was dropped in the sixteenth century, and councillors called themselves citizens first (*cives brixiae*), nobles second.[40] In the seventeenth century the term changed again to *i nobili cittadini di Brescia*, the noble citizens of Brescia.

While the eligibility restrictions established in 1488 made lineage, in addition to residence and citizenship (either original or *benemerenza*), a principal criterion for council membership, it did not preclude the stipulation of further tests designed to exclude parvenus from government responsibilities and from the honored status of civic nobility. Lifestyle and the reputation of the family also became fundamental requisites of status, and the council committee charged with screening new memberships meticulously investigated these qualities. To qualify for the council, one not only had to be a legitimate descendant of a family with original citizenship or *benemerenza*; to have had a residence in Brescia; and to have paid taxes with the city since at least 1438; one also had to maintain a lifestyle that was in *more nobilium* and to prove that one's ancestors had lived nobly for at least three generations. By the middle of the sixteenth century that signified above all else reliance upon agricultural income. There was absolute disdain for applicants associated with commerce or industry. While in the fifteenth century, as well as during a brief interval following French occupation in the early sixteenth century,[41] the council accepted families engaged in textile activities, the spice trade, or the iron and arms industries,[42] in 1528 and 1546 provisions were drawn up to exclude all aspirants engaged in trade, or whose fathers or grandfathers had practiced one, or whose relatives were still engaged in *arti vili*. A special committee in

---

[40] BMCV, Archivio Donà, N. 17, f. 79, report of Leonardo Donà, Podestà of Brescia, 1579.

[41] Ventura, *Nobiltà e popolo*, pp. 261–262; 272–273.

[42] The occupational status of city councillors in the fifteenth century is listed in ASCB, vol. 1426 1/2 A–C.

council excluded candidates who were even remotely involved in commerce and industry or had worked with their hands. The *Accuse date a patrizi di meccanica* (1551–1569) are the oldest such documents in the Terraferma regarding the exclusion of *meccanici* from the council.[43] In Brescia the intermediate orders joined together in guilds, confraternities, and other associations which gave them some public identity, but they were denied the opportunity of replenishing the ranks of the civic nobility. Elsewhere on the Italian peninusla similar processes of constriction were taking place. In neighboring Milan, by the 1560s patricians excluded individuals who practiced the *arti vili* from their ranks.[44] Parallels may be drawn with Lucca; Siena; Genoa; and Jesi, a community of the Papal States, as well.[45] The process, however, was not universal. Cremona[46] and some of the other Lombard cities retained, if at times unwillingly, merchants in council.

ARISTOCRATIZATION

There was a qualitative change in the Brescian Council that paralleled the entry restrictions of the late fifteenth and sixteenth centuries.[47] Whereas in the fifteenth century merchants and shopkeepers sat next to gentlemen in the council, by the middle of the sixteenth century a more aristocratic and professional consciousness had permeated the minds of city councillors, a transformation in values that other urban councils of the Venetian Terraferma were experiencing as well. In his *Della economica*, a treatise on urban government, the Brescian gentleman Giacomo Lanteri noted this change in 1560:

> It appears that when reforming the statutes, our ancestors (perhaps to preserve *civiltà*, I do not know) ruled that whoever exercised any kind of mechanical art could not number among the nobles of the city.

43 See Ventura, *Nobiltà e popolo*, pp. 279; 313–317.
44 Vismara, "Il patriziato milanese," pp. 156–162; for Italy see Jones, "Economia e società," pp. 367–368.
45 Berengo, *Nobili e mercanti*, pp. 252–257; D. Marrara, *Riseduti e nobiltà. Profilo storico-istituzionale di un'oligarchia toscana nei secoli XVI–XVIII* (Pisa: Pacini. Biblioteca del Bollettino Storico Pisano, 1976), pp. 158–159; R. Molinelli, *Un'oligarchia locale nell'età moderna* (Urbino: Argalia, 1976), p. 39.
46 G. Politi, *Aristocrazia e potere politico nella Cremona di Filippo II* (Milan: Sugar Co., 1976), pp. 42; 59.
47 See Berengo, *Nobili e mercanti*, pp. 252–257. For the eighteenth century, see C. Donati, "Scipione Maffei e la scienza chiamata cavaleresca. Saggio sull'ideologia nobiliare al principio del '700," *RSI* 90 (1978): 30–71. See also G. Barni, "Mutamenti di ideali sociali dal secolo XVI al secolo XVIII: giuristi, nobiltà e mercatura," *Rivista Internationale di Filosofia del Diritto* 34 (1957): 766–787.

Moreover, they ruled that if a noble exercised an art, either because of poverty or some other reason, he would be deprived of *civiltà*, that is of council membership, of obtaining offices and the city's honors; and if his heirs were doctors [i.e., graduates in law] or notaries, in the College of Doctors or Notaries, they could not in any way enter the Council either.[48]

The transformation in values within the council was part of the general discussion over the nature of chivalry which pervaded Italy during the middle decades of the sixteenth century.[49] It also presaged the general *rentier* mentality that would pervade Italy's ruling elites in the seventeenth century.[50] It is significant that Brescian city councillors did not simply abandon commerce for real estate. They focused on legal and humanistic studies and careers in the professions.[51] The professional colleges, particularly those of jurisprudence and the notarial arts, in many urban centers of north central Italy – and Venice seems to have been an exception[52] – were centers for the transmission of the culture and values of the governing classes.[53] Most of all, they were centers of preparation for those who, through their positions in municipal government, would wield political power. Control of jurisprudence and of entry into the College of Judges were, in short, strategies that

[48] "Pare che i nostri passati (forse per conservare la civiltà, ch'io non so) nella reformatione de gli statuti, ordinassero che alcuno che arte mecanica essercitasse per modo alcuno non potesse connumerarsi fra i nobili della città. Anzi, di più ordinarono, che se un nobile, ò per povertà, ò per qual si voglia altro caso si essercitasse in simil arti, fosse della civiltà privato, cioè di poter' andare a consiglio, dell'ottenere i magistrati, e gli honori della città; Et Dottore essendo, alcuno de gli heredi di lui, ò notaio, nel collegio così de Dottori, come de' notai, entrar non potesse in modo alcuno." G. Lanteri, *Della economica* (Venice: Vincenzo Valgrisi, 1560), p. 95; see also G. Barbieri, "Il trattatello 'Della economia' di G. Lanteri, letterato e architetto bresciano del secolo XVI," in *Rassegna degli Archivi di Stato* 21 (1961): 35–46; D. Frigo, "Governo della casa, nobiltà e 'republica': l'economica' in Italia tra Cinque e Seicento," in *Governo della casa, governo della città*, ed. M. Bianchini, D. Frigo, and C. Mozzarelli, *Cheiron* 4 (1985): 85.

[49] C. Donati, *L'idea di nobiltà in Italia. Secoli XIV–XVIII* (Rome–Bari: Laterza, 1988), p. 112.

[50] On the shift from commercial to landed activities in Venice and the Veneto see D. Beltrami, *La penetrazione economica dei veneziani in Terraferma. Forze di lavoro e proprietà fondiaria nelle campagne venete dei secoli XVII e XVIII* (Venice–Rome: Istituto per la Collaborazione Culturale, 1961); Woolf, "Venice and the Terraferma," pp. 175–203. For Brescia the phenomenon has been described in Pasero, "Introduzione," *Il catastico Da Lezze*, pp. 62–64.

[51] See D. Zanetti, "Università e classi sociali nella Lombardia Spagnola," in *I ceti dirigenti*, ed. Tagliaferri, pp. 242–243.

[52] See Cozzi, "La politica del diritto," pp. 79–121.

[53] See G. P. Brizzi, *La formazione della classe dirigente nel Sei-Settecento. I seminaria nobilium nell'Italia centro-settentrionale* (Bologna: Il Mulino, 1976), p. 23.

ensured the hegemony of the municipal ruling class.[54] In Brescia the productive energies of the Marini, the Rosa, and the Serina, who had been prosperous Brescian wool merchants, subsided.[55] Merchants such as the Baitelli and the Rosa turned to the study of law and entered the College of Judges in the sixteenth century. Other families such as the Soncini, furriers, textile and gold merchants in the fourteenth and fifteenth centuries, shifted to the notarial arts. In the sixteenth century Giacomo Soncini q. Domenico became a notary, and the lineage acquired the mobility for admission to the city council.[56]

Although there were not many new families that entered the council after 1488, those that did were usually represented in the Judicial and Notarial Colleges, another index of the fundamental link by the sixteenth century between these professions and the system of municipal power.[57] The study of law was an avenue of social mobility in the early sixteenth century, preparing the way for careers in urban government. For families who already enjoyed social status, law was a means of adding to the decorum of the family. Most importantly, however, it was a tool of power, since many of the more important offices in the council were the domain of law graduates. Moreover law touched the very basis of civic and family life, giving magistrates a preeminent position in society at large. This was also true for notaries, who stood at the heart of governmental, economic, civic, and family affairs.

By the sixteenth century, the Colleges of Judges, Notaries, and Physicians in Brescia served as institutions for the preparation of city councillors.[58] A prospective magistrate completed seven years of university study. The graduate subsequently applied to the Brescian College of Judges, defending a thesis in very complicated civil law before seven examiners. If the candidate performed well, he would be scrutinized before the entire college. Approval enabled him to proceed to the second examination, where he was required to argue an even

---

[54] See C. Mozzarelli, "Il sistema patrizio," *Patriziati e aristocrazie nobiliari*, eds. C. Mozzarelli and P. Schiera (Trent: Libera Università degli Studi di Trento, 1978), pp. 58–63; and compare the Brescian case with that of Milan in C. Mozzarelli, "Strutture sociali e formazioni statuali a Milano e Napoli tra '500 e '700," *Società e Storia* 3 (1978): 441–448.

[55] Marini, ASCB, vol. 1426 1/2 A, ff. 10v, 36r, 104v; Serina, *ibid.*, f. 55v; Baitelli, *ibid.*, f. 34r; Rosa, *ibid.*, f. 45r; vol. 1426 1/2 B, f. 293r.

[56] P. Guerrini, "Famiglie nobili bresciane, Soncino o De Soncino," *RA* 32 (1934): 485–490; 546–554.

[57] Compare Mozzarelli, "Strutture sociali," pp. 441–448.

[58] See A. Zanelli, "L'istruzione pubblica in Brescia nei secoli XVII e XVIII," *CAB* (1896): 23–53.

more complex theme in civil law after three days' preparation. If he passed this test, he was admitted to the college. At least until the late sixteenth century the entrance requirements of the College of Judges were identical to those of the Brescian Council.[59] Lineage was a key requisite for admission, and fathers passed their positions in the College on to their sons. Admission requirements to the College of Notaries were equally as rigorous, as were those of the corps of physicians.[60] The candidates for each of these corporations followed a prescribed course of study and underwent public examinations. If they met the essential requisites for council membership, notaries and physicians had careers in civic government in addition to their other professional duties. Unlike the College of Judges, however, the Notarial College had a two-tiered membership: some of its members were excluded from the city council, and their professional duties were confined to civil affairs outside the limits of civic government.[61] Moreover, after 1612 Venetian rectors had a hand in admissions to the Brescian Notarial College. They were also able to choose their own notaries to assist them in the state chancelleries.[62] The tight-knit structure of the three professional colleges reflected that of the city council: they were essentially closed, "aristocratic-minded" institutions, enjoying special recognition both in Brescian society and before the Venetian Republic.[63] In particular, the notaries distinguished themselves from the city's craft guilds by divorcing themselves from any association with the concept of *meccanica*. When Venice imposed an extraordinary tax (*gravezza*) on the guilds in Brescia in 1571, the notaries inscribed in the city council refused to contribute to this impost, arguing that their profession could not be considered one of the *arti vili*. The Venetians recognized their claims, giving Brescian notaries more status than the other notarial corps of the Terraferma. The members of the College of Judges were even more exclusive, and there were distinctions within the profession. Law graduates who did not enjoy its membership were

59 Report of Paolo Correr, Podestà, April 1562, in *RV*, ed. Tagliaferri, vol. XI, pp. 72–73.

60 There is very little written about the physicians. See Pasero, "Il dominio veneto," p. 117. Some of them, however, still held prestigious positions in the council in the seventeenth century.

61 Report of Paolo Correr, in *RV*, ed. Tagliaferri, vol. XI, pp. 72–73; ASV, *Senato. DRB*, F. 45, letter of Antonio Longo, Podestà, and Domenico Tiepolo, Capitano, August 28, 1643.

62 *Parte* in the Consiglio dei Pregadi, January 12, 1612, *more veneto*, in *Raccolta di privilegi, ducali, giudizi, terminazioni, e decreti pubblici sopra varie materie giurisdizionali, civili, criminali, ed economiche concernenti la città di Brescia* (Brescia: Tip. G. B. Bossino, 1732), p. 58.

63 Pasero, "Il dominio veneto," pp. 116–118.

excluded from civic government and relegated to being fiscal lawyers (fiscali) or advocates (causidici).[64]

By the sixteenth century law and the notarial arts, fundamental tools of the ruling class, helped define status and had significant impact on the Brescian Council's sense of hierarchical order. Councillors attempted to delineate boundaries within their ranks that also produced some effect on the assignment of public responsibilities. The difficulty of defining degrees of status and of demarcating its various ranks was not just a problem of the Brescian Council but part of a wider debate taking place in many cities of north central Italy as well. Lanteri's *Della economica* was part of this discussion. He wrote,

> There are four degrees of noblemen (aside from Princes), no more. In the first, and more important than the others, are nobles of the blood who possess private jurisdictions, such as counties, minor baronies, castles, and villages. In the second are those who are nobles without jurisdictions, but by merit of their virtue, or by inheritance, not by merit of their relatives, possess honored titles, such as count, cavalier, doctor, mercenary captain, colonel, or captain of rank. They are followed by those in the third [degree], born nobly with nothing but their own faculties and private *civiltà*. And in the last group are those born of ignoble relatives, or that exercise commerce, or some other activity which is not mechanical, in order to earn a living.[65]

In late sixteenth- and early seventeenth-century Brescia, though nobles and non-nobles had amalgamated into one governing class that was considered a civic nobility by definition, city councillors recognized various grades of citizenship, identified with lineage and with

---

[64] See Marrara, *Riseduti e nobiltà*, p. 136. Marrara discovers for Siena that there was a social hierarchy of functions.

[65] I have translated from the Italian. The original text is: "Le conditioni de gli huomini nobili (lasciando quella dei Prencipi) sono quattro, senza più. Nella prima, e più dell'altre riguardevole, sono coloro annoverati, i quali prima sendo nobili di sangue, posseggono poi stati privati, come sono Contati, Baronie minori, Castelli, e Villagi. Coloro che sono nobili senza stato, ma o per merito di propria virtù, o per successione, ne i meriti dei parenti loro posseggono titolo honorato, come di Conti, Cavalieri, Dottori, Condottieri di gente d'arme e colonelli, o capitani di grado, nella seconda sono compresi. Sono poscia quei della terza, coloro che nati nobilmente altro che le facoltà loro, e la privata civiltà non posseggono. Et quelli dell'ultima schiera coloro saranno, che nati ancora da parenti ignobili, essercitano la mercantie, o altro essercitio non mechanico, per cagione di guadagno." Lanteri, *Della economica*, pp. 13–14. Many treatises on nobility, modeled on the fourteenth- and fifteenth-century jurists and humanists, emerged in Italy in the period following 1560. The literature reached its apogee in the period between the sixteenth and seventeenth centuries. There was a tendency to define grades of nobility, as evidenced in texts on precedence, on titles, on coats of arms, etc. See Donati, *L'idea di nobiltà*, pp. 113; 151–152.

jurisdictions. Yet establishing criteria for intra-class differentiation did not stop here. Professional status became one of the variables in the equation as well, and jurists increasingly claimed more status. Social weight was redefined in terms of political power. There were six degrees of precedence that the council used to assign offices to six different categories of citizen. City councillors agreed that the Brescian lineages aggregated to the Venetian patriciate, the Martinengo di Padernello; the Martinengo della Pallata; the Martinengo da Barco; the Gambara; and the Avogadro held first place in the local hierarchy. The social spheres of these houses radiated beyond Brescia; they were linked to Venice and to other Italian states. Moreover, their status was a reminder that power and council membership were not synonymous: there were important families from this upper stratum of the Brescian nobility that remained uninterested in civic government, for they had carved out separate spheres of influence. City councillors also agreed that the descendants of the medieval *nobiles* with jurisdictions of *mero et mixto imperium* (supreme criminal and civil jurisdiction) and command of some part of the province followed the Brescian lineages aggregated to Venice in their hierarchy.[66] But apart from these two upper strata, there was no consensus about how to order the other 'degrees of citizenship' in the council. In the seventeenth century, the descendants of *nobiles* who possessed titles but no jurisdictions vied with the judges for third place. Their disagreement was a frequent source of tension in council, since the system of precedence was also used to assign special public functions.[67] For example, an "orator," as delegates to Venice were called in the seventeenth century, was a responsibility that carried with it both status and honor. In 1637 two Brescian councillors selected to serve as ambassadors to Venice involved the entire Brescian Council as well as the Venetian Senate in a dispute over precedence. Count Paolo Emilio Martinengo, a scion of one of Brescia's most illustrious noble houses, claimed precedence over Stefano Maria Ugone, a descendant of the *nobiles rurales* and one of the most powerful judges in council. Martinengo was a feudatory without jurisdictions. Ugone appealed the case in the Venetian Senate, which gave a verdict of *nulla decide*, leaving the matter for locals to resolve. The issue of precedence, a catalyst for violence, arose frequently throughout the period, an index of the tensions resulting from the

---

66 There is a parallel here with Milanese patricians, most of whom possessed fiefs and who practically required the acquisition of a fief as the first step toward becoming a patrician. Vismara, "Il patriziato milanese," pp. 166–169.

67 ASV, *Senato. Rettori*, F. 11, letter of April 10, 1638 and letter of January 25, 1637 attached to the former.

ambivalence over categorization – and the distribution of power – in council. As aides to higher magistracies (assessori), as envoys to Venice; as public deputies; as consuls for the various quarters of the city; as judges for indirect taxes (dazi); for victuals; and for the appeals of Brescia, the Territorio, Asola, the Riviera di Salò, the Valcamonica, and the College of Judges itself, magistrates were major figures in public life.[68]

What we have, then, in the late sixteenth century and the first half of the seventeenth century, is a relatively closed governing class of composite social origins, the product of changing admission standards that hinged primarily on degrees of citizenship and on changing concepts of civic nobility over the course of the fifteenth and sixteenth centuries. Table 4, based largely on Alessandro Monti della Corte's profile of the families enrolled in the Brescian Council, gives us some idea of the composition of the Brescian Council during the period between 1588 and 1650 by identifying the origins of the lineages for which genealogical information is available.[69] The families who entered the council prior to 1488 are broken down into nobiles, cives veteres, benemeriti, and others.

Table 4 helps us to see the variety of social groups within the council. First, it appears that the restrictions for council membership applied in 1488 were decisive: the majority of the active lineages on the council membership lists during the late sixteenth and seventeenth centuries had entered by 1488; relatively few new lineages entered after that date.[70]

[68] Another dispute arose in 1638 between Giovanni Battista Bornato, a descendant of the medieval nobiles, who held neither title nor private jurisdictions, and Dottor Onofrio Maggio, a judge whose social origins were identical to Bornato's. Bornato lost the case in the Venetian Senate with a vote of 300 to 6. BMCV, MS. Martinengo, PD/C 1180, Mazzo 21, No. 5 u.d..

[69] A. A. Monti della Corte, Le famiglie del patriziato bresciano (Brescia: Geroldi, 1960), pp. 19–79; 83–138. I was not able to obtain information for the following case: Alberti, Ardesius, Bazardi, Belacatti, Belasi, Bergognines, Bettoncelli, Bocatius, Buarni, Buratti, Calzavelia, Carrarie, Castelli, Catanei, Coccali, Fabi, Fausti, Fobelli, Gavandi, Gadaldue, Gaffuri, Glerola, Gobini, Gotij, Guerrini, Humeltate, Lolli, Lupatini, Malvetij, Marende, Marchetti, Mauri, Mercanda, de Morris Gambara, Morescus, Nazari, Nuolina, Odasi, Offlaga, Oldofredi, Oriani, Pagani, Paitoni, Papiae, Passirani, Parenti, Penne, Placentini, Prandoni, Prati, Pulusella, Roberti, Ronzoni, Rovati, Parpagni, Saiani, Scalvini, Scaramutie, de Scopuli, Seriate, Suraga, Tairdini, Tarelli, Trivella, Ustiani, Vineltatus, Zanatta, Zerbini, and Zoni.

    With few exceptions, the case listed above held an insignificant number of seats – at most one per term – in the council over the period under study. The majority appeared only briefly on the enrollment lists. The exceptions are the Belasi, Buarni, Carrara, Castelli, Guerrini, Lupatini, Mauri, Offlaga, Penne, Oldofredi, Pontevici, and Saiani.

[70] Ventura, Nobiltà e popolo, pp. 275–374, esp. p. 374.

The prevalence of old families in urban councils is characteristic of other aristocratic regimes on the Italian peninsula as well. Ventura and other historians of the Veneto have shown that the formation of urban councils in the Venetian territories was essentially complete by the end of the fifteenth century. The Bellunese Council, for example, closed around 1423 to 1426. Individuals who made their fortunes in commerce and industry in the fifteenth century did not find a seat in government.[71] Moreover, in Feltre, the council closed in 1451 with an important nucleus of families of feudal origin in control, though a group of more recent families linked to commercial activities was able to join the ranks of the governing class. Power was concentrated in relatively few families by the late fifteenth century.[72] The early fifteenth century appears to have been a cut-off period for the admission of newcomers to the Florentine Council.[73] Though the time frame for closure varied from place to place, from the fifteenth to the sixteenth centuries, there are parallel situations in Cremona and the communities of the Marche as well.[74]

Second, table 4 also suggests that relatively few non-noble families entered the council outside the period between 1438 and 1488. Those that did, particularly in the sixteenth century, had already left their commercial ventures for the professions. Moreover, by the seventeenth century, in conformity with the prescribed requirements, the new families that entered the council were entirely disassociated from the *meccanica* for three generations or more, again typical of aristocratic regimes which valued landed wealth and the professions, particularly law.

Given the variety of social groups within the Brescian Council, there is no general term that can satisfactorily describe its membership. We shall see in chapters 3 and 4 that the families in the council underwent a certain amount of amalgamation and integration which ultimately defies any attempts at social categorization. Above all, city councillors were citizens who enjoyed elite status. By the seventeenth century, the descendants of *nobiles*, *cives*, *benemeriti*, merchants, and shopkeepers were all proponents of an aristocratic consciousness which identified civic nobility with lineage, with antique citizenship status, with the

---

[71] F. Vendramini, *Tensioni politiche nella società bellunese della prima metà del '500* (Belluno: Tarantola, 1974).

[72] Corrazol, "Una fallita riforma," pp. 287–288.

[73] Litchfield, *Emergence of a Bureaucracy*, p. 20.

[74] Politi, *Aristocrazia e potere*, p. 33; Molinelli, *Un'oligarchia locale*, pp. 58–66; B. G. Zenobi, *Ceti e potere nella Marca pontificia. Formazione e organizzazione della piccola nobiltà fra '500 e '700* (Bologna: Il Mulino, 1976).

Table 4. *The social origins of the active case inscribed in the council*
(1588–1650)

Nobiles (inscribed prior to 1488)		
Arici	Fenaroli	Nassini
Averoldi	Fisogni	Oldofredi
Avogadro	Foresti	Palazzi
Bargnani	Gambara	Poncarali
Calini	Girelli	Porcellaga
Campana	Gonfaloneri	Provaglio
Caprioli	Lana	Riva
Cavalli	Lantiera di Paratici	Rodengo
Chizzola	Lodi	Sala
Confalonieri	Lodetti	San Gervasio
Coradelli	Longhena	Schilini
Covi	Maggi	Secco
Curte	Manerba	Suardi
Ducchi	Martinengo	Terzi
Emigli	Monti	Uggeri
Federici	Montini	Ugone

Cives veteres (inscribed prior to 1488)		
Armani	Cesarenus	Paitoni
Armaninni	Crottus	Paitusi
Avoltori	Feroldi[a]	Pedrocche
Barbera	Gaetani	Peschera
Barbisone	Garbelli	Pontecarales
Bocca	Ghidella	Pulusellae
Bona	Guarneri	Roberti
Bonati[a]	Luzzaghi	Rovati
Bornati	Masperoni	Scalvini
Briggia	Medici	Soncini
Brunelli[a]	Merlini	Stella
Cagnola	Montini	Tarelli
Carenzoni	Odasi	Zamara
Cazzamali	Offlaga	Zoni
Cegula	Oriani	

Benemeriti (inscribed in 1438)		
Alventi	Mazzola	Violini
Appiani	Peroni	Zola[a]

Other (inscribed prior to 1488)		
Bianchi[a]	Pizzoni[a]	Saerina[a]
Castelli[a]		

Table 4 (*cont.*)

Caravati[a]	Prati[a]	Tiberi[a]
Comotta[a]	Rosa[a]	Tomasini[a]
de Laude[a]	Saenna[a]	Trussi[a]
Fasana[a]	San Pellegrini[a]	Ulmi[a]
Ganassoni[a]	Savallo[a]	Valtorta[a]
Gandini[a]	Scanzi[a]	
Malveti[a]	Tarelli[a]	
Marini[a]		
Padovani[a]		
Pescherie[a]		
Pontevicus[a]		

Obtained membership in the sixteenth century

Baitelli[a]	Occhi
Brognoli	Pontolei[a]
Bucchi	Prandoni
Capitano	Prati
Duranti[a]	Zanetti
Grati	Zaniboni[a]
Lodetti	
Mazzuchelli[a]	

Obtained membership 1600 to 1650

Cazzamali	Pagnani
de Scopuli	Papiae
Fabi	Pedrochi de
Marchetti	Peroni
Nazari	Ustinani
	Zanucha

Note: [a]Of mercantile origins.
Sources: ASCB, vols. 1426 1/2 A–C, "Elenco delle famiglie nobili di Brescia iscritto nel Gran Consiglio fino al 1796"; A. Monti della Corte, *Le familie del patriziato bresciano* (Brescia: Geroldi, 1960), pp. 19–79; 93–128.

professions, and with modes of behavior. Yet there were differences in status within the council's ranks, and those differences were tied largely to the political (and professional) and economic weight of the family. Thus the disagreements in the council over hierarchy were in fact disagreements over the distribution of power.

CHAPTER 3

FAMILY AND POWER:
STRATEGIES OF CONSOLIDATION

By the late sixteenth century elites in a myriad of urban centers in north and central Italy had consolidated their ranks, not simply relative to the disenfranchised but also within the confines of their own respective governing circles. Studies of Milan, Siena, Venice, Cremona, Genoa, Lucca, and Verona reach similar conclusions: restricted numbers of families held high offices, separated from the rest of their order by superior wealth and in some instances by superior demographic strength.[1] The impact of these narrowing systems of power in early modern Italy was far-reaching. Contrasts in wealth and authority created divisions, making patrician regimes unstable, or, as Mozzarelli aptly put it, "precarious groups of alliances."[2] Also, the constriction of power placed the future of ruling orders in a precarious position over time: they ran the risk of lacking sufficient numbers to cover administrative offices, another factor producing social and political instability.[3]

Through the natural process of biological extinction, and cooptation, the Brescian ruling class too became increasingly concentrated into the seventeenth century. The Venetian Signoria does not appear to have interfered with this development, which was also characteristic of its

---

[1]   For Siena, Marrara, *Riseduti e nobiltà* and G. R. F. Baker, "Nobiltà in declino: il caso di Siena sotto i Medici e gli Asburgo-Lorena," *RSI* 84 (1972): 584–616; for Lucca, Berengo, *Nobili e mercanti*; for Cremona, Politi, *Aristocrazia e potere*; for Genoa, E. Grendi, "Capitazioni e nobiltà genovese in età moderna," *Quaderni Storici* 8 (1974): 403–444; for Verona, Borelli, *Un patriziato*; for the Marca pontificia, Zenobi, *Ceti e potere*; for Venice, J. C. Davis, *The Decline of the Venetian Republic as a Ruling Class* (Baltimore: The Johns Hopkins University Press, 1962); for Mediterranean society as a whole, Braudel, *The Mediterranean*, vol. II, p. 704. For a valuable review of the contributions of this literature see Cesare Mozzarelli's historiographical essay, "Stato, patriziato," pp. 421–512.

[2]   Mozzarelli, "Stato, patriziato," p. 510.

[3]   *Ibid.*, p. 495.

own ruling class. The absence of state intervention supports the notion that the Venetians did not have overall ambitions to centralize or unify the cities under their sway. Instead, ample powers of decision were left to the urban ruling orders. In contrast, the Medici exerted more control over oligarchy formation in Tuscany. This is particularly true in the Sienese case, where Cosimo I designated the members of the oligarchy.[4] Even in the Papal States, less firmly controlled at their center than Tuscany, there were instances of state intervention: in Jesi in 1587 Pope Sixtus V opened the hereditary council to doctors and jurists.[5] Local power in the Venetian territorial state, in contrast, remained relatively more autonomous.

Strategies of consolidation merit study for the light they shed on the behavior of the ruling family and, more broadly, on the role the family played in shaping systems of power during the ancien régime. The constriction of political power in Brescia found its support in family continuity and economic continuity. Size, wealth, kinship ties, and professional careers helped assure the family's survival and success in public life. Study of the strategies that Brescian families employed over the long term to plan their futures also helps illumine some of the features of early modern European family life.[6]

FAMILY DEMOGRAPHY

Through the cooptation of kinsmen, the membership of the Brescian Council steadily expanded throughout the sixteenth century and maintained its numbers into the first half of the seventeenth century. Enrollments rose from 238 individuals in 1522 to 484 in 1576[7] and 522 in 1594,[8] a result, according to Pasero, of the 1517 provision that the sons of city councillors were automatically eligible to join the council. There was no limit on the number of men who could put forward their names to serve in the biannual reforms, once they had been admitted to the eligibility lists.[9] Therefore the number of councillors to serve in each of the biannual reforms fluctuated from term to term, from as low as 355 in 1630, a plague year, to as high as 504 in 1650. The average

4   Fasano Guarini, "Principe ed oligarchie," pp. 115–116.
5   Molinelli, Un'oligarchia locale, p. 41.
6   See N. Z. Davis, "Ghosts, Kin, and Progeny: Some Features of Family Life in Early Modern France," Daedalus 106 (1977): 87–114.
7   Pasero, "Il dominio veneto," p. 356, n. 3. See also M. Romani, "Prestigio, potere e ricchezza nella Brescia di Agostino Gallo (Prime indagini)," in Agostino Gallo nella cultura del Cinquecento, ed. M. Pegrari (Brescia: Tipografia Artigiana, 1988), p. 117.
8   ASCB, Provvisioni, vol. 562, ff. 121r–126v, January 5, 1594.
9   Report of Paolo Correr, April 1562, in RV, ed. Tagliaferri, vol. XI, p. 67.

number of councillors listed in the biannual reforms for 1594 (522), 1600 (484), 1608 (432), 1620 (451), 1630 (355), 1644 (433), and 1650 (504) was 454.[10] This meant that in any given term the council represented approximately 1 percent of the urban population, which fluctuated around 40,000 during normal demographic cycles; 19,000 after the plague of 1630.

In the period between 1588 and 1650 there were 220 *case* represented in twenty-nine of the thirty-one biannual reforms (see appendix 1).[11] (It is appropriate here to define the terms *casa* and lineage. A *casa* is a group of families which belong to the same consanguineous kin group with the same surname. Lineage is defined as "descent in a line from a common progenitor."[12] There are, then, separate lineages within each *casa*.) Sixty-one *case* (*circa* 28 percent) were represented in less than five biannual reforms; forty-three of these became extinct at some point during the period under examination,[13] while eighteen were absent for long periods of time and then reappeared.[14] On the other hand, 159 *case* (72 percent) appeared on the reform lists with great regularity.

The way the numerical presence of the 220 *case* was distributed over time will furnish a more precise indication of the number of families

[10] See Romani, "Prestigio, potere e ricchezza," whose study terminates with 1636.

[11] There are twenty-nine rather than thirty-one reforms between 1588 and 1650 because the membership lists for 1640 and 1646 are missing from the council deliberations for those years. Moreover, the 1590 reform was annulled, and the council deliberated to retain the membership of 1588. ASCB, *Provvisioni*, vol. 560, ff. 74v–75r, January 5, 1590. I have made use of the membership list of 1588 for two terms, 1588–1589 and 1590–1591. The biannual reforms of the Brescian Council for 1588; 1592–1638; and 1648–1650 are listed in ASCB, *Provvisioni*, vols. 559, ff. 82v–91r; 561, ff. 143v–152r; 562, ff. 121r–126v; 563, ff. 74r–80r; 564, ff. 94v–100r; 565, ff. 129r–135v; 566, ff. 95v–107v; 567, ff. 89r–94v; 568, ff. 99v–102v; 569, ff. 20r–26v; 570, ff. 14v–19v; 571, ff. 16v–23r; 572, ff. 17v–24r; 573, ff. 38v–44v; 574, ff. 34v–41r; 575, ff. 29r–33v; 576, ff. 14r–17r; 577, ff. 30r–32r; 578, ff. 20v–22v; 579, ff. 21r–24v; 580, ff. 14r–18r; 581, ff. 180r–184r; 582, ff. 175v–178v; 583, ff. 157r–161r; 584, ff. 109r–111v; 589, ff. 32r–37v; 590, ff. 8v–13v. The reforms for 1642 and 1644 are in ASV, *Senato, Rettori*, F. 20, u.d.

[12] *Webster's New Collegiate Dictionary* (Springfield, Massachusetts, 1974), p. 668.

[13] The Aleni, Grilli, Lenij, Gaetani, Salodi (1594); the Gavandi, Gadaldue, Moreschi, Nuolina, Parenti, Vineltati (1596); the Bergognini, Bettoncelli, Ceruti, Cinalia, del Fe, Lonius (1600); the Parpagni (1602); the Burrati (1604); the Suraga, Tairdini, and Valtorta (1608); the de Humeltati (1612); the Bazardi (1616); the Gafurri (1620); the Buarni, Carravati, and Coccali (1622); the Belacatti, and the Gabbiani (1624); the Marende (1626); the Calzaveglia, Campana, de Morris, Passirani, Roberti (1628); the Gobini, San Peregrini, Trivella, and Zerbini (1630); the Seriate (1636); the Mauri (1638); the Cegula (1642). ASCB, *Provvisioni*, vols. 559–586. See n. 11.

[14] The Comotta, Fausti, Garbelli, Glerola, Pagani, Pontoli, Ponzoni, Prandoni, Prati, Ronzoni, Savalli, Scalvini, Scaramutie, Schilini, Suardi, Thomasi, Zamara, Zaniboni disappear from the registers for periods ranging from fourteen to forty-two years.

Table 5. *Number of seats per* casa *in the biannual reforms (1588–1650)*

	Range of seats per term	Number of *case*	Percentage of 220
Group I	6–12	19	8.6
Group II	3–5	20	9.1
Group III	below 3	181	82.3
Total		220	100.0

Source: See n. 11, p. 74.

with some stake in association with civic government. To calculate the demographic weight of each *casa*, I counted the number of seats it occupied in each of the twenty-nine biannual reforms under review. The preliminary results are set out in table 5.[15]

The representation in the council of these 220 *case* is divided roughly into three categories. The majority (Group III: 82 percent) occupied, on average, less than three seats per term, while a minority – less than 18 percent (Groups I and II) – held what may be interpreted as significant demographic weight consistently over time.[16] The thirty-nine *case* that comprise Groups I and II are listed in table 6 with more specific demographic data: the number of terms in which the names of these *case* appear, the total number of seats each *casa* occupied over the twenty-nine biannual reforms, the average number of seats it occupied per term, and the range of separate lineages within each *casa*.

The thirty-nine *case* listed in table 6 – 18 percent of 220 – occupied approximately 53 percent of a total of 13,166 seats (454 multiplied by twenty-nine terms = 13,166) over the six decades under study. In particular, it is the nineteen *case* that comprise Group I that merit attention, for they carried preponderant numbers in the council over the course of a half century. Collectively, they occupied 4,454 seats, or, approximately 34 percent of the total number of seats over twenty-nine

[15] The demography of 111 families, approximately half of the membership (Romani, "Prestigio," p. 122), for the years between 1486 and 1639 may be found in M. Pegrari, "I giochi del potere. Presenza e incidenza del patriziato nella società bresciana del Cinquecento," in *Arte, economia, cultura e religione nella Brescia del XVI secolo* (Brescia: Società Editrice Vannini, 1988), pp. 233–236. See also Romani, "Prestigio, potere e ricchezza," pp. 131–134. My demographic study covers the entire membership, 220 *case*, for the more concentrated period between 1588 and 1650.

[16] The spread in Group II (9.1 percent) included five *case* that occupied on average at least 5.1 seats per term; seven *case* that occupied 4.1 seats per term; and ten *case* that occupied 2.6 seats per term. The spread in Group I (8.6 percent) included five *case* that maintained on average 9.1 seats; seven that maintained on average 7.0 seats; and five *case* that averaged 6.0 seats.

Table 6. *The case with preponderant weight in the council*

Casa	Number of terms served	Total number of seats; average per term		Range of lineages
GROUP I				
1. Maggi	29	417	12	7–17
2. Lana	29	305	10	5–11
3. Luzzaghi	29	300	9	7–10
4. Ugoni	29	297	9	6–10
5. Fenaroli	29	271	9	5–9
6. Ducchi	29	245	8	4–8
7. Martinengo	29	239	7	5–11
8. Sala	29	238	8	4–12
9. Bona	29	229	8	4–9
10. Stella	29	219	7	4–8
11. Averoldi	29	213	7	5–10
12. Bornati	29	201	7	3–9
13. Nassini	29	200	6	3–7
14. Chizzola	29	189	6	3–12
15. Soncini	29	186	6	2–8
16. Montini	29	182	6	3–6
17. Foresti	29	179	6	3–8
18. Calini	29	175	6	4–6
19. Bargnani	29	169	6	2–9
GROUP II				
20. Pedrocche	29	168	5	3–6
21. Manerba	29	156	5	3–5
22. Faite	29	155	5	3–4
23. Fisogno	29	146	5	3–6
24. Pischerie ⎫	29	143	4	1–4
25. Gambara ⎭	29	143	3	1–6
26. Rodengo	29	142	5	2–5
27. Rovati	29	132	5	2–5
28. Ganassoni	29	131	5	1–5
29. Feroldi	29	128	4	2–5
30. Longhena	28	121	4	2–5
31. Coradelli	29	120	4	1–6
32. Porcellaga	28	117	4	1–5
33. Malvetij	28	116	4	2–4
34. Emigli	28	113	4	2–6
35. Federici	29	111	4	1–3
36. Marini	28	109	4	2–5
37. Mazzole	29	103	4	1–5
38. Paratici	18	93	3	2–7
39. Savalli	20	89	3	1–3
Total number of seats		6,990		

Source: See n. 11, p. 74.

terms. The Maggi, for example, were an impressively large *casa* throughout the period under study. Between 1588 and 1610 they occupied 189 seats; between 1612 and 1630, 107 seats, and between 1632 and 1650, 140 seats, for a total of 436 seats (3 percent of 13,166). By 1650 they had expanded to twenty lineages and were consistently the largest *casa* in the council. Nine of the largest *case* followed the same pattern, though in smaller proportions, while six diminished in numbers in the period after the plague of 1630 but still retained preponderant demographic weight. The Lana, for example, held 126 seats between 1588 and 1610, 111 between 1612 and 1630, but only fifty six seats between 1632 and 1650. Yet they still occupied the second largest number of seats within the council. It is significant as well that most of the thirty-nine *case* identified above were present in all twenty-nine biannual reforms, giving them the opportunity to establish firmly their presence in council with consistency over time.

We may draw some important conclusions from the evidence thus far. First, the council preserved its size over time. Second, a relatively small proportion of *case* carried preponderant demographic weight. These two trends ultimately confirm that council participation grew even more elitist over this period, constricted to a small group of *case* that had developed successful strategies over time to preserve their numerical advantages. This raises some important questions. What do these strategies tell us about the social significance and solidarity of the larger family institution of the *casa*? Did certain families in the council owe their political stature in the late Cinquecento and early Seicento to the ability of their *casa* to preserve and expand its numbers more readily than others?

One way to answer these questions is to determine the factors that the thirty-nine largest *case* held in common. The first common denominator that stands out is that they had multiple lineages represented on the council membership lists. While we are not equipped here to offer an analysis of fertility rates within the ruling class, it is evident that the larger *case* had the good biological fortune not only to escape extinction but also to multiply (see table 6). A lengthy history of council membership, the second element these families held in common, also gave the largest *case* the time to draw in consanguineous kinsmen. With respect to Group I, all but one of the *case* had appeared on the membership lists of the city council before 1488, while the Ducchi were admitted in the sixteenth century. Thirteen *case* (including the Ducchi) originated with the rural nobility of the Middle Ages while four were among the families that had governed the medieval commune, the *cives veteres*. All of the names in Group II had appeared on the council membership lists from 1438 or before. Eleven derived from the rural nobility; three were from the *cives veteres*; eight had non-noble origins and had entered the council early on: in 1438 as a reward for their military service to Brescia.[17] In sum, the *case* with the largest demographic numbers were also among the oldest families who had participated in civic affairs. The reason they had multiple lineages in the council becomes apparent when we examine the way in which the council retained its size, despite its losses. As mentioned above, forty-three *case* disappeared from the roll lists during the period under study and eighteen were absent for significant lengths of time.

We begin to have a general idea of the number of families that disappeared from the council's enrollment lists over the sixteenth century from Monti della Corte's list of the families inscribed in the Brescian Book of Gold: 108 surnames do not appear in the biannual reforms between 1588 and 1650.[18] Further evidence is supplied by Romani, who notes the disappearance of twenty-six families between 1486 and 1499 and thirty-eight families over the sixteenth century.[19] Who was replacing the extinct families? Between 1588 and 1650 only eleven new *case* without kinsmen in the council were accepted into the membership.[20] In contrast, the overwhelming majority of new additions bore the same surnames as the families in council. There appears to have been a conscious effort on the part of the members of the *case* who were consistently present in the council and who carried preponderant demographic weight, both to protect their numerical strength and to buttress the stature of this larger family institution in public life by admitting consanguineous kinsmen. Control of the screening committee for new admissions, the deputati alla civiltà, was fundamental to this objective. The efforts of these *case* are also evident in the applications for membership, conserved in the *Processi di Nobiltà*. The

[17] To determine the social origins of the *case* I consulted: ASCB, vol. 1426 1/2 A–C, "Elenco delle famiglie nobili di Brescia iscritto nel Gran Consiglio fino al 1796"; A. Monti della Corte, "Il registro veneto dei nobili estimati nel territorio bresciano tra il 1426 e il 1498," *CAB* 159 (1960): 165–270; Monti della Corte, *Le famiglie del patriziato bresciano*, pp. 19–79; 93–138; A. Monti della Corte, *Fonti araldiche e blasoniche bresciane. Il registro veneto dei nobili detti rurali od agresti estimati nel territorio bresciano tra il 1426 e il 1498* (Brescia: Geroldi, 1962); C. Manaresi, "I nobili della Bresciana," *CAB* 129 (1930): 271–421.

[18] See Monti della Corte, *Le famiglie del patriziato bresciano*, pp. 90–92. I have not included the families who were admitted post 1650.

[19] Romani, "Prestigio," pp. 118–119.

[20] Among them, the Ustinani (1628), the Gorni (1636), the Marchetti (1642), the Nazari (1642), the Papiae (1644), the Pedroche de Peroni, the de Scopuli, the Zanucha (1642).

extant records span the years from 1607 to 1797.[21] During the years
between 1607 and 1654 there were a total of 666 files in this archival
collection. A preliminary survey indicates that out of 666 files, twenty-
four, or 3.6 percent, of the surnames were parvenus, while 642, or 96.4
percent bore the same surnames as the *case* already enrolled in the
council.[22] Moreover, a relatively small number of *case* consistently
applied for membership. A careful examination of both the lists of
Processi di Nobiltà and the demographic patterns of the *case* enrolled in
the governing class confirms that the larger *case* were growing even
larger by coopting consanguineous kinsmen into their ranks: the largest
thirty-nine *case* also account for 44.1 percent of the total number of
entries in the archival collection. Their success in entering the council is
confirmed by the number of seats they gradually gained. For example,
between 1594 and 1610 the Maggi held 101 seats; between 1632 and
1650 they held 140. In the first period the Ugone held sixty-six seats; in
the second 102. The Bona jumped from forty-five to eighty-nine seats;
the Bornati from forty to ninety-four. The *case* that saw their numbers
increase were most often the same ones that filled the ranks of the
executive committee, charged with approving new admissions. There
was, then, some correlation between size and power, though we must
be careful not to overemphasize this: a *casa* could compensate for fewer
numbers by its wealth and by its marriage connections.

While it is not possible to establish how closely members of a *casa*
cooperated with one another in daily political matters (there is no
record of how individuals voted), the way in which Brescian councillors, and more specifically the members of the executive committee,
coopted consanguineous kinsmen strongly suggests that they expected

---

[21] ASCB, *Descrizione ed inventario di tutti i libri, mazzi, e documenti esistenti nell'archivio
antico municipale di Brescia (1866)*, pp. 48–51.

[22] The frequency with which these surnames appeared in the application files may be
illustrated in the table. Many of the *case* in Group I were among the largest *case* in the
council. They included the Maggi, Lana, Ugoni, Fenaroli, Luzzaghi, Bona, Ducchi, Sala,
Averoldi, Martinengo, Stella, Bornati, Soncini, Chizzola, Bargnani, Calini, Nassini.

Group	Number of *case*	Number of files	Percentage of total files
I	27	245	36.8
II	40	189	28.4
III	107	208	31.2
Total	174	642	96.4

Source: ASCB, *Descrizione ed inventario di tutti i libri, mazzi, e documenti esistenti
nell'archivio antico municipale di Brescia (1866)*, pp. 48–51 (1607–1654).

to gain political support from new recruits. Here the results of Grendi's study of the Genoese oligarchy are instructive. Families in Genoa were conscious of their demographic strength. Not only did various lineages maintain solidarity; there was also an active system of clientage.[23] It is no coincidence that in Brescia fifteen of the twenty-two *case* who filled the executive offices (listed below, table 8) most frequently during this period also figure among the largest *case* in the council. Numbers and power were closely intertwined. The interrelationship of these two elements is most visible, however, at the level of the domestic unit. A survey of the membership list of 1644, for example, reveals forty-eight pairs of brothers in the council that term; five instances of three brothers; two of four brothers; and one of five brothers plus their father. The provision of 1517 that permitted membership to the sons of city councillors[24] had a decisive effect on the political strength of the nuclear family and thus on the future composition of the city council: by having more than one member of the domestic unit on the council membership lists at the same time, the lineage could ensure its representation on the council for consecutive years. Moreover, it could avail itself of multiple votes. Still further, good relations with other members of the lineage – uncles and cousins – multiplied the odds of carrying substantial political weight.

The cooptation of consanguineous kinsmen is also a sign that the *casa* enjoyed its own collective social identity in Brescia. It conferred social identity upon prospective councillors, serving as a basis for the credentials they presented when applying for admission. The council placed a high priority on bloodline and on consanguineous kinship ties when it reviewed admission applications. When Aurelio and Lodovico Giorgi applied for membership in 1634, they were refused both because their ancestors were tainted by connections with the peasantry and because some of their kinsmen still worked with their hands.[25] Few families without relatives already in the council found their way into this municipal governing elite between 1588 and 1650.[26] The members of the civic elite were acutely interested in coopting families of their own quality into their ranks. That signified above all else families with similar genealogical dossiers and families who came from *case* that

---

[23] Grendi, "Capitazioni," p. 404, n. 26.

[24] Pasero, "Il dominio veneto," p. 356, n. 3.

[25] ASCB, *Provvisioni*, vol. 582, f. 3r, January 2, 1634; *Processi di Nobiltà*, vol. 307, No. 42 (u.d.).

[26] There were only eleven out of 220 (5 percent) between 1588 and 1650. They included the Fabi (1602); the Pagnani (1616); the Ustinani (1628); the Gorni (1636);

vaunted long histories of political experience and participation in civic affairs.[27] The applications of Giovanni Giacomo Cavallo (1640) and Lanfranco Federici (1654) for admission to the city council are good cases in point. Giovanni Giacomo's uncle had been automatically eligible to participate in civic government. Giovanni Giacomo was careful to underline that his genealogical credentials were identical to those of his consanguineous kinsmen in the council, and the deliberating body unanimously approved his admission.[28] Lanfranco Federici came from an old noble family, invested as marquises and counts by the Holy Roman Emperor in 1024. The family met the citizenship requirement. Moreover, other branches of Lanfranco's family were already in the council. The application was approved in 1654.[29]

THE DISTRIBUTION OF THE EXECUTIVE OFFICES

By the late sixteenth century power was in the hands of a select number of families who rotated the positions of the executive committee, called public deputies. This committee consisted of an abbate, who was the president of the General Council, or general deliberating body, and the Special Council; two avvocati, who, in addition to standing in for the abbate, defended public interests and approved or vetoed the proposals put forward in the General Council; two deputati ad observantiam statutorum, who devised and enforced the civil and criminal statutes, and one or two sindici, who supervised the city's revenues.[30] By alternating the executive posts, together with the more important public responsibilities (e.g., supervision of the tribunals of food provisioning and indirect taxes, of the estimi, of the Monti di Pietà, and of the Hospedale Maggiore), this small group of councillors controlled the reins of judicial, legislative, and financial power in the city.

In theory, every two years the General Council elected a group of twenty-one men to rotate the offices of the executive committee. There were twelve abbati, one for each month of the year; four lawyers who alternated the post of avvocato in groups of two every six months; two deputati ad observantiam statutorum who held office for one year; and one or two sindici, who remained in office for the entire two-year

the de Scopuli, the Zanucha, the Marchetti, and the Nazari (1642); the Cazzamali, the Papiae, and the Pedroche de Peroni (1644).

27 ASCB, *Provvisioni*, vol. 585, ff. 6v–7r, January 3, 1640.

28 *Ibid.*

29 ASCB, *Processi di Nobiltà*, vol. 319, No. 12, Lanfranco Federici (u.d.), January 15, 1654.

30 Report of Paolo Correr, in *RV*, ed. Tagliaferri, vol. XI, pp. 67–68.

term. According to established procedures, the names of council members were written on slips of paper and put into a bag, and from these names the executive committee was drawn. Adherence to these election procedures grew more lax in the latter half of the sixteenth century, for the same names appear on the committee with regularity. Moreover, the number of men who served on this committee during each biannual term was irregular, ranging from twenty-one individuals at the beginning of the period to seventeen or eighteen towards the end. Finally, the members of this inner circle became in effect a separate corps, convening without the Special Council or other special magistracies. Major proposals were frequently sent directly from the executive committee to the General Council, so that gradually the functions of the Special Council withered away and the public deputies began to undertake more political responsibilities. In practice they became an autonomous committee that controlled the nerve of urban finance and political power in Brescia.[31] Given the importance of these offices, we may identify the families that enjoyed political prominence in Brescia in the late sixteenth century and the first half of the seventeenth century by singling out the councillors that occupied them most frequently.

To arrive at a quantitative distribution of the executive seats, I extracted the names of the public deputies from the registers of the General Council deliberations for the years between 1590 and 1641.[32] These twenty-six terms, or fifty-two years, are time enough to observe two generations of council members. I tabulated their participation in the inner circle first according to *casa* and then according to individual, with the following results: 133 men representing 65 *case* (29.5 percent of the 220 *case* on the council membership lists) were represented on the executive committee over the course of this half century. At first glance, the percentage appears to be substantial. A more detailed analysis, illustrated in table 7, indicates that only a small number of *case* held these posts with any consistency over great lengths of time. Table 7 reveals that about one-third of the *case* accounted for only 8 percent of the total number of occupied seats.[33] Roughly another third

---

31   Zanelli, *Delle condizioni*, pp. 19–24; 49–52. See also report of Giovanni Battista Foscarini, Podestà, May 9, 1620, in *RV*, ed. Tagliaferri, vol. XI, p. 250.

32   To find the names of the public deputies for these years, I consulted ASCB, *Provvisioni*, vols. 560–585.

33   Eleven *case* (eleven councillors) held one seat each for a total of eleven seats: Avogadro, Brunelli, Buratti, Caprioli, Emigli, Locadelli, Nassini, Paratico, Pezani, Pischerie, Sala. Seven *case* (nine councillors) held two seats each for a total of fourteen seats: Calzavelia, Conforto, Mantua, Ponzone, Rosa, Ripa, Scalvino. Four *case* (five councillors) held three seats each for a total of twelve: Capitano, Ducco, Gambara, Zanetti.

Table 7. *The distribution of executive seats (1590–1641)*

Number of *case*	Number of men	Total seats occupied	Percentage of total seats
22	71	322	68
21	37	116	24
22	25	37	8
Total			
65	133	475	100

Source: ASCB, *Provvisioni*, vols. 560–585.

Table 8. *The* case *with preponderant weight in executive offices*

Casa	Number of councillors	Number of seats occupied
Averoldi	5	30
Lana	8	27
Stella	2	22
Federici	4	20
Luzzago	3	20
Calino	5	20
Soncino	3	19
Martinengo	8	18
Savallo	3	18
Longhena	3	13
Porcellaga	3	12
Maggi	3	11
Baitelli	2	10
Coradelli	2	10
Manerba	1	10
Saiano	3	10
Ugone	3	9
Savoldo	4	9
Feroldi	1	9
Palazzi	2	9
Barbisone	1	8
Gallo	2	8
Total	71	322

Source: ASCB, *Provvisioni*, vols. 560–585 (1590–1640).

accounted for 24 percent of the total number of seats,[34] while the first third occupied a significant 68 percent of the seats during this half century. A detailed distribution of this last group is set out in table 8.

[34] Five *case* (eleven councillors) held four seats each for a total of twenty: Appiano, Bargnani, Fenarolo, Gandini, Girelli. Five *case* (six councillors) held five seats each for a total of twenty-five: Faita, Fisogno, Pontevici, Scanzo, Trussi. Six *case*

A relatively small number of *case* – twenty-two out of 220, or, 10 percent – stood at the apogee of power during the half century under analysis. Moreover, eighteen of the men accounted for in table 8 served multiple terms on the executive committee and occupied 37 percent of the total number of seats during this period; twenty-seven men occupied 49 percent of the seats. What we have, then, is not simply rule by a few *case* but rather conditions where relatively few men could monopolize the most important offices for long periods of time.[35] The foundations of their power lay with the political behavior of their households and lineages, which acted as fundamental units of social organization within the council.

The strategy of those who held the reins of power was to keep the executive offices within the reach of the domestic unit, making control generational. The Soncini are a good example of how these offices were passed from father to son. Quinto Fabio served on the executive committee for eight consecutive terms (sixteen years) during the period between 1614 and 1628. His son Virginio first appeared on the executive committee in 1628, during Quinto Fabio's last term, and thereafter served consecutive terms until 1640, the terminal date of this survey. Thus father and son served collectively a total of fourteen terms, or twenty-eight consecutive years on the executive committee. The Soncini are not an isolated example. There are several cases where sons followed their fathers to the executive committee: Ippolito Luzzago (1590) and Giovanni Paolo (1618);[36] Gaspar Lana (1606) and Francesco (1650);[37] Bernardo Gallo (1604) and Francesco (1650);[38] Giovanni Battista Averoldi (1599) and Pompeo (1620);[39] Costanzo Baitelli (1600) and Lodovico (1618);[40] Gabriele Rodengo (1602) and

---

(eight councillors) held six seats each for a total of thirty-six: Carenzone, Covo, Foresti, Montini, Pontecarali, Sicci. Five *case* (twelve councillors) held seven seats each for a total of thirty-five: Chizzola, Cucchi, Provagli, Rodengo, Schilini.

[35] Giovanni Paolo Luzzago served 13 terms; Giulio Stella, 12; Giulio Federici and Francesco Porcellaga, 11 each; Pompeo Averoldi, Nicolò Manerba, Bartolomeo Stella, 10 each; Octavio Feroldo, Giovanni Battista Savallo, 9 each; Pietro Barbisone, Francesco Longhena, Gaspar Lana, Francesco Savallo, Quinto Fabio Soncino, 8 each; Ruttilio Calino, Francesco Saino, Virginio Soncino, Giovanni Antonio Cucchi, 7 each. If we keep in mind that each term lasted for two years, these men served anywhere from fourteen to twenty-six years on the executive committee.

[36] Giovanni Paolo Luzzago, ASCB, *Provvisioni*, vol. 574, f. 79v, March 3, 1618; Ippolito Luzzago, *ibid.*, vol. 560, f. 77r, January 11, 1590.

[37] *Ibid.*, vol. 568, f. 75r, December 9, 1605; vol. 590, f. 7v, January 13, 1650.

[38] *Ibid.*, vol. 567, f. 117r, April 21, 1604; vol. 590, f. 74, August 18, 1650.

[39] *Ibid.*, vol. 565, f. 2v, January 5, 1599; vol. 574, f. 199r, October 20, 1618.

[40] *Ibid.*, vol. 565, f. 125v, January 12, 1600; vol. 574, f. 72v, February 15, 1618.

Giovanni Antonio (1640);[41] Francesco Longhena (1618) and Orazio (1640);[42] Aloisio Federici (1602) and Giulio (1641).[43]

Marriage strategies among the councillors that frequently served on the executive committee were also designed to solidify control of these offices. Fathers and sons-in-law, and brothers-in-law,[44] formed important political alliances. Pompeo Averoldi, Ludovico Asto, and Ruttilio Calino are a good case in point. Averoldi, who served on the executive committee for ten terms during the period between 1618 and 1640, was followed by his son-in-law, Ludovico Asto, who began to appear on the executive committee in the 1640s. Moreover, Averoldi served on the executive committee simultaneously with his father-in-law, Ruttilio Calino, who appeared for seven terms between 1622 and 1640.[45] The Luzzago–Zaniboni alliance is another example of how marital ties kept the executive offices within the reach of a tight-knit family group over three generations. Ippolito Luzzago served on the committee throughout the 1590s. He was followed by his son, Giovanni Paolo, who served thirteen terms between 1608 and 1640. When Giovanni Paolo reached the twilight of his career in the 1640s, he was followed by his son-in-law, Giovanni Paolo Zaniboni.[46] The Zaniboni were a tiny *casa*: Giovanni Paolo, who became active in the council in 1632, was its only representative. Moreover, the *casa* was relatively new compared to the rest of the council membership: the Zaniboni, deriving from an old Guelf house, had been admitted in 1529.[47] Though the *casa*'s history of council membership did not match that of the Luzzago, Giovanni Paolo was conspicuously wealthy;[48] his riches furthered his political career by enabling him to conclude a fruitful marriage alliance. The Baitelli–Ugoni alliance provides a final example of how marriage ties kept the executive offices within the reach of a small family group

---

[41] *Ibid.*, vol. 566, f. 146v, August 28, 1602; vol. 585, f. 33r, March 15, 1640.

[42] *Ibid.*, vol. 574, f. 1r, January 2, 1618; vol. 585, f. 19r, January 18, 1640.

[43] *Ibid.*, vol. 566, f. 125r, April 13, 1602; vol. 585, f. 110r, March 7, 1641.

[44] For example, Paolo Manerba and Hercule Alvento (on the executive committee in the 1640s) were brothers-in-law. For Hercule Alvento q. Hercule, ASB, *Polizze d'estimo* (hereafter *PE*), 1641, B. 4, No. 250; For Paolo q. Nicolò Manerba, *ibid.*, B. 7, No. 243.

[45] For Ruttilio Calino q. Vicenzo, *ibid.*, B. 1, No. 213; for Lodovico Aste q. Antonio Maria, *ibid.*, B. 6, No. 97; for Pompeo Averoldi q. Giovanni Battista, *ibid.*, B. 2, No. 175.

[46] For Giovanni Paolo Luzzago q. Hippolito, *ibid.*, B. 1, No. 130; For Giovanni Paolo Zaniboni q. Ottaviano, *ibid.*, B. 11, No. 331.

[47] Monti della Corte, *Le famiglie del patriziato bresciano*, p. 127.

[48] Zaniboni's *campione d'estimo* was D14, placing him in the top 1 percent of the city councillors surveyed for 1641, ASB, *PE* 1641, B. 11, No. 331.

for generations.[49] Constantino Baitelli served on the executive committee without interruption between 1590 and 1600. After a six-year interval, his son, Lodovico, one of the most respected authorities on jurisprudence in the Venetian state, appeared on the lists of public deputies. Lodovico served in 1616, and then for three consecutive terms between 1620 and 1624, inclusive. His career path, however, took him outside Brescia to serve in a consultative capacity for Venice. While Lodovico himself did not have occasion to serve on the executive council again, his nephew, Stefano Maria Ugone, held this important post consistently throughout the 1630s and 1640s. Again, the Baitelli were a tiny but powerful *casa* with important family ties and wealth. Like the Zaniboni, they had found successful ways of compensating for their small numbers. These examples reflect the care that was taken by the councillors who filled the ranks of the executive committee over the course of half a century to ensure that these offices remained within a tight-knit kinship circle.

The same kinds of close-knit kinship strategies over generations were used to monopolize the more important public responsibilities, such as the city chancellors, the officials that sat with the sindici to discuss the management of city revenues and expenditure and that supervised the assignment of civic offices. According to council regulations, the two chancellors, chosen by scrutiny, would serve five-year, renewable terms. Pasero has noted for the sixteenth century that a few families (the Nassini, the Emili, the Malvezzi, the Feroldi, the Coradelli, the Pedrocca, the Faita, the Trussi, and the Calino) monopolized these offices, even though the council made concerted efforts to prevent them from becoming hereditary.[50] Indeed, in 1590 Hieronimo Ugone bemoaned this problem in one of the General Council's deliberations. The chancellors would not give up their positions, nor would others come forward to be selected for this post. Ugone moved that the chancellors be constrained to step down, but the General Council turned down the motion by a wide margin, 230 to 55, a sign of the support the families of the chancellors held in the council. Two years later Ludovico Calino q. Calimero and Adriano Pedrocca were again selected for these posts.[51] Calino, who came from an old, powerful

[49] Lodovico's sister, Marta, married Pietro Ugone. They had three sons: Costanzo, an abbot; Stefano Maria, a lawyer who frequently served as a public deputy, and Lucretio. For the Baitelli, ASB, *PE 1641*, B. 9, No. 213; for the Ugoni, ASB, *ibid.*, B. 11, No. 204.

[50] Pasero, "Il dominio veneto," p. 114.

[51] The vote was 105 yes and 233 no. ASCB, *Provvisioni*, vol. 560, ff. 68v–69v, January 2, 1590; vol. 561, f. 263v, December 19, 1592.

casa, was also connected to the executive committee. His son, Pietro, served eight of the nine possible terms between 1590 and 1610, while Ludovico served the only two-year term (1604–1605) when Pietro was absent from the executive lists. In 1618 Benetino Calino took Ludovico's place as chancellor. He had served four terms on the executive committee before moving into this coveted post.[52]

What we find, thus, in this survey of the most important offices, is that a small group of families, sustained by close kinship ties, monopolized political power, particularly the executive offices. A closer examination of some of the councillors who rose to prominence in council also reveals that they were rotating the most important public responsibilities simultaneously while rotating in and out of the executive committee. For example, Gaspar Lana, who served eight terms on the executive committee over the first three decades of the seventeenth century, also supervised the tribunals of food provisioning (1605) and indirect taxes (1632), served as Deputy of Sanitation (1630), as Prior of the Hospedale Maggiore (1618), and as the city council's lawyer (1618). Giovanni Paolo Luzzago, who served thirteen terms on the executive committee, followed the same pattern. In the two-year period between 1626 and 1628, while rotating in and out of the executive committee, Luzzago served as Prior of the Hospedale Maggiore (1626; 1628) and as Deputy of the Estimo (1626). Again, these are not isolated examples. Rather they represent a pattern: the councillors who most frequently served on the executive committee also simultaneously rotated all the other important magistracies as well.[53] Thus, a select group of *case*, sustained by consanguineous and marital kinship ties forged over generations, enjoyed the privileges that came with supervising the most important public responsibilities: the administration of public monies, the design and execution of the direct tax system and the *annona* (system of food provisioning), and the control of judicial organs that dealt with food provisioning and indirect taxes.

The narrow distribution of power within the governing class explains in part why council membership held no more than honorific value for a great majority of the *case* that appear on the membership lists throughout the course of the late sixteenth and early seventeenth centuries. There were distinct signs of reluctance to serve. In 1608 the council discussed disciplinary measures to check absenteeism in the

[52] *Ibid.*, vol. 574, ff. 323r–323v, August 17, 1619.
[53] Francesco Longhena served as a public deputy in 1616 and as *conservatore* of the Monte Nuovo in 1618; he repeated these offices in 1626–28. Giulio Stella did the same in 1626, serving as a public deputy, the *conservatore* of the Monte Nuovo, and *deputato all'estimo* all in the same year.

podestarie maggiori.[54] That same year it failed to meet the quorum of councillors required to deliberate.[55] Eight years later, in 1616, the council complained that young lawyers were reluctant to undertake public responsibilities.[56] The following year the council ruled that *dottori* (university graduates) who came of age must serve on the deliberating body or lose their rights of membership. What conditions prompted young professionals to avoid the communal governing hall? For some families, the financial responsibilities of some of the less desirable offices outweighed the social advantages. Most public responsibilities came with only a small honorarium. The important ones, such as the podestarie maggiori, required large financial resources.[57] Others, such as the massari (financial administrators) for the Monti or for the *sussidio* (a direct tax) were risky because the funds were difficult to collect, and often the massari were left with pledges in hand. But beyond these drawbacks, reluctance to serve in daily meetings was a symptom of the concentration of power. There was little incentive for newcomers without the necessary kinship ties to throw their hats into the political arena.

The narrow bases of power had also created divisions within the council itself, particularly over the question of precedence. This was not simply a social issue; it was a political one that often led to violence and discouraged some of the citizenry from attending council meetings. The disagreement over precedence, ostensibly a dispute over degrees of "citizenship," was in fact an expression of the tension in the council over the division of offices. The judges had the lion's share of authority, and nobles with no outside jurisdictions contested their monopoly over food provisioning and commerce.[58] The thirteen dissenters with comital titles held few significant responsibilities in public administration: Count Alfonso Provaglio held six seats on the executive committee over the fifty years observed, while Count Ottavio Martinengo and Count Camillo Capriolo held only one seat each. There were eight Martinengo who served on the executive

---

[54] ASCB, *Provvisioni*, vol. 569, ff. 73r–74r, May 17, 1608.
[55] A quorum of 160 was required. The council was divided over how to impose this rule, often turning down disciplinary measures. *Ibid.*, vol. 573, ff. 12r–12v, January 8, 1616.
[56] *Ibid.*, vol. 573, ff. 12r–12v.
[57] Zanelli, *Delle condizioni*, pp. 50–52.
[58] ASV, *Senato. Rettori*, F. 11, letter of Count Francesco Martinengo, April 10, 1638. The dispute is brought up again in BMCV, MS. Martinengo, PD/C 1180, Mazzo 21, No. 5 u.d..

committee, but only two derived from comital branches of the family, while six – more significantly – were judges. Thus titles of nobility carried less weight in the council than legal qualifications. Brescian councillors held high regard for the status of feudatories, but the latter were not heavily represented in council: between 1590 and 1640 there were only seven to fourteen councillors per term who derived from the comital branches of the Martinengo, the Gambara, the Calini, the Caprioli, and the Provagli on the council roll lists, a mere 1 to 3 percent of the membership in any given term. This did not necessarily signify that these *case* held no political sway within the council, simply that their influence was not visible. Because the public deputies made a practice of consulting advisors outside their committee, it is entirely plausible that the prestigious *case* had the opportunity to exert political influence through this informal arrangement. The marriage ties between the Gambara and the Calini, for example, provided the setting for such an exchange to take place. Rutilio Calino q. Vincenzo served on the executive council throughout the 1630s. His daughter Ortensia married Pompeo Averoldi, also a member of the inner circle, while his son Vincenzo married into one of Brescia's prestigious houses, the Gambara. Calino's son-in-law, Count Alemanno Gambara, who appears on the council membership lists but was not conspicuously active in public office, thus was directly tied to members of the inner circle.[59]

The relatively small percentage of feudatories within the Brescian Council is also a sign that their social and political orientation was not directed towards civic government. The Martinengo and the Gambara were equipped with arms, with men and with vast financial resources that made membership in the Brescian civic council rather incidental to their power and illustriousness. The most prestigious of these *case* (the Avogadro, the Gambara, the Martinengo da Barco, and the Martinengo della Pallata) were aggregated to the Venetian patriciate and enjoyed command of some part of the province with the jurisdiction of *merum et misto imperium*, supreme civil and criminal jurisdiction. The Martinengo da Barco and the Martinengo della Pallata, as well as several other branches of this family, enjoyed a history of preeminence both in Venice and in the province of Brescia.[60] The Venetians were beholden to countless Martinengo for their military service to the Republic, and they rewarded these families generously with privileges

---

59 ASB, *PE* 1641, B. 1, No. 213.
60 See Guerrini, *Una celebre famiglia lombarda;* Guerrini, "I Conti di Martinengo e il feudo di Urago d'Oglio," *Brixia Sacra* 15(1924): 52–96; the Martinengo Da Barco had married into the upper ranks of the Venetian ruling class. In 1498 the daughter of

and with feudal jurisdictions.[61] In particular, the Martinengo di Padernello, who had joined the Venetian ruling class in 1517, received large fiefs and pensions in the fifteenth century in compensation for military service and political action. Antonio Martinengo di Padernello had conquered the powerful Gambara family for Venice, and as a reward his family was given *merum et mixtum imperium* in Urago, Pavone, and Gabbiano. Additionally, the Martinengo di Padernello had received a vicariate, with civil and criminal jurisdiction.[62] In later centuries, particularly the sixteenth and seventeenth centuries, when the state was attempting to consolidate its hold over Terraferma resources, the Republic would attempt to reduce the privileges of the Padernello and others, but the Martinengo emerged from this policy relatively intact.[63] In the seventeenth century the *casa* still enjoyed large privileges and concessions on the lands bordering the left bank of the Oglio, especially at Orzinuovi, Roccafranca, and Rudiano, where they drew large incomes from their extensive agricultural domains and ecclesiastical benefices. Thus the power of this important *casa* rested on its feudal jurisdictions, and on its ties to ecclesiastical and secular powers outside the confines of municipal government.[64] Finally, several branches of the Martinengo enjoyed the benefits of a wide support network in both city and countryside, making them some of the most powerful *case* in the province.

No less illustrious were the Gambara, who occupied 143 seats in the council between 1590 and 1650, but only one on the executive committee. Contemporaries regarded this *casa* as the equal of the Gonzaga of Mantua, the Scaligeri of Verona, and the Visconti of

---

Leonardo q. Giovanni Martinengo Da Barco married the Venetian Doge Nicola Marcello. This branch of the Martinengo entered the Venetian patriciate in 1517. V. Spreti, ed., *Enciclopedia storico-nobiliare italiana* (Milan: Unione Tipografia di Milano, 1931), vol. II, pp. 426–428.

[61] Guerrini, *Una celebre famiglia lombarda*, pp. 133; 265–266; 282; 285–286.

[62] *Ibid.*, pp. 265–266; BMCV, *Codice Donà delle Rose*, No. 17, ff. 94r–95v, report of the Venetian Podestà, Leonardo Donà (1579); report of Paolo Correr, in *RV*, ed. Tagliaferri, vol. XI, p. 76.

[63] See P. Guerrini, "Un codice bresciano di privilegi nobiliari," *RA* 25 (1927): 454–460; G. Zulian, "Privilegi e privilegiati a Brescia al principio del '600," *CAB* 137 (1935): 69–137. The Venetians periodically reviewed, reduced or confirmed the privileges of the families of the Brescian nobility. A printed copy of the review of 1648 may be found in *Dichiaratione, & revisione dell'Illus. & Ecc. Sig. Zorzi Contarini, Podestà & Giovanni Alvise Valier, Capitano, Rettori di Brescia. In proposito di privilegij, & essentione di datij di Sua Serenità* (Brescia, 1648), ff. 7v–15r, in ASV, *Senato. DRB*, F. 50.

[64] Guerrini, *Una famiglia celebre lombarda*, p. 124.

Milan.[65] The Gambara possessed vast landed estates, privileges, and princely honors in the Bresciano. They held preponderant economic interests in Pralboino, Ostiano, Milzano, Verola Alghisi, Leno, Remedello, Volongo, Pavone, and other neighboring communities, where they had ample power. In addition, they filled the ranks of the high clergy in Brescia, in Rome, and in other Italian regional states,[66] thus availing themselves of powerful secular and ecclesiastical networks throughout the Peninsula. Though they kept a few kinsmen within the city council, a tactic designed to cover all bases of power, the illustrious members of the Gambara and the Martinengo families clearly remained in a social order whose prestige was linked to arms, to princely courts, and to ecclesiastical sees, far from the meeting hall of the Brescian Council. The latter was more the domain of law graduates, notaries, physicians, humanists, and other professionals.[67]

THE DISTRIBUTION OF WEALTH

As there was a certain disparity in the distribution of power within the council, there was also a disparity in the distribution of wealth, another critical foundation of power which, like family continuity, ensured secular domination. The *estimo* of 1641, which is particularly rich and virtually complete, enables us to reconstruct a relatively clear picture of the distribution of wealth among the *case* who appeared on the council membership lists during the first half of the seventeenth century.[68] It is not an absolutely complete picture, since the *estimo* is an inherently limited source. First, it should be noted that the Brescian *estimi* were not compiled with any regularity. While the municipal statutes stipulated that they be renewed every ten years, the tax registers of 1641 were completed after an interval of fifty-three years. Second, the tax assessments, expressed in numerical coefficients, do not reflect any measure of liquid wealth but rather income from property, rents, and credit operations. Further, the assessments of the ruling families were no doubt conservative, reflecting the privileged position of the politically enfranchised. Despite these limitations, the coefficients supplied in this tax census are useful for their relative value. Moreover, since nobles and

---

65 See Guerrini, "Per la storia dei Conti Gambara di Brescia," pp. 307–314; 370–374; 398–404.

66 BMCV, *Codice Donà delle Rose*, No. 17, ff. 72v–73v.

67 On Brescian councillors' accomplishments in letters and their participation in the city's academies, V. Peroni, *Biblioteca bresciana*, 3 vols. (Bologna, 1818). In particular, Virginio Soncino, vol. III, p. 234; Camillo Palazzo, vol. III, p. 23; Achille Pontoglio, vol. III, p. 66; Francesco Porcellaga, vol. III, p. 67 ; Camillo Medici, vol. II, p. 272.

68 The *estimo* of 1641 is preserved in the Archivio di Stato di Brescia. The individual tax declarations, or *polizze*, for urban inhabitants are organized according to

Table 9. *The distribution of wealth in the Brescian Council (1641)*

	Percentage of total wealth	Number of households	Percentage of sample
Group I	33.0	24	8.0
Group II	39.0	72	24.0
Group III	28.0	201	68.0
Total	100.0	297	100.0

Sources: ASCB, vol. 188, "Estimo della Sola Città", u.d.; ASV, *Senato. Rettori*, F. 20, Enrollment List of 1644, u.d..

merchants alike had sunk much of their capital into real estate and credit after 1590, these records serve quite well to illuminate the foundations of family fortunes.[69]

This analysis is based on the coefficients of 363 out of the 420 councillors (86 percent) on the membership list for 1644.[70] Together they comprised 297 tax households and represented 129 of the 156 *case* (83 percent) on the membership list for that term.[71] To chart the distribution of wealth, I added together the numerical coefficients of the 297 tax households, then roughly divided this sum into thirds, and then tabulated the number of households that comprised each of the three parts. The results are indicated in table 9.

Table 9 helps us to see the contrasts in family fortunes within the council. Twenty-four households (Group I) held 33 percent of the total wealth, while 201 (Group III) households accounted for only 28 percent. In fact, fifty-three of the households in Group III had very low assessments: below one *denaro d'estimo* (see appendix 2 on direct taxes), in contrast with the families in Group I, whose coefficients ranged

neighborhood. There are a total of thirteen *buste* (*Polizze*, 1641, *Buste* 1–13). The register of coefficients assigned to each tax household for 1641 is stored in another archive, the ASCB, in vol. 188, "Estimo della Sola Città." Despite the limitations inherent in all documentation of this kind, the numbers are useful for their relative value.

[69] The individual tax declarations are very rich in information, allowing us to reconstruct, in part, the world of the domestic unit. They list the location, quantity, and quality of land; crops cultivated; and income derived from agriculture and rents. They describe in detail all edifices in both city and countryside. They specify the donors and beneficiaries of loans, the amount of these loans and the interest rates. They describe the lenders and borrowers in credit operations, and they describe the domestic household.

[70] ASV, *Senato. Rettori*, F. 20, u.d.

[71] For the status of 111 families in the *estimi* of 1486, 1517, 1548, 1588, Romani, "Prestigio," pp. 125–134 and Pegrari, "I giochi del potere," pp. 233–237.

anywhere from nine to thirty-one *denari d'estimo*.[72] The contrasts in wealth recall the characteristics of other ruling elites in Italy's major urban centers – Venice, Genoa, and Florence – where there were rich and poor among the politically enfranchised. However, it is important to keep some perspective on the wealth of Brescian councillors. This sample of Brescian *case* was very wealthy relative to the rest of the urban population: 185 households (62 percent of the sample) had a coefficient of two *denari* or more, placing their taxable assets in the upper 10 percent of the urban population of 1641 (8,225 households), and only 53 households, slightly more than a sixth of the sample, failed to reach a *denaro*.

Who were the wealthiest *case* in the council? To be methodologically consistent with the sections on family demography and officeholding, it is necessary to begin by assessing the relative wealth of the *casa* (table 10) as opposed to the individual household. This yields only crude results, since the ranking represents the sum total of the household coefficients within this larger family institution. The enormous wealth of one household, in the case of the Martinengo and the Chizzola for example, or the presence of multiple households, as in the case of the Luzzaghi, the Maggi, the Foresti, the Sala, the Soncini, and the Lana, might bolster the numerical ranking of the *casa*. An examination of some of the tax coefficients of the individual councillors mentioned above who enjoyed

[72] The coefficients of the tax households listed in Group I ranged from 9 to 31 *Denari d'estimo*; those in Group II ranged from 4 to 8; those in Group III ranged from 0 to 3. The actual distribution of taxable assets among the 297 households, according to these tax assessments, was as follows:

C	H	C	H	C	H
I		II		III	
31	(2)	–		–	
17	(1)	8	(8)	3	(37)
16	(1)	7	(9)	2	(52)
15	(1)	6	(10)	1	(59)
14	(3)	5	(18)	below	(53)
13	(1)	4	(27)	–	–
12	(2)	–		–	–
11	(5)	–		–	–
10	(3)	–		–	–
9	(5)	–		–	–
319	(24)	385	(72)	274	(201)

Source: ASCB, vol. 188, "Estimo della Sola Città," (u.d.). C = coefficient; H = number of tax households.

Table 10. *The wealthiest case*

Sum of coefficients	Casa	Sum of Coefficients	Casa
1 (66)	Martinengo	10 (22)	Manerba
2 (45)	Luzzago	(22)	Fisogni
3 (39)	Chizzola	11 (18)	Conforti
4 (37)	Maggi	12 (16)	Federici
5 (35)	Averoldi	13 (14)	Ganassoni
(35)	Soncini	14 (13)	Foresti
6 (30)	Sala	(13)	Medici
7 (29)	Lana	(13)	Gambara
8 (28)	Ugone	15 (12)	Stella
9 (23)	Nassini	16 (11)	Rodengo
(23)	Calino	17 (10)	Ducchi
		18 (9)	Longhena

Sources: ASCB, vol. 188, "Estimo della Sola Città (u.d.)"; ASV, *Senato. Rettori,* F. 20, Enrollment list of 1644 (u.d.).

political power offers a more refined picture of the correlation between wealth and power.

Table 10 confirms the relationship between wealth and power. Twelve of the *case* listed in this table also figure among those who held the office of public deputy most frequently: the Averoldi, the Lana, the Stella, the Federici, the Luzzago, the Calino, the Soncino, the Martinengo, the Longhena, the Maggi, the Manerba, and the Ugone. The tax coefficients of the councillors who served on the executive committee for multiple terms provide further evidence of this. Giovanni Paolo Luzzago, who served thirteen terms, had a tax coefficient of seventeen *denari*; his son-in-law Giovanni Paolo Zaniboni had a coefficient of fourteen. Quinto Fabio Soncino, who served on the executive committee for eight terms, and his son Virginio, who served for seven, had a tax coefficient of fourteen. The Public Deputy Francesco Lana, whose father Gaspar served eight terms at the beginning of the seventeenth century, had a tax coefficient of fifteen. Rutillio Calino, who served seven terms, had a coefficient of fourteen. The Public Deputy Paolo Manerba, whose father Nicolò served ten terms, had a coefficient of ten.[73] Lodovico Baitelli, one of Brescia's most prominent councillors, had a coefficient of ten.[74] The fortunes of these councillors stood well

[73] ASCB, vol. 188: Manerba, 5 S. Giovanni, No. 243; Soncini, 7 S. Faustino, No. 22; Zaniboni, Cittadella Vecchia, No. 331; Lana, 2 S. Giovanni, No. 275; Averoldi, 5 S. Faustino, No. 175; Calino, 3 S. Faustino, No. 213.

[74] *Ibid.,* 1 S. Alessandro, No. 213.

above those of other council members. Of the 297 tax households surveyed, only 6 percent (Group I in table 9) were assessed at ten *denari* or above, and the majority (Group III, table 9) fell well below this figure. Moreover, only 1 percent of the 8,225 urban households assessed in 1641 reached this level of assessed taxable wealth. The data confirm that wealth and political power within the council went hand in hand. Wealth was a requisite of power, necessary both to sustain the expenses of a public career and to forge alliances of social and political value. Moreover, the privileged status that came with political power served to protect if not to augment family fortunes.

THE FOUNDATIONS OF POWER

To recapitulate, the families that sustained the city's most important governmental responsibilities in Brescia owed their political preeminence to five major factors: family continuity; antiquity, both in terms of time served in council and in terms of social status; professional standing; wealth; and beneficial marriage connections. All five factors were tied to the behavior of household and lineage; the first factor was also tied to the behavior of the *casa*. With respect to the first factor, there was a direct correlation between the demographic weight of the family institution and its representation on the executive committee. Sixteen out of the twenty-two *case* (table 8) that served most frequently on the executive committee appear among the thirty-nine *case* with preponderant demographic weight. Moreover, nine of these *case* figure among the thirteen largest in the council. Power rested to some degree on large numbers. Thus the families of note made a conscientious effort to coopt kinsmen. The second factor, antiquity, also helped determine the political stature of the *casa*, giving it the time both to establish a reputation and to execute political strategies that would preserve its weight in council. Only two of the *case* (the Baitelli and the Capitano) represented in the executive committee between 1590 and 1640 derived from lineages that had not been involved in civic affairs since at least 1426, the year Venice annexed Brescia.[75] Moreover, thirteen of the *case* who dominated the seats of the executive committee (Averoldi, Lana, Longhena, Stella, Federici, Calino, Martinengo, Porcellaga, Maggi, Coradelli, Manerba, Ugone, Palazzi) derived from the old rural nobility that had transferred to the city in the Middle Ages, establishing residences between the porta di Torlonga, Via Tosio, Via Antica Mura,

---

[75] Monti della Corte, *Le famiglie del patriziato bresciano*, pp. 97–98; de Capitani di Scalve, p. 101.

the Broletto, and the Castello.[76] These families, which still enjoyed strong social and economic bonds with the countryside, exhibited a specifically urban orientation, dominating the political, social, and cultural life of the city. They became, for example, the leading members of the city's professional corporations.[77] The Luzzago, and the Barbisone, on the other hand, derived from the first citizen elite of the medieval commune, the *cives veteres*. Only five of the sixty-five *case* that served on the executive committee between 1590 and 1640 were of non-noble origins: the Soncini (nineteen seats), carders, gold and cloth merchants-turned-notaries and lawyers in the sixteenth century;[78] the Feroldi (nine seats), who derived from fifteenth-century arms merchants;[79] and the Baitelli (ten seats), the Brunelli (one seat), and the Rosa (two seats), who again all derived from mercantile origins.[80] Eighty-one percent (383/475) of the seats filled on the executive committee went to men whose *casa* derived either from the rural nobility or from the *cives veteres*, while 9 percent (41/475) went to non-nobles (10 percent, fifty-one seats, are unknown). Antiquity, both in terms of time served in council and in terms of social status was also a common denominator among the thirty-nine largest *case*: only one had entered in the sixteenth century (the Ducchi); only three were non-noble (the Feroldi, the Ganassoni, and the Soncino). Few new families and few non-nobles rose to power. The political formations of the medieval period had left a permanent imprint on the sixteenth- and seventeenth-century councils. That imprint was the product of political strategies engineered and conducted through family institutions – most visibly through household and lineage but also through the *casa* – for generations.

The power of the top families also rested heavily on their professional status. In particular, those at the apogee of power were widely represented in the city's judicial and notarial colleges. Forty-eight of the 133 councillors (36 percent) who served on the executive committee

---

76 ASV, *Collegio, Relazioni*, B. 54, *fasc.* 5, f. 6, report of the Sindaci Avogadori Inquisitori Leonardo Moro and Marco Giustiniani, August 9, 1621. See also Von Schullern-Schratthenhofen, "La nobile famiglia bresciana Calini di Calino," pp. 243–257; Von Schullern-Schratthenhofen, "Cenni sulla nobile famiglia Maggi di Brescia," pp. 241–249; P. Guerrini, "Gli Ugoni di Brescia," *RA* 18 (1920): 127–132; 299–302; 324–327; 371–377; 19 (1921): 63–69; 137–143; 183–188.

77 Report of Paolo Correr, *Podestà*, April 1562, in *RV*, ed. Tagliaferri, vol. XI, p. 67; see also P. Guerrini, "Il nobile collegio dei giudici di Brescia e la sua matricola dal 1342 al 1796," *RA* 24 (1926): 485–493.

78 See Guerrini, "I Luzzago," pp. 198–205; 297–304; 341–348; P. Guerrini, "Famiglie nobili bresciane, Soncino o de Soncino," *RA* 32 (1934): 485–487.

79 Monti della Corte, *Le famiglie del patriziato bresciano*, p. 40.

80 I was unable to determine the origins of the Pezani.

between 1590 and 1640 were law graduates.[81] It is significant as well that the structure of the executive committee and of the major offices was constructed to reflect the importance of judges. Many Venetian podestà in Brescia reiterated the complaints of Leonardo Donà, who upon completing his term in 1579 wrote in his summary report, "some doctors and notaries meet and elect officers, that is, the deputies, before the council deliberates. And they aim to keep city income in the hands of a few."[82] And further, "all is reduced to physicians and notaries and doctors, who by virtue of their position exercise the office of avvocato together and make greater progress."[83] Between 1588 and 1650 there were at least forty judges present (9 percent of the membership) on the rolls of the city council for any given term. The Venetian Podestà, Paolo Correr, conveyed the centrality of the judges' powers in 1562: "all causes in city and Territorio that are committed to the Consiglio di Savio cannot be judged by other doctors save those from their College."[84]

In practice, the eighty notaries who enjoyed council membership during the first half of the seventeenth century were no less influential than the judges, for they recorded all the proceedings of the city's civil and criminal tribunals. By creating obstacles in the judicial process, the notaries, in collusion with the judges, were able to control the political and economic life of the city. Two registered the acts of the podestà and four transcribed the proceedings of the podestà's vicar. These scribes were able to check Venetian authority effectively, for at their will the rectors' judgments could be lost or hidden, rendering them null and void. Other notaries served on the Councils of Justice, or in the Maleficio, the tribunal for serious crimes. They could conceal the crimes of family members and friends, ensuring that the criminal evidence never reached the tribunals, and those who recorded judgments concerning food provisioning and tax collection could postpone or cancel debts.[85] Through the notaries' adept manipulation, legislation

---

[81] There was no way of determining the number of notaries who were represented on the executive committee. We must rely on the descriptive reports of the Venetian rectors.

[82] "Alcuni dottori e nodari fano li loro conventicoli et ilegono prima che venghino in Consiglio li offici cioè è li deputati. Et procurano di tener tra alcuni pocchi il governo delle entradi pubblici." BMCV, *Codice Donà delle Rose*, No. 17, ff. 94v–95r.

[83] "Tutto è ridotto in fisici(?) et nodari e dottori li quali in virtù che questi loro officio essercitando insieme l'Avocato si fanno maggior stradda." *Ibid.*

[84] "Tutte le cause sì della Città come del Territorio che sono comesse a Consiglio de Savio non possono esser giudicate da altri dottori che da loro del collegio." Report of Paolo Correr, April 1562, in *RV*, ed. Tagliaferri, vol. XI, p. 72.

[85] Report of Giovanni Soranzo, Podestà and Vice-Capitano, October 2, 1638 and report of Antonio Longo, Podestà, March 25, 1644, in *RV*, ed. Tagliaferi, vol. XI, pp. 383–385; 435.

became hopelessly lost in a web of legal entanglements, without any conclusive results. Their absence from the civil and criminal tribunals, for example, could delay the judicial process *ad infinitum*. Even more overtly, they could make decrees "disappear," effectively obfuscating the announcements of the public criers, for every public announcement was sent to their deputy *ad hoc* to preserve and record.[86] Hence the notaries, together with the judges, enjoyed preponderant political weight in the Brescian Council and in society at large because of the enormous influence they wielded in both civil and criminal affairs. With such ample powers, the families that monopolized the city's civil and criminal magistracies could act as patrons, constructing a wide network of beholden clients from all levels of society.

It is not surprising then that the Brescian councillors who stood at the apogee of power placed a high priority on an education that prepared them for the professions, particularly law, which was without doubt an important dimension of the prestige of the upper-class family. This was typical of the ruling elites of north and central Italian cities. Milan, Siena, and Pescia are three examples.[87] Giovanni Paolo Luzzago, his father Ippolito, and his grandfather Giovanni Paolo all held distinguished offices in civic government as well as in the College of Judges.[88] Should there be three sons in the family, it was not uncommon to find one in each of the professional colleges, a means of covering all bases of power within the urban center. The family of Quinto Fabio Soncino, a judge, provides an excellent example of career patterns. His son Virginio, also a judge, was a distinguished member of the Brescian Council who, following his father's footsteps, frequently served on the executive committee and as the city council's lawyer, while another son, Giovanni Battista, belonged to the College of Fisici (physicians).[89] In this way the family was represented in two of the city's most powerful corporations.

Finally, kinship ties supported and sustained the political preeminence of the families that continually directed civic affairs, first through the lineage, then through marriage. This subject, however, will be treated in greater detail in the following chapter. It will suffice to

---

[86] F. Capretti, *Mezzo secolo di vita vissuta a Brescia nel Seicento (1600–1649)* (Brescia: Scuola Tipografica Opera Pavoniana, 1934), p. 143.

[87] Cf. Zanetti, "Università," pp. 236; 242–245; Marrara, *Riseduti e nobiltà*, p. 180; Brown, *Pescia*, p. 178.

[88] See B. Faino, *Arbore gentilizio historico della nobile e antica famiglia Luzzago* (Brescia: Rizzardi, 1671). Other examples are the Peschera, who specialized in jurisprudence, ASB, *PE* 1641, B. 11, No. 84; and the Grato, who specialized in the notarial arts, *ibid.*, B. 11, No. 125.

[89] ASB, *PE* 1641, B.3, No. 22.

mention here that endogamy was one of the fundamental social and political strategies that preserved and enhanced the position of the ruling family.

What about those families at the helm of government who lacked antiquity, either in terms of the time their *case* had been associated with the council or in terms of social status? What factors enabled the few non-noble families we have mentioned to rise in power and to integrate with families of more prestigious social origins? Professional success, wealth, and kinship ties were important avenues of social and political mobility. Though there are some excellent examples it is important to keep in mind that they were few. The Baitelli, prosperous merchants from the Val Sassina, shifted to law in the sixteenth century and within three generations, through the accomplishments of Girolamo, Costantino, and Lodovico, had distinguished themselves in jurisprudence and, as we have seen above, in the executive offices of the city council.[90] Costantino married into an old Brescian family, the Bargnani, and concluded very prestigious marriage alliances for his three daughters with the Ugone, the Martinengo, and the Barbisone. In 1641 Lodovico, together with his brother and his nephew, had a distinguished residence in San Alessandro, a rural estate – la Baitella – in Castegnato, with 178 *piò*; another residence in Trenzano with 162 *piò*, as well as some smaller properties in Ludriano and Marocchina (Comezzano).[91] Their *estimo* coefficient, ten *denari*, made them one of the wealthiest families in Brescia.

Quinto Fabio Soncino, one of the most prominent city councillors of the early seventeenth century, derived from a family of sixteenth-century merchants. Quinto Fabio studied law; married into a family that was more prestigious than his own, the Zanetti, and began to accumulate wealth.[92] His son Virginio followed the same career path and made a conspicuous matrimonial alliance with Lucrezia Sala. Both the Baitelli and the Soncino, then, were able to amalgamate with some of the older and more prestigious families in the council because of their wealth and their professional success.

Wealth in the sixteenth and the seventeenth centuries was still an avenue of social and political mobility within the council itself. The Capitano and the Zaniboni, for example, were very small but wealthy *case*. Both families did not appear regularly on the council membership

90 O. Rossi, *Elogi historici di bresciani illustri. Teatro di Ottavio Rossi* (Brescia: Bartolomeo Fontana, 1620), pp. 409–410.
91 F. Lechi, *Le dimore bresciane in cinque secoli di storia*, vol. V: *Il Seicento* (Brescia: Edizioni di storia bresciana, 1976), p. 44.
92 *Ibid.*, vol. III: *Il Cinquecento* (Brescia: Edizioni di storia bresciana, 1974), pp. 175–176.

lists until the 1630s; both families did not occupy more than one or two seats in the council per term. The tax assessment of nine *denari* of Francesco Capitano, who served three terms on the executive committee in the 1630s, and of fourteen *denari* for Giovanni Paolo Zaniboni, reflect the large fortunes at their disposal, fortunes that helped them slowly rise to power.

The families of noble descent did not shut the non-nobles with conspicuous fortunes out of their kinship circles; they became virtually indistinguishable. Besides the Baitelli and the Soncino, the Zaniboni, the Scanzo, and the Ganassoni provide good examples of this. By 1641 Giovanni Paolo Zaniboni ranked among the wealthiest citizens. He married Marta Luzzago, the daughter of Giovanni Paolo, in the 1630s and thereafter followed in his father-in-law's footsteps, serving frequently on the executive committee in the 1640s. The Scanzo also came from mercantile origins. Andrea Scanzo,[93] with seven *denari d'estimo*, concluded a valuable marriage alliance with the daughter of Giulio Stella (Stella served twelve terms on the executive committee in the seventeenth century). Scanzo enjoyed a number of important offices in council. The Ganassoni, whose origins were identical to the Baitelli, also intermarried with the older families in the council, in particular the Ugone.[94] The Brunelli, wool merchants in fourteenth-century Brescia who entered the council as *benemeriti* in 1438, also intermarried with older families, such as the Bocca, in the seventeenth century.[95]

What this demographic, political, and economic survey has demonstrated is that association with the Brescian Council was very important to a restricted number of families who for generations had made civic government an integral part of their public lives and their social success. Though the prestige of those families rested in large part with their *case*, the strategies they implemented to preserve their place in Brescian public life – university degrees and professional careers that gave them a wide range of authority in civil, criminal, economic and family affairs; the preservation and expansion of patrimony; passing positions of importance from father to son or from fathers-in-law to sons-in-law; fruitful marriage alliances – were designed and executed within the smaller kinship circles of household and lineage.[96] We shall turn to their inner workings in the next chapter.

[93] On the Scanzi, Monti della Corte, *Le famiglie del patriziato bresciano*, pp. 125–126.
[94] Lechi, *Le dimore*, vol. V, p. 63.
[95] *Ibid.*, vol. II: *Il Quattrocento* (Brescia: Edizioni di storia bresciana, 1974), p. 228.
[96] Litchfield, *Emergence of a Bureaucracy*, pp. 16–20. Wealth and old qualifications for office were keys to success for the families of the Florentine ducal bureaucracy. The lineages kept links with collateral branches of their families, but the patrician household was predominantly nuclear.

CHAPTER 4

MARRIAGE BONDS, PATRIMONIAL STRATEGIES, AND FAMILY RELATIONS

The activities of Brescian councillors over the course of the late sixteenth and early seventeenth centuries provide evidence of collective solidarity within the body as a whole. It emerged in the defense of municipal interests, especially fiscal interests, against the capital city or against the Territorio. It surfaced as well when networks of judges and notaries carefully guarded their jurisdictional prerogatives before state authorities. In such instances there were firm lines of cooperation, based upon the defense of corporate liberties and common interests. But the city council must be conceptualized in terms other than a corporate association, for there were also many smaller units of organization at work within it. In particular, there were multiple groups, bound together both by a complex web of kinship ties and by social and financial relations that moved in concert with the everyday rhythms of political life. The cohesiveness of these groups was fluid, depending strictly upon the degree to which the interests of the individual lineages that comprised them intersected. While the *casa* (for the distinction between *casa* and lineage, see chapter 3) conferred a family name and reputation, offering the basic credentials for council membership, it is difficult to assess its cohesiveness, for its political behavior was elusive. There was, moreover, a great deal more latitude for discord within this larger family institution, where patrimonial interests did not always converge. Ultimately, for city councillors considerations of lineage took priority above all else, and these considerations are highly visible.

Settlement patterns within the seventeenth-century urban space underline the interests of lineage (family relations descending from a common progenitor, e.g. father–son; brothers; uncle–nephews) over any sort of collective institution such as the medieval clan (a family association united by common interests). There were still many upper-class households situated in ancestral districts, vestiges of the fifteenth

7. Floriano Ferramola. "The Bride and Groom." Photograph
courtesy of the Civici Musei d'Arte e Storia di Brescia. Protocol No.
1239/14.

century or before, surrounded by closely related families. In particular,
the area around the foot of the castle and to the southeast, Cittadella
Vecchia, which had traditionally contained enclaves of the Maggi, the
Luzzaghi, the Ugoni, the Rodengo, the Oldofredi, and the Gambara.[1]

[1]   Lechi, *Le dimore*, vol. V, p. 15, note 2.

Yet another enclave of prominent families included the seventh district of San Faustino, on the Via Marsala, where several branches of the Lana had lived since the fifteenth century or before;[2] and the second district of San Faustino, where various branches of the Bocca family had established residences.[3] By the seventeenth century, however, choice of residence was not guided by ties to any clan, nor was it constrained by any sort of political configurations. It was instead a reflection of the contemporary social values of the ruling class. The family residence was a means of publicly representing the honor, decorum, and position of the lineage, and above all it was a way of displaying its rank and quality of nobility or of citizenship. Lanteri devoted special care in his *Della economica* to explaining how the location, architectural structure, and decor of the residence should reflect the social station of the upper-class family.[4] The treatise is set in a specifically Brescian context. Feudatories, or nobles with titles and jurisdiction, should elect a large site, where they could construct grand courtyards and loggie, spacious rooms, and magnificient gardens that reminded the public – including other segments of the nobility – of their superior rank. Domestic architecture was a measure of social position. Thus, families who enjoyed titled but not feudal jurisdictions, the second degree of nobility according to Lanteri, should build residences in function of their activities. Two kinds of nobility fit this category: those who studied law and letters and devoted themselves to the governance of the city; and those who bore arms. The latter, according to Lanteri, would have fewer public functions and therefore needed fewer servants. Their residences should reflect their ties to the sword, displaying arms and symbols of valor. The former, on the other hand, who devoted themselves to study and to governing the city, should have residences that were "rather ornate." Size was not as important as decor or style. It was important, for example, to have a library and a room to receive clients and public officials near the entrance of the residence.

Lanteri's treatise on household management suggests that building in Brescia reflected social position and public activity. A century before Lanteri, the architects of Brescia's ruling families had abandoned the tower-house motif of the communal era for a two-story dwelling with

---

[2] A group of Lana families descending from Giuscardo and Paribono, vavasors from the Bergamasc community of Terzo, had established their residences in the fifteenth century around the Via Marsala. In the seventeenth century three branches still lived in this neighborhood: Agostino and Pace Lana q. Alessandro; Count Girardo; and Giovanni Battista and Faustino Lana. *Ibid.*, pp. 184–186, note 1.

[3] *Ibid.*, p. 480.

[4] Lanteri, *Della economica*, pp. 14–22.

painted facades and large windows.[5] Throughout the sixteenth century, a period of sharp demographic expansion, there was a flourish of building activity in Cittadella Vecchia, the second section of San Giovanni, and the seventh section of San Faustino. In the middle of the century, the noted architect Beretta decorated the city with the palaces of the Terzi-Lana, the Martinengo, the Ganassoni, the Maggi, the Martinengo-Cesaresco, the Monti della Corte, and the Pedrocca. Construction slowed in the seventeenth century. Still, a number of prestigious families from old lineages, in particular the Martinengo dalle Palle, Cesaresco, da Barco, and Colleoni, embellished the city with sumptuous palaces that occupied large stretches of urban space in the fifth, sixth, and seventh sections of San Faustino; in the first and second sections of San Alessandro; in the third section of San Giovanni; and in Cittadella Vecchia, the area which incorporated the old Roman quarter of the city.[6] Their stately palaces and elaborate gardens, ostentatious symbols of aristocratic wealth and status, stood proudly amidst the more moderately sized edifices of other members of the local ruling class, such as the Brunelli, the Luzzago, and the Fenaroli;[7] and the more humble structures of the wool manufactures, silk weavers, millers, and tanners in Cittadella Vecchia.[8]

Lechi's meticulous survey of urban construction in seventeenth-century Brescia reveals that by this time some branches of the city's more prestigious families had spread out, leaving the more densely built neighborhoods of their ancestors in search of more space, where their new, opulent constructions would stand out. Branches of the Luzzago, Maggi, and Poncarali, for example, began to rebuild the neighborhood around the Via C. Cattaneo, in Cittadella Vecchia, where they could buy ample space at convenient prices. In this old neighborhood, which had largely been inhabited by the popular classes in the Middle Ages, these families built large palaces, which occupied horizontal rather than vertical space in order to distinguish their preeminence.[9] Two other seventeenth-century sources suggest that family partriarchs were not particularly motivated to remain in the same neighborhood with members of their *casa*: Da Lezze's census, which maps noble households in the various districts of the city from 1609 to 1610; and the *estimo* of

---

[5] Panazza, "Il volto storico," pp. 1, 113; 1,129–1,130. The Calzavellia, the Porcellaga, the Brunelli, the Martinengo da Barco, the Oldofredi, the Appiani, the Cigola, the Averoldi, the Terzi-Lana, and the Calini built urban dwellings during the late fifteenth and sixteenth centuries.

[6] See Lechi, *Le dimore*, vols. IV and V.

[7] Panazza, "Il volto storico," p. 1,135.

[8] *Ibid.*, p. 1,137, n. 1.

[9] Lechi, *Le dimore*, vol. V, p. 55.

1641. I used this last source in conjunction with a list of the 156 *case* in the council of 1644 to gain some perspective on the settlement patterns of the ruling class. Council members with the same surname had more often than not spread out across the city, establishing residences in two, three, or four quarters.[10] Moreover, brothers who had set up different households could live in different quarters of the city as well. These dispersive settlement patterns strongly suggest that although the *casa* gave council members a common heritage – a name, a common ancestral district, holdings in the same rural community – [11] it was not necessarily a prime unit of social organization by the seventeenth century. To find out what linked the families of the ruling class together we must turn to how their very focused interests of household and lineage intersected.

WEALTH CONSERVATION AND FAMILY ALLIANCES

Strong domestic groups, wealth, honorable and decorous lifestyles, and marriage connections were all critical factors that gave the lineages in the Brescian Council the possibility of making powerful and prestigious alliances and of maintaining preeminent positions in public life. The efforts of each lineage to meet the standards that its position demanded in effect helped shape the internal structure of the family. Because wealth was a fundamental requisite of power, the foremost

[10] To conduct this survey, I used the membership list of 1644 in ASV, *Senato. Rettori*, F. 20, u.d. and the register of tax coefficients for 1641 in ASCB, vol. 188. The Lana and the Sala are good examples. Giovanni Agostino q. Alex. and Giovanni Battista q. Guerrero lived in 7 S. Faustino (ASCB, vol. 188, 7 S. Faustino, Nos. 181 and 190); Francesco and Terzio lived in 2 S. Giovanni (*ibid.*, 2 S. Giovanni, No. 275), and Cesare q. Alphonsus lived in Cittadella Vecchia (*ibid.*, CV, No. 547). The Sala were spread out as follows: Horatio q. Philippini, 4 S. Faustino (No. 248); Giovanni Battista q. Giovanni Paolo, 7 S. Faustino (No. 68); Federico q. Vicenzo, 6 S. Giovanni (No. 5); Ottino q. Pietro, 6 S. Faustino (No. 109); Ulixes q. Mario, 2 S. Giovanni (No. 248); Giovanni Battista q. Lodovico, 4 S. Giovanni (No. 468); Carlo q. Pietro, 3 S. Giovanni (No. 165).

[11] The most common example of this is contiguous property holdings. In the seventeenth century, eleven branches of the Ugone held property in Campazzo, a *frazione* (village) of Pontevico. Lechi, *Le dimore*, vol. V, p. 451. In the sixteenth century nine branches of the Barbisone had holdings in Offlaga. *Ibid.*, pp. 50; 447. The Provaglio had a feudal investiture in Monticelli. Up to the middle of the seventeenth century four branches of this family held it in subdivision. *Ibid.*, p. 467. From the fourteenth century onwards, the Luzzago were preeminent landowners in Manerbio. *Ibid.*, p. 56. The Fenaroli had owned property in Provezze since the fifteenth century. *Ibid.*, p. 349. The Brunelli had residences in Bagnolo from the sixteenth to the nineteenth centuries. *Ibid.*, p. 443. The Palazzi had property in Longhena for generations. *Ibid.*, p. 473.

preoccupation of every lineage that belonged to the Brescian ruling class was its economic stature. Economic continuity was a consideration that bound the destinies of agnatic kin together, giving domestic groups a certain cohesion and logic based on what historians have described as a patriarchal orientation. The structure of the domestic group reflected this consideration: many Brescian councillors, like other urban elites of northern and central Italy,[12] tended to live at least a part of their lifetimes in complex households. As Davis' study of the Venetian Donà family has illustrated, this was in part a function of wealth conservation: the complex household allowed family patriarchs to economize on daily living expenses; and it kept family patrimony intact for as long as possible.[13] At the same time a large domestic group, especially sons, living under the same roof was a way of publicly representing the family's cohesion and power in society at large.[14] In Brescia, extended families (a conjugal couple living with other relatives) were particularly common following catastrophic mortality: the plague of 1630 left many truncated households in its wake. During normal demographic cycles multiple-vertical families (two conjugal couples consisting of parents and a married son) seem to have been very common as well. Eventually when the older couple died the multiple-vertical family became a nuclear one.

The principal challenge facing family partriarchs was how to prevent the dispersion of wealth among offspring. In fifty households of the ruling class I examined using the tax declarations of 1641,[15] the average

---

[12] M. Barbagli, *Sotto lo stesso tetto. Mutamenti della famiglia in Italia dal XV al XX secolo* (Bologna: Il Mulino, 1984), pp. 142; 167; 170; 189–195.

[13] J. C. Davis, *A Venetian Family and Its Fortune, 1500–1900* (Philadelphia: American Philosophical Society, 1975), pp. 6–8; Barbagli, *Sotto lo stesso tetto*, p. 190.

[14] Davis, *A Venetian Family*, pp. 6–8.

[15] I examined the tax declarations of fifty of the most active Brescian councillors. Their declarations are in ASB, *PE* 1641.

Aste, Lodovico, B. 6, No. 97
Averoldi, Pompeo, B. 2, No. 175
Avogadro, Francesco and Scipione, B. 9, No. 397
Baitelli, Lodovico, B. 9, No. 213
Belasi, Pietro, B. 6, No. 247
Borgondio, Theodosio, B. 4, No. 123
Calino, Giovanni Andrea, B. 11, No. 124
Calino, Horatio, B. 5, No. 131
Calino, Ruttilio, B. 1, No. 213
Capitaneo, Francesco and Scipione, B. 9, No. 387
Carenzone, Hercole, B. 1, No. 107
Cazzago, Giulio, B. 9, No. 174
Chizzola, Galeazzo, B. 10, No. 253
Chizzola, Pompeo, B. 10, No. 252

number of children was three. Ten households were childless and four were without a conjugal couple, making the average in fact slightly higher for the other thirty-six cases. The women in these households gave birth at regular intervals of 1.5 to 2 years. Although we know from the studies of historical demographers that many of these children would not survive beyond infancy, nonetheless family partriarchs would have to plan meticulously the futures of those that did. While they followed no set pattern, one common strategy employed in Brescia during the first half of the seventeenth century, which emerges from close scrutiny of the *estimi*, hinged upon restricted marriage.

Even though nuptial bonds were an indispensable political and social

Conforto, Lodovico, B. 7, No. 79
Covo, Gieronimo and Horatio, B. 11, No. 7
Ducchi, Antonio and Gieronimo, B. 4, No. 266
Emigli, Emiglio, B. 12, No. 559
Emigli, Lodovico, B. 6, No. 1
Faita, Ottavio, B. 10, No. 62
Federici, Giulio, B. 7, No. 35
Fenaroli, Giovanni Maria, B. 11, No. 52
Fenaroli, Giovanni Maria, Luca, Geronimo, B. 3, No. 206
Feroldo, Eneo, B. 11, No. 186
Foresti, Carlo, B. 5, No. 109
Foresti, Glisente and Giuliano, B. 2, No. 5
Gallo, Francesco, B. 7, No. 194
Lana, Francesco, B. 4, No. 275
Lana, Giovanni Agostino, B. 3, No. 181
Longhena, Oratio and Gieronimo, B. 7, No. 137
Lupatini, Giovanni Battista, B. 2, No. 48
Luzzago, Agostino, B. 12, No. 613
Luzzago, Carlo, Hieronimo, Joseffo, Vicenzo, B. 11, No. 196
Luzzago, Giovanni Paolo, B. 10, No. 130
Maggi, Achille, B. 11, No. 301
Maggi, Brunoro, B. 11, No. 341
Maggi, Lodovico, B. 11, No. 63
Maggi, Nicolò, B. 11, No. 227
Manerba, Paolo, B. 4, No. 243
Martinengo da Barco, Count Giovanni Battista, B. 10, No. 284
Martinengo-Cesaresco, Camillo, Count Francesco, Count Carlo, B. 11 (u.d.).
Martinengo-Villagara, Count Francesco, B. 4, No. 272
Medici, Francesco, Cristoforo, and Giorgio, B. 5, No. 27
Ponzone, Agostino, B. 13, No. 120
Portulaga, Francesco, B. 1, No. 38
Rodengo, Giovanni Antonio, B. 1, No. 26
Scanzo, Andrea, B. 1, No. 179
Soncino, Quinto Fabio, B. 3, No. 22
Ugone, Stefano Maria, B. 11, No. 204
Violino, Lodovico, B. 2, No. 125
Zanatta, Ottaviano, B. 3, No. 67
Zaniboni, Giovanni Paolo, B. 11, No. 331

tool among the families of the Brescian ruling class, the number of children who married impinged upon the economic equilibrium of the family. Choices were guided in part by political exigencies, financial capacity, and cultural norms, but patriarchs could not lose sight of the necessity of protecting the fortunes of the lineage. This was not a simple task given the common Brescian practice of partible inheritance among male offspring and the legal obligations to dower daughters. Elsewhere in Italy, according to Barbagli, the wealth-conserving practices of entail (*fidecommissum*: a deed of trust; the heir was the custodian of the inheritance and was obliged to hold it and then return it on his death) and primogeniture were coming into use.[16] Legal historians do not entirely agree on the reasons why the first institution became widely diffused during this period. Davis has suggested it was probably a product of an unpromising economic picture.[17] By the late sixteenth century upper-class Italian families had sunk the preponderance of their fortunes into landed investments, which rendered steady but certainly not brilliant returns. The prospects of making large profits over a short time span were limited, as was the possibility of circulating large sums of liquid capital. Under these circumstances the *fidecommissum* was designed to prevent dispersion and keep wealth within the lineage. It also protected patrimony against confiscation by the state. While Brescian patriarchs availed themselves of the option of *fidecommissum*, they did not practice primogeniture. Instead their inheritance practices fit the Venetian model, studied by Davis,[18] whereby possessions were left to all sons equally. Still there was collaboration: there might be tacit agreement that one son should manage the family fortunes. It appears that fathers educated sons from an early age to keep their wealth together as much as possible, for brothers tended to remain under the same roof for as long as possible and, like the ruling classes in Venice, Florence, and Milan, to practice restricted marriage.[19]

Two types of restricted marriage were prevalent in the fifty Brescian declarations of taxable assets examined here. In the first, one son (not necessarily the oldest, but perhaps the one most disposed to marriage) married, while his brothers remained single and eventually left their possessions to their married brother's children. In this way the family

[16] Barbagli, *Sotto lo stesso tetto*, pp. 196; 199; 240–41.
[17] J. C. Davis, *The Decline of the Venetian Nobility as a Ruling Class* (Baltimore: The Johns Hopkins University Press, 1962), pp. 68–69.
[18] *Ibid.*, pp. 68–71.
[19] In sixteenth- and seventeenth-century Florence, 60 percent of the nobility remained unmarried; in Milan between 1600 and 1649 50 percent did so. Barbagli, *Sotto lo stesso tetto*, p. 199.

patrimony remained intact. According to the Brescian statutes, the married son would live under his father's authority, together with his siblings, coming into his inheritance upon the death of the patriarch. It was very rare to find emancipated sons. There was only one such instance in the fifty cases examined.[20] Perhaps there was no reason for it in an age where wealth was concentrated in immovables and where fathers were not engaged in the risk-taking ventures that might compel them to use emancipation as a means of protecting the lineage's financial legacy. In the second type of restricted marriage, where the family estate was large enough to sustain division and it was not locked up in entail, two brothers (rarely more than two) married and set up separate households. To have some idea of how frequently this second option was practiced, I examined the membership list of the Brescian Council of 1644. Among the 312 households for which I found tax information[21] there were twenty-four cases (7.7 percent) where brothers had divided their wealth and set up separate tax households,[22] and there were twenty-nine (9.3 percent) cases where brothers remained under the same tax household. Three factors appear to have had some impact on these choices. The first was the financial capacity of the family (actually fiscal, since we are using fiscal evidence; the *estimi* do not disclose the actual financial capacity of the family). In the twenty-four cases of division there were only five individuals whose assessed taxable wealth fell below one *denaro*, and in each of these cases the other brother(s)' assessed wealth surpassed this figure. A second factor was the critical importance of bonding the politically active families together through marriage, for indeed the brothers that divided their wealth and took spouses figured prominently in public life. A third factor that may have induced brothers to divide their wealth and set up new households was the financial opportunities that came from dowry resources. After Agostino and Giorgio Federici divided their wealth, for example, Giorgio continued to have large assets at his disposal, for the dowry resources his wife Maddalena Gambara brought to the marriage equalled his entire taxable assets.[23]

The most common alternative for men and women who did not marry was of course to join religious orders. It has been widely argued

[20] ASB, *PE* 1641, B. 3. No. 181, Giovanni Agostino and Pace Lana.
[21] The council of 1644 had 422 councillors, in 369 tax households. ASV, *Senato. Rettori*, F. 20, u.d.
[22] ASCB, vol. 188: the Armani, 6 S. Faustino, No. 51 and 3 S. Faustino, No. 177; the Brognolo, Cittadella Vecchia, Nos. 474 (Anibale q. Alfonso) and 518 (Scipione q. Alf.); the Calini, Cittadella Vecchia, No. 124 and 2 Alessandro, No. 208.
[23] ASCB, vol. 188, 5 S. Giovanni, No. 261 (Agostino); 1 S. Alessandro, No. 132 (Giorgio and Maddalena Gambara).

that this option was a capital-saving device for fathers constrained to limit the number of children for whom they could arrange marriages. It was also both politically and economically important to have well-placed sons in the ecclesiastical hierarchy. More attention, however, needs to be devoted to the role that children – both sons and daughters – who belonged to religious orders played in family-estate management. Without a systematic study of ecclesiastical records, at this point it is only possible to suggest what some of those roles might be. In the Bresciano, as on the Italian peninsula at large, ecclesiastical entities were rich sources of capital during this period, and they functioned as important lending institutions. The tax declarations of Brescia's ruling families reveal that almost all were borrowing capital from convents and monasteries. This was a common means of obtaining liquid funds – not necessarily because the borrowers were short of capital but rather because the loans were made under advantageous conditions. For example, the capital was lent at relatively low interest rates and over long periods of time. Who consented to such conditions? The heads of Brescia's religious orders were often members of the city's ruling families. Kinsmen could engage in credit operations that were mutually beneficial: the religious institution would earn a slow but steady income on what would have been in essence unfruitful capital, and the borrower acquired liquid capital on easy terms which could be employed in other investments, such as the purchase of property, land improvement, or the assemblage of dowries.[24] There seem to have been many other benefits to families with kinsmen in ecclesiastical entities. Release from actually making payment on spiritual dowries was one of them. Bartering and exchanging property was another.[25] Still further, family members in religious institutions could serve as financial custodians for their lay kinsmen. Faustina Soncino Maggi, for example, left 9,200 *lire* in trust with her granddaughter, Sister Paola Faustina Maggi, to be distributed to her grandchildren upon her death.[26] These examples are all too few but are highly suggestive: we must be cautious in casting aside the roles of second and third sons and daughters assigned sacred celibacy, for they had access to large financial assets and could potentially offer benefits to their natal kin.

[24] See G. Borelli, *Un patriziato*, p. 365; G. Borelli, "Aspetti e forme della ricchezza negli enti ecclesiastici e monastici di Verona tra secoli XVI e XVIII," in *Chiese e monasteri a Verona*, ed. G. Borelli (Verona: Banca Popolare di Verona, 1980), pp. 130–137; 165.

[25] ASV, *Provveditori da Terra e da Mar*, F. 272, letter of the *Deputati sopra l'estimo*, August 22, 1644.

[26] ASB, *Hospedale Maggiore. Atti di Eredità e Processi* (hereafter *HM.AEP*), *Famiglia Maggi*, Mazzo 4, No. 23, f. 1r, September 12, 1658.

Brixiana Nobilis ex Titiano.

8. A Brescian noblewoman. From Raffaello Savonarola. *Universus Terrarum Orbis Scriptorum Calamo Delineatus* (Patavii, 1713), vol. I, p. 197. Photograph courtesy of the Biblioteca Nazionale Marciana, Venice.

WOMEN AND PROPERTY

Where did daughters fit into this patrilineal framework of family inheritance? One general rule stands out in the Brescian statutes concerning fathers who died intestate: family patrimony served the lineage, passing through the male line, first to sons, and in their absence to brothers and nephews, then to the closest agnatic kin. Only when there were no close male heirs in the line did the patrimony pass to female issue. Moreover, with respect to dowry resources, in Italy they served as a daughter's primary share of the family patrimony. Upon their receipt, whether she took marital or spiritual vows, a daughter renounced all claims to her father's and/or brother(s)' estate. Statutes, however, can be misleading, for in practice families expressed a variety of choices. Women often inherited patrimony from their mothers or other female relatives, and from their fathers if there were no brothers in the line of succession. Further, we must be cautious too in placing dowry resources in a secondary position to that of male legacies: many daughters became brides of Christ during this period because the marriage market commanded dowries whose size and substance could jeopardize the fortunes of the male line. Because dowries brought vital social and political connections, their content and worth were economically substantial. This meant of course that dowries could significantly influence the fortunes of a groom's lineage. But it also meant that women, primarily widows, could play some role both in the Brescian marriage market and in the social and financial relations of the ruling class. Thus the functions and importance of the dowry, of women's property in general, and of women's role in strengthening the reputation and fortunes of the family merit further assessment.

Recent historical literature has emphasized that the importance of the brideprice went beyond aiding the husband with the cost of matrimony: it was instrumental in forging important social and political alliances among the Peninsula's ruling elites.[27] It is well worth investigating how this applied to Brescia, if we are to understand the bonds among council members, the strengths behind political alliances, and strategies of consolidation. Moreover, the ways in which the dowry benefited the patrimonial strategies of the lineages in council also merit careful attention, for they were an integral part of the logic behind the ruling family's economic behavior.[28] What was the dowry's role in land accumulation? In credit operations? In what other ways did it economically serve the interests of lineage? In Brescia the disposition of the dowry, and women's property in general, was a

---

[27] See L. Martines, *The Social World of the Florentine Humanists, 1390–1460* (Princeton, NJ: Princeton University Press, 1963), pp. 18–19; 38–39; F. W. Kent, *Household and Lineage in Renaissance Florence: The Family Life of the Capponi, Ginori, and Rucellai* (Princeton, NJ: Princeton University Press, 1977), pp. 92–93.

[28] See F. Lane, *Andrea Barbarigo. Merchant of Venice, 1418–1449* (Baltimore: The Johns Hopkins University Press, 1944), pp. 28–29; F. Lane, "Family Partnerships and Joint Ventures," in F. Lane, *Venice and History. The Collected Papers of Frederick C. Lane* (Baltimore: The Johns Hopkins University Press, 1966), pp. 38–39; Davis, *A Venetian Family*, pp. 106–108; B. Pullan, "The Occupations and Investments of the Venetian Nobility in the Middle and Late Sixteenth Century," *Renaissance Venice*, ed. J. R. Hale (London: Faber and Faber, 1973), pp. 379–408.

critical part of estate planning. The dowries of upper-class women were important for their size, for their landed assets, and for the ways in which they furthered the patrimonial ambitions of the groom's lineage.[29] Yet they did far more than simply perform a vital economic service for the male line. Because women were both the recipients and often the donors of these dowries, we can also discover instances where economic resources were passed through the maternal line.[30] The legacies women received from their mothers, coupled with the dowries provided by their fathers, made it possible for them to become economically substantial persons whose resources had a significant impact on the financial and social relations of the Brescian ruling class.

I shall concentrate on the dowries of thirty women whose natal and marital families were inscribed in the Brescian city council.[31] The data comes from the fifty declarations of taxable assets mentioned above as well as the family papers in the Hospedale Maggiore. The first archival

---

[29] Husbands had the legal right to administer and invest dowry resources; however, they could not alienate property. Moreover, they were obliged to return the equivalent value of movables to their wives. As a guarantee, a lien could be placed on their property for this purpose. The husband's male kin were also held responsible. On the legal status of the dowry in Italy, F. Ercole, "L'istituto dotale nella pratica e nella legislazione statuaria dell'Italia superiore," *Rivista Italiana per le Scienze Giuridiche* 45 (1909): 191–302; 46 (1910): 167–257, both of which are bound in the volume dated 1908. On husbands' rights and limitations see 46 (1910): 167–182; 222–223; 246.

[30] Compare Davis, *A Venetian Family*, p. 107.

[31] I extracted information about the dowries of the following list of women from ASB, *PE* 1641 (when possible, both maiden and married names are given): Olimpia Maggi Ugone, B. 11, No. 301; Marta Luzzago Zaniboni, B. 11, No. 331; Paola Fisogna Ponzone, Barbara Fisogna Chizzola, Pellegrina Fisogna Avoltore, B. 10, No. 253; Lucrezia Sala Soncino, B. 3, No. 22; Caterina Averoldi Aste, B. 6, No. 97; Aurelia Zanetti Fenarolo, B. 3, No. 206; Theodora Martinengo Emiglia, B. 4, No. 313; Madalena Ducchi Faita, B. 5, No. 266; Camilla Calino Monte and Hortensia Calino Averoldo, B. 1, No. 213; Lidia Roccio Lana, B. 3, No. 181; Cecelia Federici Pavone, B. 7, No. 33; Masimilla Stella Scanzo and Lucia Scanzo Emigli, B. 1, No. 179; Marta Baitelli Ugone, Eleonora Baitelli Martinengo and Camilla Baitelli Barbisone, B. 9, No. 213; Bertolomea [?] Porcellaga, B. 1, No. 38; Leonora Longhena Luzzago, B. 7, No. 137; Margarita Bornato Medici, B. 5, No. 27. I gathered information about the dowries of the following list of women from ASB, *HM.AEP:* Paola Fe Maggi, *Famiglia Maggi, Mazzo* 7, No. 5, f. 13v and F. 1, No. 131–132, January 19, 1626, u.d.; F. 1, No. 153, May 19, 1646, u.d.; Faustina Soncino Offlaga, *Famiglia Maggi, Mazzo* 9, *Repertorio*, f. 41v, December 20, 1632; Chiara Ugone Gallo and Francesca Ugone Violino, *Famiglia Ugone, Carlo* (hereafter *Famiglia Ugone*), F. 1, No. 69, April 10, 1624, u.d.; No. 75, u.d.; Giulia Omi Ugone, *Repertorio Ugone*, f. 11r, September 27, 1611; Lucia Aringhina Chizzola in Terzio Lana q. Gaspar, *Famiglia Lana*, F. 4, No. 25, December 23, 1636, u.d.; Aurelia Lana Longhena, *ibid.*, F. 3, No. 65, November 26, 1604. Virginia Avogadro Martinengo Da Barco's dowry is in ASB, *Fondo Avogadro*, B. 9, u.d.

source frequently furnishes detailed descriptions of the landed assets, credit operations, debts and credits of dowry resources. However, it has two limitations. First, it does not list mobile property. This limits our analysis to land and credit operations. On balance, however, it is important to note that these were primary forms of income among Brescia's ruling elites during this period. Second, the passive income quantified in the tax declarations must be used with reservation, since tax documents often conceal or minimize assets with the obvious purpose of escaping the state fisc. The rich descriptions in these declarations can be used primarily to reconstruct marriage and kinship ties, to study dowry levels, and to trace the social and financial relations that stemmed from the assemblage and use of dowry resources. The tax declarations also supply demographic data on the nuclear family: the number of members, their respective ages, a list of the domestic help and the cost of its maintenance. The second archival source, the *Hospedale Maggiore. Atti di Eredità e Processi*, contains the personal papers of several families in the Brescian ruling class. I have consulted the family papers – wills, marriage contracts, account books, *estimi* – of branches of two Brescian families whose civic prominence harks back to the medieval period, the Maggi and the Ugone. The assemblage and use of dowry resources in these two families often mirror the strategies which emerge from the *estimi*. I do not maintain that these sources offer us an exhaustive survey of the patrimonial strategies which stemmed from dowry resources but they do shed light on what some of those strategies were.

In general, as the basis of power in patrician and noble regimes narrowed, few families married outside their closed circle.[32] In Brescia, because of council admission standards, lineage considerations were among the major catalysts behind class endogamy:[33] after 1488 only candidates who descended through the male line from original citizens or *benemeriti* would be accorded membership in the council. Thus the families active in civic government married almost exclusively within their ranks, and by the seventeenth century the Brescian body politic was in essence composed of a multiple number of extended families whose kinship ties are too complex to trace. Within the ruling class marriage ties offer some evidence of intra-class differentiation: the Brescian *case* aggregated to the Venetian patriciate – the Avogadro, the

[32] Stumpo, "Ceti dirigenti," p. 187.
[33] For political reasons, citizens were forbidden to marry foreign women without the permission of the government. Violators would lose the patrimony they possessed within the state. A. Pertile, *Storia del diritto italiano dalla caduta dell'Impero Romano alla codificazione* (Padua: Tipografico alla minerva dei Fratelli Salmin, 1874), vol. III, p. 253.

Martinengo da Barco, and the Martinengo-Padernello often married within their ranks.[34] Occasionally Venetian rectors or their wives acted as godparents for the offspring of these families.[35] Yet the evidence of intra-class differentiation at this level is not overwhelming: some Brescian families aggregated to the Venetian patriciate did not seek one another out in marriage.[36] Moreover, whether they married within their social rank or not, what stands out is their local orientation. The branches of the Martinengo aggregated to the Venetian patriciate, for example, chose Brescian marriage partners, married in Brescian churches, and often chose Brescians both as witnesses to their nuptial ties and as godparents.

It is more difficult to find marked inter-class differentiation among the families in the council who actively undertook public responsibilities and who had enjoyed social distinction in the city for generations. The families at the helm of power tended to intermarry with one another irrespective of whether their ancestors were rural nobles, *cives veteres*, or from the intermediate orders. This suggests that, at least within the inner circle, social origins were subordinated to the necessity of making connections of political and/or financial value. The Baitelli are a prime example. This wealthy family, deriving from mercantile origins, joined the Brescian Council in the sixteenth century. Gerolamo began a distinguished career in law and civic offices which became a family tradition. His son Costanzo, a public deputy from 1597 to 1599, was able to marry into an old Brescian family, the Bargnani.[37] In the early seventeenth century Costanzo had arranged marriages for his three daughters with families that were far older than the Baitelli: the Barbisone, the Ugone, and the Martinengo. Other examples of families

[34] See, for example, ASV, *Avogaria di Comun. Processi per nobiltà*, B. 328, *fasc.* 18 and 38. On the marriages of the Martinengo da Barco, see Lechi, *Le dimore*, vol. V, p. 79; on the Gambara, *ibid.*, pp. 18–20.

[35] Giovanni Battista Foscarini was the godfather of Hieronimo Martinengo Padernello's son, Bernadino Andrea (b. 1625). ASV, *Avogaria di Comun. Processi per Nobiltà*, B. 328, *fasc.* 31, March 15, 1624. Andriana, the wife of Francesco Corner, a Capitano in Brescia, was godmother to Federico, the son of Count Carlo Camillo Martinengo da Barco q. Ercole in 1635. *Ibid.*, B. 328, *fasc.* 36, October 31, 1635. The Contessa Canale and Andrea Soranzo were godparents to the first-born son of Count Hestor Martinengo in 1593. *Ibid.*, *fasc.* 11, February 11, 1593.

[36] Lodovico Martinengo, a Venetian noble, married Medea Ganassoni, March 1, 1575, *ibid.*, *fasc.* 8; Carlo Camillo Martinengo da Barco, *Nobile Veneto* (hereafter NV), married Veronica Porcellaga, May 18, 1632, *ibid.*, *fasc.* 35; Hercole Martinengo da Barco, *NV* married Laura, daughter of the jurist Camillo Calzaveglia, February 2, 1600, *ibid.*, *fasc.* 14; Gerolamo Martinengo, *NV* married Camilla Calina, September 18, 1624, *ibid.*, *fasc.* 34; Count Leopardo Martinengo da Barco, *NV*, married Lavinia Caprioli, March 24, 1582, *ibid.*, *fasc.*6.

[37] Lechi, *Le dimore*, vol. V, p. 144.

deriving from mercantile origins who concluded nuptial bonds with older families of distinction include the Scanzo, who intermarried with the Emigli and the Stella;[38] the Violino, who intermarried with the Ugone;[39] the Rosa, who intermarried with the Carenzone;[40] the Alvente with the Borgondi and the Manerba;[41] the Ganassoni with the Ugone,[42] the de Sena with the Brognoli;[43] and the Soncino. In this last case Giovanni Battista Soncino, a leather merchant, married Maddalena Foresti in 1534. Two of their sons, Fausto and Quinto Fabio, studied law. Quinto Fabio, the last of eleven children, rose to the pinnacle of power during the second decade of the seventeenth century, serving as Podestà of Salò in 1610 and as a public deputy four times between 1619 and 1628. His youngest son Virginio would follow the same career path in the third and fourth decades of the seventeenth century, making a prominent marriage with Lucrezia Sala q. Giovanni Battista.[44]

Marriage and family served as a primary means through which the more powerful lineages of the civic leadership preserved their political weight in council over generations. Kinship ties between fathers and sons-in-law and between brothers-in-law underlay important political relationships within the executive leadership. In-laws guarded the interests and welfare of their families, acting as godfathers and potential guardians for one another's children, and as witnesses for important family occasions such as the conclusion of marriage contracts and the writing of testaments. Together they also guarded their families' representation in the key offices. A close examination of the individuals who repeatedly stood at the helm of government between 1595 and 1650 reveals strict family ties. Horazio Longhena, a member of the executive committee throughout the 1640s, and Agostino Luzzago, the nunzio (Brescian representative in Venice), were brothers-in-law who worked very closely together defending municipal interests before the capital city.[45] Two other members of the executive committee during this period, Giovanni Paolo Luzzago (a public deputy for nine biannual

---

38 Lucia Scanzo Emili; Masimilla Stella Scanzo, ASB, *PE* 1641, B. 1, No. 179.
39 Francesca Ugone Violino, ASB, *HM.AEP, Famiglia Ugone,* F. 1, No. 69, u.d. Testament of Giovanni Antonio q. Scipione Ugone, April 10, 1624.
40 Flaminia Rosa Carenzone, ASB, *PE* 1641, B. 1, No. 107.
41 Sara Alventa Borgondi; Isabella Manerba Alvento. *Ibid.*, B. 4, No. 123; B. 4, No. 243.
42 Lechi, *Le dimore*, vol. V, p. 63.
43 *Ibid.*, p. 425.
44 Lechi, *Le dimore*, vol. III, pp. 175–76; Spreti, "Soncino (Corvini)," in *Enciclopedia storico-nobiliare italiana*, ed. Spreti, vol. VI (Milan: Unione Tipografia di Milano, 1932): 369–70.
45 ASB, *PE* 1641, B. 7, No. 137.

reforms) and Giovanni Paolo Zaniboni (also a public deputy), were father and son–in–law, respectively. This important political union was forged when Marta Luzzago married Zaniboni at the tender age of fourteen.[46] Pompeo Averoldo (a public deputy who served ten terms between 1618 and 1642), Lodovico Aste (a public deputy from 1644 to 1645 and 1646 to 1648), and Ruttilio Calino (a public deputy from 1626 to 1631, 1634 to 1635, 1640 to 1641) – were also joined by family bonds: Averoldo's daughter married Aste[47] and Calino wed his daughter to Averoldo.[48] The marriage connections of these three councillors meant that the immediate family circle would be represented on the executive committee consecutively over long blocks of time. Costanzo Baitelli, father of the distinguished seventeenth-century judge, Lodovico, created the same kind of powerful family alliance. His three daughters brought him important family alliances with Pietro Ugone, Vicenzo Barbisone, and Giovanni Battista Martinengo, while his fourth daughter, Angelica, became the abbess of Brescia's most prestigious convent, Santa Giulia. Costanzo's case is one of the best examples of how patriarchs used the marriage of their children to bring the lineage valuable political connections.[49] Fathers like Costanzo Baitelli were willing to contract nuptial bonds for as many as two or three daughters (a formidable financial commitment) in order to secure the political position of their lineages on the executive committee for future generations.[50] Stefano Maria Ugone, the son of Pietro and Marta Baitelli, was a public deputy, elected in the biannual reforms of 1636, 1638, 1640, 1646, while his uncle, Lodovico Baitelli, served on the executive committee in the reforms of 1618, 1624, and 1626, and his grandfather Constanzo Baitelli served in this position for several terms at the beginning of the century. In the Baitelli's case, marriage connections not only gave them continuous representation in the key offices; it also compensated for the relatively small size of the family. The Baitelli were not very heavily represented in council, with three seats in each reform between 1596 and 1616, two seats between 1618 and 1634, rising to four or five seats between 1636 and 1650. However through marriage they were allied with houses such as the Ugone, who enjoyed preponderant demographic weight. The Ugone held no less than ten seats in council in each reform between 1618 and 1650.

---

[46] *Ibid.*, B. 11, No. 331.

[47] *Ibid.*, B. 6, No. 97.

[48] *Ibid.*, B. 1, No. 213.

[49] *Ibid.*, B. 9, No. 213.

[50] Virginio Ugone arranged for his daughters to marry the cream of the city council: Pompeo Chizzola, ? Manerba and Giovanni Battista Sala. *Ibid.*, B. 10, No. 252.

The importance of continuing the male line, of forging important social and political alliances, and of preserving and building the family patrimony encouraged members of the Brescian civic leadership to arrange marriages for their children as early as possible. In the tax households of the fifty Brescian councillors I examined, the common age at marriage for women was the late teens, and seven were married just after puberty.[51] While the legal age of marriage for Brescian women was fifteen,[52] some of the earlier marriages, concluded during post-plague years, probably reflected the sense of urgency following a period of catastrophic mortality to start new families and/or to repair broken lineages.[53] There is further support for this in the 1641 *estimi*, which reveal that births came frequently and at regular intervals. Barbara Fisogna q. Carlo was married by the age of sixteen. At age twenty-three she had five children, aged four months to six years.[54] Lodovica Giulia Foresto q. Lelio at age nineteen had a six-year-old plus two other children.[55] Olimpia Gambara, who married Vincenzo Calino q. Ruttilio, must have been married at fifteen, for at age twenty she had a four-year-old plus one other child.[56] Marta Luzzago had eight children, all but the last at intervals of one to two years.[57]

The price of these important family alliances among the council's power holders was high: in the first four decades of the seventeenth century, dowries ranged anywhere from 8,000 to 42,000 *lire*. Their contents commonly included immovables as well as movables: credit from loans, real estate, trousseaus, and liquid capital. Stumpo's investigation of the seventeenth-century Florentine patriciate, Gullino's study of the Pisani Dal Banco and Moretta, Davis' monograph on the Donà, and Pullan's investigation of the sixteenth-century Venetian nobility all conclude that dowries rose over the sixteenth and seventeenth centuries.[58] Elsewhere, Amelang's investigation of Barcelona's honored citi-

---

[51] See ASB, *PE* 1641: Medici, B. 5, No. 27; Zaniboni, B. 11, No. 331; Calino, B. 1, No. 213; Foresto, B. 5, No. 109; Borgondi, B. 4, No. 123; Terzi Lana, B. 3, No. 208; Avogadri, B. 9, No. 397.

[52] *Statuti civili*, Capo CLX, f. 157r.

[53] On the other hand, the ages supplied in the tax declarations may not be precise, as heads of household were sometimes casual about reporting these matters.

[54] ASB, *PE* 1641, B. 10, No. 253.   [55] *Ibid.*, B. 5, No. 109.

[56] *Ibid.*, B. 1, No. 213.   [57] *Ibid.*, B. 11, No. 331.

[58] Compare Stumpo, "Ceti dirigenti," pp. 187–189; G. Gullino, *I Pisani Dal Banco e Moretta* (Rome: Istituto Storico Italiano per l'Età Moderna e Contemporanea, 1984), pp. 420–423; Davis, *A Venetian Family*, p. 106; Pullan, "The Occupations and Investments," p. 390.

zens also shows that dowries were growing larger.[59] However, inflationary trends make it difficult to demonstrate the rate at which dowries were rising, or to make meaningful comparisons of the dowry figures in one period with those of another. A further complication in assessing dowries is that they were sometimes augmented years after the marriage took place. For example, Paola Fe Maggi's dowry of 30,000 *lire*, assembled in 1625, was augmented in 1646, twenty-one years after her marriage.[60] We may attempt to determine the relative worth of these dowries by using the data in the *estimo* of 1641. The assessed value of some of the city's most sumptuous residences was around 10,000 *lire*, the lower range of upper-class dowries.[61] Moreover, one city councillor, Carlo Lana, reported in his tax declaration a yearly cost of 3,900 *lire* to feed seventeen servants.[62] Other tax declarations reveal that the private tutors of the upper class earned approximately 96 *lire* a year; coachmen earned 123 *lire* a year; and farm-bailiffs (*fattori*) earned anywhere from 113 to 142 *lire* a year. A second source, the census of the Venetian Podestà Giovanni Da Lezze, compiled in 1609 to 1610, provides a detailed summary of the salaries of those employed by the Venetian fiscal organ, the Camera Ducale. At the top of the list were the Venetian rectors in Brescia, who received yearly salaries of 432 ducats each.[63] That would mean that the dowry of 42,000 *lire* Virginia Avogadro brought to Giovanni Battista Martinengo Da Barco in 1613 represented approximately fourteen and a half years of a Venetian rector's salary from the Camera Ducale.[64] This was, however, the top

---

[59] J. Amelang, *Honored Citizens of Barcelona* (Princeton: Princeton University Press, 1986), p. 79.

[60] ASB, *HM.AEP, Famiglia Maggi, Mazzo* 9, No. 35, *Repertorio Maggi*, f. 38v, January 11, 1625; f. 45r, May 19, 1646; F. 1, No. 153 u.d., May 19, 1646. She had inherited the addition – one-third of some real estate in Tener di Manerbio, which could not be divided into parts with the other heirs, Veronica Luzzaga and Giovanni Battista Cigola – from her mother. The inheritance was assessed at 4,660 *lire* in 1671, when Paola's brothers paid off her dowry. *Ibid., Mazzo* 9, *Repertorio*, f. 51r.

[61] ASB, *Estimo* 1641, Cittadella Vecchia: Estimo delle Case, Reg. 5, u.d. provides a detailed list of property values in this quarter of the city where many upper-class residences had been established since the Middle Ages. Most palaces were assessed at well below 10,000 *lire*, with the exception of Count Cesare Martinengo's residence in San Zeno, assessed at 10,000 *lire*, and Count Carlo Antonio Gambaresco's residence, again in San Zeno, assessed at 13,120 *lire*.

[62] ASB, *PE* 1641, B. 3, No. 208.

[63] *Il catastico Da Lezze*, ed. Pasero, vol. I, p. 486. Each Venetian ducat contained 7.43 *lire italiane*. Martini, *Manuale di metrologia*, p. 819. Therefore each Venetian ducat was equivalent to 6.7 *lire imperiali*.

[64] 42,000 *lire* divided by 6.7 equals 6,268 Venetian ducats. 6,268 divided by 432 equals 14.5 years. Virginia Avogadro's dowry is in ASB, *Fondo Avogadro*, B. 9, No. 1, u.d.

range of Brescian dowries, reflecting both the social station and financial possibilities of these two families: both were among the very few families aggregated to the Venetian patriciate. Their son's nuptial union further exemplifies how these families sought one another out and distinguished themselves from other ranks of nobility by concluding lucrative and prominent family ties. Francesco Leopardo Martinengo da Barco wed into another family of Venetian patricians, the Martinengo della Pallata, and Cecilia brought Francesco 59 hectares in Bagnolo,[65] 41 hectares in Pontoglio, and 26 hectares in Gottolengo.[66] (According to Marino Berengo, 2 to 5 hectares during this period constituted a small farm; 300 hectares or more, a large property.[67]) Not all dowries were as opulent as those of the Avogadro and the Martinengo della Pallata. Dowry levels were yet another reflection of sociopolitical hierarchy. But even the more modest dowry of 8,000 *lire* that the betrothal of Giulia Omi q. Giovanni Francesco brought to Giovanni Antonio Ugone in 1611 represented a large financial commitment for her natal kin, large enough for the dowry to be paid off gradually over eighteen years.[68] Paola q. Antonio Fe's dowry of 30,000 *lire*, promised to Lodovico Maggi q. Scipione in 1625, was paid over several decades: her brother issued the last installment in 1671, after forty-six years.[69]

Paying dowries in installments, some with interest, over long periods of time is a sign of the enormous efforts families expended to meet this important responsibility.[70] This practice, no doubt, gave a woman's natal kin the time gradually to absorb the expense of the dowry or to accumulate additional income to meet this commitment. At times legacies were designated for dowry resources, but the recipient had to wait until the death of the testator. Moreover, the economic climate of the period may have influenced the way dowry commitments were fulfilled. In the early seventeenth century, land values and income

---

[65] All figures in hectares have been converted from the Brescian unit of measuring land, *piò*. One *piò* equalled 0.3255 hectares. A. Martini, *Manuale di metrologia ossia misure, pesi e monete* (Turin: Ermanno Loescher, 1883), p. 101.

[66] Lechi, *Le dimore*, vol. V, pp. 95–96; 99, n. 11.

[67] Berengo, "A proposito di proprietà fondiaria," *RSI* 82 (1970): 132.

[68] *Ibid.*, *Famiglia Ugone*, F. 1, *Repertorio Ugone*, ff. 11r–12v.

[69] *Ibid.*, *Famiglia Maggi*, *Mazzo* 7, No. 5, f. 13v, January 11, 1625; F. 1, Nos. 131–132, u.d.; No. 153, u.d., May 19, 1646; *Mazzo* 9, No. 35, *Repertorio Maggi*, ff. 38v, 45r, 51r.

[70] Other examples of this are the dowry of Olimpia Maggi, ASB, *PE* 1641, B. 11, No. 301; the listings in note 31; and *HM.AEP*, *Famiglia Maggi*, *Mazzo* 9, No. 35, *Repertorio Maggi*, ff. 37r–37v (Offlaga).

from agriculture stagnated; after 1630 they dropped.[71] At the same time Venetian fiscal pressure rose.[72] Under the circumstances heads of households who relied primarily on real estate for income would expend their resources with extreme caution in order to protect both the family's standard of living and the lineage's financial integrity.

The practice of paying off dowries in installments made intra-family financial relations complex, and possibly generational. If, for example, a father did not meet his entire obligation to dower his daughter, the responsibility passed to his sons and in turn to his grandsons, who would then be responsible for making payments to their uncle or cousins for their aunt's dowry. Fulfilling the obligations of one's ancestors was no doubt less compelling than those pledged during one's lifetime. Thus the tax declarations are filled with the lamentations of heirs who awaited full payment of the dowries of female kin.

How did women's natal kin meet the high costs of these important marriage alliances? One way was of course to acquire large dowries, thus compensating for outgoing land and capital. Davis found that the head of the Donà family in Venice, for example, kept a list of incoming and outgoing dowries.[73] Dowry income came not only from brides, but also from mothers and stepmothers. In Brescia, for example, Francesco, Giorgio, Cristoforo, and Ignatio Medici q. Federico collected a sizeable income from the expected dowries of their mother, two stepmothers, and Francesco's wife.[74] The nature of the Brescian "constitution," with its emphasis on bloodline, reinforced a distinctly patrilineal orientation, compelling patriarchs to conserve as much patrimony as possible for the lineage. This was sustained by the statutes regarding inheritance in Brescia and by laws on the Italian peninsula as a whole, which clearly favored the direct male line and agnatic kin.[75] Female issue, on the other hand, had a legal right to be dowered.[76] What is more, fathers and brothers had a vested interest in making new family alliances. Much has been written about fathers' or brothers' fright at assembling large dowries which threatened to ruin the financial

[71] Romano, "La storia economica," pp. 1,828; 1,832. See also Sella, *L'economia lombarda*, pp. 55; 72; 94–95; 123–124; for Desenzano, G. Zalin, "Il mercato granario in Desenzano nei secoli XVI e XVII," pp. 44–45.

[72] See Gullino, "Considerazioni," pp. 66–67; M. Knapton, "Il Territorio vicentino," pp. 67–68.

[73] Davis, *A Venetian Family*, p. 107.

[74] ASB, *PE* 1641, B. 5, No. 27.

[75] *Statuti civili*, ff. 197–201; Pertile, *Storia del diritto*, vol. IV, pp. 76–79.

[76] Ercole, "L'istituto dotale," *Rivista Italiana per le Scienze Giuridiche*, 45 (1909): 197–198.

solvency of the male line.[77] Without underestimating the reality of such preoccupations, it is also important to underline that the task of assembling the dowry did not fall entirely upon the resources of Brescian fathers or brothers.[78] If possible, the dowry was customarily assembled from both the paternal and maternal estates. As such the Brescian case parallels that of Venice in the early Renaissance, studied by Chojnacki.[79] By law, the dowry in both of these cities was not earmarked exclusively for the husband's lineage.[80] Instead, it benefited both male and female offspring alike, for the Brescian statutes stipulated that all children, regardless of gender, were entitled to equal shares of their mother's dowry. This meant that dowries had an economic impact on the status of the upper-class family which extended beyond the lineage. They could, for example, perform a matrilinear function, as mothers passed all or a portion of their dowries to their daughters, who in turn did the same with their female offspring. Davis also found this practice in Venice among women in the Donà family.[81]

The disposition of the Maggi estate is typical of how the responsibility of assembling the dowry was shared by both parents. In 1658 Scipione Maggi q. Lodovico, the older son of Lodovico, one of the most politically active city councillors during the third and fourth decades of the seventeenth century, calculated how much of his paternal and maternal inheritances could be used to assemble dowries, which he distinguished using the terms maternal dowry (*dote materna*) and congruent paternal dowry (*dote congrua paterna*), for his two sisters.[82] His father Lodovico, who had died in 1649, had left 182 hectares[83] in the rural community of Frontignano, together with two barns and five small houses for laborers. The "possession" was valued at 50,000 *lire*. Lodovico also left property in Manerbio, valued at 25,000 *lire*; a family palace in Brescia worth 15,000 *lire*; 10,000 *lire* in silver, jewels, and furniture; and a credit of 8,000 *lire* for the rest of his wife

[77] See S. Chojnacki, "Dowries and Kinsmen in Early Renaissance Venice," *Journal of Interdisciplinary History* 4 (1975): 41; Berengo, "Patriziato e nobiltà," pp. 514–515.
[78] *Statuti civili*, p. 198. Compare with other areas of Italy in: Ercole, "L'istituto dotale," 45 (1909): 261.
[79] Chojnacki, "Dowries and Kinsmen," pp. 41–70, esp. p. 47.
[80] For Brescia, *Statuti civili*, p. 197. Brescian laws in this matter are not, however, exemplary of Italy as a whole. While in most places the dowry primarily benefited the children, in Brescia, Milan, and Lodi this was only the case if the father predeceased the mother. Otherwise the father was entitled to half his wife's dowry. Ercole, "L'istituto dotale," *Rivista Italiana per le Scienze Giuridiche* 46 (1910): 215, n. 3.
[81] Davis, *A Venetian Family*, p. 107.
[82] ASB, *HM.AEP, Famiglia Maggi, Mazzo* 4, No. 23, September 12, 1658, u.d.
[83] Lodovico Maggi's last testament is in ASB, *HM.AEP, Famiglia Maggi*, F. 1, No. 161, Testament of August 31, 1649.

(Paola Fe)'s dowry. Scipione deducted from the paternal estate the entire value of his mother's dowry, 30,000 *lire*, as well as 11,000 *lire* that belonged to his grandmother (Faustina Soncino)'s estate.[84] Property inherited from the maternal line was clearly to be treated separately. (This was also true for tax purposes. Men listed their female relatives' property separately. Moreover, in contradistinction to dowry resources, women were not obliged by law to bequeath the property they inherited to their children.) Scipione also excluded some land tied up in entail, valued at 15,000 *lire*. After these deductions, the entire paternal inheritance amounted to 52,000 *lire*. Half of that inheritance was reserved for Scipione and his brother. The other half was divided into equal shares among Scipione, his brother and his two sisters. Scipione's sisters would thus receive for their dowries 6,500 *lire* each, or approximately 12.5 percent each of the paternal estate, while Scipione and his brother each inherited 19,500 *lire*, or approximately 37.5 percent. As such the dowries were not "congruent," that is, equal to a full share of the paternal estate.[85] The patrimony deriving from the maternal inheritance, Paola Fe's dowry of 30,000 *lire*, however, was. It would be divided equally among the two sons and two daughters. Scipione's two sisters would thus receive another 7,500 *lire* each, or 25 percent each of their mother's estate. In sum, Scipione would be able to provide a modest dowry of 14,000 *lire* for each of his sisters; collectively the two dowries represented 34 percent of his parents' combined assets.

The Maggi case underlines an important function of the dowry, and of women's property in general: it helped provide for the dowries of female offspring. In drawing up his testament, Lodovico Maggi counted on both his mother's[86] and his wife's resources, for 6,500 *lire* would hardly have brought his daughters marriage partners congruent with their family station.[87] Moreover, he displayed both trust and affection for these women in his will. He left his wife and mother with responsibility for managing the household and asked his sons to obey them. Further, although Lodovico named his sons his "universal heirs," he stipulated that his wife Paola would have use of his estate throughout her lifetime, a provision that Brescian husbands quite commonly made

---

[84] Faustina Soncino Maggi left her estate in equal shares to her grandchildren. ASB, *HM.AEP, Famiglia Maggi, Mazzo* 4, No. 23, u.d.

[85] See S. Chojnacki, "Patrician Women in Early Renaissance Venice," *Studies in the Renaissance* 21 (1974): 186; Chojnacki, "Dowries and Kinsmen," p. 45; Ercole, "Istituto dotale," *Rivista Italiana per le Scienze Giuridiche* 45 (1909): 212–213; 231–35.

[86] Lodovico stated in his will that his mother, Faustina Soncino Maggi, was quite generous to her granddaughters. ASB, *HM.AEP, Famiglia Maggi*, F. 1, No. 161, ff. 26r–29r, Testament of August 31, 1649.

[87] *Ibid.*

for wives during this period. In widowhood Paola Fe thus had the opportunity to make an important decision, which would ultimately have some bearing on dowry levels in the Brescian marriage market: she would see that her contribution to her daughters' dowries (which derived not simply from her own dowry, already destined to go in part to her daughters, but also from her own mother's legacy) was not supplemental. It would actually surpass the contribution which derived from the paternal estate, more than doubling the amount of the brideprice.[88]

Giulia Ugone's dowry also played a decisive role in the marriages of her two daughters, Chiara and Francesca.[89] As a widow, Giulia was free to dispose of her patrimony as she chose.[90] Her late husband Giovanni Antonio Ugone had bequeathed each of his daughters 6,000 *lire*.[91] This was a very modest sum for the late 1630s, again insufficient to attract one of the more prominent scions of the ruling class. Giovanni Antonio was silent as to whether this represented the limits of what he was disposed to expend or whether he counted on his wife's fortunes to make up the difference. Perhaps the decision came as a combination of both circumstances. Indeed Giulia's own marriage to Giovanni Antonio in 1611, which brought a house in Brescia and property holdings in the community of Rodengo, had significantly augmented the fortunes at the groom's disposal, for Giulia was the last in the Olmi line and her dowry was substantial.[92] Since Giulia's dowry resources were destined to go in part to female heirs, Giovanni Antonio may have decided to conserve as much of his own patrimony as possible for his male offspring. What is apparent is that Giulia's contribution to her daughters' dowries, three times that of her husband, was decisive in attracting two prominent members of the ruling elite, Francesco Gallo and Carlo Violino. Giulia stipulated that each daughter would receive 18,000 *lire* from her own property in addition to the amount that came from her husband's estate, despite the fact that her only son Carlo, the "universal heir" to his father's estate, felt that this was a large commitment. Carlo wanted his sisters to be content with their maternal

[88] Paola Fe Maggi's last testament is in ASB, *HM.AEP, Famiglia Maggi*, F. 1, No. 172, u.d., June 28, 1682.

[89] ASB, *HM.AEP, Famiglia Ugone*, F. 1, No. 75, u.d., June 16, 1640.

[90] *Statuti civili*, f. 159; Ercole, *Rivista Italiana per le Scienze Giuridiche,* "L'istituto dotale," 46 (1910): 222–223. It was customary for widows to conduct business with the aid of male advisors, or *tutori*. Oftentimes their brothers assumed this role, giving a woman's natal kin a further opportunity to guide the direction of family fortunes. See Pertile, *Storia del diritto*, vol. III, p. 241.

[91] ASB, *HM.AEP, Famiglia Ugone*, F. 1, No. 69, u.d., August 10, 1624.

[92] Compare the tax declarations of 1588 and 1637 in ASB, *HM.AEP, Famiglia Ugone, Mazzo* I, No. 9., u.d.

dowries alone.[93] Giulia, perhaps unsure of whether her young son would meet his responsibilities to his two sisters, had taken measures in her will to see that her daughters were adequately dowered. This kind of maternal participation (there are also examples of grandmothers and aunts who assumed responsibility for the dowries of female kin) in the assemblage of the dowry, exemplified in Giulia Ugone and Paola Maggi, illumines womens' role in the Brescian marriage market: they shared responsibility for providing dowries with male kin; moreover, the substantive contributions they gave their daughters from their own legacies helped keep dowry levels high. Finally, large dowries in turn made women who reached widowhood an important economic force both within the family unit and within the Brescian ruling class. There was a good chance that women would reach widowhood, since their husbands were often significantly older than they were. Paola Fe Maggi is a case in point: she outlived her husband Lodovico by forty-nine years.

The dowries of married women, however, primarily served to forge important political and economic alliances. Because of their size and nature, dowries were vital financial tools, especially for land accumulation. The world of the families who governed Brescia during the late sixteenth and early seventeenth centuries was far from the maritime ventures and manufacturing activities that occupied patricians in the capital city of Venice. It revolved largely around the professions, credit operations (in the form of personal loans) and landed resources (rents and agriculture). As such the lifestyles of these local power holders was characterized by a dual orientation. The countryside constituted the basis of their wealth, as symbolized in the stately villas and expansive fields under intense cultivation. The city, on the other hand, offered important social, political, professional, and cultural outlets. The marriage politics of Brescia's ruling families reflected this dual orientation: suitable partners were selected for the social and political ties they would bring to the family alliance; at the same time they were chosen with an eye towards building family wealth, in particular that which derived from the rich landed patrimonies situated in the Po Plains just south and southeast of the urban center.

By the late sixteenth and early seventeenth century centuries, land constituted the vital basis for upper class fortunes in the Venetian state and in many parts of the Italian peninsula as a whole.[94] It not only furnished a stable income from rents and agriculture but also provided

---

[93] *Ibid.*, F. I, Nos. 69 and 75, u.d.
[94] D. Beltrami, *La penetrazione economica;* Pullan, "The Occupations and Investments," pp. 379–408; Berengo, "A proposito di proprietà fondiaria," pp. 121–147.

collateral for loans.[95] Moreover, it was a relatively secure investment against inflation. At the same time real estate gave the ruling elites of urban centers in northern Italy economic as well as political leverage over the surrounding countryside. Finally, it was a symbol of social prestige among the ruling classes, for it was part of the general decorum of the nobility.[96] Thus a dowry which brought with it landed patrimony represented a critically important asset.

A few examples will illustrate how. Giovanni Paolo Brunello, a Brescian councillor in the early decades of the seventeenth century, had been left with rather insignificant land holdings in the rural community of Bagnolo. A century earlier his father Ettore, a rich cloth merchant from Rovato, had established the family in this rural community with a modest possession of 17 hectares. Giovanni Paolo's brother, Alessio, (b. 1584) had enlarged the Brunelli holdings in Bagnolo in the early years of the seventeenth century, but the property was dispersed after his death. Giovanni Paolo was left with a mere three hectares, but was able to repair the family's landed fortunes in Bagnolo by marrying a wealthy heiress, Ottavia Rosa, the daughter of Ottavio Rosa (fifteenth-century wool merchants) and Lucrezia Rodengo (rural nobility). Ottavia brought with her dowry several landed possessions in Bagnolo which totaled 186 hectares, making the Brunello household a substantial economic presence in this rural community.[97] In another instance the dowry of Lucrezia q. Giovanni Battista Sala furnished the Soncini household (Virginio q. Quinto Fabio) with valuable landed assets.[98] In his tax declaration Quinto Fabio stated that his daughter-in-law's dowry contained 105 hectares of land,[99] including a 33-hectare farm at Montichiari which produced sources of food and energy which could be used both for consumption and also for sale: 2,918 dry liters of rye, 584 dry liters of vegetables; 1,459 dry liters of millet; 4,775 liquid liters of wine; 107 cubic meters of hay; and 322 cubic meters of wood; another 19-hectare farm in Cluzane valued at 6,615 *lire*; yet another 17-

---

[95] See G. Corazzol, *Livelli stipulati a Venezia nel 1591* (Pisa: Giardini editori, 1986), p. 89.
[96] Berengo, "Patriziato e nobiltà," p. 502.
[97] Lechi, *Le dimore*, vol. V, p. 444.
[98] The Sala derived from the rural nobility during the Middle Ages. The *casa* appears in the lists of city council members between the twelfth and the seventeenth centuries. Monti della Corte, *Le famiglie del patriziato bresciano*, p. 69. The Soncino, originally from the Cremonese, were one of the most distinguished families in the Brescian Council because of marriage and kinship ties as well as because of their participation in civic affairs until the end of the Venetian Republic. *Ibid.*, p. 75.
[99] Arable: 72.5; olives: 0.81; pasture: 4.5; forest: 17.0; meadow: 1.5; arable and irrigated: 8.8. ASB, *PE* 1641, B. 3, No. 22.

hectare farm in Cluzane which produced 1,751 dry liters of rye, 1,167 dry liters of millet, 584 dry liters of vegetables; 4,775 liquid liters of wine; 537 cubic meters of hay; and 537 cubic meters of wood; several houses and loans (*censi*) on capital of 6,160 *lire* which yielded annually 305 *lire*. For another city councillor, Andrea Scanzo, land was such an attractive incentive that he took Masimilla Stella q. Giulio (a prominent public deputy at the turn of the century) as his wife *and* included his wife's sister in his household as well. The Stella sisters owned a large, impartible inheritance.[100]

Dowries such as the ones mentioned above could do more than simply augment the landed income at a conjugal couple's disposal. Strategies of land accumulation were even more finely nuanced: under ideal circumstances the holdings women brought with their dowries were contiguous or at least in the same community with those of their husbands. This was a way of building up blocks of territory, of ensuring substantive presence or even hegemony in rural communities, and of sharing vital resources. The marriage of Carlo Josefo Foresto q. Theodosio to Lodovica q. Lelio Foresto is a case in point. According to Carlo's tax declaration,[101] the couple had married very early: Lodovica around twelve, for at nineteen she had a six-year-old child; and Carlo at around nineteen. (It is possible, however, that individuals expressed a rather casual attitude about keeping accurate track of age.) Carlo held 23 hectares of land in the rural community of Capriolo. Lodovica brought with her dowry yet another 22 hectares in the same community, just about doubling the land in Capriolo that was at Carlo's disposal. Of equal significance, the land of both husband and wife[102] was exempt from direct taxation. This was both financially advantageous and it carried with it a high degree of social prestige. During this period the Venetian state was trying to reduce the privileges and exemptions of local ruling elites, periodically checking their claims of exemption.[103] Moreover, the period witnessed heigtened fiscal pressure on the part of the state. The families of this conjugal couple were obviously trying to keep their exempt land together.[104]

[100] ASB, *PE* 1641, B. 1, No. 179.
[101] *Ibid.*, B. 5, No. 109.
[102] The couple bore the same surname. I was not able to determine whether they were related.
[103] See Gullino, "Considerazioni," pp. 63–77.
[104] A dowry that brought with it exempt land was highly desirable. This is evident in the nuptial union of Giovanni Andrea Calino and Chiara Avogadro. ASB, *PE* 1641, B. 11, No. 124; and the marriage of Carlo Camillo Martinengo Da Barco and Veronica Porcellaga, *ibid.*, B. 11, No. 336.

If the dowry did not always bring the groom landed patrimony in the same rural communities where he and/or his natal kin were proprietors, it could instead tie his newly acquired landed fortunes to those of his in-laws in a kind of economic association. Though cetainly not as financially beneficial as the mergers brought about through nuptial bonds, which directly enhanced the fortunes of the lineage, this arrangement could produce fruitful results if – and it cannot be assumed – fathers and sons-in-law, or brothers-in-law, remained on good terms. Again the dowry would serve to create a solid patrimonial block which endured over time. The way this was done was to give as part of the dowry land that was inalienable and indivisible with other siblings. A father might dower three daughters with an impartible holding. A mother might bequeath her indivisible holding to her children, male and female alike, thus tying their fortunes and those of their respective spouses together. There was more than one reason to follow this strategy. To begin with, sometimes there was no choice: the land had already been made inalienable, and the heir was simply its custodian throughout his or her lifetime. Second, some of these land holdings no doubt would have lost their qualitative and thus quantitative value had they been partible. Third, although a woman's dowry was legally protected against the potential rapacity of her husband, impartibility served as further insurance. Fourth, the father or mother who dowered their daughters with impartible land founded a kind of economic association by tying the fortunes of their daughters' natal and marital kin together for future generations. Not coincidentally, the economic tie was linked to a political union. For example, Carlo Fisogno dowered his three daughters, Barbara, Pelegrina, and Paola, with indivisible land in the rural community of Cremezano. The dowries of these women linked the landed fortunes of three brothers-in-law who were members of the inner political circle together, Giovanni q. Galeazzo Chizzola, Francesco Avoltore, and Agostino Ponzone.[105] Virginio Ugone made the same provisions for his three daughters, dowering them with land in Seniga, Pralboino, Gottolengo, and Pavone. The property in common again tied members of the political elite together: Ugone, together with his three sons in-law Pompeo Chizzola, Paolo Manerba, and Giovanni Battista Sala.[106] Finally, dowering daughters with indivisible holdings ultimately created a lasting bond with their natal lineages that could perhaps return benefits to their families. On the other hand, there were serious drawbacks to this arrangement, for in the long run the parcel of

[105] *Ibid.*, B. 10, No. 253.
[106] *Ibid.*, B. 10, No. 252 (*Polizze* Pompeo Chizzola).

land would be the property of multiple owners, a source of discord and division.

Besides land, dowries often contained large sums of capital that were committed to two forms of personal loans, called *censi* and *livelli* (a *censo* was a loan linked to an immovable on which the creditor had no rights; a *livello* was an annual sum paid on the direct dominion of a property in order to enjoy its use).[107] Technically, to avoid the church's prohibition against usury, *livelli* took the form of a lease of real property rather than a loan.[108] For example, a borrower would fictitiously sell some real estate to a lender for 5,000 *lire* and then "rent" the holding back at an annual rate of 375 *lire*, which corresponded with 7.5 percent "interest" without violating the church's prohibitions against usury. The borrower's land in effect served as collateral for the loan. This form of investment was attractive in the early seventeenth century because it represented a stable form of income in a period when land values were stagnating. De Maddalena's study of the Belgioso estate in Lombardy places the returns on land in the third decade of the seventeenth century at about 1 to 3.5 percent.[109] The yields on *censi* and *livelli* in the Bresciano, on the other hand, ranged anywhere from 5 to 7.5 percent. Husbands and widows used dowry resources for this type of investment, creating a wide network of financial relations that included but were not limited to both their natal and marital kinsmen as well as other members of the ruling class. *Censi* thus laid the foundation for the same kind of economic partnerships among members of the city council that land did. Moreover, *censi* could also return benefits to the wife's natal family, by providing liquid capital in loans on some of the capital they had initially relinquished.[110] Thus marriage and the disposition of women's property was of critical importance to the patrimonial and political strategies of Brescian councillors. Dowries helped build blocks of territory; they helped forge economic associations that complemented political alliances; they provided investment resources; and they aided fathers in assembling dowries which would bring the family fruitful marriage alliances. Dowries wove the

---

[107] See G. Corazzol, *Fitti e livelli a Grano. Un aspetto del credito rurale nel Veneto del '500* (Milan: Franco Angeli, 1980).

[108] Pullan, "The Occupations and Investments," p. 380.

[109] See A. De Maddelena, "I bilanci dal 1600 al 1647 di una azienda fondiaria lombarda," *Rivista Internazionale di Scienze Economiche e Commerciali* 2 (1955): 510–525; 671–698.

[110] For example, Barbara, Pelegrina, and Paola Fisogno issued a *censo* in the amount of 1500 *lire* to their paternal uncle Marc Antonio Fisogno. ASB, *PE* 1641, B. 10, No. 253.

interests of kinsmen and non-kinsmen of the ruling class together in a complicated network of financial relations.

The property women inherited, or the dowry resources returned to widows, served the same functions that dowries did, with the difference that women played a more direct role in their disposition. For example, Bianca Martinengo, the widow of Conte Estore, aged forty-four in 1641, disposed of a large and rich patrimony. Both her husband and her son had died, and she was responsible for the care of her young grandson, Teofilo, aged eight. Bianca made payments on her daughter Theodora's large dowry of 42,000 *lire* to Massimiliano Emigli. She also supported another daughter, a nun in the convent of Santo Spirito, with a small *livello* of 70 *scudi* a year (a servant earned 24 *scudi* per year), and she provided for another female relative in the order of Santa Giulia.[111] In another case, Alessandro Zanetti received his sister's financial help in dowering his daughter. She provided her niece, Aurelia, with 15,000 *lire* from her own legacy to help assemble the 30,000 *lire* dowry.[112] Silvia Lodreno Palazza q. Hipolito Lodreno also provided money to her niece Aurelia to help pay her dowry to Glisento Foresto q. Giovanni Battista.[113]

In many ways marriage bound the interests of multiple family clusters within the Brescian ruling class together. However, we must be cautious in carrying this idea too far. During this period the exchange of property and capital among kinsmen was also a source of division, sometimes violent division, and thus a source of instability which gave the kinship groups at work within the ruling class a certain fluidity.[114] In the end it was the interests of household and lineage which prevailed over that of the wider family network. Successful estate planning would thus include laying the foundations for inter-familial cooperation by seeing that the interests of more than one lineage converged.

[111] *Ibid.*, B. 4, No. 313.   [112] *Ibid.*, B. 3, No. 206.
[113] *Ibid.*, B. 2, No. 5.
[114] See *Ibid.*, B. 3, No. 206, where Luca Fenaroli q. Hercole was in a long dispute with the Zanetti family over their failure to make payments on his wife's dowry. Lodovico Violino had the same problem. *Ibid.*, B. 2, No. 125.

PART III

ARISTOCRATIZATION AND THE GOVERNING POLICIES OF THE VENETIAN STATE

CHAPTER 5

KEEPING CIVIL ORDER:
FAMILIES AND FACTIONS

In 1611 the Provveditore et Inquisitore in Terraferma, Leonardo Mocenigo, reported to the Venetian Senate on conditions of civil disorder in the Bresciano. The special Venetian official, charged with correcting disorders in the system of justice, informed the state authority that the squares of Brescia were lined with important men and their armed factions. Townsmen, hired assassins, and a legion of other individuals on the fringes of society stood ready to take up arms at their faction leader's command. Mocenigo underlined the firm grip Brescian *grandi* – a name given by contemporaries to members of the most prestigious lineages – held over the local population. "Husbands and fathers cannot protect their wives and daughters," he wrote with alarm. "In their own homes and in their own beds men are not safe, shops must close before dusk, and the reputation of being just, truthful, and zealous is enough to invite one hundred enmities and bring on one's own ruin."[1] The State Inquisitor's report concerning *grandi* and factions in Brescia a decade later was no less dramatic. "No one living in the city," wrote Leonardo Moro,

> can be sure of his life or his home if he does not join one of the many factions. People elect to join one so that they do not have to fear them all. Women live in constant peril of rape. Crimes go unpunished because the men of importance march through the city flanked by twenty to forty armed supporters. If the Venetian officers of justice order them to stay in their homes, they send out their hired reinforcements to carry out their misdeeds, and the Venetian Republic lacks both the men and the

---

[1] ASV, *Collegio. Relazioni*, B. 54, *fasc.* 7a, ff. 4v–5v, report of L. Mocenigo to the Senate, August 8, 1611. On Mocenigo's visit to Brescia see Pasero, "Introduzione," *Il catastico Da Lezze*, pp. 36–37.

resources to control the situation. In fact, the *grandi*[2] so intimidate public officials that the latter prefer to stay in their palaces.

"The Brescians," Moro added, coming to his main point, "would like to see more central government. The wisest, and those who hold public office feel that the Republic has forgotten them, and many, feeling alienated, abandon the Bresciano because they do not have public protection."[3]

The two reports reflect the preoccupations of Venetian rectors, provveditori, and inquisitori of the late sixteenth and early seventeenth centuries.[4] The Republic of Venice, concerned with the order and stability of the territorial state, confronted an alarming number of homicides, assaults and riots associated with the struggles of Brescia's ruling families. The Avogadro, the Gambara, the Porcellaga, and several branches of the Martinengo[5] stood at the helm of large factions which periodically transformed Brescia as well as the surrounding hinterland into theatres of war. Their violence and *vendette* (the term is used by Venetian representatives) fill the reports of Venetian representatives. Thus they have become a centerpiece of the city's local history, almost a part of its folklore. The vicissitudes of Brescia's principal families have been viewed as a product of the violent character of their social order; and their behavior has been linked to the pejorative notion of decadence.[6] Such readings of archival collections have not taken full advantage of the rich material in these sources. In particular the reports of the podestà, who presided over Brescia's criminal tribunal, to the Council of Ten, Venice's supreme organ of criminal

[2] *Grande:* in the sixteenth century, a noble. Prior to the sixteenth century, someone powerful. An important man. My translation from Cortelazzo and Zolli, *Dizionario etimologico della lingua italiana*, vol. II, pp. 516.

[3] ASV, *Collegio. Relazioni*, B. 54, ff. 6v–7r, report of the *Sindaci Avogadori Inquisitori* Leonardo Moro and Marco Giustiniani, August 9, 1621. On the competencies of the Sindaci and Inquisitori, see G. Maranini, *La costituzione di Venezia* (Florence: La Nuova Italia, 1974), vol. II, pp. 478–490.

[4] After the governmental reforms of 1582 to 1583, the Council of Ten took charge of all serious crimes against the Venetian state or its subjects. On the competencies of the Ten see Maranini, *Costituzione di Venezia*, vol. II, pp. 422–424; on the reforms, see G. Cozzi, *Il doge Nicolò Contarini: Ricerche sul patriziato veneziano agli inizi del Seicento* (Venice and Rome: Istituto per la Collaborazione Culturale, 1958). For a summary of the new institutional climate during this period, see C. Povolo, "Processo contro Paolo Orgiano e altri," *SS* 29 (1988): 321–324.

[5] On the various branches of the Martinengo, Guerrini, *Una celebre famiglia lombarda*; on the Martinengo-Colleoni, G. M. Bonomi, *Il Castello di Cavernago e I Conti Martinengo Colleoni* (Bergamo: Stabilimento Fratelli Bolis, 1884); on the Porcellaga, Capretti, *Mezzo secolo*, pp. 1–10.

[6] Capretti, *Mezzo secolo*; for other sources see Pasero, "Introduzione," *Il catastico Da Lezze*, p. 33, n. 83.

justice, together with testimonies from victims and witnesses, teach us as much about the social fabric of Brescian life during this period as they do about the violence of the ruling class. These reports document the patrimonial concerns of Brescia's ruling families at the close of Italy's "Indian Summer." Further, they offer a means of studying social organization in the Venetian hinterland: Brescia's principal families availed themselves of wide support systems which included but were not limited to friends and kinsmen. The descriptions of patron–client relationships that welded together their support networks, like social orders, occupation and family structure, shed important light on the ways in which Terraferma society was knit together. Finally, these sources illuminate the relationship between Brescia's ruling families and the Venetian state.

Looking in the direction of the capital city, the writings of Venetian officials about the struggles of Brescia's ruling families reveal much about state priorities. To state magistrates, public order in the provinces was of critical concern. Thus the intra- and inter-familial violence of Brescian elites was not simply a personal or moral offense but above all a threat to internal stability because it involved more than just the disputing parties. Firmer state control over the judicial process on the mainland, where Venetian representatives worked with local magistracies and local judges, was also an important priority, linked to that of public order.[7] It required not simply tightening administrative structures but, of equal importance, working around the local social arrangements that stemmed from ties of kinship, friendship, and patronage. The way the state intervened in family affairs thus is a means of studying another dimension of its relationship with local power holders. Finally, it is important to note that the state did not always initiate intervention in family disputes: often Brescian families, using Venetian rectors as mediators, requested the Ten to settle their differences and to redress their injuries.

FAMILY SCHISMS

Berengo's astute observation that the family was in many ways the real protagonist of Italian urban history in the Cinquecento[8] aptly fits

---

[7] For changes in the Venetian administration of justice see G. Cozzi, "Considerazioni sull'amministrazione della giustizia nella Repubblica di Venezia (sec. XV–XVI)," in *Florence and Venice: Comparisons and Relations* (Florence: La Nuova Italia, 1980), vol. II, pp. 101–133; Cozzi, "La politica del diritto," pp. 17–152; Povolo, "Aspetti e problemi," pp. 155–258.

[8] Berengo, "Il Cinquecento," p. 493.

Brescia. The late sixteenth and early seventeenth centuries are marked by family schisms, especially among kinsmen from different lineages, who quarreled over the rights and property they had to share. Differences in wealth, a fundamental requisite of power, separated one family from another. Poorer families would be extruded from the inner circles of power. Thus, dowries, inheritance,[9] water rights,[10] and especially land – a source of power over the rural communities directly subject to the city – were among the causes for conflict. It is plausible too that general economic developments helped shape family behavior, making the lineages of the ruling class anxious to secure and reinforce their material resources. The period witnessed a fundamental shift in direction of the Venetian economy:[11] commercial and industrial activity slowed down, and the Republic began to rely increasingly on the economic resources of the Terraferma. Moreover, the cost of warfare heightened Venetian fiscal pressure, prompting the state to expand its bureaucratic organs and to make strenuous efforts to reduce the fiscal privileges and exemptions of the local elites.[12] Further, conjunctural adversity in the agrarian sector may have caused families whose fortunes rested largely on income from agriculture, rents, and private loans to become more cautious and competitive with one another than they would be under more promising economic circumstances. The criminal records of the period, some of which are presented in narrative form in Capretti's survey of early seventeenth century Brescian life, provide ample testimony of this. Capretti narrates at least twenty-five major conflicts disrupting civil order in Brescia and the surrounding hinterland during the period between 1599 and 1626 alone.[13] A tangled web of patrimonial disputes not only broke down intra- and inter-family relations but also created warring factions and armed zones within the urban space. Certain members of

[9]   ASV, *Consiglio dei Dieci. Lettere ai Capi dai Rettori di Brescia* (herefter *LCRB*), B. 27, No. 303, letter of Francesco Morosini, Podestà to the Ten, May 27, 1617. The rectors ruled in favor of Domicilla Martinengo. ASB, *Cancelleria Pretoria. Ducali*, Reg. 42, f. 158r, November 27, 1618.

[10]   ASV, *Consiglio dei Dieci. LCRB*, B. 28, No. 297, letter of Giovanni Capello, Podestà and Andrea Da Lezze, Capitano, February 28, 1626.

[11]   There is a large body of literature on the transformation of the Venetian economy. Briefly, see Sella, "Rise and Fall," pp. 106–126; D. Sella, "Crisis and Transformation in Venetian Trade," in *Crisis and Change*, ed. Pullan, pp. 88–105; and Pullan's introduction in *Crisis and Change*, ed. Pullan, pp. 1–21. On the shift to landed activities, Woolf, "Venice and the Terraferma," pp. 175–203.

[12]   On fiscal evasion, Gullino, "Considerazioni," pp. 69–77. On Venetian efforts in the second and third decades of the seventeenth century to control and tax interest income see Corazzol, *Livelli stipulati*, pp. 8–9; 90; 114–115.

[13]   Capretti, *Mezzo secolo*, pp. 9–348.

the ruling class, backed by powerful support systems, drew large segments of the city council into their family quarrels, causing it to break into splinter groups.

Beyond the violent antagonism reported in the criminal documents of the period, both fiscal records and family papers reveal in a less dramatic mode the same kinds of tensions and fissures among kinsmen over the division of patrimony. Lapsed dowry payments, inheritance disputes, and other forms of indebtedness all threatened the integrity of wider family relations, which were prone to the centrifugal force of generational disputes and ultimately subordinate to the immediate interests of the lineage. Patrimonial disputes divided the Brescian ruling class. A few examples will illustrate how diffuse, complex, and tedious these divisions were. The Fenaroli brothers (Giovanni Maria, a cathedral canon; Geronimo, a member of the city council; and Luca) were involved in long legal disputes with three other families in the council. The brothers held a 29-year-old grievance against the heirs of Gherardo Lana and the Pontevici, heirs of q. Olimpia Lana. Further, Luca, married to Aurelia Zanetti q. Giovanni Andrea, had filed a suit against his in-laws over the lapsed payment of her dowry.[14] In another case Ottaviano Zanatta q. Ambrosiano was in litigation for twenty years with Carlo Foresto, over a debt.[15] In yet another Lodovico Baitelli and his siblings were involved in a generational dispute first with Scipione Maggi and then with his son Lodovico during the early decades of the seventeenth century over a piece of land in Frontignano, where the Maggi family had accumulated sizeable holdings.[16] Finally, Terzio Lana q. Gaspar, whose three brothers and father were also active members of the city council, filed a suit in 1634 against Quinto Fabio Soncino over an outstanding debt for a land purchase in Bagnolo.[17]

We have seen in the last chapter how matrimonial alliances helped defend the economic integrity of the lineage. The bride who brought a substantive dowry, or inheritance, to her marriage could potentially augment the fortunes of the groom's lineage and/or counterbalance the deficits it suffered from outgoing dowries. The sources describing inter-familial conflict in Brescia, however, reveal considerable latitude between the dowry and inheritance provisions that individuals made and the actual fulfillment of those provisions: women did not necessar-

---

[14] ASB, *PE* 1641, B. 3, No. 206.
[15] *Ibid.*, B. 3, No. 67.
[16] ASB, *HM.AEP, Famiglia Maggi, Lodovico* (hereafter *Famiglia Maggi*), *Mazzo* 2, No. 2, u.d., (1598); *Mazzo* 3, No. 3, u.d., (1648; 1669).
[17] *Ibid., Famiglia Lana, Giovanni Antonio* (hereafter *Famiglia Lana*), *Mazzo* 11, No. 13, u.d.

ily receive all the property they were legally entitled to. This is also confirmed in fiscal documents, which indicate that women's natal kin could fail to meet both dowry obligations and obligations relating to the transmission of property, a sign if not of precarious finances then of reluctance to jeopardize the fortunes of the lineage, even if it meant alienating in-laws.

Women's property was a tempting prize, and it was vulnerable. Thus it was one of the common catalysts for inter- and intra-familial conflict.[18] The feud between Giovanni Battista and Cesare Martinengo-Colleone q. Prospero and Sansone and Paolo Porcellaga, Theofilo Martinengo da Barco, and Calimerio Cigola between 1618 and 1628 over patrimony their wives had inherited but had not received from the Porcellaga is an example of the first kind of conflict.[19] Yet another example is the feud in 1618 between Annibale Gambara and his brothers-in-law Cesare and Antonio Martinengo-Cesareschi over the estate of Gambara's deceased wife, Domicilla.[20] There are also vivid examples of the second type of conflict. In 1624 Corrado Bornato murdered his mother-in-law, Lucia Fisogna, and her servant Mattia. The Venetian rectors gathered many testimonies against Bornato and against his accomplices, Giovanni Battista and Achille Cazzaghi. They were able to persuade fifteen-year-old Monica, Corrado's wife, to testify against her husband. Monica explained that Corrado was set on having the 10,000 *lire* liquid capital her mother had saved after providing her with a dowry. Corrado also wanted Lucia to change her testament. First he offered to take his mother-in-law into his own home if she would relinquish the money. When she refused, Corrado threatened and beat her regularly. When Lucia still would not submit, Corrado, together with the Cazzaghi brothers, took her life.[21] In another case, the rectors gathered testimony against Count Giovanni Battista Provaglio, accused of poisoning his wife, Lucrezia Medici, and their four children. Lucrezia's kin, whom the rectors described as

[18] See ASV, *Consiglio dei Dieci. LCRB*, B. 29, No. 53, letter of Domenico Ruzzini, Podestà, to the Ten, September 8, 1623; No. 54, unsigned letter to podestà, n.d.; No. 60, letter of Domenico Ruzzini, Podestà, and Martinengo Vallaresco, Capitano to the Ten, September 22, 1627; B. 28, No. 261, letter of Marco Fausti for Livio Feroldo to the rectors, February 17, 1625; Nos. 219–220, letter of Marc Antonio Correr, Capitano and Vice-Podestà to the Ten, January 14, 1624; B. 30, No. 138, letter of Gerolamo Pesaro, Podestà to the Ten, September 15, 1641.

[19] ASB, *Cancelleria Pretoria. Ducali*, Reg. 42, ff. 155v–156r, 1618, no date, and Reg. 43, ff. 310v–314r, January 26, 1628.

[20] *Ibid.*, Reg. 42, ff. 158r–159r, November 27, 1618.

[21] ASV, *Consiglio dei Dieci. LCRB*, B. 28, Nos. 219–220, letter of Marc Antonio Correr, Capitano and Vice Podestà, to the Ten, January 14, 1624.

honorati and *qualificati,* underlined that she had brought Provaglio a rich dowry, her entire paternal inheritance, which yielded 2,000 *scudi* annually. According to her uncles, the dowry was not enough to satisfy her husband's greed.[22]

Women attempted to defend their claims, initiating civil litigation against brothers and sons. For example, in 1618 Caterina Martinengo-Cesaresco petitioned the Council of Ten to aid her in obtaining the patrimony that her mother, Lodovica Porcellaga, had bequeathed her as part of her dowry. Her brothers, Sansone and Paolo Porcellaga, had refused to honor this obligation.[23] Women like Caterina did not have to stand alone; there were male kinsmen who were willing to support them, sometimes sacrificing their lives. In one instance, Lavinia Simoncelli, mistreated by her husband Cristoforo Ottinelli, procured a separation and demanded the restitution of her dowry. She relied upon her sister's husband, Giacomo Feroldo, for protection. When Feroldo attempted to aid her, the entire Ottinelli clan set out to destroy the Feroldi, and Giacomo lost his life on the last day of Carnival in 1625, murdered by men from the Ottinelli clan who enjoyed the support of the city's *grandi.*[24] Cases such as the ones recounted above came before the Venetian rectors and the Council of Ten because they often involved more than the disputing parties; they drew in many other important families as well, and the potential for violence and civil disorder in Brescia was immeasurable.

Family disputes in Brescia were at times the result of transfers in wealth that did not strictly favor patriliny. Two cases stand out in particular: the conflict between the Martinengo-Padernello and the Martinengo-Cesaresco and that between the Martinengo-Colleone and the Avogadro. In the first case, the brothers-in-law of these two aristocratic households convulsed Brescia and the surrounding hinterland during the years between 1597 and 1604. At the root of their private war was a long and tedious dispute over the division of real and personal property of two of their female kin. In 1602 Cesare Martinengo-Cesaresco filed a suit against his brother-in-law, Andrea Martinengo-Padernello, for half the dowry of his deceased wife, Margarita Martinengo-Padernello. Legally, Cesare's claim to his wife's dowry was

---

[22] *Ibid.,* B. 29, No. 53, letter of Domenico Ruzzini, Podestà, to the Ten, September 8, 1623; No. 54, unsigned testimony, n.d., attached to No. 53; No. 60, letter of Rectors Ruzzini and Vallaresco to the Ten, September 22, 1627.

[23] ASB, *Cancelleria Pretoria. Ducali,* Reg. 42, ff. 93v–94v, March 6, 1618.

[24] ASV, *Consiglio dei Dieci. LCRB.* B. 28, No. 260, letter of Antonio Da Ponte, Podestà and Marc Antonio Correr, Capitano and Vice-Podestà to the Ten, February 18, 1625; No. 261, letter of Marco Fausti for Livio Feroldo to the rectors, February 17, 1625.

not out of line. According to the Brescian statutes, when a wife predeceased her husband, and there were no children, her spouse was entitled to retain one-half of the dowry. If there were children, the husband was entitled to keep the entire dowry intact for their issue.[25] Margarita's natal family, however, posed violent objections to Cesare's claim, refusing to pay the remainder of her dowry. Her death signified that either part or all of this patrimony would have to be transferred to her husband's lineage, and the Martinengo-Padernello stood to suffer a substantial loss. Cesare made further claims for his children: 6 per cent of his mother-in-law's dowry, which she had willed them. Again there was a legal basis for his claim: as a widow, Cesare's mother in-law, Giulia Ganassoni, was entitled to bequeath her dowry resources as she saw fit.[26] The Brescian tax declarations for 1641 often reveal that women exercised this option, making provisions for their children, grandchildren, or sometimes other female kin in their natal families.[27] It was not unusual, then, that Giulia should have designated a part of her estate for her daughter's children. Yet Giulia's last wishes were clearly disadvantageous to her sons' agnatic line: Andrea and Hieronimo Martinengo-Padernello would see their property shifted into their brother-in-law's lineage under this arrangement. Thus Andrea Martinengo-Padernello objected both to his brother-in-law's claims and to his mother's bequest. The patrimony under dispute was substantial, including income from rents and credit operations, pledges to the Monte di Pietà and other credits which, according to the podestà, amounted to more than 36,000 ducats.[28] To have an idea of the relative weight of 36,000 ducats, this sum well exceeded the entire Bresciano's share of the *sussidio*, a direct tax of 25,000 ducats, for 1609.[29] Andrea filed a counter-suit, where he attempted to argue that Cesare, who had lived with Giulia Ganassoni for years, had manipulated his mother-in-law into leaving her grandchildren a part of her estate. Moreover, Andrea claimed that Giulia had expended funds to support Cesare and

[25] *Statuti civili della magnifica città di Brescia. Volgarizzati* (Brescia: Pietro Vescovo, 1776), f. 159r.

[26] *Ibid.*

[27] See Chojnacki, "Dowries and Kinsmen," pp. 66–67.

[28] The details of the litigation are in ASB, *Cancelleria Pretoria. Ducali*, Reg. 41, ff. 80r–80v, March 27, 1604; ASV, *Consiglio dei Dieci. Parti Comuni*, F. 247, March 27, 1604; *Consiglio dei Dieci. LCRB*, B. 26, No. 80, letter of the rectors to the Ten, February 18, 1602; Nos. 82–86, March 18–21, 1602, Testimonies of Cesare Martinengo Cesaresco and Andrea Martinengo-Padernello; No. 93, letter of Nicolò Donado, Capitano and Vice-Podestà to his nephew Piero, June 6, 1602; No. 94, letter of Nicolò Donado to the Ten, June 25, 1602.

[29] See Da Lezze, *Il catastico Da Lezze*, vol. I, p. 482.

his family for years, and the Martinengo Padernello expected compensation for this. While the podestà attempted to resolve the civil differences of these two important families, friends, clients and kin chose sides, the city council literally split in half, and a series of assaults, homicides, and riots rooted in the quarrel grew to alarming levels.

The Martinengo-Padernello–Martinengo-Cesaresco dispute draws attention to the reluctance on the part of upper-class women's natal families to jeopardize the interests of the lineage by meeting dowry obligations; it also illumines the practical problems associated with such women disposing of property. Because the Brescian statutes sanctioned widows' disposition of their dowries,[30] they had the capacity to influence family fortunes significantly. Chojnacki has argued for an earlier period of Venetian history that when women drew up their testaments, family considerations were as important or even more important than lineage considerations; that women expressed a more flexibile social attitude, inclined to give equal regard to both their natal and marital kinsmen.[31] Giulia Ganassoni's choices exemplify the kinds of inter- and intra-familial problems that could result from such social flexibility in Brescia. The differences between the Martinengo-Padernello and the Martinengo-Cesaresco became explosive when this widow made provisions that favored her daughter's issue and thus allowed property to be diffused into her son-in-law's lineage.

Men could also express the kind of flexibility that caused conflict. According to the Brescian statutes, if a man died intestate, his patrimony was designated for the patriliny, or the closest male kin, however remote. However, Brescian fathers with no male offspring at times opted to leave their estates to daughters. During the years between 1616 and 1618 a branch of the Avogadro (Paolo, Matteo, and Sforza) and the Martinengo-Colleoni (Francesco and his son, Gaspar Antonio) assumed adversary positions over this issue. The Marchese Gaspar Antonio Martinengo-Colleone was promised to Emilia Avogadro, the last in Roberto Avogadro's line and his designated heiress. Emilia would bring to her matrimony a weighty fortune – an annual income of 8,000 ducats. Of particular social and economic significance, Emilia's real estate holdings were exempt from Venetian taxation. Moreover, she enjoyed a small army of servants, a castle, a mill, water rights, and property holdings in Meano and Ghedi, where she had a palace.[32] The

---

[30] *Statuti civili. Volgarizati*, f. 159r.
[31] Chojnacki, "Dowries and Kinsmen," pp. 66–67; see also Berengo, *Nobili e mercanti*, p. 39.
[32] Emilia later married into another branch of the Martinengo. Her taxable assets are listed in ASCB, *Polizze d'estimo: Martinengo, Bartolomeo q. Estore*, 1637, B. 85, u.d.

huband-to-be and his father, Francesco, claimed the right to dispose of Emilia's rich patrimony, while the Avogadro brothers – her first cousins and her father's closest surviving agnatic kin – contested her inheritance. The three brothers argued that their grandfather's will had stipulated that the property in question was entailed to male heirs exclusively. Roberto Avogadro's testament had allegedly been destroyed, making the civil proceedings difficult, if not impossible.[33] The prospective matrimonial alliance of the Martinengo-Colleoni represented a new alignment of economic power, one which triggered a negative reaction among the Avogadro, who competed for control of the same territory and the same resources. The Martinengo-Colleoni and the Avogadro resorted to violence, and according to Venetian representatives, the climate of unrest in the province reached alarming levels.[34]

The conflicts of the Martinengo-Padernello–Martinengo-Cesaresco and the Martinengo-Colleone–Avogadro – and there are many more – emphasize the critical importance of securing the fortunes of the patriliny. Because the patrimony of the women involved in these two cases could significantly enhance or threaten these interests, it became the object of violent antagonism. At the same time the two cases draw attention to the kind of flexibility that worked within the patriarchal structure and the ambivalence, depending on who stood to lose and who stood to gain, over women disposing of property and inheriting property.

The complicated civil litigation between the Martinengo and the Cigola between 1635 and 1738 over Lucrezia Cigola's dowry provides a final case in point. A good part of this dispute was triggered by the testament of Lucrezia's maternal grandmother, Barbara Luzzago. When Lucrezia received a substantial portion of her grandmother's estate, her husband Battista Martinengo demanded that her dowry of 20,000 ducats be augmented with Luzzago properties in Brescia, the Chiusure, and the Territorio. The Cigola, Lucrezia's natal family on her paternal side, refused to augment the dowry. Though the Cigola and the Martinengo disagreed as to how Lucrezia's inheritance should be apportioned, they defended her legacy. In contrast, the Luzzago (Lucrezia's maternal kinsmen) tried to contest the principle of inheritance through the female line. As a result of this general lack of consensus over who was entitled to what, tied not to any overriding principle but rather to individual interests, Lucrezia's paternal, maternal

[33] ASV, *Consiglio dei Dieci. LCRB*, B. 27, No. 303, letter of Francesco Morosini, Podestà, May 27, 1617. See also Capretti, *Mezzo secolo*, pp. 224–225.
[34] Capretti, *Mezzo secolo*, pp. 230–235.

and marital kin, and then their heirs, did not come to a final agreement over the substance of her dowry for more than a hundred years.[35]

The inter- and intra-familial struggles over the division of patrimony in Brescia underline the potential subordination of wider family interests, especially those created through marriage ties, to those of individual lineages. They also accentuate cases of flexibility within the patriarchal structure. Finally, that women's property became a prize to fight for and that brothers-in-law were frequently the antagonists in these violent disputes suggests that in-laws did not necessarily benefit from matrimonial alliances. Not all families enjoyed the kind of strong bonding that stemmed, for example, from holding important public offices within their circle for generations. For the families of the *grandi*, for example, ties with in-laws were rather fluid because they were able to construct other support systems to defend their interests. Those support systems will be treated below.

SUPPORT NETWORKS OF BRESCIAN FAMILIES

While disputes over dowries, over legacies, and over other patrimonial concerns reflected the lineage's preoccupation with protecting its economic status and the economic basis of its power, they also provided Brescia's ruling families with occasions to vaunt their support networks and to act out in public the true relationships of power in the local community. Not only did the grieving parties come to blows in these domestic quarrels. The associations of ruling families and their supporters took sides and participated in the conflicts as well. Thus faction leaders such as the Martinengo-Padernello and the Martinengo-Cesaresco created units for the perpetration of violence.[36] The Venetian Podestà, Marcantonio Memmo, wrote to the Senate with a sense of urgency in 1602, declaring that Brescia's peace and tranquility depended upon the resolution of the differences of the four brothers-in-law.[37] The disputing parties were able to mobilize large and dangerous followings.[38] The Martinengo-Padernello availed themselves of Pietro Avogadro's faction, reputed to be the largest and most dangerous,[39] while the Martinengo-Cesareschi enjoyed the backing of the Porcellaga.

[35] ASB, *Fondo Avogadro*, B. 10, No. 7, April 29, 1656; November 26, 1738, u.d.

[36] See L. Stone, *The Family, Sex and Marriage in England, 1500–1800*, abridged edition (New York: Harper Torchbooks, 1979), p. 77.

[37] ASV, *Consiglio dei Dieci. LCRB*, B. 26, No. 80, letter of Marcantonio Memmo, Podestà, and Nicolò Donado, Capitano to the Ten, February 18, 1602.

[38] Capretti, *Mezzo secolo*, pp. 74; 224.

[39] "Diari dei Bianchi" (July 14, 1607), in *Le cronache bresciane inedite*, ed. P. Guerrini (Brescia: Istituto artigianale, 1930), vol. IV, pp. 72–73.

Included in these factions were the names of many of the most important families in the Brescian ruling class.[40] Memmo warned the Senate that if peace were not concluded between the Martinengo-Padernello and the Martinengo-Cesareschi, it could not be concluded for the city.[41] In fact, over the next five years the differences between these families generated several more conflicts, and Memmo and his successors were allowed no respite. Andrea and his brother Hieronimo Martinengo-Padernello commanded many men.[42]

Why was it that a domestic disagreement between the Martinengo-Padernello and the Martinengo-Cesaresco could literally polarize the local community? The answer to this question reveals a great deal about the larger concerns of the members of the Brescian ruling class. Further, it sheds light upon the capacity of the city's leading families to influence, mobilize, and discipline a wide cross-section of local society. In the first place, the relatively high proportion of ruling families who participated in the struggles of the Martinengo-Padernello and Martinengo-Cesaresco is an index of the fissures which existed among members of this group. While the Brescian elites played no formal role in the state political structure, their power was entrenched in local urban and ecclesiastical institutions and in the landed property of the Territorio. Hence the "politics" of this Venetian subject city turned largely upon the relationships and rivalries of the principal families. The patrimonial disputes of the Martinengo, Avogadro, and others indicate that the contest for local influence, status, and economic resources within the ruling class was played out publicly in "family politics": matrimonial alliances, dowries, testaments, etc.

The competition among Brescia's ruling families was also expressed by a display of physical force, sustained by kinship and clientage

[40] BMCV, *Codice Donà delle Rose*, No. 160, *fasc.* 30, ff. 155r–156v, May 1601. This document furnishes a detailed list of the followings of the Avogadro, who were supporters of the Martinengo-Padernello, and the Martinengo-Cesareschi. For Vicenza cf. C. Povolo, "Crimine e giustizia a Vicenza. Secoli XVI–XVII. Fonti e problematiche per l'approfondimento di una ricerca sui rapporti politico-giudiziari tra Venezia e la Terraferma," in *Atti del Convegno Venezia e la terraferma attraverso le relazioni dei rettori*, ed. A. Tagliaferri (Milan: Giuffrè, 1981), pp. 421–425. Povolo underlines the relationship between noble violence and the fissures in the Vicentine city council.

[41] ASV, *Consiglio dei Dieci. LCRB*, B. 26, No. 80, letter of Marcantonio Memmo, Podestà, and Nicolò Donado, Capitano to the Ten, February 18, 1602; Senato. *APRB, Dispacci del N. H. Marcantonio Memmo, Podestà di Brescia, 1601–1602*, dispatch to the Ten, ff. 90r–90v, March 29, 1602; ff. 97v–98r, dispatch to Serenissimo Prencipe, April 21, 1602.

[42] The Padernello lost the case: in 1604 the Council of Ten supported the Martinengo-Cesaresco's legal claims. ASV, *Consiglio dei Dieci. Parti Comuni*, F. 247, August 30, 1602; July 11, 1603; March 27, 1604.

networks. Factions were, in essence, the public representation of family support systems. It is particularly significant that Brescian families did not confine public displays of force to the countryside, the seat of their landed patrimonies and often the object of their quarrels. The city was a central stage for their wars and their terror tactics. They staked out armed zones in Brescia, claiming the urban space as their domain. Members of old noble lineages such as the Martinengo and other *grandi*, followed by their kinsmen, clients, and allies in the city council, set the tenor of inter/intra familial relations,[43] for the rectors reported on many occasions that peace could not be concluded among families belonging to rival factions unless it was concluded between the faction leaders themselves.

What held family support networks together? Friendships and common interests among the ruling families, no doubt, played a large role in fostering alliances. The *grandi* covered all bases of power in both city and countryside. For example, one brother might devote himself to study and civic government while another retained a distinctly rural orientation, living as a *signore* with significant control over the rustics in his vicinity. Further, Brescian citizens, including members of the city council, sought the patronage and the social prestige that resulted from association with the old noble houses who stood, according to contemporaries, at the pinnacle of the provincial social hierarchy. A few of the Martinengo and the Gambara enjoyed some juridical autonomy, holding civil and criminal jurisdiction *citra penam sanguinis* in their territories.[44] They also provided vital military leadership for the Venetian Republic.[45] In short, they held significant resources, authority and social prestige. Thus they were able to cultivate a support network from the ranks of the top citizen families, not only for the political and social benefits such an association would bring but also because in a world where violence was frequently the means through which differences were resolved the faction furnished its members with mutual protection as well. Finally, there was also a financial dimension behind community support of family rivalries: many creditors stood to lose or gain from the financial outcome of a dispute between families such as the Martinengo-Padernello and the Martinengo-Cesaresco.

---

[43] Berengo, "Il Cinquecento," p. 494.

[44] Report of Paolo Correr, Podestà, April 1562, in *RV*, ed. Tagliaferri, vol. XI, p. 76.

[45] Geronimo Avogadro was a *Capitano di corazze*, "Diari dei Bianchi," in *Le cronache bresciane*, vol. IV, p. 85, January 1615. Conte Pietro Avogadro was governor of Crema in 1617. *Ibid.*, p. 101, January 10, 1617. Pietro Avogadro; Francesco Martinengo-Colleoni; Bartolomeo, Estor and Pietro Martinengo-Colleone led companies of *corazze*, ASV, *Provveditori da Terra e da Mar*, F. 45, letter of Benetto Moro, *Provveditore Generale in Terraferma*, January 31, 1606, *more veneto*.

Brescian faction leaders had both *adherenze*[46] and *dipendenze*. Though we have little or no information about the organization of these factions, we know something of their composition. The *grandi* drew together various levels of society, both from the mainstream and from the marginal, forging vertical as well as horizontal ties. Recruits in the armed factions were inscribed on both a voluntary and an involuntary basis. Among the former, were the renowned Manzonian *bravi*,[47] the armed men of the *signore*, a phenomenon particularly characteristic of this period. They were not necessarily Brescians, but came from other Italian and European states as well. Any number of reasons may have impelled them to join the services of the *signore*, such as economic dependence. It is also possible, however, that these *bravi* were developing a political consciousness of their own, as a dangerous group that was able to sell its services.[48] "Do not think, Your Excellency, that if the banished did not have the support and stimulus of this or that faction that they would dare stay within these borders, and commit the misdeeds that they commit," wrote the Podestà Giovanni Corner in 1603.[49] Also among the voluntary recruits were the sons of Brescian artisans, who were trained to bear arms at an early age. The flagging activity of certain Brescian industries (e.g., wool) during this period might help explain their involvement in factions.[50] An equally compelling argument may be made, however, that association with a powerful faction served as a channel of mobility: the support of the *signore* and his *bravi* gave the artisan's son leverage as well as physical protection. It is plausible that other youth from the more prosperous ranks of the intermediate orders who also joined these factions did so for the leverage it brought, too.

While the desire for social mobility and physical protection cut across generational lines, motivating Brescia's youth to join factions, material concerns prompted certain segments of the financially emarginated population to participate in the quarrels of Brescia's ruling

[46] *Aderènza:* authoritative relations, friendship in high places (Machiavelli, 1513–21). My translation from Cortelazzo and Zolli, *Dizionario etimologico della lingua italiana*, vol. I, p. 20.

[47] Alessandro Manzoni, *I promessi sposi* (*The Betrothed*) (New York, P. F. Collier and Son, 1909).

[48] Why this form of violence surfaced at this point in time is an important question which merits further research. See Povolo, "Aspetti e problemi," pp. 233–234; 236.

[49] "Ne credano V. Ecc. se le banditi non havessero l'appoggio et fomento chi di questa, chi di quella fattione ardissero di star à questi confini, et venir a commetter le sceleratezza che commettono." ASV, *Consiglio dei Dieci. LCRB*, B. 26, Nos. 165–166, letter of Giovanni Corner, Podestà and Vice-Capitano to the Ten, August 8, 1603; Capretti, *Mezzo secolo*, pp. 76–77.

[50] On Brescian industries see Pasero, "Introduzione," *Il catastico Da Lezze*, pp. 71–77.

families.[51] Brescians, foreigners, and itinerant bands flocked to the city, seeking sustenance where they could, even as retainers or hired assassins.[52] Because poverty and transience were not just problems in Brescia but were widely diffused in all the urban centers of early modern Italy, the vagrants, gypsies, and unemployed soldiers who served the interests of Brescia's ruling families presented a problem that extended far beyond Venetian jurisdiction; they were the concern of every Italian regional state.

There were also involuntary recruits in Brescia, impelled by fear of the *grandi* and their *bravi* to join with a faction.[53] They relied upon the protection of powerful patrons for sheer physical survival. The necessity for virtually everyone within the urban space to attach himself to powerful patrons for protection made vertical as well as horizontal social bonds a distinct characteristic of Brescia's urban factions.

The Martinengo-Colleone–Avogadro feud over Emilia Avogadra's inheritance offers an example of the difficulty of controlling the violence associated with the differences of Brescia's ruling families. Venetian representatives found this dispute particularly alarming because the faction leaders, using coercion and fear tactics, terrorized the subject population. On June 18, 1618 the Ten received an anonymous letter from "one who wishes peace."[54] It contained a long list of injuries committed by *bravi* and *banditi* under the tutelage of the Martinengo-Colleoni. The author complained that Francesco Martinengo-Colleone exercised absolute authority in Brescia, the Territorio, and the Brescian valleys, controlling the lives of everyone who supported his arch enemies, the Avogadro family. Martinengo-Colleone employed his own militia (*compania di corazze*) to carry out his misdeeds. He also hired outlaws, and within a few short months, Francesco's hired assassins had committed a long list of homicides: Antonio Longo, a prosperous Brescian merchant, was shot in a public square because he was walking with the Avogadri; the Marchese Rampinello from Gardone di Val Trompia lost his life after providing

---

[51] ASV, *Collegio. Relazioni*, B. 54, *fasc.* 7a, ff. 4r–4v, report of Leonardo Mocenigo to the Senate, August 8, 1611.

[52] For the economic conditions which contributed to the rising level of poverty in the last decade of the sixteenth century see N. S. Davidson, "Northern Italy in the 1590s," in *The European Crisis of the 1590s*, ed. P. Clark (London and Boston: G. Allen and Unwin, 1985), pp. 167–170.

[53] ASV, *Collegio. Relazioni*, B. 54, f. 6v, report of Leonardo Moro and Marco Giustiniani, *Sindaci, Avogadori et Inquisitori*, August 9, 1621; *Consiglio dei Dieci. LCRB*, B. 28, No. 17, letter of Francesco Morosini, *Podestà*, and Antonio Morosini, *Capitano*, to the Ten, June 30, 1618; No. 18, anonymous testimony, n.d., attached to No. 17.

[54] See Capretti, *Mezzo secolo*, pp. 232–235.

food and lodgings to Matheo and Sforza Avogadri; one of Matheo Avogadro's auxiliaries, Francesco Odalio, was killed in Barbarigo by Martinengo-Colleone and his soldiers; Gabriel Buccelleno was knifed and shot because of his friendship with the Avogadri; Martinengo-Colleone's gunmen (they used arquebuses) paid a visit to Bernadino Bressiano, the servant of Giovanni Antonio Catanio, because he had taken a walk with Matheo Avogadro; even the renowned bandit Francesco Riva had not escaped Martinengo-Colleone's lethal grasp. With a sense of futility and desperation, the author explained that many individuals were forced against their will either to choose sides in the conflict between the Martinengo-Colleone and the Avogadro or flee. Francesco Martinengo-Colleone could influence the Brescian ruling class and compel participation by the popular orders. He was certain that he did not need to fear retribution from the law because the Venetians were at war and had need of his military reinforcements. The author implored the Council of Ten to intervene before the population was bathed in blood. The podestà attached his observations to this letter. He felt the supplication would be difficult to satisfy because the younger Martinengo-Colleone commanded a company of one hundred men (*corazze*), and under the orders of Francesco Erizzo, defended the borders of the Cremasco. The Venetians would encounter serious difficulties in disciplining him because he had great influence and powerful alliances.

What stands out immediately in this testimony is the author's apprehension that the forces of the state could not overturn those of the Martinengo-Colleone. The Venetian organs and officers of justice had more than the powerful to contend with in this struggle; they were dealing with a healthy cross-section of society at large, which Martinengo-Colleone had been able to draw into his sphere of influence. His accomplices were recruited not just from fearful Brescians but from his own personal military reinforcements as well as a wide pool of vagrants that roamed the countryside bordering the Bresciano and the Cremonese.

Thus, factional conflict among Brescia's ruling families was fueled by followers who sought mutual protection and prestige. It also converged with the wider social problems (e.g., *bravi*, poverty) that furnished the *grandi* with large numbers of dependents. Finally, it ran full force because the need for protection impelled many to associate themselves with factions. The task of maintaining order and stability within the urban space was daunting in the extreme.

STATE ACTION

It was important for Venetian representatives to correct the image that state authority was weak and distant compared to that of local power holders, even if in fact the state's forces of physical repression often could not match those of the Brescian *grandi*.[55] Faction leaders such as the Martinengo-Padernello, the Martinengo-Cesaresco, the Porcellaga, and the Avogadro, taking advantage of their strength in numbers, treated Venetian officials with disdain, openly defying the ministers of justice. They also intimidated the local population, making it difficult for Venetian representatives to gather testimonies against them. The behavior of Lelio Martinengo-Cesareschi is a case in point. In 1621 he provided a group of twenty-five to thirty gypsies with food and lodgings in one of his barns in the community of Pavone. In exchange the gypsies terrorized the community, robbing it for their protector. When the Venetian Podestà Michele Foscarini heard of these misdeeds, he sent the capitano di campagna (captain of rural police) and twenty armed men to arrest the offenders. Lelio greeted the forces of public order with seven or eight of his own hired *bravi*. He sounded a bell and within minutes the number of his supporters who gathered round grew to such proportions that the state officials were compelled to flee for their lives.[56]

The Ten perceived that the state must dispense civil justice, rather than simply concentrating on methods of repression, in order to eradicate the roots of violence sponsored by Brescia's ruling families. Civil justice, Cozzi has noted, was a means of asserting control over the important families.[57] The state's tactic was to try and resolve the civil litigation between adversaries in order to extinguish the violence. In

---

[55] See E. Basaglia, "Il controllo della criminalità nella Repubblica di Venezia. Il secolo XVI: un momento di passaggio," in *Atti del convegno Venezia e la terraferma*, pp. 65–78; Povolo, "Aspetti e problemi," pp. 207–216. Brescian *grandi* frequently shot at the *capitano di campagna*. ASV, Senato. *APRB, Registro di tutte le lettere publiche scritte nel corso del Reggimento dell'Ill.mo Michele Foscarini, Podestà di Brescia principiate a 4 Maggio 1620 et finito a 2 Ottobre 1621*, letters of Foscarini to the Ten, August 19, 1620; January 17, 1621; and to Serenissima Prencipe, April 25, 1621.

[56] ASV, Senato. *APRB, Lettere publiche dell' Ill.mo Michele Foscarini*, letters of Foscarini to the Serenissima Prencipe, March 22 and April 15, 1621. Foscarini also reported that the Chizzola family availed itself of outlaws and *malfattori*, in *ibid.*, letter to the Ten, September 19, 1620. There are many other examples; among them, Camillo Martinengo-Cesareschi, ASV, Senato. *APRB, Di lettere secrete del Capitanato di Brescia, 1599*, letter of Nicolò Dolfin, Capitano, to the Ten, September 3, 1599, ff. 43r–44r. The Ten began to legislate specifically against housing *malfattori*. See note 74.

[57] See G. Cozzi, *Repubblica di Venezia e stati italiani* (Turin: Giulio Einaudi, 1982), pp. 167–168.

addition to Venetian representatives and the Ten, Venice used the friends of grieving parties as arbitrators to settle family differences.

At the same time the Venetians understood that in order to preserve order equal emphasis would have to be placed on tightening up the judicial apparatus. The self-confidence of the Brescian *grandi* and their associates stemmed not only from their strength in numbers but also from the fact that they had access to the administrative short-cuts and judicial expedients that could free them from the arms of the state. The duplicity of the judicial system made it particularly difficult to bring members of the ruling families to justice. Venice did not command the system of justice autonomously, but rather employed the members of the Brescian Colleges of Judges and Notaries to execute this important task. Protagonists of factional violence in Brescia held vital links with these local power holders.

What was the wider legal significance of such kinship and patronage structures? How did Brescian judges and notaries view the violence associated with the struggles of Brescia's principal families? When it came to members of the ruling class, or to family and friends, social networks redefined the boundaries of violence and "crime." The status of a noble faction leader who was guilty of homicide, or of hiring someone to commit murder, or of instigating riots was ambiguous. Because he was linked to the local power structure or capable of inflicting physical harm, there was neither total consensus nor total aversion to his behavior. Kinship and patronage ties between faction leaders and the local ministers of justice established firm lines of cooperation, providing the means for protection against prosecution and punishment.

The way Brescian elites availed themselves of the city's notarial corps is an important example. When the podestà and the praetorial court acted under ordinary jurisdiction in the respective cities of the Venetian mainland, the proceedings for criminal cases were prepared by the notaries of the Maleficio, a local bureaucratic organ. In Brescia members of the College of Notaries under the direction of a judge from the Brescian College ran the Maleficio.[58] The proceedings were then sent, if the rules were followed, to the podestà. This is the point where the local kinship and patronage structure could obstruct the administration of justice. Brescian notaries (who were also members of the city council), responsible for recording criminal offenses, judicial proceedings, sentences and decrees, often took the proceedings home, altered

---

[58] See Povolo, "Aspetti e problemi," pp. 156–164; L. Mazzoldi, "Gli ultimi secoli del dominio veneto," in *Storia di Brescia*, vol. III, pp. 10–11.

them, hid them, or even destroyed them before they could reach the Venetian podestà.[59] Such behavior was not peculiar to Brescian notaries but was characteristic of scribes in the other Venetian subject cities as well.[60] Testimonies from the Brescian citizenry, which are included in the rectors' letters to the Ten, frequently mention how the networks between the notarial corps and the *grandi* impeded the dispensation of justice.[61] For example, in 1618 Octavio Feroldo, a member of the inner circle of the Brescian Council, protected his nephew, Francesco Feroldo, "a ferocious man, a principal of Brescia, with many supporters and dependents." The rectors complained to the Ten that they could not persuade anyone to testify against Francesco because of his powerful support system.[62] Again, in 1655 the podestà complained to the Ten that he could not initiate action in the civil dispute between Girolamo Maggio and Ottavio Ognibene because the notary in the Maleficio, a relative of the Maggi, was not cooperating.[63] In the same year Giovanni Paolo Brunello pleaded with the Ten for protection against Ottaviano Bocca, a "rich young man with many relatives who are notaries in the Maleficio and who are trying to kill him." Brunello claimed Bocca was responsible for many homicides, but the notaries had either disguised the truth or hidden the evidence.[64]

One of the ways the state attempted to intervene in the judicial systems of the various subject cities was to grant the podestà extraordinary jurisdiction and to exclude the local notaries from the judicial process.[65] In 1569 the Council of Ten ruled that in cases delegated to the Venetian rectors only the podestà's chancellor could write and manage the records of judicial proceedings.[66] This was, in effect, an institutional response to local social arrangements that produced

59 Mazzoldi, "Gli ultimi secoli," p. 22. More than one podestà attempted to compile a *catasto criminale* in order to keep track of these cases. ASB, *Cancelleria Pretoria. Ducali*, Reg. 41, ff. 329–330v, report of Pietro Barbarigo, June 17, 1611; report of Domenico Ruzzini, July 1628, in *RV*, ed. Tagliaferri, vol. XI, p. 315.

60 See Povolo, "Aspetti e problemi," pp. 163–164, for other examples.

61 ASV, *Consiglio dei Dieci. LCRB*, B. 30, No. 181, letter of Antonio Longo, Podestà to the Ten, March 1, 1642; No. 182, Testimony of Silvestro Ceretti to the podestà, January 17, 1642.

62 "huomo feroce, principale di Brescia, pieno di adherenze e dipendenze." ASB, *Cancelleria Pretoria. Ducali*, Reg. 42, ff. 142v–144r, September 18, 1618.

63 ASV, *Consiglio dei Dieci. LCRB*, B. 32, No. 86, letter of Rectors Morosini and Bassadona to the Ten, May 30, 1655; No. 87, unsigned testimony to the rectors, n.d., attached to No. 86.

64 *Ibid.*, No. 48, testimony of Brunello to the rectors, March 10, 1655.

65 Povolo, "Aspetti e problemi," pp. 192–199.

66 *Ibid.*, p. 196.

conflict between center and periphery in many of the subject cities, especially Brescia and Padua, during the late sixteenth and early seventeenth centuries. The intensity and duration of these conflicts depended largely on the relative status and power of the local notarial corps.[67] In Brescia the attempt to curb local notarial jurisdictions was met with tenacious resistance. Throughout the last decades of the sixteenth century and the first half of the seventeenth century, the Brescian College of Notaries, with at least eighty representatives in the city council, objected to the notaries in the service of Venetian rectors' handling of civil and criminal cases. They defended their traditional prerogative to prepare the proceedings for the podestà, and the city council defended them, sending envoys to Venice to request that the authority of Venetian rectors in this matter be curtailed, that they be delegated the powers of *rito* – gathering testimonies in secret – as little as possible. The powers of *rito*, councillors argued, were of prejudice to the College of Notaries.[68] The city council also objected to the extraordinary rigor of the sindaci in Terraferma, whom they accused of trampling on the local tribunals' prerogatives. For example, Brescian judges wanted to act as an appeals court for the sindaci's decisions, but the Senate refused them.[69] Indeed, the influence of the sindaci grew throughout the Venetian Terraferma during this period, a reflection of the state's need to curtail administrative abuse in the local judicial systems.

Whether the state was successful in breaking through local social arrangements can only be evaluated on a case-by-case basis. While Venice made efforts to strengthen its own judicial authority – in particular that of the praetorial courts in the respective subject cities[70] – it also worked through the local judicial system, respecting customary laws and practices and using local judges and notaries. Under these circumstances, the state could only realistically hope to monitor the system of justice and not to intervene effectively. State actions and rulings were not the product of any set policy, but rather were made on an individual basis.

Besides arbitrating between grieving parties and tightening the system of justice, Venice proceeded vigorously against faction leaders, for their terror tactics created a widespread climate of insecurity. The brazen acts

[67] *Ibid.*, pp. 196–199.
[68] ASCB, *Provvisioni*, vol. 559, ff. 54r–54v, May 9, 1587; *ibid.*, vol. 568, ff. 249v–250v, December 22, 1607; *Lettere Pubbliche*, vol. 54, November 26, 1642, letter to Lorenzo Morosini, Podestà; *Lettere Autografe*, vol. 1235A, ff. 70r–71v; 72r–72v, letters of Agostino Luzzago, Nunzio, April 15 and 19, 1642; ASV, *Senato. DRB*, letter of October 23, 1602.
[69] ASV, *Senato. Rettori*, F. 7, May 2, 1635.
[70] Povolo, "Aspetti e problemi," p. 243.

of the *grandi* and their followers served as an avenue of social control in Brescia. The Ten made strenuous efforts to bring these faction leaders to justice: those convicted of homicide were banished, and their possessions were confiscated and used to pay damages to the victims of their aggression.[71] Punishment, however, was not necessarily a deterrent, for there were many ways of winning one's freedom relatively quickly.[72]

What of the accomplices of the Brescian *grandi*, the members of the city's armed societies and the groups of hired dependents? Venice attempted to check and control factionalism in Brescia and on the mainland not only by prosecuting the leaders of these factions but also by attempting to deprive them (and also rid the state) of their voluntary recruits, the *bravi* and the paid assassins (*sicarii*) who served as their auxiliaries. *Bravi*, *forestieri*, and *vagabondi* are key words in Venetian legislation dealing with the control of homicide during the late sixteenth and early seventeenth centuries.[73] In the eyes of the law it appeared that vagabondage, foreigners (*forestieri*), and violent crime went hand in hand.[74] The state was, in effect, trying to deprive local power holders

---

[71] On September 28, 1578 the Council of Ten ruled: "Che in tutti li Casi d'Homicidii pensati, overo di mala qualità, et attroci per i quali questo Consiglio, overo per il Senato sarà data auttorità a i Rettori Nostri di Bandir di Terre, e Luoghi, e confiscarli Beni, siano li Beni confiscati . . . asignati tutti in feudo alli offesi, cioè alli più prossimo delli morti," in *Leggi criminali del Serenissimo Dominio Veneto in un solo volume raccolte e per pubblico decreto restampate*, ff. 62v and 63r. On banishment see Cozzi, *Repubblica di Venezia e stati italiani*, pp. 82–86.

[72] The Ten applied the tactic of divide and rule: a person banished for *homicidio puro* could gain absolution by killing another person guilty of the same crime. Still further, members of the upper social orders could buy their freedom with money, arms, and men, and/or military service. See E. Basaglia, "Aspetti della giustizia penale nel '700: una critica alla concessione dell'impunità agli uccisori dei banditi," *Atti del Istituto Veneto di Scienze, Lettere ed Arti* 142 (1979–80): 1–16.

[73] The language in a *Parte* of the Council of Ten, dated 1577, April 26, read: "Li molti homicidij, violentie, e altri atrocissimi delitti che ben spesso si intendono esser commessi nel stato nostro, sono causati per la maggior parte, e passano per mano di huomini sicarij, e sanguinolenti forestieri." *Parti e terminazioni prese in vari consigli della Repubblica in materiale criminali* (Venice, Stampatori ducali vari, Sec. XVI–XVIII), No. 60.

[74] On April 15, 1574, for example, the *Parte* of the Council of Ten stated, "tutti gli huomini vagabondi, che non cavano il viver loro, e vestir, o da sue intrade, o da qualche honesto esercitio, e arte, e specialmente quelli che servono per bravi, accompagnando particolari con le armi, debbono essere usciti delle Città, e poi in termine di doi altri giorni di tutto lo stato nostro." *Ibid.* And on December 11, 1604 at St. Marks, "tutti li forestieri di aliena giuriditione, che servono a particolari persone per Bravi, et quelli, che vivono senza essercitio, arte, o proffesione alcuna fuori, che di Bravi, debbano esser usciti fuori delle città, Terre o Castelle dove si trovassero et dentro il termine di altri giorni doi usciti di tutto il Stato Nostro." ASB, *Cancelleria Pretoria. Ducali*, Reg. 41, ff. 106v–108r, January 8, 1605.

from availing themselves of the wide network of collaborators, both within and outside the bounds of local society in two ways: first, by banishing their auxiliaries from the Republic; and second, by punishing them for offering sustenance and refuge to the undesirables.[75] While these laws could potentially affect patronage and clientage, they could not of course respond to the epidemiology of phenomena such as vagabondage and *bravi* and thus to the epidemiology of the wide support system for violence among Brescia's ruling families.

A key to maintaining order in Brescia rested with the resolution of civil litigation among the families with preponderant power and social weight. Often it was the discord that arose from patrimonial disputes that gave rise to riot and civil unrest, as the more powerful families had the ability to mobilize large followings. Thus the Venetian rectors in Brescia devoted much attention to settling disputes which involved the transfer of property and other economic resources before those conflicts mushroomed into physical violence. Preserving order rested as well with the establishment of cooperative ties between Brescia's principal families and Venetian statesmen. Without executive structures in the provinces, this was an important means for the Venetian government to maintain peace and stability. Thus Venetian statesmen would turn at times to influential Brescian noblemen to arbitrate in family disputes and to persuade adversaries to settle their differences through peaceful means. Finally, order and stability depended on more Venetian intervention in the local judicial apparatus. While Venice made significant strides in this area during the late sixteenth and early seventeenth centuries, in the Brescian case the more powerful families could still avail themselves of kinsmen, friends, and clients to shield them from legal proceedings, conviction, and punishment. Family ties, important foundations of local power, proved a formidable challenge to the effective administration of justice.

[75] See ASV, *Consiglio dei Dieci. Parti Comuni*, Reg. 50, ff. 59v–60v, August 18, 1600.

CHAPTER 6

THE BENEFITS OF CIVIC OFFICE

The importance of council membership to the ruling elites of the Venetian subject cities has sparked lively historical discussion over the last two decades. Berengo set the parameters for debate with several fundamental questions concerning the nature and expression of nobility. "Between the seventeenth and eighteenth century public life in the subject cities of the Venetian Terraferma was reduced to little, and council membership at that point had honorific value."[1] Other historians of the Venetian state, on the other hand, have emphasized that council membership conferred advantages that, at least for the sixteenth and seventeenth centuries, extended beyond honorific value.[2] There is no universal answer to this question. The importance of council membership must be evaluated city by city and office by office. In Brescia, a seat on the city council potentially conferred political, fiscal and juridical advantages over the disenfranchised, yet membership was not sought out by all local power holders. Some important families preferred to remain detached from municipal government, sustained by their own social and political ties, antiquity of lineage, wealth, and strong support systems. Moreover, by the late

---

[1] "Tra Sei e Settecento la vita pubblica delle città suddite della terraferma veneta è ridotta a poca cosa, e l'appartenenza al Consiglio civico ha ormai un significato onorifico." Berengo, "Patriziato e nobiltà," p. 500.

[2] Cf. Ventura, *Nobiltà e popolo*, pp. 349–350; Borelli, "Introduzione," *RV*, ed. Tagliaferri, vol. IX, pp. xlvi–xlvii; xlix–xl and G. Borelli, "Patriziato della dominante e patriziati della Terraferma," *Atti del convegno Venezia e la terraferma*, p. 87; Tagliaferri, "Introduzione," *RV. Podestaria e capitanato di Vicenza*, ed. Tagliaferri, vol. VII, pp. xxv–xxviii; S. Zamperetti, "Quadrare il cerchio. Note sulle vicende politiche e sociali a Vicenza negli ultimi decenni del '500," in *I ceti dirigenti in Italia in età moderna e contemporanea*, ed. A. Tagliaferri (Udine: Del Bianco, 1984), pp. 109–111. For Italy, see also the review of historical literature on this subject by Mozzarelli, "Stato, patriziato," pp. 448–451.

sixteenth century the advantages of the more important public responsibilities were not open to all council members.

Brescian councillors at the head of civic government disposed of
multiple residences in city and countryside, rental properties, vast lands
under cultivation, a substantial network of private lending activities,
and full domestic staffs, complete with liveries, private tutors, and
chaplains. Tax records, which were probably conservative, paint a
vivid picture of high living standards; they are sustained by the tax
quotas assigned each household in 1641, again probably conservative,
where 82 percent of the households on the council's matriculation lists
for 1644 had assessments, quantified in coefficients called *denari* (see
appendix 2 for an explanation of tax assessments), which placed their
taxable assets in the upper 17 percent of the urban population. How
these families sustained their fortunes is an important area of inquiry
which not only helps to define their character but also sheds light on
how the aristocratic power system worked. This chapter aims to show
how the governing methods of Brescian councillors served their
economic exigencies. First, they had the opportunity both to invest in
the civic institutions they supervised and to employ the capital in these
repositories for their own private interests. The administration of the
Monti and the hospitals is a good example of this. Second, councillors
also had the opportunity to design and execute grain provisioning and
fiscal policies that directly favored their own economic interests.
Third, as judges and notaries, city councillors ran the local tribunals of
food provisioning, of indirect taxes, and of civil and criminal justice. In
these capacities they enjoyed ample latitude to protect the interests of
family and friends. Ultimately, cooperation among judges, notaries,
and massari (financial officials) in the supervision of urban charities, the
system of grain provisioning, and the fisc constituted the real strength of
the ruling oligarchy. The benefits of office in Brescia probably extended
far beyond the urban magistracies that will be considered in this
chapter. For example, the provincial podestarie that were under the
jurisdiction of city councillors undoubtedly offered strong advantages
as well, and they merit specialized study in themselves.

CHARITY AND PROFIT

The Monti di Pietà

The Christian campaign against usury in fifteenth-century Italy, aimed
particularly at Jews, had encouraged the establishment of lending
institutions under the control of urban authorities. The sermons of

Michele di Aquis and Bernardino da Feltre,[3] which fueled negative sentiment towards usury in Brescia, became linked with the need to assist poor and middle-income families in times of financial hardship. The city founded its first Monte di Pietà in 1489, modeled after the Vicentine Monte established in 1486. The Brescian Monte became the city's primary source of credit, particularly after 1509 when much of the mainland's Jewish population resettled in Venice.[4] In 1587 Brescia established a second Monte, or Monte Nuovo, which operated in conjunction with the Monte Vecchio until 1595 when it was made into a separate body.[5] The Monte Nuovo's range of financial operations was quite diverse from its predecessor, which continued to operate for the most part as a source of credit for the needy. It acted both as a savings bank for depositors and as a credit bank, especially for the city of Brescia. Further, it was more a lending institution for prosperous citizens than a charitable institution for the poor.[6] The Monte Nuovo was not limited to lending capital on pledges of property, but could also circulate capital, borrowing and lending at interest. The Monte Vecchio lent sums of up to three ducats per household on adequate pledges that had to be worth at least one-third more than the sum lent on their security. The officials of the Monte Vecchio were to lend for periods of six months, with no interest; the borrower was only required to pay back the principal. But the Monte Nuovo adopted the system of interest-bearing deposits. In Brescia in the early seventeenth century, it borrowed at 4.5 or 5 percent and lent at 7 percent. The capital it earned was used to pay for its administration. Any surplus was designated for the poor and for other Brescian charities. This new system effected two fundamental changes: first, while the original purpose of the Monte di Pietà was to lend money to the poor, the Monte Nuovo came to serve all ranks of the community; second, the Monte Nuovo served as a

---

3 M. Pegrari, "L'anima e la tasca. Etica economica e bisogni reali nelle attività del Monte di Pietà e del Monte Nuovo nei secoli XV–XVII," *Piazza della Loggia. Una secolare vicenda al centro della storia urbana e civile di Brescia*, ed. I. Gianfranceschi (Brescia: Grafico edizioni, 1986), p. 215.

4 B. Pullan, *Rich and Poor in Renaissance Venice* (Oxford: Basil Blackwell, 1971), p. 475.

5 The Monte Vecchio, together with the Monte delle Biade and the Opera dei Poveri, was governed by seven conservatori elected from the General Council. The procedures are in ASCB, *Provvisioni*, vol. 563, ff. 37v–38r, May 27, 1595.

6 The fundamental work on charitable institutions in Venice and the Veneto for the Renaissance period is Pullan, *Rich and Poor*, and on Brescia in particular, pp. 464–465; 598; 609; 617–618. The Monte di Pietà in Crema suffered from problems that were analogous to those in Brescia. Cf. P. Lanaro Sartori, "Introduzione," *Podestaria e capitanato di Crema, provveditorato di Orzinuovi, provveditorato di Asola*, vol. XIII of *RV*, ed. A. Tagliaferri (Milan: Guiffrè, 1979), pp. xxxix–xli.

means of investment for the wealthy, and gradually the capital of which it disposed grew in value.[7]

City councillors such as Giulio Federici and Francesco Lana were very willing to combine Christian goodwill with opportunities for profit by investing in the city's charities. Liquid capital over the course of the late sixteenth and early seventeenth centuries was losing its purchasing power; interest rates of 5 percent were a small hedge against inflation. Moreover, they bore slightly higher fruits (5 as opposed to 3 percent) than did landed investments during this period. Federici invested 10,000 *lire* in the Monte Nuovo, 12,000 *lire* in the Hospedale Maggiore, and 4,000 *lire* in the Casa di Dio. At rates of 5 percent, he earned 1,300 *lire* annually.[8] Francesco Lana, son of Gasparo, both public deputies for long intervals during the seventeenth century, invested 12,000 *lire* in the Monte Nuovo under very special provisions. The Lana claimed that the annual fruits of this investment, 600 *lire*, were exempt from direct taxes because of a pledge (*promissione*) made in the Brescian Council in 1588.[9]

The Monti, particularly the Monte Nuovo, were more than investment outlets for their caretakers in the city council. A study of their administration illuminates how some councillors disposed of community funds either for private purposes or to repair city finances. Not simply in Brescia but in most early modern European municipalities, it was difficult clearly to demarcate public from private patrimony, as power holders availed themselves of the resources under their supervision. Administration of the Brescian Monti (and the Brescian hospitals, for that matter) is a good case in point. As in several Venetian subject cities, particularly Padua and Verona, the Brescian Monti came under the supervision of city councillors, though the Venetian rectors enjoyed the right to monitor their administration.[10] In 1548, the council had combined the administration of the Monte Vecchio with two other charitable institutions, the Monte delle Biade (grain) and the Opera dei Poveri (poor relief), placing them under the direction of one committee.[11] The rationale behind this decision was to improve and coordinate the administration of these institutions by removing any overlapping jurisdictions. But the result of the reform was to constitute

---

[7]   Pullan, *Rich and Poor*, pp. 582–589.
[8]   ASB, *PE* 1641, B. 7, no. 35.
[9]   ASB, *PE* 1641, B. 4, no. 275.
[10] See Ventura, *Nobiltà e popolo*, pp. 423–424; cf. Pullan, *Rich and Poor*, pp. 581–582.
[11] C. Pasero, "Notizie sul sacro monte delle biade di Brescia e sugli istituti di beneficenza bresciani durante il secolo XVI," *Atti e memorie del III congresso storico lombardo* (Milan: Giuffrè, 1939), p. 397.

well-organized elites, small enough to collaborate in secret and to exploit the capital and goods in these repositories. Henceforward small circles of families which also appeared on the council's executive committee rotated the offices of the conservatori (caretakers of Monte funds) and the massari (officials who accepted and assessed pledges and dispensed funds to lenders). By the early seventeenth century, effective control of the Monte Nuovo resided with a tightly knit group of prominent citizen families, among them the Lana, the Averoldi, the Soncino, the Calino, the Luzzago, the Federici, and the Stella.[12] This explains why the system suffered: the accountants and the conservatori belonged to the same elite of massari that they were supposed to supervise.[13] Conservatori allowed massari to embezzle funds they were theoretically watching over; public deputies and conservatori collaborated in removing gold and capital from the Monte, under the pretense of paying the city's expenditures. Venetian rectors complained that the custodians of the Monti used these resources for their own purposes.[14]

The case of Ludovico Luzzago, the cashier (pagador) for the Monte Nuovo who was accused by the Venetian Sindaci e Inquisitori of embezzlement in 1635 illuminates quite well the kind of cohesion and cooperation among Monte officials. Although the Avogaria di Comun (a Venetian appellate court) found Luzzago innocent, we learn from the testimonies of city councillors who had served as custodians of the Monte that the office of pagador was a difficult one, and that it was "easy" to make accounting errors and to lose track of pledges.[15] Some pagadori, Venetian rectors found in 1644, were guilty of altering their books and transferring deficits to the accounts of bankrupt massari.[16]

From its founding in 1587, then, some custodians of the Monte Nuovo used its funding for personal benefit or for the benefit of friends and kinsmen, accepting pledges of land, grain, or liquid capital in exchange for loans. In 1644 the Venetian Podestà Bernardino Renier reported to the Venetian Senate that the caretakers of the Monte were either kinsmen or clients (*dipendenze*) of those in debt to the institu-

---

[12] In 1595 the Brescian Council complained that the Monti were in disorder because the same men who governed the Monte Nuovo governed the Monte Vecchio, ASCB, *Provvisioni*, vol. 563, ff. 37v–38r, May 27, 1595.

[13] For the Venetian mainland, Pullan, *Rich and Poor*, pp. 610–621.

[14] ASV, *Senato. DRB*, F. 46, letter of Bernardino Renier, Podestà and Girolamo Venier, Capitano, October 29, 1644.

[15] ASV, *Avogaria di Comun*, B. 484 *Penale (nero), fasc.* 15, February–March, 1635. Luzzago, according to the testimony of D. Aurelio Corte, had exercised all the offices of the Monte. *Ibid.*, March 5, 1635.

[16] ASV, *Senato. DRB*, F. 46, letter of Bernardino Renier, Podestà and Girolamo Venier, Capitano, October 29, 1644.

tion.[17] Other reports of Venetian rectors abound in descriptions of abuse on the part of these officials. To summarize, the massari frequently lent out money on fictitious pledges, called *partite abuse* or *partite morte*.[18] They also dispensed sums of money which exceeded the actual value of the pledge, or they handed out more than one claim ticket. In some cases, they allowed the pledge to remain in the hands of the proprietor.[19] Pledges belonging to influential gentlemen were seldom or never sold and interest payments on them lapsed.[20] The books were not balanced regularly, allowing the debts of the massari to go unchecked for lengthy periods of time.[21] By neglecting to sell unredeemed pledges promptly, the massari tied up capital and reduced the sums available for further loans. The massari also engaged in monetary speculation, loaning debased coinage and collecting debts in good currency (*moneta di buona valuta*). Year after year Venetian rectors furnished a similar list of transgressions, which were not particular to Brescia alone.[22] Ventura and Pullan cite numerous examples of abuse in management of the Monti in Brescia and other Venetian subject cities,[23] and Lanaro-Sartori has documented the Veronese case.[24]

The Monte Nuovo suffered serious deficits over the first half of the seventeenth century when councillors began to use its resources to bail the city out of debt, particularly for the arrears on direct taxes.[25]

[17] ASV, *Collegio V (Secreta), Relazioni*, B. 37, April 12, 1645; also in *RV*, ed. Tagliaferri, vol. XI, p. 444.

[18] In 1617 the council ruled that the essatore could not make use of or loan out pledges to either laymen or clergy. Transgressors would lose their salaries, one-third of which would go to those who testified against them. ASCB, *Provvisioni*, vol. 573, f. 202r, January 21. In 1618 the council ruled that the conservatore could not accept money in *censi* without its approval. *Ibid.*, vol. 574, f. 52r, February 3. Often the council tried to impose sanctions on transgressors, which were turned down. For the essatori see *ibid.*, vol. 567, ff. 84r–84v, January 12, 1603.

[19] ASCB, *Provvisioni*, vol. 583, f. 91v, January 1, 1637.

[20] Pullan, *Rich and Poor*, p. 617.

[21] Venetian rectors found that the accounts of the *massari* had not been balanced between 1616 and 1627. ASV, *Senato. DRB*, F. 28, letter of Giovanni Capello, Podestà and Alvise Vallaresso, Capitano, April 8, 1627.

[22] For a recent study of the Brescian Monti as institutions for speculation and abuse, see M. Pegrari, "L'immagine e la realtà. Attività di credito e vicende dei Monti di Pietà bresciani (secoli XV–XIX)," in *Per il quinto centenario del Monte di Pietà di Brescia (1489–1989)*, ed. D. Montanari (Brescia: Officina grafica artigiana Travagliato, 1989), pp. 105–106; 114–120; 151.

[23] Ventura, *Nobiltà e popolo*, pp. 424–428; Pullan, *Rich and Poor*, pp. 604–621.

[24] P. Lanaro Sartori, "L'attività di prestito dei Monti di Pietà in Terraferma veneta: legalità e illeciti tra quattrocento e primo seicento," in *Studi Storici Luigi Simeoni* 33 (1983): 181–189, and especially pp. 161–177.

[25] On the mounting debt of the Monte Nuovo see accounts in ASCB, *Provvisioni*, vol. 580, ff. 33r–34v, February 23, 1630; ASV, *Senato. DRB*, F. 45, letter of B. Renier

Between 1602 and 1615 Brescia borrowed 18,793 ducats:[26] in 1609 to pay the salaries of the district podestarie and vicariates;[27] in 1610 to supplement the costs of sustaining the Casa di Dio;[28] in 1612 to defray the costs of the fair in Brescia;[29] in 1616 to finance the troops offered to Venice and in 1619 to settle the city's accounts for the *sussidio*;[30] in 1620 to purchase grain;[31] in 1631 to cover expenses for sanitary measures during the plague;[32] in 1632 to pay the salaries of the district podestarie;[33] and in 1640 to make payment on a direct tax, the *ordine di banca*. The Venetian Podestà Girolamo Civran recounted to the Senate in April 1640,

> The city on various occasions borrowed significant sums of money from the Monte, without public knowledge or permission, with the promise of repaying the loan at an annual interest rate of 5 per cent. It has never met its obligations, so that the interest due is twice that of the principal borrowed. Added to that, the city has borrowed even more, without any obligation of interest.[34]

By 1644, the city had borrowed a total of 40,681 ducats and accumulated a debt of 30,000 ducats in interest.[35] The following year the total debt rose to 74,000 ducats.[36] Brescia was unable to cover its extraordinary expenses with regular income, let alone replenish the shrinking coffers of the Monte.

Five years earlier, in 1635, the public deputies, with the approval of the General Council, had devised a solution for the reconstitution of the Monte Nuovo: to impose a direct tax (*taglia*) on urban inhabitants on top of their obligatory grain contributions (on these contributions, see

and D. Tiepolo, December 26, 1643; *Senato. Rettori*, F. 20, "Sommario delli provi delli cose contenuto nell'resposto dell' Il.mi et Ecc. mi Sig. Rettori di Brescia alla Scrittura di Sig.ri Ambasc. della Med.ma Città," ff. 64r–66r, 1644, n.d.

26 A. Zanelli, "Le condizioni economiche di Brescia nei primi anni del seicento. A proposito di due recenti pubblicazioni," *Archivio Storico Lombardo* 15 (1937): 252. Zanelli reported the debt as 177,637 *lire planet*. The calculation in ducats is at the rate of 9.45 *lire planet* per Venetian ducat.

27 ASCB, *Actum Deputatorum*, vol. 833, ff. 132v–133r, April 2, 1609.

28 ASCB, *Provvisioni*, vol. 570, f. 60v, April 24, 1610.

29 *Ibid.*, vol. 571, ff. 143v–144r, December 6, 1612.

30 ASCB, *Actum Deputatorum*, vol. 835, ff. 117r–117v, April 20, 1619.

31 *Ibid.*, vol. 835, f. 170v, May 30, 1620.

32 ASCB, *Actum Deputatorum*, vol. 839, f. 63v, April 9, 1631.

33 *Ibid.*, vol. 839, f. 120v, March 18, 1632.

34 ASV, *Collegio V (Secreta) Relazioni*, B. 37, report of Girolamo Civran, Podestà and Vice-Capitano, April 26, 1640; in *RV*, ed. Tagliaferri, vol. XI, pp. 389–390.

35 ASV, *Senato. DRB*, F. 46, letter of B. Renier, Podestà and Girolamo Venier, Capitano, July 8, 1644.

36 ASV, *Collegio V (Secreta), Relazioni*, B. 37, report of Bernardino Renier, Podestà and Vice-Capitano, April 12, 1645; in *RV*, ed. Tagliaferri, vol. XI, pp. 443–444.

the section on grain provisioning below). The supplementary tax was to be at the rate of four *gazzette* per obligatory share of grain, based on the tax register of 1588.[37] The tax was to provide 4,000 Venetian ducats annually towards restoring the principal. The Senate approved the proposal in 1640, to be implemented the following year.[38] In the final analysis, this solution was pernicious for the disenfranchised, who in effect were paying direct taxes, under different guises, because the funds of the Monte Nuovo had been misused. Collection of the *taglia* proved difficult, as a similar tax had been placed on grain in 1637 to help defray the costs of the *estimo*. The second part of the council's solution was to repay outstanding interest to the Monte with the profits of Brescia's annual fair as well as with the funds deriving from the various fines the city collected. This too proved unsuccessful, prompting Venetian rectors to propose that yet another tax, the *taglione*, be levied to restore Monte funds.[39]

Between 1640 and 1653, the city's debts gradually exceeded its assets, making it difficult for its financial caretakers to find new sources of income. The urban tax base showed signs of reaching its fiscal limit: the yields of *taglie* were diminishing. Shrinking fiscal resources were not a simple reflection of conjunctural adversities in the economic sector, but of slipshod tax administration as well. The tax assessments had not been updated for more than half a century, producing multiple inequalities that prevented the city from efficiently tapping fiscal resources. Moreover, tax evasion was a serious problem. In 1652, the city council reported that the *taglia* of four *gazzete* instituted to restore the Monte Nuovo had been unsuccessful.[40] The council attributed the defeat to the imperfections of the tax census, famine, and plague, reasons of some legitimacy. Yet it brushed over the widespread problem of tax evasion. Some families of the ruling class consistently refused to acknowledge their fiscal responsibilities to the community. In particular, the *taglia* on the grain contributions, which specifically hit landowners, invited evasion since it cut into profit margins from the sale of agricultural

[37] ASV, *Senato. Terra*, Reg. 122, ff. 204v–205r, September 7, 1640; ASCB, *Provvisioni*, vol. 582, ff. 111v–113r, February 7, 1635. The massaro's salary was 2.5 percent of the obligatory quota of grain. He risked a penalty of 20 percent if he fell short of his pledge.

[38] ASV, *Senato. Terra*, Reg. 122, ff. 330v–331r, January 3, 1640.

[39] ASV, *Senato. DRB*, F. 46, letter of B. Renier, Podestà and Girolamo Venier, Capitano, September 20, 1644. The public deputies tried to avoid this. See their letter to the city's ambassador in Venice in ASCB, *Actum Deputatorum*, vol. 844, f. 61r, February 24, 1644.

[40] ASCB, *Provvisioni*, vol. 591, ff. 45v–46r, February 24, 1652.

produce. Reticence in providing the required grain in turn reduced the tax yields levied to restore the Monte.[41]

The Monte Nuovo reached a crisis point in 1643 when its coffers were completely empty. One Venetian podestà estimated in his report to the Senate in 1643 that if the Monte Nuovo continued to operate at the current deficit, by 1657 it would be totally annihilated.[42] Part of the capital had gone to pay the city's debts but a great deal was also lost to sensational cases of embezzlement on the part of massari who were attempting to redress their own financial reversals. The most acclaimed instances involved two massari, Camillo Luzzago in 1629, and Lodovico Ghidella in 1631, who were found to have taken 40,458 *lire* and 23,523 *lire*, respectively.[43] The Brescian Council wished to make an example of the two "citizens who have forgotten their birth, against their *patria*." It offered a bounty of 500 *scudi* for each offender, dead or alive; removed them from the council; and would deprive their progeny of office for three generations if they did not restore the capital they had robbed from the Monte.[44] The Venetian Senate also used a firm hand against the massari, banishing Luzzago and Ghidella from Brescia and confiscating their property. However, Ghidella was heavily in debt, and most of his property was in entail, "where nothing can be taken," wrote the podestà. The rectors also pursued the estate of Bernardino Barbisone, another city councillor to whom Ghidella had illicitly transferred 6,000 ducats. Like Ghidella, Barbisone's debts exceeded his assets.[45] Finally, Camillo Luzzago was also seriously in debt. Moreover, some of his property, tied up in entail, was secure against confiscation. The Venetian rectors who were assigned to take stock of Luzzago's assets reported that the massaro had a mere ninety-three *campi bresciani* with a few small houses and a country house which Luzzago co-owned with his brothers. The property was indivisible.[46]

---

41 ASV, *Senato. DRB*, F. 46, letter of B. Renier, Podestà and Girolamo Venier, Capitano, September 20, 1644.
42 ASV, *Senato. Rettori*, F. 20, "Sommario," ff. 65–66r, 1644, n.d.
43 ASV, *Senato. DRB*, F. 41, letter of Girolamo Civran, Podestà, and Nicolò Donato, Capitano, June 8, 1639; ASB, *Cancelleria Pretoria. Ducali*, Reg. 44, ff. 222r–222v, January 10, 1634.
44 ASCB, *Provvisioni*, vol. 582, ff. 155v–156r, September 1, 1635; Ventura, *Nobiltà e popolo*, p. 426, n. 93.
45 ASV, *Senato. DRB*, F. 41, letter of Girolamo Civran, Podestà, and Nicolò Donato, Capitano, June 8, 1639.
46 BNMV, MS. It VII 1155 = (7453), ff. 296r–297v, "Registro di lettere commune-mente scritte in publico dagli Ecc.mi Sig.i Rettori di Brescia," letter from the coadiutore of the praetorian tribunal to the Senate, April 19, 1645. On the precautions massari took to protect their property, see Pullan, *Rich and Poor*, p. 613.

From these properties Luzzago had an income of 1,000 *lire*, after expenses and direct taxes, inadequate to cover his debt to the Monte. Luzzago and Ghidella had apparently robbed the coffers of the Monte Nuovo to repair their personal fortunes. There was a long list of indebted custodians of the Monte during the first half of the seventeenth century.[47] Some had diverted capital into their own pockets, into those of kinsmen, or of those to whom they were beholden. Others, such as Nicolò Poncharale, were the victims of circumstances: it was difficult, for example, to collect pledges during and immediately after the plague.[48] Giovanni Battista Bona left his office in 1620 with a debt of 3,000 *lire*;[49] Stefano Baitelli with 6,000 *lire* in 1618; Scipione Ugone with 2,440 *lire planet* in 1620;[50] Nicolò Poncharale with 2,970 *lire* in 1628;[51] and the list continues in the council's deliberations throughout the period.

For almost every year in the first half of the seventeenth century the massari left their offices with debts in hand. Because of the high risk factor, it was difficult to convince more scrupulous councillors to take on the duty of collecting pledges to the Monte.[52] In 1594 the conservatori of the Monte Nuovo made a motion in council to constrain members to accept the position of massaro on penalty of a 100 *lire* fine. The proposal was overwhelmingly turned down, by 205 votes to 30.[53] As a further incentive to accept this responsibility, the council made the massaro's salary more substantial: 600 *lire* the first year, and 400 the second, yet the official was required to keep the pledges at his own risk and to provide a security deposit of 6,000 ducats.[54] The council also made efforts to discipline delinquent massari. Giovanni Battista Bocca, for example, who left his office in 1618 with a 1,000 *lire* debt to the Monte Vecchio, lost his salary, and the council launched criminal proceedings against him[55] In sum, there were efforts within

[47] For a list of indebted massari for the late sixteenth and early seventeenth centuries, see ASCB, *Provvisioni*, vol. 569, ff. 135v–137v, January 16, 1609.

[48] Poncharale was given the chance to make up for his deficit because after the plague pledges had to be sold at half price. Moreover, there was much confusion. ASCB, *Provvisioni*, vol. 582, f. 28r, March 20, 1634.

[49] ASCB, *Actum Deputatorum*, vol. 835, f. 142r., January 3, 1620.

[50] ASCB, *Provvisioni*, vol. 578, f. 18r, January 14, 1626.

[51] *Ibid.*, vol. 582, f. 28r, March 20, 1634.

[52] It was difficult to find assessors for the pledges, *ibid.*, vol. 569, f. 146r, February 5, 1609; or pagadori, *ibid.*, vol. 582, f. 129v, March 6, 1635.

[53] ASCB, *Provvisioni*, vol. 562, ff. 214r–214v, December 22, 1594. In the same meeting councillors voted that massari must keep pledges at their own risk and guarantee as security 6,000 ducats of their own resources.

[54] *Ibid.*

[55] ASCB, *Actum Deputatorum*, vol. 836, ff. 6v–7r, October 31, 1620.

the municipal body to monitor good governing practices; the initiative to supervise the Monte did not just emanate from the Venetian Signoria.

The disorder of the Brescian Monte Nuovo became a festering grievance for the upper ranks of the non-privileged citizens during the first half of the seventeenth century. Protest issued in part from the public deputies' attempt to compensate for the improper use of Monte funds by increasing the number of *taglie*, a policy that particularly hit the upper strata of the non-privileged citizenry. Some protest was voiced at the fact that capital in the Monte was being siphoned off. Several citizens who had deposited large assets in this credit bank held dim prospects of recovering their investments and protested.[56] No doubt the prospects of losing invested capital were not limited to the Monte Nuovo, but extended to other charitable institutions managed by city councillors as well. Thus the capital of Brescian protesters such as Gabriel Arighini, who placed money in the Pii Luoghi and the Hospedale degli Incurabili, may have been dissipated by similar acts of fraud and embezzlement.[57] Moreover, since city councillors had a hand in the administration of most of Brescia's charities, they followed the practice of "robbing Peter to pay Paul." For example, to remedy the Casa di Dio's serious deficit in 1596, the council borrowed from the Monte Vecchio;[58] in 1610 the Monte Nuovo bailed the Casa out of debt.

The Venetian Senate responded to these protests from Venetian rectors and Brescian citizens against maladministration of the Monte Nuovo by consistently urging the former to make the massari collect outstanding debts and to punish delinquency with stiff fines ranging around 10 percent of the capital due for the custodians of the Monte and around 15 percent for the city itself.[59] It was not, however, simply a two-way dialectic between state and periphery: groups of Brescian councillors also tried to monitor the government of the Monte,

---

[56] To cite some examples, the tax records of Francesco Albani in 1632 and 1660 both listed a deposit of 11,400 *lire planet*, ASCB, *Polizze d'estimo:* Albani; Odasio Odasi had deposited 2,000 *lire planet*, *ibid.*, Odasio (1659); that of Giovanni Battista Lurano, 30,129 *lire planet*, ASB, *PE* (1641), B. 2, no. 115; that of Ippolito Buzzone, 818 *lire planet*, *ibid.*, B. 12, no. 641; and that of Livio Metello 600 *lire planet*, *ibid.*, B. 6, no. 202.

[57] ASCB, *Polizze d'estimo:* Arighini (1653).

[58] ASCB, *Provvisioni*, vol. 563, ff. 121r–121v, August 9, 1596.

[59] ASB, *Cancelleria Pretoria. Ducali*, Reg. 43, ff. 218v–219r, October 19, 1627; *ibid.*, Reg. 44, ff. 218r–219v, March 6, 1635; *ibid.*, Reg. 45, f. 29v, June 11, 1639; *ibid.*, Reg. 46, f. 82v, February 16, 1643; ASV, *Senato. Terra*, Reg. 122, ff. 330v–331r, January 3, 1640 *more veneto*.

proposing stern penalties for malfeasance that were sometimes but not always defeated in the council. Nonetheless, some councillors continued to use public patrimony for private purposes. The Brescian Monte Nuovo, the domain of small oligarchic circles that monopolized the major civic magistracies, continued to be the object of speculation. In 1644 malgovernment sparked criticism and protest from citizens who wished to break the monopoly of oligarchic rule and serve in public offices. Mismanagement of the Monti, as we shall see in the next chapter, was one of the key targets in this protest movement.

Grain provisioning

Control over other urban institutions besides the Monte Vecchio and the Monte Nuovo afforded city councillors the opportunity to protect and advance their own private economic interests. In no other sphere is this more evident perhaps than in the system of grain provisioning, which touched the very basis of councillors' fortunes. It revolved around a very dynamic set of relationships between the Brescian Council, which represented propertied citizens, and the representatives of the Territorio (the rural communities subject to the city), both of whom exerted pressure on the capital city to endorse tax policies which would favor their respective interests; and between Brescian landed elites, who aimed as far as possible to sell the grain from their estates where demand was high and prices were best, and the state, concerned that Brescia receive an adequate supply of grain at low prices.

Two opposing economic philosophies shaped the system of grain provisioning in Brescia: protectionism and free trade. On the one hand, Venice wanted to ensure that an adequate supply of grain was reaching its subject cities and thus enjoined the council elites to regulate trade in their respective areas. On the other hand, however, the protective measures of the capital city conflicted with the economic interests of urban authorities, landed elites who wanted a free market. Hence, the system of grain provisioning in urban centers such as Brescia was in part a tug-of-war between the Venetian officials who tried to ensure that the grain did not leave the districts of the subject city, and local landed proprietors, heavily represented in the municipal council, who preferred to sell their grain outside the Venetian state at more advantageous prices. Yet there was a further dimension to the dynamics between state and periphery: it was the responsibility of city councillors to ensure that Brescia be well stocked with low-priced grain, a task that could not be neglected and that required a kind of selective protectionism that would not compromise their own economic interests.

Conditions east of the Mincio, where the Venetians themselves owned extensive properties, were different from those in the Lombard cities of Brescia, Bergamo, and Crema.[60] The provinces nearest Venice were compelled to furnish the capital with grain. A free market was out of the question, as the Venetian Signoria was concerned to keep reasonable food prices in the *Dominante*.[61] The more distant Lombard cities, on the other hand, remained outside the immediate sphere of Venetian economic control and thus were not required to supply grain to the *Dominante*. Instead, they were obliged to provide a fixed quota biannually to their own inhabitants. For Brescia, this quota was 70,000 *somme* (one *somma* is equal to 145.92 liters, dry weight) until 1548, when it was increased to 80,000 *somme*. Landowners were assigned shares of this overall quota that were calculated on the basis of their individual tax assessments (*estimi*). For example, in 1542, for every 100 ducats of assessed income, each household had to contribute sixteen *somme*. Bergamo, on the other hand, was an exception to the model practiced west of the Mincio. Because the region was incapable of producing ample grain supplies to meet the city's needs for more than one-third of the year, it was granted liberty of trade and drew most of its supply from the Milanese.[62]

The task of ensuring adequate grain supplies for the city of Brescia was not simple: the Venetians were caught time and again between the contradictory demands of customary practices and state regulations. In order to ensure a high profit margin, city councillors created dearth by lax enforcement of the obligatory grain quotas. Population trends in Brescia certainly did not warrant a reduction of grain provisions: demographic numbers had steadily risen since the plague of 1576. Moreover, subsistence crises had stricken the region at regular intervals between 1590 and 1610. Nonetheless, those whose incomes rested heavily on agriculture resisted the protective measures of the *Dominate*, circumventing initiatives by Venetian rectors to have grain brought into

---

[60] See Ventura, *Nobiltà e popolo*, pp. 375–405.

[61] On the Venetian system of grain provisioning, see L. Dal Pane, "La politica annonaria di Venezia," *Giornale degli economisti e annali di economia*, N.S. 5 (1946): 335–338; G. Zalin, "La politica annonaria veneta tra conservazione e libertà (1744–1797)," *Rivista di Storia dell'Agricoltura. Atti del Congresso Nazionale di Storia dell'Agricoltura*, Milan, 7–9 May 1971, vol. II, pp. 391–423; also published in *Economia e Storia* 2 (1972): 207–229; R. Molesti, "Il problema del commercio dei grani nell'economia veneta del '700," *Studi Economici e Sociali* 7 (1972): 165–174. For the Bresciano, G. Zalin, "Il mercato granario di Desenzano," *Il Lago di Garda: Storia di una comunità lacunale* (Salò: Ateneo di Salò, 1969), pp. 117–145; A. De Maddalena, *Prezzi e aspetti di mercato in Milano durante il secolo XVI* (Milan: Malfasi, 1950), which compares the institutions of grain provisioning in Brescia and Milan.

[62] Ventura, *Nobiltà e popolo*, p. 382.

the city and sold in the public market (instead of being hoarded in private granaries) and to supervise public warehouses. The abbate, as head of the Brescian Council, together with the two anziani, determined the price of grain every Saturday morning.[63] They communicated the sum to the Victuals Tribunal, whose two judges in turn fixed the price of bread. These grain prices were supposed to be below those outside the city.[64] Hence the landowners' reluctance to consign their surplus to the city.

Without a detailed survey of agricultural yields in the Territorio – the rural areas directly subject to the city, including the fertile plains – it is difficult to know how frequently production actually met local demand. In periods of normal harvests, contemporaries furnished positive estimations of the lower plains' productive capacity. The Podestà Giovanni Da Lezze assured the Senate in 1610 that the province was "well stocked with all that one could desire."[65] Similarly, the Brescian envoy to Venice Lorenzo Averoldi informed the government that under normal circumstances the lower plains could provide the entire province with adequate grain supplies.[66] That would have included the city, which demanded between 70,000 and 80,000 *somme* per year; the valleys, where the terrain permitted only limited grain cultivation; and the Riviera di Salò, which was perennially in want of cereals.[67] Further yet, the Venetian Capitano Nicolò Donato lauded the fertility of the plains a decade after the plague of 1630: "First, I reviewed the plains of the Territorio, which for the quality of the land, for the salubrity of the air, for the irrigation system, and for good technology, is very fertile and abundant in victuals."[68]

Naturally these descriptions referred to agricultural production during optimal conditions. In his survey of Italian agriculture De Maddalena concludes that the Bresciano maintained only a modest cereal production in the sixteenth and seventeenth centuries.[69] In

---

[63] *Statuti civili della magnifica città di Brescia. Volgarizzati* (Brescia: Pietro Vescovo, 1776), p. 32.

[64] *Raccolta di privilegi, ducali, giudizi, terminazioni e decreti pubblici . . . concernenti la città di Brescia* (Brescia: Tip. G. B. Bossino, 1732), p. 275.

[65] "Abbondante di tutte quelle cose che si possino desiderar." Report of Giovanni Da Lezze, Podestà, December 27, 1610, in *RV*, ed. Tagliaferri, vol. XI, p. 199.

[66] Pasero, "Introduzione," *Il catastico Da Lezze*, pp. 66; 66, n. 194.

[67] Zalin, "Il mercato granario in Desenzano nei secoli XVI e XVII," p. 34.

[68] "In primo grado reviddi la pianura del territorio, che per la qualità del terreno, per la salubrità dell'aria, per l'irrigationi dell'acqua et per la cognitione di buona coltura che hanno quelle genti, è fertilissimo et abbondante de viveri." Report of Nicolò Donato, Capitano, September 22, 1640, in *RV*, ed. Tagliaferri, vol. XI, p. 407.

[69] De Maddalena, "Mondo rurale," pp. 414–415.

Lombardy, Emilia, and the Veneto the ratio of seed planted to yields oscillated between 1:5 and 1:6. In the seventeenth century the ratio dropped to between 1:4 and 1:5.[70] Further, we know from studies of the early modern European agrarian economy that conditions were not always ideal. Inclement weather, drought, limited technology, and soil exhaustion, among other problems, ruined harvests and subjected the population to periodic subsistence crises. This was certainly true of the Bresciano, which suffered serious grain shortages once or even twice a decade: in 1590 to 1591, in 1610,[71] again in 1620 to 1621, in 1628 preceding the plague, and then in 1648. The Venetian Podestà Lorenzo Capello worriedly alerted the Senate in 1621: "the last two harvests have been so poor that most of the territory has suffered great famine, particularly the valleys, which are nourished for the most part on millet."[72]

The adequate provisioning of grain supplies on the mainland was a constant preoccupation of Venetian rectors. Especially in the middle and later decades of the sixteenth century, with a swollen population, Venice favored the cultivation of cereals above all else,[73] a preference shared by large landed proprietors, which in the long run exhausted the soil.[74] Although there was much discussion about improving agricultural methods in the Cinquecento, owing to a decline in yields, there seem to have been no technological watersheds either in the Venetian territories[75] or on the Italian peninsula as a whole.[76] The new principles of agriculture proposed by two of the sixteenth century's most celebrated agronomists, Agostino Gallo and Nicolò Tarello, both Brescians, were more theoretical discussions than practical maxims.[77] Even in neighboring Lombardy, where agrarian methods were among

---

[70] A. De Maddalena, "L'Europa rurale (1500–1750)," in *Storia economica di Europa*, ed. C. Cipolla (Turin: UTET, 1979), vol. II, p. 266.

[71] The Brescian city council reported a rise in the cost of living. ASCB, *Provvisioni*, vol. 570, ff. 111v–112r, August 14, 1610.

[72] "È però stata così cattiva la staggione delli due raccolti passati, che la maggior parte del medesimo territorio ha patito grandissima carestia et le Valli in particolare, che per il più si nutriscono di migli." Report of Lorenzo Capello, Capitano, May 7, 1621, in *RV*, ed. Tagliaferri, vol. XI, p. 263.

[73] See A. Ventura, "Considerazioni sull'agricoltura veneta e sulla accumulazione originaria del capitale nei secoli XVI e XVII," *SS* 9 (1968): 674; 692.

[74] De Maddalena, "Mondo rurale," pp. 414–415.

[75] D. Beltrami, *Saggio di storia dell'agricoltura nella Repubblica di Venezia durante l'età moderna* (Venice–Rome: Istituto per la Collaborazione Culturale, 1955). See also Woolf, "Venice and the Terraferma," pp. 175–203.

[76] De Maddalena, "Mondo rurale," pp. 349–426.

[77] *Ibid.*, pp. 414–415.

the most technologically advanced in Europe, subsistence was not guaranteed in the late sixteenth and seventeenth centuries.[78]

It was thus no easy task for Venice to balance arguments of supply and demand when the city's population levels were in dramatic flux. The perennial argument of city officials, especially after an epidemic, was that a decline in population had reduced the demand for grain. While in fact this was true, the argument did not take into account demographic recuperation, nor periodic subsistence crises. Venetian rectors in Brescia were mindful of the need to accumulate grain supplies in times of abundance for times of famine.

Negotiations on the question of grain supplies between city councillors, Venetian rectors, and the Senate became particularly urgent in the early 1630s. Conjunctural adversities interrupted the steady flow of grain supplies to the city: the plague had decimated a significant portion of the rural work force, and the region was threatened by bad harvests.[79] According to contemporary assessments, Brescia itself had suffered heavy losses due to the plague,[80] a development which reduced its demand for cereals. The Brescian chronicler Pluda noted in his diary in 1634 that grain prices were disadvantageous for citizens who relied upon them for income.[81] Though it would stand to reason that a fall in both rural production and urban demand would balance itself out, the Venetian rectors proceeded cautiously. While the Podestà Francesco Zen confirmed Brescia's heavy demographic losses to the Senate in 1630, he also pointed out that numbers in the city were subject to flux. The demand for cereals could be greater than expected. Zen pointed out that Brescia had fed 6,000 troops with its grain supplies that year. He also mentioned that there were large numbers of country people in the city, exchanging goods or appearing before the tribunals, and there were many foreigners and other travelers. Zen maintained that it was better to have a surplus of grain supplies in the city than face a shortage and argued for regulations to ensure this.[82]

Brescian landed proprietors, on the other hand, argued strongly for a free market during the post-plague years. In April 1633 the city sent a delegation to Venice to inform the Senate that the grain in its

[78]   Sella, *L'economia lombarda*, pp. 55–59.
[79]   Report of Angelo Contarini, Podestà and Vice-Capitano, 1632, *RV*, ed. Tagliaferri, vol. XI, p. 361.
[80]   On the population of Brescia, cf. Pasero, "Dati statistici," pp. 71–97; K. J. Beloch, "Bevölkerungsgeschichte der Republik Venedig," *Jahrbuchern fur National Ökonomie und Statistik* (Jena: G. Fischer, 1899), p. 20.
[81]   "Diari dei Pluda," *Le cronache bresciane*, ed. P. Guerrini, vol. II, pp. 360; 375.
[82]   ASV, *Collegio V (Secreta), Relazioni*, B. 37, report of Francesco Zen, Podestà and Vice-Capitano, February 1630; in *RV*, ed. Tagliaferri, vol. XI, pp. 337–339.

warehouses was sufficient. Brescian representatives argued that reduced demand did not warrant the pre-plague obligatory grain quota and that citizens should have the liberty of selling their surplus on a free market. They also objected to Venetian limitations on the export of grain from community to community within the Bresciano, arguing that productivity levels in the Territorio could supply the population with grain supplies for two or three years. If surplus grain could not be sold, they argued, rural inhabitants would come to financial harm.[83] Venetian rectors responded firmly, however, that local officials compiled their reports with something less than objectivity. The Podestà Vicenzo Gussoni wrote to the Venetian Senate in 1633:

> they know quite well how to explain things to their own advantage . . . these citizens are interested in keeping grain prices high, that grain be rather scarce rather than abundant, and one sees the effects. During the six months that I have been here I have seen an abundance of grain in the Territorio, where grain prices decline daily, but the public deputies who are obliged to regulate the price of grain for bread, have not once altered these prices accordingly.[84]

Indeed, Venetian rectors were compelled to monitor record-keeping in the city, because descriptions of grain supplies from council officials often conflicted with those of state representatives.

The distribution of the obligatory grain quotas, a form of direct taxation, was another problem for Venetian rectors. Brescian councillors had the possibility of manipulating the *estimo* so that their grain obligations did not necessarily reflect their contributive capacity. To begin with, the *estimi* were not updated with any regularity. The tactic of delaying their renewals, in effect postponing new tax assessments, signified that those households that had made new landed acquisitions would enjoy a lengthy period of tax immunity. Meanwhile original proprietors were obliged to supply a quantity of grain that was based on assets that had been alientated. The inequalities of this system ultimately reduced the quantity of grain the city was able to collect.

City councillors' design of the *estimo* also aimed to unload a heavy share of the burden of obligatory grain contributions on the residents of the Territorio.[85] The portion of 9,000 *somme* the Territorio was required to supply to Brescia was consistent over the second half of the

---

[83] ASCB, *Actum Deputatorum*, vol. 839, f. 195r, April 17, 1633; on this theme see also ASCB, *Lettere Autografe*, vol. 1156, letter of the nunzio to the public deputies, November 30, 1630; *Lettere Pubbliche*, vol. 54, unsigned letter to Ambassador in Venice, September 20, 1642.

[84] ASV, *Senato. DRB*, F. 35, March 15, 1633.

[85] See Ferraro, "Proprietà terriera," pp. 159–182.

sixteenth century, despite changes in the distribution of property. Lawyers and representatives for the rural communities perennially complained to Venice over the unequal fiscal burden, over the constraint to supply Brescia with grain at below market prices, and over the fact that local power holders exported grain from their communities, leaving others to supply the obligatory quotas to the city.[86] Propertied citizens were the major beneficiaries of these practices.[87] Citizens who had acquired land on a big scale throughout the sixteenth century were conveniently exempt both from grain contributions and from other forms of direct taxation through the delayed tax assessments. Brescian citizens had acquired two-thirds of the property in the Territorio over the course of the fifteenth to early seventeenth centuries, yet their tax quotas did not necessarily reflect the weight of their landed acquisitions. Once the urban *estimi* were renewed, in 1588 and subsequently in the 1640s, it was the council elites in Brescia that actually conducted the tax assessments for those registered in the urban *estimo* and assigned the tax quotas, an occasion to favor members of their own class.

There were also serious problems concerning the collection of obligatory grain contributions. Procedures were under the control of the public deputies, who in turn appointed two judges from the council to handle all legal affairs pertaining to the *annona*, such as delinquent grain contributions, smuggling, illegal prices, etc. A large corps of other officials elected from the Brescian Council assisted the public deputies and the two judges: a vicar and a grain supervisor (granarolo); a chancellor with three notaries who recorded all incoming grain contributions; seven deputies charged with controlling the quality of the grain brought into the city; and two vicars for the supervision of the grinding of grain, together with two notaries, posted at the city gates to weigh the incoming grain.[88] As city councillors controlled every avenue of grain provisioning in the city, they had every opportunity to allow friends and kin to avoid paying their required quotas.[89] The officials at the city gates often marked down fictitious contributions, or recorded a larger quantity of grain than was actually introduced, or accepted low-

[86] ASV, *Consiglio dei Dieci. LCRB*, B. 26, Nos. 175–176, letter of Giovanni Corner, Podestà and Vice-Capitano, September 19, 1603.
[87] The city council discussed a measure to prevent the export of grain from the Territorio. ASCB, *Provvisioni*, vol. 563, ff. 124r–124v, September 30, 1596.
[88] Da Lezze, *Il catastico Da Lezze*, vol. I, pp. 275–353.
[89] The city council and the podestà attempted to regulate this. ASCB, *Provvisioni*, vol. 571, ff. 261v–263r, June 5, 1613.

quality grain and allowed substitutions.[90] At times large landed proprietors avoided shipping their quota of grain into the city by simply paying a fine, since the profits from the sale of grain more than compensated for the penalty.[91] Venetian officials tried to discourage this practice by waiving fines and insisting on the requisitions.

Some local authorities neglected at times to discipline those who failed to consign grain. Notaries inscribed in the city council concealed records, making it difficult to trace offenders; massari charged with collecting fines made special concessions to friends, falsifying records;[92] judges in the Victuals Tribunal also did favors for friends and kinsmen, absolving offenders without consulting the Venetian rectors.[93] Yet as with the Monte Nuovo, so with grain provisioning, regulation of disorders did not come exclusively from the state. In January 1607, for example, the Brescian Council made careful provisions to monitor the city's granaroli;[94] and in 1613 the city council voted in new regulations against the disorders in collecting and recording grain contributions.[95]

Neglect in disciplining tax evaders seriously damaged city revenues, since part of Brescia's income derived from the penalty fees of those who failed to consign grain. Thus Venetian governors in Brescia insisted on managing these fines. In the third and fourth decades of the seventeenth century city councillors attempted to win control over these revenues, reminding the Venetian Senate of the privilege (which state representatives had apparently forgotten for convenience's sake more than a century before) that made penalties and fines their jurisdiction. The podestà on the one hand and Brescian councillors on the other made their points of view known to Venice on this issue. The Brescian Nunzio Agostino Luzzago cited examples of other mainland cities to buttress his arguments, noting that in Verona the podestà did not handle penalties for delinquent grain contributions. There was a similar provision for Crema, but Venetian rectors did not honor it; this

---

[90] The notaries who recorded grain contributions had a monthly salary of 18–21 *lire* in 1613. *Ibid.*, vol. 571, ff. 262v–263r, June 5, 1613.
[91] Report of Bartolomeo Gradenigo, August 3, 1635, in *RV*, ed. Tagliaferri, vol. XI, p. 368.
[92] ASCB, *Provvisioni*, vol. 569, ff. 144r–145r, February 5, 1609. Provides a list of the illicit activities of the massari.
[93] BMCV, *Archivio Donà delle Rose*, No. 17, f. 155, report of the Venetian Podestà Leonardo Donà, 1579.
[94] ASCB, vol. 568, ff. 219v–221r, June 16, 1607.
[95] ASCB, *Provvisioni*, vol. 571, ff. 261r–263r, June 5, 1613.

was the case in Brescia as well.[96] Venetian rectors wished to employ the fines to restore the ailing Monte Nuovo, while city councillors claimed that the capital – if collected – was designated for sanitary measures and for the poor.

Smuggling was another important problem related to the city's grain provisioning. The harvests that never reached Brescia were smuggled out of the Territorio along two main thoroughfares: the lakes and the mountains of the Riva di Trento, which carried the grain into the Alto Adige; and Desenzano, one of the largest markets for contraband goods in the Venetian state. Other grain left the Territorio through the Veronese.[97] It was difficult for Venetian officials to control the flow of contraband, for the smugglers were protected by the powerful. For example, in 1591, following a year of bad harvests and extreme grain shortages, the Venetian rectors complained to the Council of Ten that the Martinengo were harboring grain smugglers on their lands. The properties of this important family, bordering the Duchy of Milan and the Cremonese, were strategically difficult to monitor.[98] Moreover, the Martinengo claimed superior jurisdictions over this territory, founded on concessions the della Scala had granted their ancestors. Thus the landed estate of Urago and Barco had grain dealings with the Milanese and the Cremonese, respectively.[99] Other powerful families were engaged in the same activities, notably the Porcellaga, the Avogadro,[100] and the Schilini.[101]

The financial gain from smuggling made it particularly difficult for the Venetian state to control. In fact, one of the most common criminal charges reported to the Ten during this period was the murder of Venetian police sent out to check the flow of contraband. It was

---

[96] ASV, *Senato. DRB*, F. 35, letter of Vicenzo Gussoni, Podestà, March 14, 1633; for Brescian negotiations with Venice over grain contributions and over penalties for delinquent contributions, ASCB, *Lettere Autografe*, vol. 1159, letters of the Nunzio Galeazzo Barbisone to the public deputies, May 10, June 28, 1633; *ibid.*, vol. 1163, letter of Brescian Ambassadors, May 17, 1633; letter of the Nunzio Agostino Luzzago, March 21, 1643; ASB, *Cancelleria Pretoria. Ducali*, Reg. 46, f. 63r, February 22, 1643.

[97] On grain smuggling, ASV, *Senato. DRB*, F. 17, letter of Giustinian Badoer, Capitano, September 16, 1617; ASV, *Collegio V (Secreta), Relazioni*, B. 37, report of Agostino Bembo, Podestà, February 26, 1631, in *RV*, ed. Tagliaferri, vol. XI, p. 342; ASV, *Senato. Terra, Reg.* 125, ff. 126v–127r, July 28, 1642.

[98] Capretti, *Mezzo secolo*, p. 427.

[99] ASV, *Consiglio dei Dieci. Lettere dei Rettori di Brescia ai Capi*, B. 25, No. 32, letter of Thomaso Morosini, Podestà, to the Ten, September 14, 1591.

[100] Capretti, *Mezzo secolo*, p. 391.

[101] ASV, *Consiglio dei Dieci. LCRB*, B. 26, Nos. 175–176, letter of Giovanni Corner, Podestà and Vice-Capitano, to the Ten, September 19, 1603.

difficult for these officials to penetrate some of the landed estates of the Bresciano, where nobles enjoyed powerful support systems. For example, some of the minor officials employed by the Venetian government to control contraband activities also seem to have had strong financial incentives to act in collusion with smugglers and with large landowners. The Venetians kept armed boats on Lake Garda to thwart the illicit transport of grain, but local officials overlooked infractions of the law in exchange for bribes, and offenders were able to build grain warehouses outside the province of Brescia.[102]

The Venetian judicial system was not adequately prepared to curb the bands of smugglers that were sponsored by large, prestigious *case*. The Martinengo, the Porcellaga, and the Chizzola, to name a few, were fortified by wealth, by the prestige of their family names, and by a strong sense of local autonomy. They enjoyed the support of a large network of clients, drawn both from the local community and from the bands of outlaws and vagabonds that traveled from regional state to regional state during this period. As we have seen in the section on public order, the *signori* employed salaried guards who lived under their command, and independent mercenaries to defend their interests.[103] The Venetians had difficulty controlling these bands for several reasons. First, they lacked adequate arms and men to cover so vast a territory. Second, the powerful families, using retainers and fear tactics, held strong control over the villages and the peasantry, making it difficult for the Venetian rectors to gather testimonies. Finally, the geographical configuration of the Bresciano – mountains in the north and northeast – served as an ideal refuge for smugglers. Since many large landed estates bordered neighboring states, it was easy for the smugglers employed by landed proprietors to cross over state boundaries and escape punishment.

When it came to the important provincial families, the Venetian administration of justice was ambivalent. On the one hand, the noble had committed a legal transgression, but on the other he was linked to the local power structure, to the financial and military resources of the province, and to important contacts with neighboring Italian states.[104] Thus Venetian justice could be rather ambiguous and sometimes even accommodating. The offender had the option of bargaining with the state, either buying his freedom or furnishing the Republic with arms

[102] ASV, *Senato. DRB*, F. 23, letter of Benetto Zorzi, Capitano, October 14, 1622; see Ventura, *Nobiltà e popolo*, pp. 390–391.
[103] P. Molmenti, *I banditi della Repubblica veneta* (Florence: R. Bemporad and Figlio, 1898), pp. 171–172, n. 2.
[104] Molmenti, *I banditi*, pp. 160–161.

and men. Thus the same legal force that supposedly controlled contraband would then grant asylum to important provincials.

While city councillors as large landed proprietors were interested in selling their grain outside the city, to maintain civil order they were also compelled to procure grain for the urban center at below market prices. There were no major food uprisings in Brescia during this period, a sign that the strategies local authorities devised to meet this responsibility, if not equitable by present standards, were relatively effective. One such strategy was to proceed against the exempt in times of famine. In 1600 the Brescian Council sent two envoys to Venice to challenge the exemption Giulio Martinengo had received in 1588 for grain contributions. The Senate voted in the city's favor.[105] Another strategy, which has already been reviewed above, was to place as much of the burden of supplying grain to the city's warehouses as possible on inhabitants registered in the Territorio's *estimo*. A final strategy hinged on the large network of devotional associations in the city that pledged victuals to the needy. Reluctant to leave these associations, which often disposed of large assets, in the hands of the ordinary citizens, the Brescian Council established a supervisorial committee from within its ranks, the deputati alle discipline, to prompt them to meet their social responsibilities. For example, the Disciplina di San Mathia, a confraternity founded in the sixteenth century, had made the commitment of supplying grain to the poor in its section of the city and of having a mass said daily. In 1614 it came under the investigation of the Deputati alle Discipline Aloisio Guainari and Girardo Averoldo, who had discovered that between 1554 and 1614 the quota of grain supplied by this confraternity had progressively diminished. Until 1570 the Disciplina had supplied twenty to twenty-five *somme* of grain annually in three distributions. Between 1570 and 1600 it consigned fifteen *somme*, and between 1600 and 1614 it made only one rather than the promised three annual apportionments. It is entirely plausible that the smaller distributions were a reflection of the agrarian crises that troubled the region during these years. Nonetheless, when the deputati alle discipline reviewed the declarations of taxable assets of the Disciplina for the last half of the sixteenth century and determined that the association was fully capable of meeting its duties, they obliged it to meet a quota of twenty *somme* annually henceforward.[106]

The charities supervised by the city councillors had been erected for pious purposes, yet they could also be manipulated to the advantage of

[105] ASV, *Senato. Terra*, Reg. 70, f. 57r, July 18, 1600.
[106] ASCB, *Actum Deputatorum*, vol. 834, ff. 161r–162v, December 12, 1614.

their supervisors. The Monte delle Biade, founded in 1505 to sell grain to the needy at subsidized prices in times of famine, appears to be a case in point.[107] Few documents are available to describe this Monte's operations. Moreover, after 1595 the institution lost its autonomy, coming under the auspices of the Monte Vecchio. Hence, we are left without a complete picture of its administration. Pasero's study of its operations during the sixteenth century, however, is particularly illuminating. The entire administration of the Monte delle Biade was in the hands of appointed members of the city council, who were free to buy and sell grain as they chose. The council imposed a *taglia* to raise the initial capital to establish the Monte delle Biade.[108] Concerned that those without genuine need might exploit free handouts, it then established a committee to determine whether applicants were indeed worthy of borrowing grain, and to supervise the Monte's transactions. The Monte would consign grain to borrowers on condition that the loan be repaid (sometimes with and sometimes without interest) the following year; the surplus earned would be sold to the poor at below market price. This system was designed to protect the needy from borrowing grain from private speculators who asked up to 12 percent interest. The results, however, were negative: first, because the poor were usually incapable of repaying their debts; second, because the loans were not necessarily made to the indigent. Pasero's evidence suggests that city councillors were beginning to use the Monte delle Biade for personal speculation around 1548. The Conservatore Giovanni Battista Portulaca, with the authorization of the council, consigned all the millet in the Monte to Gerolamo Baitelli, Guerrerio Maggio, and Giacomo Chizzola – not the indigent, but rather members of illustrious citizen families.[109] The only stipulation was that the grain be repaid at the next harvest; there was no mention of interest. However, the borrowers were given the option of repaying the loan with capital rather than with grain. These conditions could be clearly advantageous, for it was more profitable to sell borrowed grain on the open market or to lend it at high rates of return and then to repay the debt with a portion of the profits. The proposal of city craftsmen to found an alternative institution further suggests that the Monte delle Biade was at times the object of speculation. In 1552, following a year of famine, the guilds and *scuole* in Brescia requested the institution of a new Monte.[110] It was the fourth time in twenty-five years that they had issued such a

---

[107] See Pasero, "Notizie sul sacro monte delle biade," pp. 381–406.
[108] *Ibid.*, p. 386.   [109] *Ibid.*, p. 391.
[110] *Ibid.*, pp. 393–394.

request. They pointed to the indigence of the religious associations and artisan guilds and complained that the Monte delle Biade and Monte delle Farine did not loan grain and flour to the needy, particularly in years of famine, but rather that it was the object of speculation for the wealthy. They offered the Venetian Republic 1,000 ducats for the privilege of setting up a similar institution under the direction of the *scuole, discipline*, and *arti* with the supervision of the Venetian rectors. The Council of Ten asked the Venetian rectors to verify the allegations of the guilds and *scuole*, while the Brescian Council sent messages to their nunzio in Venice to defend its interests. The request of the *scuole* was denied for the fourth time. Venice monitored but fundamentally supported the dominance of city councillors over the popular orders. Besides protecting their own individual interests, however, councillors would have to design policies that addressed the needs of the poor.

The hospitals

While the latitude Brescian councillors enjoyed in the governance of urban institutions afforded them investment opportunities and conferred political, judicial, and fiscal advantages, it did not blind them to the critical need to maintain civil order and social equilibrium. As leaders of the lay community, city councillors coordinated the work of pious institutions and lay confraternities that bore responsibility for social welfare. At the same time, their bequests to pious institutions and causes are testimony that they too joined in the spirit of these associations. A multitude of lay associations as well as religious congregations in Brescia devoted to charitable works may help explain why the city suffered no serious popular protests during a period noted for economic adversities. Brescia had indeed embraced the Catholic Reformation's spirit of lay devotion and social responsibility: in the early seventeenth century there was a formidable array of institutions of social welfare, sustained by investments from pious donations, to tend the needs of the middle and lower ranks of the community.[111] Twelve *discipline* (of considerable economic substance, according to the Venetian Podestà Giovanni Da Lezze[112]) and twelve charities (congregationi), located in various quarters of the city, supplied clothing, victuals, and at times vocational training to the poor. There were also several important hospitals in Brescia to administer to the sick and needy: the Hospedale degli Incurabili, which cared for women; the

---

[111] See Da Lezze, *Il catastico Da Lezze*, vol. I, pp. 141–154.
[112] *Ibid.*, p. 143.

Hospedale della Misericordia, an institution that taught vocational skills to the children of the poor (though it is difficult to know the meaning of poor in this context); the Hospedale delle Orfanelle, which in 1611 supported more than 200 orphans, mostly with bequests and donations; the Soccorso, a house for reformed prostitutes; and the Zittelle, a *compagnia* which trained young women to serve as domestic help in upper-class households. The merchants of the city, with the aid of investments from pious donations and bequests, cared for elderly artisans, children, and the poor in the Casa di Dio.[113] There were also two hospitals that aided victims stricken with plague, the Hospedale dei Ciechi et Stropiati and the Hospedale di San Bartolomeo.[114]

The Brescians centralized the administration of their hospitals,[115] and city councillors held a firm hand in their supervision, notably the Luogo della Misericordia, the Casa di Dio, the Hospedale delle Orfanelle, and the Hospedale Maggiore.[116] This last institution, which administered to the needs of adult males and children of both sexes, was one of Brescia's principal hospitals.[117] Founded in 1441 with state exemptions from *gravezze*,[118] the Hospedale Maggiore was under the governance of the Brescian Council, with the assistance of 101 confrati. Each year in the presence of the Venetian rectors, the city council elected a prior, two rectors, and three accountants (calculatori). It also supplied the 101 confrati, with a restriction of two members per *casa*, representing a total of fifty-two ruling families. The confrati had two sindici who served three-year non-renewable terms and two presidents who served one-year terms. These officers governed the operations of the Hospedale, including management of its properties. There was also a Special Council of twelve, restricted to one representative per *casa*, that, together with the presidents, had the authority to administer the Hospedale's contracts, with the approval of the Brescian Council. A massaro ordinario collected the monies for the Hospedale's mainten-ance.[119] In the seventeenth century the Hospedale Maggiore fed and clothed approximately 300 orphans until the age of ten, whereupon they were taught vocational skills. It also dispensed medicine to the

[113] ASB, *Cancelleria Pretoria. Ducali*, Reg. 43, ff. 110v–111r, October 3, 1625.
[114] Da Lezze, *Il catastico*, vol. I, pp. 151–153.
[115] Pullan, *Rich and Poor*, p. 630.
[116] ASCB, *Actum Deputatorum*, vol. 834, f. 44r, September 16, 1611.
[117] ASB, *HM. AEP. Famiglia Ugone, Mazzo* 3, No. 3, "Origini e Regola del Governo del Hospitale Maggiore," n.d.; u.d. The document appears to be from the late seventeenth century; *ibid*., letter to Venice from the presidents and governor of the Hospedale, February 14, 1629.
[118] Venice also exempted the Hospedale from *dazi* in 1538 and 1612. *Ibid*.
[119] ASCB, *Provvisioni*, vol. 570, f. 67r, May 2, 1610.

poor, furnished food and lodgings to transient pilgrims, made weekly
distributions of bread and wine to the poor and to prisoners, provided
dowries for young women, gave funding to the indebted families of
prisoners, and paid wet nurses for mothers who were incapable of
feeding their young. In 1629 the presidents and the governor of the
Hospedale reported to the Venetian Senate that the institution supported 1,000 children outside the city at a monthly cost of 1,000 ducats;
it also supported another 500 children at an annual cost of fifty *scudi*,[120]
100 sick, and 100 disabled persons, many of whom were soldiers. It
dispensed bread and wine to the poor every Wednesday, gave donations of 5,000 *scudi* per year to the Casa di Dio and to children under the
care of pious institutions, such as the Miserecordia and the Pietà.

The Hospedale Maggiore, like the Monte Nuovo, also provided
occasions for city councillors to combine Christian charity with profit.
Though some public monies were available, it was sustained largely
through donations that were often substantial: some households of the
ruling class, facing extinction, left their entire legacies to the Hospedale.
Its custodians invested capital in loans, making the Hospedale, like the
Monte Nuovo, a credit bank for the wealthy. The Hospedale also
possessed rich properties in the Territorio.[121] City councillors who
compiled direct tax assessments argued with the Territorio over
whether the Hospedale enjoyed exemptions from *gravezze, dazi*, and
other imposts, as such exemptions protected substantial investments.

Like the Monte Nuovo and the Hospedale Maggiore, the Casa di Dio
also served as a credit bank for the wealthy. The Casa's tax declaration
for 1641 reveals that members of the city council were borrowing large
sums from it at the rate of 7.5 percent for *censi* and 5 percent for
livelli.[122] This explains why such an important source of credit and
property came under the supervision of the families that held the most
important civic responsibilities: they were borrowing from the very
institutions they were charged with watching over. The Venetian
Podestà Antonio Longo wrote to the Senate in 1644:

> I have also observed the hospitals in that city, which have very large
> assets. They are governed by important citizens, who violate the laws
> prohibiting communities and guilds from alienating property or accept-
> ing capital with interest without state license. At any rate, not only do
> they alienate property on a daily basis; they also accept capital with

---

[120] The Venetian *scudo* was equivalent to 5.23 *lire Italiane*. Martini, *Manuale di metrologia*, p. 820.

[121] ASV, *DRB*, F. 48, letter of Giovanni Alvise Valier, Capitano and Vice-Podestà, August 31, 1646.

[122] ASB, *PE* 1641, B. 7, no. 247.

interest without state license, as they have a despotic government which is not subordinate to the commands of public representatives.[123]

Besides serving charitable purposes, then, the Brescian hospitals, like the Monti, were very important sources of capital and credit. They could, and did, serve the financial interests of Brescian councillors. For these reasons councillors kept them under their exclusive and careful supervision.

THE FISC

Indirect taxation and the Dazi Tribunal[124]

Supervision of the Dazi Tribunal was another area where city councillors could protect their own private interests. *Dazi*, or indirect taxes on foodstuffs and manufactured goods, were a primary source of revenue for the Venetian state. Moreover, they were a primary form of taxation, which hit all social orders across the board. Their overall administration was the competency of the Venetian Camera Ducale for Brescia, under the supervision of two chamberlains who were Venetian patricians. These officials in turn relied upon a host of Brescian fiscal lawyers, accountants, notaries, and tax farmers to assist them in the administration of indirect taxes. Unlike the direct taxes, collected by the Brescian Council, the *dazi* were auctioned off by the Camera Ducale to local tax farmers, making their administration more difficult to monitor. Among the potential tax farmers were the chamberlains themselves, who could undertake these duties when they found other bids unacceptable; and at times city councillors. Brescia had a restricted number of tax farmers – only five or six in 1644 – working in cooperation with one another. They divided up all the *dazi* among themselves and agreed on keeping their bids as low as possible in order to ensure high profits.

Neither indirect taxes nor tax farmers were popular in the Venetian state, or in the ancien régime for that matter. Brescian elites were notorious for evasion, and Venice had to make large efforts by the seventeenth century to reduce the fiscal privileges it had conceded

---

[123] Report of March 25, 1644, in *RV*, ed. Tagliaferri, vol. XI, pp. 435–436.

[124] On the organization of the fisc in the Venetian state for the fourteenth to sixteenth centuries, see M. Knapton, "Il fisco nello stato veneziano di Terraferma tra '300 e '500. La politica delle entrate," in *Il sistema fiscale veneto*, eds. Borelli, Lanaro, and Vecchiato, pp. 15–57; for the Bresciano, particularly in the eighteenth century, M. Knapton, "Cenni sulle strutture fiscali nel Bresciano nella prima metà del Settecento," in *La società bresciana e l'opera di Giacomo Ceruti*, ed. M. Pegrari (Brescia: Comune di Brescia, Tipografia Mario Squassina, 1988), pp. 53–104.

them in times past. For example, in the fifteenth century the state had granted privileges and exemptions from *dazi* to original citizens and to *benemeriti*; by the seventeenth century these privileges were no longer recognized.[125] Moreover, in response to complaints by Venetian rectors that *dazi* were poor because nobles were abusing privileges, the state was carefully checking the claims of the Martinengo, Avogadro, Gambara, Manerba, Federici, and others. Venice ordered a complete review of these families' privileges and immunities in 1613, and then again in 1633 and 1642.[126] Some powerful nobles not only claimed fiscal immunities. They also met tax farmers with violent resistance.[127] The Venetian Captain Giorgio Badoer suggested in 1629 that Venetian agents accompany the farmers. The captain himself had had to collect the *dazio* on wine because no one had offered to undertake the commission.[128]

Tax evasion and other disorders related to indirect taxes were the domain of the Dazi Tribunal, a strictly local structure. As in the administration of the Victuals Tribunal, so in the administration of the Dazi Tribunal, the state had to confront problems of abuse linked to the social arrangements of local power holders.[129] Disorders stemmed from private arrangements among tax farmers, Camera officials, and smugglers; between tax farmers and notaries; and between tax evaders and judges of the Dazi Tribunal. Here the jurisdictions of judges in the Brescian Council were a central issue. Venice had generously delegated authority to these magistrates in the 1470s, a period when the city council had also acquired more latitude in the selection of new councillors, by revising the *patto dei dazi*.[130] The *patto* of 1430 had stipulated that the judge in charge of the Dazi Tribunal would be a law graduate chosen by the Venetian rectors, exclusively. In 1470, however, the *patto* was revised to favor the interests of city councillors. It established that the judge for *dazi* had to be a member of the Brescian College of Judges, and a city councillor. Venetian delegation of judicial power for the *dazi* to judges in the city council placed an important part

[125] Zulian, "Privilegi e privilegiati," pp. 69–137.
[126] Report of A. Lando, Capitano, May 23, 1611 in *RV*, ed. Tagliaferri, vol. XI, pp. 205–216; report of Stefano Viaro, May 13, 1613, in *ibid.*, vol. XI, pp. 223–236.
[127] Report of G. P. Gradenigo, January 12, 1607 in *ibid.*, vol. XI, pp. 169–180; report of Giorgio Badoer, June 30, 1629, in *ibid.*, vol. XI, pp. 325–334; report of B. Renier, April 12, 1645, in *ibid.*, vol. XI, p. 445.
[128] ASV, *Senato. DRB*, F. 46, letter of Bernardino Renier, Podestà and Vice-Capitano, May 19, 1644.
[129] ASV, *Senato. Terra*, Reg. 99, ff. 247r–248r, October 19, 1627.
[130] ASV, *Senato. DRB*, F. 45, letters of Bernardino Renier, Podestà and Domenico Tiepolo, Capitano, February 16, 1644; May 19, 1644.

of the administration of these imposts into the hands of local power holders: the judge over *dazi* was responsible for interpreting the *patti dei dazi*, for ruling over cases of tax evasion and contraband, and for deciding whether fiscal exemptions were valid or not. Problems between state and periphery arose when local judges kept the Venetian Camera Ducale ill-informed of agreements made with tax farmers and when they protected kinsmen and other power holders guilty of fraud and evasion in exchange for a share of the *dazi*.

Notaries had a hand in these disorders, too. For example, Andrea Zambello, the chief notary of the Camera Ducale in the early 1640s, was responsible, according to the rectors, for inestimable losses. Zambello omitted recording the names of debtors; he credited fraudulent sums to friends in order to reduce their fiscal obligations; he accepted funds from smugglers in exchange for favors; he speculated on the sale of property that had been confiscated from debtors; he embezzled monies from the Camera Ducale in the amount of 26,054 *lire*, which he used to pay his collaborators – e.g., 7,000 *lire* to the Venetian chamberlain Giacomo Parozzi – as well as to fill his own pockets.[131]

Venetian financial exigencies in the middle decades of the seventeenth century, coupled with a decline in *dazi* yields, moved the state to intervene in these private arrangements in order to tighten administration. Competition for jurisdictions among two groups of Brescian notaries, those serving Venetian rectors and those representing the interests of the Brescian Council, was a central issue in this struggle.[132] On the one hand Venetian rectors aimed to have cases before the Dazi Tribunal prepared by their own preselected notaries, who may have been College members but were not city councillors. The rectors were sustained by the avvocati fiscali, lawyers who served Venetian interests and who at the same time served as advocates for the Territorio.[133] On the other hand, the local judges for the *dazi* wished to rely on the notaries in the Brescian Council – allies and kinsmen – to perform these important duties. The Venetian capitans frequently complained to the Senate that the judges on the Dazi Tribunal dispensed special favors to acquaintances, suspending their sentences. Moreover, the notaries in the

---

[131] ASV, *Senato. DRB*, F. 45, letter of Domenico Tiepolo, Capitano, February 16, 1644.

[132] ASV, *Senato. DRB*, F. 44, letter of Antonio Longo, Podestà and Girolamo Foscarini, Capitano, April 2, 1642; F. 45, letter of Antonio Longo, Podestà and Domenico Tiepolo, Capitano, August 28, 1643; ASCB, *Lettere Autografe*, vol. 1163, letter of Nunzio Agostino Luzzago, November 22, 1642. See the *Transazione* between the Fori Pretorio and Prefettizio of June 6, 1664 in *Raccolta*, pp. 62–64.

[133] One Brescian protester, Aloisio Benzolo, a notary in the prefettizia, championed their interests. ASCB, vol. 1235A, *Lettere Autografe*, letter of Nunzio Agostino Luzzago, ff. 72r–72v, April 19, 1642.

Brescian Council deliberately neglected to record infractions of the law. Still further, the public deputies and the city's chancellor overrode the rectors' competencies by signing the accounts of the *dazi* sent to the Senate.[134] Venetian officials sought permission from the Avogadori and the Venti Savi to intervene and to use their own avvocati fiscali and their own notaries to handle these cases.[135] Brescian councillors, however, clung to the *patti dei dazi* as a defense of their jurisdictions.[136] Meanwhile tax evaders exploited the confusion resulting from the struggle over jurisdictions by not meeting their fiscal obligations.

Tax farming

The collection of direct taxes such as the *sussidio* was also farmed out. City councillors could undertake these posts provided they were not simultaneously serving a term in the council. Collecting direct taxes was not an easy assignment unless one had a powerful support system, and the city council had difficulty finding tax farmers without such leverage. In 1623, for example, the council informed the Senate that even after it offered an extra 100 ducats in salary, it was unable to auction off the *sussidio* because of the risks inherent in this reponsibility. It requested permission to select its own massaro.[137] This was repeated in 1628 and 1644.[138] The lists of massari inevitably ended up being filled with the names of council families who found ways to exploit this responsibility despite its inherent risks. Massari elected by scrutiny from the Brescian Council did not establish efficient collection procedures; they granted postponements or even exemptions on payments; they neglected to forward all of the funds they had pledged to the Camera; and they made large withdrawals of collected tax funds, called *intacchi*. At the end of their terms they left with large debts. Lodovico Mantua (1626), Hieronomo Bornato (1638), and Nicolò Maggi (1640) failed to collect the obligatory grain contributions for those years;[139] Aurelio Calini (1626), Pietro Bona (1642), and Fausto Placentio (1642) did not

[134] *Senato. Terra*, Reg. 113, f. 334v, January 9, 1635; Reg. 105, ff. 242r–242v, July 12, 1631.

[135] ASCB, vol. 1235A, *Lettere Autografe*, ff. 72r–72v, letter of Agostino Luzzago, April 19, 1642.

[136] See for example, ASV, *Senato. DRB*, F. 45, letter of Domenico Tiepolo, Capitano, February 16, 1644.

[137] ASCB, *Provvisioni*, vol. 576, ff. 163r–163v, November 18, 1623.

[138] *Ibid.*, vol. 579, f. 76r, November 20, 1628; ASCB, *Actum Deputatorum*, vol. 844, f. 86r,. August 9, 1644.

[139] ASCB, *Actum Deputatorum*, vol. 837, ff. 116r–116v, January 14, 1626; *ibid.*, vol. 842, f. 61r, February 11, 1638; *ibid.*, vol. 843, f. 40v, January 13, 1640.

meet their pledges for the *sussidi* and *taglie*. Again, delegation of authority at the local level made it difficult for the state to tap fiscal resources efficiently and left a certain degree of latitude for city councillors to repair, protect, or enlarge their fortunes.

Designing fiscal structures: the 'estimi'

The direct taxes of the Venetian state were apportioned primarily on the basis of taxable assets deriving from immovables. The most important of these taxable assets was real estate; it was also the primary basis of citizen wealth. Brescian councillors, thus, like all of the urban elites of the Venetian Terraferma, were interested in designing fiscal structures that sheltered their assets from state taxation.[140]

Well before Venetian annexation of Brescia, prosperous citizens had begun to purchase property in the Territorio, the communities of the plains that lay south of the city, and the areas of Franciacorta and Pedemonte.[141] Some families had had large holdings in this area since the Middle Ages, which they continued to expand in later centuries; others penetrated the area in the fifteenth and sixteenth centuries. By the middle of the sixteenth century, Brescian citizens had firmly established their presence in these rural communities. At this point land ownership was a promising investment, offering some security during a cycle of inflation. Demographic expansion and land shortages had caused property values to rise, and the jump in food prices made agriculture a particularly attractive investment.[142] Aside from agricultural income, property offered possibilities of financial gain through dues, tolls, speculation, and monopolies of mills. It also served as

[140] This argument is treated more fully in Ferraro, "Proprietà terriera," pp. 159–182 and in J. Ferraro, "Feudal-Patrician Investments in the Bresciano and the Politics of the *Estimo*, 1426–1641," *Studi Veneziani*, N.S. 7 (1983): 31–57. I would like to thank the editors of *Civis* and of *Studi Veneziani* for permission to republish the material in my articles, with some revision, in this book. For other areas of the Veneto, cf. M. Knapton, "L'organizzazione fiscale di base nello stato veneziano: estimi e obblighi fiscali a Lisiera fra '500 e '600," in *Lisiera. Immagini, documenti e problemi per la storia e cultura di una comunità veneta. Strutture, congiunture, episodi*, ed. C. Povolo (Vicenza: Parrocchia di Lisiera, 1981), pp. 377–418; Knapton, "Il Territorio vicentino," pp. 33–115.

[141] The Territorio was a federation of rural communities, represented by a council. It was present by the third decade of the fifteenth century, earlier than most rural federations in the Venetian Terraferma. On its early formation and organization in the fifteenth century see D. Parzani, "Il territorio di Brescia intorno alla metà del Quattrocento," *Studi Bresciani* 12 (1983): 51–75, and esp. pp. 73–75; and for the sixteenth century, A. Rossini, "Il territorio bresciano dopo la riconquista del 1516," in *Studi Brescriani* 12 (1983): 79–96.

[142] Romano, "La storia economica," pp. 1,901–1,902; 1,904.

collateral for credit operations. Beyond financial incentives, there were strong social and cultural foundations behind building up landed assets: rentier mentality encouraged disassociation with the *arti meccaniche* in favor of agriculture, and landed wealth became a fundamental requisite for upward social mobility.[143] Thus, urban elites throughout the Venetian Terraferma, and in the capital city as well, were investing in real estate. This attraction to the land as both an investment and as a means of social elevation is evident in a wide body of sixteenth-century literature that extols the virtues of pursuing agriculture.[144] Several Brescians, notably Agostino Gallo, Camillo Tarello, and Giacomo Lanteri, participated in this discussion.

In the absence of statistical studies of property transfers in the Brescian Territorio during the centuries of Venetian rule, historians have relied on the descriptive accounts in the census of the Podestà Giovanni Da Lezze.[145] In 1609 and 1610 Da Lezze reported to the Senate that between 1440 and 1610 the proportion of land held by the urban and rural populations, respectively, had inverted. While in the fifteenth century rural owners held 66 percent of the Territorio, by 1610 acquisitions by the citizenry had reduced that percentage to a mere one-fourth of all holdings. The acquisitions were made either through purchase, through long-term leasing, through alienation, or through usurpation.[146] There are parallels elsewhere in the Venetian Terraferma. By 1635 the rural population possessed only one tenth of the Vicentine *contado*;[147] by 1588, according to Piero Badoer, Venetians owned approximately one-fourth of the Padovano, 18 percent of the Trevigiano, and 3 percent of the Vicentino-Veronese, and their investments in these areas increased into the third decade of the seventeenth

[143] See Lanteri, *Della economica*, p. 61.
[144] See P. Lanaro Sartori, "Gli scrittori veneti d'agraria del Cinquecento e del primo Seicento tra realtà e utopia," in *Atti del convegno Venezia e la Terraferma attraverso le relazioni dei rettori*, ed. A. Tagliaferri (Milan: Giuffrè, 1981), pp. 261–310.
[145] Pasero, "Introduzione," *Il catastico Da Lezze*, pp. 62–63.
[146] Ferraro, "Proprietà terriera," pp. 173–174. The race for common lands was a trend in the Venetian state during this period as well. In the eastern provinces prosperous Venetians acquired 89,008 hectares of *beni comunali* between 1646 and 1727. Beltrami, *Forze di lavoro*, pp. 74; 77; for Italy see Romano, "La storia economica," p. 1,923; for the Veronese: P. Lanaro Sartori, "Il mondo contadino nel '500: ceti e famiglie nelle campagne veronesi," in *Uomini e civiltà agraria in territorio veronese dall'alto medioevo al secolo XX*, ed. G. Borelli (Verona: Grafiche Fiorini, 1982), vol. I, pp. 312; 327; F. Vecchiato, "Il mondo contadino nel Seicento," in *ibid.*, vol. I, pp. 372–375.
[147] S. Zamperetti, "Aspetti e problemi delle comunità del territorio vicentino durante il XVI secolo nell'ambito dei rapporti città-contado nello stato regionale veneto," in *Lisiera. Immagini, documenti e problemi per la storia e cultura di una comunità veneta*, ed. C. Povolo (Vicenza: Parrocchia di Lisiera, 1981), p. 508.

century.[148] In the neighboring province of Cremona in the sixteenth century citizens owned 865,000 *pertiche* of land, while country people had only 213,000, yet the latter paid more than their fair share in direct taxes.[149]

Urban political and fiscal prerogatives, defended by the respective city councils on the Venetian mainland, were instrumental both in protecting and in consolidating citizens' landed interests. The strategy of those who held the reins of fiscal administration was to delay the renewal of the *estimo*, or tax census, which involved an updated assessment of real property and other immobile income.[150] In Brescia, though the local statutes prescribed that the tax census be renewed every ten years, the 1588 census was not updated until 1641. In the Brescian Territorio, the renewals took place in 1573 and 1641. Despite Venetian attempts to expedite the renewal of the *estimi*, disputes over the criteria to be used in the fiscal assessments, over the value of currency, and over the bureaucratic procedures and legislative norms established by the Venetian government delayed the process. The delays caused much confusion, deflecting the fiscal burden from households whose fortunes had risen while those whose assets had diminished received no proportional tax relief.

There was another strategy tied to local practices that safeguarded citizen holdings in the Brescian Territorio: the tax rates remained the same for one or even two centuries. Thus new property owners enjoyed both a lengthy period of exemption and tax rates that did not entirely take into account the redistribution of wealth among tax divisions. The nine tax divisions of the Bresciano – the city, the Territorio, the Val Trompia, the Valsabbia, the Valcamonica, Salò and the Riviera, Asola, Lonato, and the clergy – were each responsible for a fixed portion of the total of any given direct tax, called a *caratto*, which theoretically represented their assessed fiscal capacity. That percentage was then distributed within the division according to the individual tax coefficients (again, representing a percentage) assigned to each household. Controversy over direct tax distribution arose because some divisions held certain advantages over others.[151] Specifically, the Valcamonica and the Riviera di Salò paid the same *caratto* in 1641 as they had

---

[148] Woolf, "Venice and the Terraferma," p. 182.

[149] G. Vigo, "Alle origini dello stato moderno: fiscalità e classi sociali nella Lombardia di Filippo II," in *Studi in Memoria di Mario Abrate* (Turin: Università di Torino, 1986), vol. II, p. 767.

[150] ASV, *Collegio (Secreta). Relazioni*, B. 37, report of Giorgio Badoer, June 30, 1629, in *RV*, ed. Tagliaferri, vol. XI, pp. 325–334.

[151] The Venetian Republic tended to grant more fiscal concessions to border areas in order to keep their loyalties. See Knapton, "Il fisco," p. 19.

paid in 1430.[152] The *caratti* of Asola, Lonato, the Val Trompia, and the Valsabbia remained the same over these two centuries as well. Moreover, the portions of overall taxes these six divisions contributed were relatively small compared to both the city and the Territorio.[153] Only the *caratti* of the city and the Territorio changed over the fifteenth to seventeenth centuries, giving rise to disputes between the two divisions over sustained periods, which Venice tried to arbitrate. The city, defended by its councillors, consistently aimed to unload as much of the tax burden as possible on the Territorio; the latter attempted to escape the disadvantageous fiscal designs of the city and to win tax relief.

The Territorio not only fought fiscal structures but strove also for partial administrative autonomy. In 1531 Venice granted it a General Council and the right to elect four deputies for the administration of the *estimo*.[154] This was a true watershed. In the rest of the Venetian Terraferma, the urban councils reserved the right to compile and calculate the taxable assets of their rural dependencies.[155] Gradually the Brescian Territorio began to register some small but significant successes. In 1541 its portion of the *sussidio* relative to that of the city was reduced; in 1591 it succeeded in having its *caratto* adjusted; in 1599 citizens were obligated to pay *gravezze* levied on the rural communities in which they held property, an obligation, however, that they tried to forget and that was to be reversed after adjustments were made in the *estimo* of 1641; in 1628 the Territorio was given partial relief from the obligatory grain contributions to the city.[156] From the middle of the sixteenth century onwards, Venice was attempting to establish a more direct relationship with the Brescian Territorio, and generally with the *contadi* of the respective mainland provinces.[157] Much research on this subject has focused on the Vicentine, where it has been demonstrated

---

[152] BNMV, MS. It VII, 1155 = (7453), ff. 168–190.

[153] The Riviera in 1426, the Valcamonica in 1428, and the Val Trompia and the Valsabbia in 1440 were only contributing one twenty-fifth of the taxes they were responsible for. These divisions paid the *limitazione dei dazi*, a portion of the *gravezze*, and beginning with 1529 the *sussidio*. Asola paid the *tasse di soldati*, the *limitazione dei dazi*, and the *sussidio*. It shared the tax for military expenditures with the city, paying one-sixteenth. *Ibid.*, ff. 3, 111–128; 168–190.

[154] Pasero, "Il dominio veneto," p. 386; Rossini, "Territorio," pp. 94–95; cf. G. Vigo, *Fisco e società nella Lombardia del Cinquecento* (Bologna: Il Mulino, 1979), p. 163.

[155] Rossini, "Territorio," p. 94.

[156] ASV, *Provveditori da Terra e da Mar*, F. 272, agreement of December 7, 1628.

[157] Cf. F. Vendramini, *Le comunità rurali bellunesi. Secoli XV–XVI* (Belluno: Tarantola. Librario Editore, 1979); Zamperetti, "Aspetti e problemi," pp. 501–532; Knapton, "Strutture fiscali nel Bresciano," pp. 68–69. For Lombardy, C. Porqueddu, "Le origini delle istituzioni 'provinciali' nel principato di Pavia," in *Annali di storia Pavese* 2–3 (1980): 9–36.

that military and fiscal exigencies drove the state to establish a more collaborative relationship with the Corpo Territoriale, a rural institution that carried out administrative functions at the provincial level and that represented rural interests before the capital city. Rural institutions in the Vicentine and Bresciano, rather than metropolitan centers, could act as mediators between Venice and the countryside.[158] Almost everywhere in the Venetian state during the middle of the sixteenth and the middle of the seventeenth centuries, the rural areas became politicized, forming representative bodies that could voice their concerns before the capital, and they attempted to redress the political and fiscal imbalance that had traditionally privileged the cities.[159]

While the Venetian state utilized these rural institutions in the provinces as mediators between itself and the population of the respective *contadi*, it had no intention of dismembering urban institutions or entirely removing their privileges and prerogatives. The elites of the Venetian subject cities still remained in privileged positions, and they continued to augment their landed wealth, despite Venetian tendencies to tighten fiscal administration. Moreover the plurality of forces that characterized the distribution of power within the Venetian regional state remained intact. Here the contrast with contemporary developments in the Milanese state is quite striking. Fiscal inequities between the cities and their respective *contadi* in Lombardy parallel the Brescian case. Inefficiencies in the fiscal system were resulting in a reduction of revenues for the Milanese state. Military exigencies and financial pressure moved the Emperor Charles V in 1543 to begin a reform of the fiscal system, a long-term process which was completed, because of the same pressures, by Charles' successor, Phillip II. There were two levels of reform, one regarding relations between cities and their respective *contadi*; the other regarding the distribution of fiscal obligations within the Lombard cities. With respect to the first level, under Phillip II the representative organs of the *contadi* consolidated and exerted pressure on the state to redress the inequities in the fiscal system. The state responded. In 1561 the *contadi* received their own respective institutions (Congregazioni) to oversee the division of direct taxes. Gradually, fiscal privileges eroded in the Lombard cities; the rural

---

[158] Knapton, "Il Territorio vicentino," pp. 54; 104; Knapton, "L'organizzazione fiscale," pp. 389; 417; 417–418; Zamperetti, "Aspetti e problemi," p. 504.

[159] Knapton, "Il Territorio vicentino," pp. 40–41. See also S. Zamperetti, "I 'sinedri dolosi'. La formazione e lo sviluppo dei corpi territoriali nello stato regionale veneto tra '500 e '600," *RSI* 99 (1987): 269–320; S. Zamperetti, "Per una storia delle istituzioni rurali nella terraferma veneta: il contado vicentino nei secoli XVI e XVII," in *Stato, società e giustizia*, ed. G. Cozzi (Rome: Jouvence, 1985), vol. II, pp. 61–131.

regions received more equitable fiscal quotas; citizen holdings could no longer pass from rural to urban tax registers; and citizens were made to share the financial burden of housing troops. With respect to the second level of reform, the state attempted to spread the fiscal burden more evenly in an effort to tap fiscal resources more efficiently by constraining merchants to contribute direct taxes, too. Economic historians Giovanni Vigo and Domenico Sella argue that these reforms, which attempted to eliminate the fiscal privileges associated with status, were a step in the direction of modern finance. Moreover, the establishment of representative organs for both city and countryside, they suggest, helped overcome political fragmentation and lay the basis for a more centralized state.[160] Centralizing intentions, though not fully realized, were more apparent in the Tuscan state of Cosimo I as well, where the prince attempted to limit the autonomy of urban centers, to erode the position of landed proprietors, to have a more equitable distribution of taxes, and to redress certain peasant grievances.[161]

In the Venetian state, despite the Brescian Territorio's strides in the sixteenth century, or those of the rural Vicentine for that matter, city councillors continued to design direct tax structures that would protect their large landed investments. The Brescian design was persistently defended in Venice over the late sixteenth and seventeenth centuries by lawyers for the city, nunzi, and Brescian ambassadors. As a result, the Territorio's *caratto* did not necessarily correspond with its fiscal capacity, while those listed in the city's *estimo* enjoyed a certain degree of fiscal immunity. Factors that hurt the Territorio's contributive capacity and favored the Brescian citizenry were the extensive land transfers from the rural population to citizens; the quality and cultivability of lands belonging to the citizenry, which were relatively superior to those of the rural population; tax exemptions for some citizens with large holdings in the Territorio;[162] and tax apportionments that did not reflect land transfers to the citizenry. Moreover, there were significant differences in methods of tax assessment. The deputies who compiled the tax census manipulated their assessments and those of kinsmen and

---

[160] Vigo, "Origini," pp. 769–772; G. Vigo, "Solidarietà e conflitti sociali nella Lombardia spagnola," in *I ceti dirigenti in Italia in età moderna e contemporanea*, ed. A. Tagliaferri (Udine: Del Bianco, 1984), pp. 247–258; D. Sella, "Sotto il dominio della Spagna," in *Il Ducato di Milano del 1535 al 1796*, vol. XI of *Storia d'Italia*, ed. G. Galasso (Turin: UTET, 1984), pp. 27–28; 56–59.

[161] E. Fasano Guarini, "Potere centrale e comunità soggette nel granducato di Cosimo I," *RSI* 89 (1977): 490–538.

[162] Achille Maggio, on the executive committee between 1637 and 1644, had several land holdings that were exempt. ASB, *PE* 1641, B. 11, No. 301.

other council members, keeping them low and concealing assets.[163] For example, the Venetian deputies who checked the tax declaration of Stefano Maria Ugoni (on the executive committee in the third and fourth decades of the seventeenth century), noted a list of properties Ugoni had neglected to report.[164] Moreover, in 1643 the special magistracy sent out by the Republic to supervise the correction of the 1641 tax census found more than 5,849 hectares that the citizenry had neglected to report.[165] Further, representatives for the Territorio speculated that only one-third to one-half of the lands citizens possessed had been actually accounted for, practices which could deprive the fisc of over 3,000,000 ducats over the long term.[166]

Indirectly, the imperfections of the *estimo* aided the consolidation of citizen holdings in the Brescian Territorio, and played some role, along with a complex set of other factors (e.g., the geographical position and natural resources of each community, rising inflation, faulty administration and abuse by local power holders, the loss of common lands and community property, and the hardships resulting from periodic cycles of famine and disease), in the growing indebtedness of rural communities during the late sixteenth century and early seventeenth centuries. Rising fiscal pressures also added to the burden of an anachronistic and inequitable tax system. In the last two decades of the sixteenth century and the first half of the seventeenth century the fiscal responsibilities of the Territorio multiplied, a burden that the entire Venetian Terraferma experienced.[167] The increase was due primarily to the escalation of Venetian military operations.[168] At the end of the sixteenth century the Republic, preoccupied with Hapsburg hegemony, took costly measures to fortify its position on the European front. In the second decade of the seventeenth century it waged war against the Austrian archduke (1615–1617) in order to defend its eastern borders against the Uskoks (the Uskoks, Christian refugees from Bosnia and the areas of Dalmatia conquered by the Turks, were pirates who plundered the northern Adriatic).[169] Then in 1620 and 1621 Spanish maneuvers to take the Valtellina, Venice's principal gateway to northern Europe,

---

[163] See the observations of the Podestà Leonardo Donà for 1588 in BMCV, *Codice Donà*, No. 17, ff. 47; 88.

[164] ASB, *PE* 1641, B. 11, No. 204.

[165] *Raccolta dei privilegi*, p. 224.

[166] BMCV, *Codice Cicogna* 2525, No. 33, "Memoriale in proposito dell'estimo della città di Brescia, e suo Territorio. Assessori, una informazione," n.d., u.d.

[167] See Gullino, "Considerazioni," pp. 66–67; Knapton, "Il Territorio vicentino," pp. 67–68.

[168] Mallett and Hale, *The Military Organization*, pp. 177–178.

[169] Lane, *Venice*, pp. 386–387; 398–400.

prompted the Republic to fortify its western borders.[170] A decade later the Republic participated in the military debacle of the Mantuan Succession.[171] Finally, by the fourth decade of the seventeenth century the Turks seriously threatened the Republic's maritime power. Venice mustered together all its resources in preparation for a conflict that would turn out to be long (lasting on and off until 1718) and costly.

Research is not at a stage where we can identify or quantify which strata of rural society crossed the boundaries of financial insolvency during this period. It is not unreasonable to conclude that the landless were in the most precarious financial situation. The urban *estimo* of 1641 helps us to see this. Scanning the lists of *miserabili* listed in the tax census, we frequently find *coloni, lavoranti dei campi*, and occasionally *mezzadri* included among the ranks of the urban poor.[172] The latter flocked to Brescia in search of sustenance and employment, sometimes attaching themselves to the city's factions. They preoccupied Venetian rectors and Brescian councillors alike, who strove to maintain order. On the other hand, there is evidence to suggest that certain segments of the rural communities – salaried workers, small and medium proprietors, craftsmen and professionals – were able to weather the strains of the period much better than others. The political efforts of the Territorio to improve its tax situation relative to that of the city, particularly in the last half of the sixteenth century and in the decades leading up to the renewal of the tax census of 1641, are one index of this.[173] Further research must seek to elucidate this process by attempting to identify both the participants of the political cells in the rural communities and the principal protagonists of the Territorio's General Council.

The progressive accumulation of debts in the rural communities made it more difficult for them to meet their fiscal and financial obligations, creating a fertile market for private lending activities. The communities, as well as individuals, resorted to borrowing from prosperous citizens (and no doubt prosperous inhabitants of the

---

[170] R. Cessi, *Storia della Repubblica di Venezia* (Florence: Giunti Martello, 1981), p. 610.

[171] Lane, *Venice*, p. 400.

[172] The *coloni* and *lavoranti dei campi* listed as *miserabili* in the eight districts of San Faustino may be used as examples. They do not have tax coefficients. ASB *Polizze d'estimo*, 1641, San Faustino: Third District, Miserabili, Nos. 96, 103, 116, 120, 122, 149; Fifth District, Miserabili, No. 41; Sixth District, Miserabili, Nos. 22, 25–26; Seventh District, Miserabili, Nos. 1, 40, 65–66; Eighth District (Mompiano), Miserabili, Nos. 6, 7, 9, 11, 14, 16, 18, 19–20, 22, 25, 40, 43, 49–50, 58. Besides the *miserabili*, many other *coloni* with relatively low taxable assets were listed in these districts.

[173] Ferraro, "Proprietà terriera," pp. 178–179.

Territorio), from feudatories, and from ecclesiastical entities.[174] In 1611 the Venetian capitano in Brescia related in his report to the Senate that the communities of the Territorio were in debt to the Camera Ducale to the tune of 100,000 ducats. Marc Antonio Corner noted that the communities of the plains alone owed 300,000 *scudi* with an annual interest rate of 20,000 *scudi*.[175] Elsewhere in the province, Lonato, Asola, Orzinuovi, and Salò exhibited similar financial difficulties throughout the first half of the seventeenth century.[176] The problem, common to other areas of the mainland as well, attracted the serious attention of the Venetian state.

A survey of the tax records of Brescian councillors, their wives and other female kin, as well as a host of other speculators, reveals that they made numerous personal loans to rural communities at rates of 7.5 percent, yields (if actually collected) that surpassed the 3 percent returns from agricultural income. Should the borrowers default on repayment of their loans, speculators would seize their land as collateral. Thus, personal loans under the guise of leases were a thriving business activity during this period.

Rural capital and landed resources were not flowing into the hands of the Brescian citizenry alone. Ecclesiastical holdings in the Bresciano were expanding during this period as well, a phenomenon that might well be linked to the upper-class family's search for tax shelters. Moreover, this trend, if viewed in terms of the economic behavior of the upper-class family, was not entirely separate from citizen penetration of the countryside. The vast ecclesiastical holdings in the Venetian dominions[177] preoccupied the state, for the clergy had a separate tax register from the lay population and enjoyed special exemptions that subtracted from state revenue. The problem was

---

[174] The fundmental studies on credit operations in the Veneto during this period are Corrazol, *Livelli stipulati*; Corrazol, *Fitti e livelli a Grano*; on the credit operations of the Veronese ruling class, Berengo, "Patriziato e nobiltà," pp. 510–512; and in the sixteenth-century Padovano, Berengo, "Africo Clemente, agronomo padovano del Cinquecento," *Miscellanea Augusto Campana*, eds. R. Avesani, G. Billanovich, M. Ferrari, and G. Pozzi (Padua: Editrice Antenore, 1981), pp. 30–33.

[175] Pasero, "Introduzione," *Il catastico Da Lezze*, p. 63, n. 184.

[176] For the debts of Lonato: ASV, *Senato. Terra*, Reg. 113, ff. 5v–6r, March 6, 1635; f. 268v., October 31, 1635; and Reg. 107, ff. 105r–105v, May 1, 1632. For Orzinuovi: *ibid.*, Reg. 113, f. 209r, September 1, 1635. For the Veronese, cf. Lanaro Sartori, "Ceti e famiglie nelle campagne veronesi," pp. 322–327; Vecchiato, "Mondo contadino nel Seicento," pp. 364–372. The fundamental works on rural indebtedness in the Veneto during the sixteenth and early seventeenth centuries are Corrazol, *Fitti e livelli a Grano;* Corrazol, *Livelli stipulati.*

[177] A. Stella, "La proprietà ecclesiastica nella Repubblica di Venezia dal secolo XV al XVII," *Nuova Rivista Storica* 42 (1958): 23

common to all Catholic European states during this period, but Venice had acquired a particularly outstanding reputation for trying to stop the gradual erosion of taxable assets caused by the expansion of ecclesiastical property. Even before the famous Interdict of 1605 the *Serenissima* had initiated a policy that limited the growth of clerical holdings. The state passed laws in 1531, 1536, 1561, 1591, and 1598 that ordered the clergy to sell all property acquired from the laity as pious donations, but these laws had been ignored.[178] Venetian policy became even more stringent in the three years preceding the Interdict. First, in May 1602 the state abolished the right of clerical preemption on perpetual leases. Then, in January 1604 it prohibited the construction of churches, monasteries, or other edifices without the Senate's permission. Finally, in March 1605 Venice forbade the laity to leave, donate, or alienate property to religious entities, and compelled the clergy to sell all property acquired from lay persons after 1536.[179] Further, any new acquisitions required a special license from the Senate.[180] Again, these rulings often went unheeded.

An index of resistance to Venetian legislation in the Bresciano was the delayed renewal of the clerical *estimo*, which remained unchanged from 1564 to 1647, making it difficult to keep track of property transfers. Not simply the clergy, but also their kinsmen – the members of Brescia's ruling families – had a vested interest in delaying the compilation of a new census. Borelli's findings for Verona are instructive for Brescia. There members of the city council supported the delayed renewal of the clerical *estimo* because they were attempting to conceal land holdings acquired from the clergy. Veronese city councillors thus had a direct interest in preserving the *estimo* compiled in 1479 into the seventeenth century and in keeping the clergy's portion of direct taxes the same.[181]

In Brescia, as elsewhere on the mainland, Venice attempted to prevent the listing of temporal assets in the separate *estimo* of the clergy. The Senate had ruled that ecclesiastical property acquired prior to 1564 could remain in the clerical register while property purchased after that date had to be included in the lay *estimo*. But this did not resolve the

---

[178] *Ibid.*, p. 27.

[179] The Senate's *parti* of January 22, 1534, March 4, 1581, and June 11, 1605 are in ASB, *Cancelleria Pretoria. Ducali*, Reg. 41, ff. 185v–187r, June 11, 1605; ff. 249v–251v, June 8, 1609; f. 295r, May 15, 1610.

[180] Stella, "Proprietà ecclesiastica," p. 28. On Brescia and the Interdict, see F. Capretti, "L'Interdetto di Paolo V a Brescia," *Brixia Sacra* 6 (1915): 224–239; F. Capretti, "Una controversia fra la città e il clero di Brescia nel secolo XVII," *Brixia Sacra* 3 (1912): 3–19.

[181] Borelli, "Aspetti," pp. 136–137.

difficulty of tracing land ownership in the Bresciano. The deputies for the *estimo* reported in 1644 that this task was especially difficult because aside from the sale and donation of property there were multiple exchanges between clergy and laymen.[182] Ecclesiastical entities were thus able to accrue holdings despite civil legislation.

The lending activities, under the guise of leases, conducted by ecclesiastical entities with the laity were also a Venetian preoccupation. Borrowers' failure to repay loans was resulting in the alienation of lay property. In 1620 Venice insisted that the laity acquire a state license before making a contract or loan with an ecclesiastical entity, but the law was difficult to enforce.[183] A study of the conditions of these loans – who was borrowing, and whether or not they were being repaid – would be a fruitful area of inquiry, for it would furnish a sharper picture of the direction in which land and capital were flowing.[184] Moreover, it would shed more light on the economic behavior of the upper-class families that were party to these credit operations. Was the lender the only beneficiary of these credit operations? The tax declarations of city councillors and other members of the laity (including women) reveal a network of borrowing operations with ecclesiastical entities. The contracting parties were very often connected by ties of kinship . On the surface it appears that the clergy were eager to put what would have been dormant capital to fruit, accruing small but steady returns, and that laymen – often kinsmen – found borrowing at advantageous interest rates with little pressure to meet obligations of repayment quickly a convenient way of confronting expenses, such as large dowries. Other benefits of such transactions, particularly for family-estate management, still need to be explored with the help of ecclesiastical records.

How did a place in the Brescian Council during the late sixteenth and seventeenth centuries serve the interests of the upper-class family? Families who stood at the helm of municipal government aimed to monopolize the more lucrative offices and avoid those that endangered their fortunes, to invest in the institutions they watched over, and to speculate with political capital. They built structures, such as the systems of grain provisioning (*annona*) and fisc, which protected their

---

[182] ASV, *Provveditori da Terra e da Mar*, B. 272, letters of Marco Contarini, Giovanni Morosini, Pietro Diedo, deputies of the estimo, August 17 and 22, 1644.

[183] ASV, *Collegio (Secreta). Relazioni*, B. 38, report of Antonio Bernardo, January 24, 1654, in *RV*, ed. Tagliaferri, vol. XI, pp. 461–466. See also Corrazol, *Livelli stipulati*, pp. 8–9; 90; 114–115; 118.

[184] See Borelli, *Un patriziato*, p. 365; Borelli, "Patriziato della dominante," pp. 90–91; Borelli, "Aspetti," pp. 130–131; 165.

patrimonial interests, sending lawyers and nunzi to Venice to defend their designs. Finally, they held firm roots, either directly or through kinship ties, in the judicial apparatus, which safeguarded their interests and protected them from punishment. While the economic orientation of these families was distinctly rural, the municipal council served as a key to their financial success.

CHAPTER 7

THE CHALLENGE TO OLIGARCHY: THE "REVOLUTION OF THE DISCONTENTED"

In the fourth decade of the seventeenth century, a conflict arose in Brescia over the restriction of political power to the narrow municipal elite.[1] At the same time, on another level, there was friction between the authority of the Venetian government and the power of the local oligarchy, which sought to resist the political and fiscal intrusions of the capital city. Partly in response to the rising costs of warfare and partly in response to a contraction of commercial and industrial activity,[2] Venice was attempting to exert greater fiscal control over her mainland territories.[3] In Brescia it was difficult for the Venetian state to command the fiscal resources that it required. State power, without an executive apparatus in the provinces, was by no means autonomous; as we have seen, finances in Brescia were largely managed by the members of the city council.[4] Tensions surfaced in 1644 and 1645, taking the form of a struggle between the Brescian oligarchy and the forces of the state. Their struggles in turn created conditions in which the intermediate orders (a second-rank social group of composite origins, which

This chapter, with some revision, appears in *The Journal of Modern History* 60 (1988): 627–653. I would like to thank the editors of this journal for their permission to reprint the article here.

[1] Local chroniclers, in particular Lodovico Baitelli, the Brescian judge who wrote a history of the motion for reform, dubbed this episode in Brescian history the "Revolution of the Discontented." BQ, MS. D:I. 7, L. Baitelli, "Istoria della rivoluzione dei malcontenti sediziosi contro la nobiltà e Consiglio di Brescia – l'anno 1644."

[2] For a brief summary of the commercial and industrial downturn in seventeenth-century Venice see Lane, *Venice*, pp. 400–402; and for the rising public debt, Ventura, "Considerazioni sull'agricoltura veneta," pp. 714–718.

[3] Knapton, "Il Territorio vicentino," pp. 67–69. Venetian desire for more economic and fiscal control over the Terraferma began after Agnadello in 1509. *Ibid.*, pp. 48–54; G. Del Torre, *Venezia e la Terraferma dopo la Guerra di Cambrai. Fiscalità e amministrazione, (1515–1530)* (Milan: Franco Angeli, 1986), pp. 59–139. On the growth of Venetian fiscal organs see Gullino, "Considerazioni," pp. 63; 71; 77.

[4] Ferraro, "Feudal-Patrician Investments," pp. 32–35.

enjoyed wealth but was politically disenfranchised) in Brescia could challenge the closure of the municipal council and propose a more broadly based government. The protesters called upon the central government to reform the city council by putting the clock back, and restoring the more fluid entry requirements that had prevailed in the fifteenth century. Venice was faced with the difficult task of reconciling both the members of the municipal council and the advocates of conservative reform.

A study of the conflict between Brescia's intermediate orders and the local ruling class in 1644 and 1645 is instructive. First, it exemplifies the kinds of tensions resulting from the consolidation of municipal power that smouldered just below the surface of Terraferma society. Secondly, it provides an example of how the Republic of Venice resolved conflicts between social orders on the mainland in order to preserve peace and political continuity. Finally, it sheds some light on why the Venetians and their neighbors accepted the myth of good governance. Brescia's case suggests that the social and political networks the Venetian patriciate utilized to deal with the administration of the subject city were relatively stable, even if they were beset with tensions, difficulties and contradictions. The Venetian – and Brescian – constitutions endured; from a seventeenth-century point of view this was reason for praise.

GRIEVANCES OVER MALGOVERNMENT

In July 1644 a group of Brescian citizens from the intermediate orders openly criticized the administrative practices of the local city council.[5] They objected in particular to the monopoly of municipal power by a few families. They also criticized the expanded authority of the committee of public deputies, which had largely assumed the governance of the city.[6] At the same time, the protesters challenged the Brescian city council's standards of admission and requested that the central government in Venice open up a place for them in the political life of the subject city. To the Brescian ruling class, this startling proposition implied dissolving the entire municipal and state frame-

---

[5] ASV, *Senato. Rettori*, F. 20, report of Bernardino Renier and Girolamo Venier, July 27, 1644, u.d.; *ibid.*, unnumbered *fasc.* entitled "Scritture dei Eccellentissimi Rettori di Brescia mandati per occasione dellj risposta sopra la scrittura dei Signori Ambassiadori di detta città," n.d., ff. 1r–73r; *ibid.*, letter of Ottaviano Buccelleno to the rectors, December 15, 1644, u.d.; BQ, MS. D:I. 7, ff. 2; 117; Zanelli, *Delle condizioni*, pp. 7–24; 172–180; 190–203. See also L. Mazzoldi, "Gli ultimi secoli," in *Storia di Brescia*, vol. III, pp. 62–64; Ventura, *Nobiltà e popolo*, pp. 469–471.

[6] It is difficult to define the Brescian "oligarchy" precisely. See chapter 3.

work, since Venice and its territorial dominions widely subscribed to the principles of aristocratic closure.[7] Hence local chroniclers of the period dubbed the motion for reform the "Revolution of the Discontented." The citizenry's protests, however, did not merit the name of "revolution": the disgruntled elements did no more than present a petition to the Venetian Senate. The voices of the lower orders were nowhere to be heard. The petition was signed primarily by lawyers, notaries, fisici, rentiers, and civil servants of the Venetian Republic who had become wealthy and now sought the prestige associated with membership in the Brescian city council. They asked that the Venetian Senate reinstate a more broadly based governing body, modeled on the Brescian Council of the middle of the fifteenth century. The last vestiges of this form of government in Brescia had been swept away in the 1470s and 1480s, when the system of cooptation had replaced open enrollment. Other grievances stemmed from this central inequity: the protesters objected to the executive council's corrupt methods of government, which had left the city in chronic indebtedness, and the erosion of their personal fortunes, undercut by the inequitable system of direct taxation. The protesters sought, on the one hand, to alleviate these tensions by enlisting Venice's help to break the Brescian oligarchy's monopoly of power, and on the other, to modify the entry requirements to the city council for their own benefit. This reform program would enable citizens of the intermediate ranks to wield political and fiscal power.

The petition of the discontented Brescian citizenry immediately received the careful attention of the Venetian Senate. Relations between the state and the Brescian city council were particularly strained during these years over fiscal matters; thus the protesters' complaints over maladministration were timely. Throughout the preceding decade Brescia's payments to Venice for direct taxes (the *sussidio*; the *tasse delle gente d'arme*; the *ordine di banca*; the *carrette, alloggi, e guastadori*; the *imposizioni*) had been continually in arrears.[8] Several problems contributed to the city's indebtedness. Among them, anachronistic tax assignments had made it difficult to tap fiscal resources efficiently.[9] Further, many Brescians from the upper orders

---

7   Ventura, *Nobiltà e popolo*, pp. 39–114; 278–279; Ventura, "Introduzione," *Dentro lo "stado italico,"* p. 10.

8   ASV, *Senato. DRB*, F. 46, letter of Domenico Tiepolo, January 14, 1644.

9   Tagliaferri, "Introduzione," *RV*, ed. Tagliaferri, vol. XI, pp. xxiii–xxvii; Ferraro, "Feudal-Patrician Investments," pp. 31–57. On the social significance of the tax assignments, A. Tagliaferri, *L'economia veronese secondo gli estimi dal 1409 al 1635* (Milan: Giuffrè, 1966), p. 37. On the fiscal inequalities that resulted from the administration of the *estimi*, cf. Knapton, "L'organizzazione fiscale," pp. 384–386.

had simply refused to pay direct imposts such as the *sussidio*.[10] Finally, there was also the problem of inefficient local administration. The central government had grown so impatient with the way the municipal ruling class had managed Brescia's assets that it sequestered the city's income in 1638 and again in 1643.[11] Meanwhile the city had accumulated other debts, and on the eve of the citizenry's protests it faced a severe financial crisis: communal expenditures exceeded revenues, and the municipality was incapable of raising the income to pay off its financial obligations.[12]

The financial crisis in Brescia lent credibility to the citizenry's disgruntlement. Of equal significance, the loss of tax revenues moved the Senate to investigate the administrative practices of the urban elite. Further, while the Venetians favored aristocratic rule, they had displayed a certain wariness towards the constriction of power in the mainland municipalities, especially if it led to malgovernment.[13] The *Serenissima* no doubt also felt impelled to respond to its subjects' open expression of discontent. For all these reasons the central magistracy appointed a committee of Venetian statesmen to substantiate the allegations of the protesters. The committee quickly drew attention to the activities of the narrow circle of public deputies. This executive body had had the opportunity to manipulate every lever that moved public finance: city revenues and properties, the systems of direct

[10] ASV, *Senato. DRB*, F. 46, letter of B. Renier and D. Tiepolo, June 25, 1644; for the names of the individuals who had not paid the *sussidio* for 1643 and 1645, ASV, *Collegio. Relazioni*, B. 37, lists attached to the report of Girolamo Venier, November 27, 1645. The problem of arrears for direct imposts was widely diffused in the Venetian Terraferma during this period. See G. Gullino, "Nobili di terraferma e patrizi veneziani di fronte al sistema fiscale della campagna, nell'ultimo secolo della Repubblica," in *Atti del convegno Venezia e la terraferma attraverso le relazioni dei rettori*, ed. Tagliaferri, pp. 204–207; for Vicenza, Knapton, "Il Territorio vicentino," p. 107. Vicenza's arrears during the War with Candia, Knapton suggests, were a "segno di cattiva volontà e magari imbrogliata amministrazione, piuttosto che di povertà." This appears to be the case in Brescia, too.

[11] ASCB, *Provvisioni*, vol. 586, f. 132r, December 22, 1643; report of Nicolò Donato, September 22, 1640 in *RV*, ed. Tagliferri, vol. XI, pp. 401–402; report of Girolamo Venier, November 27, 1645, in *ibid.*, p. 453.

[12] For Brescia's debts in 1644–1645 see ASV, *Senato. Rettori*, F. 20, report of B. Renier and G. Venier, March 10, 1645, f. 12v; cf., *RV*, ed. Tagliaferri, vol. XI, p. xxii.

[13] For example, the Republic did not support a movement in Feltre in 1567 to restrict admissions to the city council severely. Corazzol, "Una fallita riforma," pp. 287–299, and in particular pp. 291–293. Further, Venice stopped the monopoly of office in Padua in 1626. Ventura, *Nobiltà e popolo*, pp. 280–281. The Vicentine Council, on the other hand, moved in the direction of oligarchy in the last half of the sixteenth century, despite Venetian reservations. Povolo, "Crimine e giustizia a Vicenza," pp. 421–425; Zamperetti, "Quadrare il cerchio," pp. 99–100.

taxation and grain provisioning, and the institutions of credit and social welfare. Because the public deputies often acted autonomously, ignoring central representatives and neglecting to consult or obtain the approval of the General Council in Brescia, it was their methods of financial administration that came under scrutiny.[14]

Venetian criticism centered foremost on the local administration of direct taxation. Since Brescia's annexation in 1426, the Republic, concerned more with fiscal yields than with the actual methods of tax collection, had left this important task to the members of the city council. By the second decade of the seventeenth century, however, military and fiscal exigencies made the efficiency of tax administration one of the Republic's primary concerns. Venetian reliance upon the Brescian municipal council to design and execute the direct tax system was resulting in a reduction of revenues and depriving the state of income that it desperately needed.[15] Thus it became imperative to monitor the governing methods of the municipal elite more carefully.

Venetian concern also focused on the anti-fiscal hostility resulting from the local administration of direct taxation. It appeared that the architects of tax administration, members of the inner circle who also served as public deputies, had precipitated this political challenge from below because the citizenry were pressed by climbing tax rates.[16] Brescia's debts had grown out of proportion in the years following the plague of 1630. Large expenditures for public health and sanitation, combined with the city's routine financial obligations, had made municipal finance more precarious. Thus the public deputies had tried to compensate for the city's shortages of funds by levying *taglie*, extraordinary taxes based on the total assets of the tax household, at the rate of 5 percent. This policy was doubly pernicious for those subject to paying direct taxes: because the quotas for direct imposts due to Venice were fixed, Brescia had to pay the arrears on them in full. The upper

14 ASV, *Senato. Rettori*, F. 20, report of B. Renier, July 27, 1644 u.d. On the competencies of the public deputies see report of Paolo Correr, April 1562, in *RV*, ed. Tagliaferri, vol. XI, pp. 67–68; Pasero, "Il dominio veneto," pp. 113–114; on how they were elected, Da Lezze, *Il catastico Da Lezze*, vol. I, pp. 284–286; on the consolidation of their power, report of Girolamo Civran, April 26, 1640, in *RV*, ed. Tagliaferri, vol. XI, pp. 390–391; report of Antonio Longo, March 25, 1644, in *ibid.*, pp. 433–434.

15 On the renewal of the *estimi* and the repartition of direct imposts, Ferraro, "Proprietà terriera," pp. 159–182.

16 Report of Girolamo Civran, April 26, 1640, in *RV*, ed. Tagliaferri, vol. XI, p. 391; Ferraro, "Feudal-Patrician Investments," pp. 46; 49–51; Zanelli, *Delle condizioni*, pp. 96–115; 121–130; Mazzoldi, "Gli ultimi secoli del dominio veneto," p. 60.

classes and the clergy contributed to the rising public debt because they were unwilling to pay the *taglie*, claiming exemptions. Further, Brescian councillors who supervised the tax assessments and assigned the tax quotas presumably had the means to shelter their fortunes and those of friends and kin. This meant that the rest of the taxable population was left to make up the difference. The *taglie* were in effect taxing households listed in the urban *estimo* repeatedly, even though they had already met their obligations, to make up the arrears caused by the refusal of the privileged elite to pay their share of direct taxes.[17]

The actual distribution of direct taxes further aggravated this social and fiscal inequality. The delayed renewal of the *estimo* meant that fiscal resources were not being tapped efficiently. Individuals whose fortunes had declined were being subjected to excessive taxes, based upon anachronistic assessments and anachronistic tax rates.[18] They were reluctant, or perhaps unable, to pay direct taxes or extraordinary *taglie* until they received a revision of the tax quotas. Meanwhile those saddled with high tax rates, in this case the Brescian protesters, had to compensate for the exempt and for the poor.

The methods that the public deputies used to combat the rising budgetary deficit also contributed to the city's dire financial situation. Since it became increasingly difficult to collect extraordinary taxes, the ruling elite borrowed money, often without ratification from the General Council, either from the Monte Nuovo or from wealthy individuals, pledging city property as security. As mentioned in the last chapter, the Monte, Brescia's central lending institution, was on its way to extinction, for the public deputies returned neither the interest nor the principal. In this manner they had expended much of the city's assets by 1643. Meanwhile members of the ruling oligarchy benefited from the municipality's fiscal difficulties by loaning their own capital at

---

17 Zanelli, *Delle condizioni*, pp. 47–48; 137; 170; See also Pasero, "Introduzione," *Il catastico Da Lezze*, pp. 46–47. Cf. P. Lanaro Sartori, "L'esenzione fiscale a Verona nel '400 e nel '500: un momento di scontro tra ceto dirigente e ceti subalterni," in *Il sistema fiscale veneto*, eds. Borelli, Lanaro, and Vecchiato, pp. 189–215. On tax evasion in the Venetian dominions and the state's efforts to reduce fiscal exemptions, see Gullino, "Considerazioni," in *ibid.*, pp. 69–77.

18 Ferraro, "Proprietà terriera," pp. 164–167. We lack a detailed study of the seventeenth-century Brescian economy. Contemporary reports furnish some evidence of a drop in commercial and industrial activity by the second decade of the seventeenth century, but they must be read with caution, since they were written to win tax relief. BQ, MS. F. II.11. f.80, "Rappresentanza fatta l'anno 1619 al principe dagli ambasciatori della città. Averoldi, Baitelli e Ugoni," pp. 80r–85r; BQ, MS. F. II. 11., "Supplica della città fatta l'anno 1648 per sollievo di gravezze," ff. 94r–100r.

high interest rates, and then accumulating public patrimony by default when the debts could not be repaid.[19]

The year 1644 was an appropriate moment for the discontented segments of the Brescian citizenry to forge ties with Venetian representatives. The protesters could legitimately point to maladministration in local government, and the Signoria, suffering from the financial strains of endemic warfare, had strong motives to take action against the Brescian oligarchy.[20] The Venetians had grown intolerant of the subject city's financial delinquency. What is more, financial pressure in Venice was so great during this period that in 1646, just two years after the Brescian reform, the Venetian patriciate itself decided to open its ranks to new families who could afford the steep entry fee of 100,000 ducats.[21] Thus in July 1644 members of the Venetian Senate formed an alliance with the Brescian protesters and seemed ready to force a program of fiscal and administrative reform onto the unwilling oligarchy.

PROFILE OF THE PROTESTERS

While the central power in Venice aimed to check maladministration in Brescia, the group of Brescian protesters had challenged the established order for separate reasons. Complaints over taxes, financial maladministration, and rule by the few – indeed, fundamental sources of dissatisfaction – served to gain the attention of the central government. The protesters emphasized the deficiencies of public administration, hoping that the breakdown in relations between the local oligarchy and the forces of the state would work in their favor. But this was not simply an anti-tax protest, nor was it by any means an attempt to dismantle municipal government.[22] Rather, it was the attempt of

---

[19] Ferraro, "Feudal-Patrician Investments," pp. 46–48. For example, one member of the Brescian elite, Rutilio Calino q. Vicenzo, lent the city 11,414 *lire planet* in 1629 to meet its debt of 29,984 *lire planet* for the remainder of the *sussidio*. ASCB, vol. 773, ff. 23r–23v.

[20] The Republic had been under pressure to finance the War of the Mantuan Succession while confronting the fearsome plague epidemic of 1630. The naval war with the Turks followed in 1638. Moreover, the Thirty Years War was in its twenty-sixth year and the War with Candia (commencing in 1645) was imminent. Lane, *Venice*, pp. 398–400; 407–409.

[21] Davis, *The Decline*, pp. 106–114.

[22] The late nineteenth-century historian, Agostino Zanelli, characterized the protest movement of 1644 as a *moto* of the *popolo*, primarily against the maladministration and monopoly of office of the civic elite. Zanelli, *Delle condizioni*, pp. 15; 171. I agree, in part, with Zanelli's analysis of the reasons for the protest but would place more emphasis on the protesters' desire for social mobility. Moreover, the members

relatively prosperous, ambitious citizens to gain membership in the municipal council. The leaders of the group that had voiced its complaints wanted to effect a relaxation of the city council's entry requirements.

Why was the Brescian city council so attractive to the intermediate orders? The honors associated with council membership may have been a strong incentive for the upwardly mobile family. The commercial recession in Italy had undermined the self-confidence of merchants and professionals alike. Those who sought upward mobility were attracted to the values and lifestyles of the nobility. The *coscienza nobiliare* characterized not only the value system of the ruling classes; it had become the prevalent psychology of bourgeois society as a whole.[23] Contemporaries in seventeenth-century Brescia viewed membership in the city council as a condition of civic nobility, a status which would attract those seeking titles and honors.

Membership in the Brescian Council may also have attracted the intermediate orders because it offered the possibility of directing important municipal institutions. Those who had capital to invest in land and credit operations – in this case the beneficiaries of the sixteenth-century cycle of economic expansion – had incentives to participate in such operations as the administration of direct taxation, the formulation of provisioning policies or the management of the city's central lending institution, the Monte Grande. It is also possible that the dreary economic climate of the 1640s not only provoked a negative response to maladministration in Brescia but also fostered the desire and the necessity of finding other means to cushion family fortunes. In this case access to the formal channels of municipal power could be an important asset.[24]

Council membership in Brescia, however, had ceased to be an option for the intermediate orders at the end of the fifteenth century, with the revisions of 1473 and 1488. In 1644 these revisions became the target of

---

of the group taking action cannot be so broadly defined as *popolari*. A sociological analysis of the group taking action reveals that many of them approximated the members of the municipal ruling class in terms of wealth, occupation, and in some instances even birth.

[23] On the changes in social ideals in early modern Italy see Barni, "Mutamenti di ideali sociali," pp. 766–787; Jones, "Economia e società," pp. 357; 367–368; Ventura, *Nobiltà e popolo*, pp. 275–374. On the defection of the bourgeoisie to the nobility see Braudel's comments in *The Mediterranean*, vol. II, pp. 725–733.

[24] See G. Borelli, "Un caso di crisi urbana nel secolo della decadenza italiana," *La pittura a Verona tra Sei e Settecento*, ed. L. Magagnato (Vicenza, 1978), pp. 247–263 and particularly p. 262.

Brescian protesters who were attempting to persuade the central government to open the city council to their ranks. With respect to 1473, they argued that the modifications of Statute 36 were invalid because the Venetian Doge had not endorsed them. To support their argument they referred to chapter 29 of the privileges Venice had granted to Brescia in 1440, where the Doge was authorized to approve all statutory amendments. There were several issues at stake here. First, the 1473 revisions of Statute 36 had implicitly given Brescian council-lors more scope for defining the requisites for council membership. Gradually lineage had taken precedence over every other qualification, and the Brescian Council had been able to establish a system of cooptation.[25] The protesters hoped to change that system by having the rectors participate in the selection process. They relied upon precedent to support their stance: in 1427 the Venetians had stipulated that the rectors participate in the selection of councillors.[26] During the early years of Venetian rule, central representatives had designated men who were *apti et idonei* to the Brescian Council, and that meant especially men who were loyal to the Venetian state.[27] Second, since it was the Venetian Podestà Bernardino Renier who was supporting the protest group of 1644, it was imperative to strengthen his authority over that of the municipal council in Brescia. To nullify the revisions of 1473 meant in effect to do away with the screening process of the deputati alla civiltà and have the rectors play a more direct role in nominating candidates for the city council. This would give strong political backing to the advocates of reform in 1644. Finally, the protesters hoped that more central control over the selection of new councillors would open the council's ranks to the intermediate orders. Thus, the protesters aimed to resurrect past political practice, demanding a more precise application of the statutes in force prior to 1473.

Criticisms of the provisions of 1488, the traditional closing date of the Brescian Council, centered around the fact that the revised citizenship requirements had never been written into the statutes. They contradicted the statutes of 1473, which simply required prospective councillors to have held citizenship for thirty years, and made no

---

[25] Zanelli, *Delle condizioni*, pp. 22; 182–186. In 1517 the Council ruled that the sons of Brescian councillors had the right to membership. Pasero, "Il dominio veneto," p. 356, n. 3.

[26] The rectors based their proposals for reform upon that provision. ASV, *Senato. Rettori*, F. 20, letter of B. Renier and G. Venier, March 10, 1645, ff. 5r–5v.

[27] Menniti Ippolito, "La dedizione di Brescia," pp. 49–50; 52–53. See also Pasero, "Il dominio veneto," pp. 113; 210–211.

mention of *cittadinanza originaria* or *cittadinanza benemerita*.[28] Further, custom had kept the 1488 provisions in force, but they had never been formally endorsed by the Doge. Neither had later provisions which excluded candidates whose fathers (1546) or grandfathers (1617) had engaged in the mechanical arts. To all of these objections Lodovico Baitelli, the Brescian judge who represented the city councillors, responded that the Republic had entrusted the government of the city to the *originari* and *benemeriti* and that approval from the Doge was a mere formality.[29]

The revisions of Statute 36 in 1473 and the provisions of 1488, 1546, and 1617 had restricted the avenues of social mobility open to merchants, manufacturers, and professionals of the sixteenth and seventeenth centuries. Those who would have met the eligibility criteria prior to these reforms no longer qualified for council membership. The protesters were a short step away from civic nobility save that the conciliar elite had shut its doors, locking them into their social stations. Their only hope was for the state to reform the structure of power, and thus civic nobility, in this subject city. It is well worth reviewing the occupational and economic status of the group advocating reform, if we are to understand the impetus behind their demands for change.

The tax records of 1588, 1627, and 1641, together with other local documents allow us to compose a socioeconomic profile for seventy-two of the individuals who wished to break the Brescian ruling class's monopoly of status and power in 1644.[30] The activities of the

---

[28]   The fifteenth-century civil statute, still in effect in 1644, read: "Et quod nullus Civis, tam Paesanus, quam Forensis, factus, vel de cetero fiendus possit esse de Consilio Civitatis Brixiae, nec aliquod officium habere a Communi Brixiae, nisi steterit Civis, et solverit onera, et factiones cum Communi Brixiae, per triginta annos continuos." *Statuta Magnificae Civitatis Brixiae cum reformatione novissima anni 1621* (Brescia: Joannis Mariae Ricciardi, 1722), p. 104.

[29]   BQ, MS. D:I.7, ff. 119; 177. Baitelli emphatically argued that the term *bonorum civium* in Statute 36 signified original citizens. *Ibid.*, ff. 123–124.

[30]   The Venetian rectors admitted a total of 264 new individuals to the Brescian city council in October 1644. A list of the reformed council of 1644 is in ASV, *Senato. Rettori*, F. 20, u.d. Approximately 103 of these men actually participated in the meetings of the reformed city council between October 1644 and April 1645. Their names are in Zanelli, *Delle condizioni*, pp. 250–253. See also P. Guerrini, "Il moto della borghesia bresciana contro la nobiltà nel 1644 ed una satira inedita," *RA* 25 (1927): 176–178. I was able to find information on 72 individuals from this group of 103. To construct a socioeconomic profile of them, I consulted their tax declarations. The tax declarations for 1588 and 1627 are in ASCB, filed alphabetically and chronologically under *Polizze d'estimo*. Those for 1641 are in ASB, *Polizze d'estimo*, B. 1–12, organized according to neighborhood. To construct a legal profile

protesters fell primarily into one of three categories: professionals (lawyers, notaries, fisici [physicians]), seventeen; rentiers, thirty-six; and servants of the Venetian Republic, seven (four of the latter may also be classified as professionals: two were lawyers and two were notaries). There were also two soldiers, one merchant, and nine unspecified. What stands out immediately is that the occupational and economic activities of the professionals and rentiers were almost identical to those of certain segments of the municipal ruling body. Protesters in the first category probably had professional contacts with lawyers, notaries, and fisici who were members of the city council.[31] Those in the second category shared the economic if not the social attributes of segments of the ruling class. Council members were forbidden to participate in the *arti meccaniche*;[32] thus they drew their income primarily from real estate and from credit.[33] The protesters availed themselves of both of these options. What is more, whether the protesters were rentiers or not, their fortunes approximated those of the city councillors: fifty-five of these same seventy-two individuals (76.4 percent) were assessed in the urban *estimo* of 1641 at one or more *denari d' estimo* (see note on taxation in appendix 2). Only 838 of the 8,186 households listed in the urban *estimo* of 1641 (10.2 percent) were assessed at this economic level. Of the families enrolled in the city council in 1644, we find that 256 of the 391 tax households (65.5 percent) fell into the same

of these individuals, I consulted BQ, MS. Codice di Rosa, No. 79, f. 175; BQ, MS. Codici Odorici, No. 105, "Catalogo delli descritti nel libro d'oro, cioè di quelli che ingiustamente pretendono d'essere aggregati al Consiglio generale della città" u.d.; ASCB, vol. 1023a, ff. 161r–168r.

[31] It is unlikely that the protesters were members of the College of Judges, for at least until the late sixteenth century the entrance requirements of this corporation were identical to those of the city council. Report of Paolo Correr, April 1562, in *RV*, ed. Tagliaferri, vol. XI, pp. 72–73. It appears that the College of Notaries included both members and non-members of the municipal council. *Ibid.*; ASV, *Senato. DRB*, F. 45, letter of Antonio Longo and Domenico Tiepolo, August 20, 1643. Many fisici enjoyed council membership. I was unable to find the membership requirements for their college.

[32] Ventura, *Nobiltà e popolo*, pp. 279; 313–317. This was a general trend in Italy. Jones, "Economia e società," pp. 367–368.

[33] These are only preliminary observations, based on the individual tax declarations of the members of the Brescian Council prior to the reform of 1644. The printed membership list was taken from ASV, *Senato. Rettori*, F. 20, dated 1644, u.d.; the tax declarations are in ASB, *Polizze d'estimo*, 1641, B. 1–12. These fiscal documents offer us a limited perspective of the basis of the Brescian councillors' wealth, since they only list assets derived from real estate and from credit operations. On the use of *estimi* to construct a profile of the ruling class see Berengo, "Patriziato e nobiltà," pp. 501–513.

economic category.[34] The protesters' investments in real estate and in credit were on a par with those of some Brescian councillors both in quality and in quantity. Because the fortunes of families enrolled in the city council were by no means equal, there was also more than one case where the wealth of certain segments of the protesters exceeded that of council members.

The professional activities of a few of the protesters – lawyers and notaries in the service of the Venetian state – had at times conflicted with the interests of the local municipal body. One segment worked directly with the Venetian fisc, among them, Giorgio Gagliardi, Procuratore Fiscale, and Ippolito Buzzone, Avvocato Fiscale, who supervised the exaction of public revenues in Brescia for the Venetian Camera Ducale.[35] Both Gagliardi and Buzzone had won the esteem of Venetian rectors for their service to the state. In Brescia, however, they had generated a great deal of ill-will among the local elites because they reported tax evaders to the Venetian government. Further, they were well abreast of the serious financial problems troubling the city and kept Venetian representatives well informed. Finally, both Gagliardi and Buzzone had served as lawyers for the Territorio,[36] which had been in constant litigation with the city, staunchly defended by the municipal council, over the division of direct tax quotas. City councillors would be reluctant to allow lawyers representing a rival corps to be privy to their meetings.[37] In fact, the rectors had complained to the Venetian Senate on previous occasions that individuals serving the Venetian state, such as the fiscal advocates, were ineligible for the city council.[38] The central officials felt that this limitation would make it difficult for the state to recruit men of quality into their service. In 1644 the rectors argued that Buzzone and Gagliardi should be admitted to the

---

[34] In 1641, one *denaro d'estimo* corresponded with 2,609 ducats in taxable assets. Ferraro, "Feudal-Patrician Investments," p. 51. To find the tax coefficients of the Brescian councillors for 1641 I consulted the lists in ASCB, vol. 188.

[35] On the duties of the avvocato and procuratore fiscali see the report of Domenico Priuli, 1572, in *RV*, ed. Tagliaferri, vol. XI, p. 127; "Ordini e Regole per le obbligazioni dei Signori Avvocato e Procuratore Fiscali della Città di Brescia (January 24, 1658, *more veneto*)," in *Raccolta di privilegi*, pp. 86–88.

[36] ASV, *Provveditori da Terra e da Mar*, F. 272, letter of the Delegati sopra l'Estimo to the Senate, May 1, 1647 u.d.; ASB, *Archivio Territoriale Ex Veneto*, B. 282, *Mazzo* 217, No. 13, u.d., letter from the Territorio to the rectors, July 27, 1674.

[37] In Verona the city council attempted to exclude the avvocato fiscale from its membership, and the rectors intervened. Report of Girolamo Corner, May 5, 1612, in *RV*, ed. Tagliaferri, vol. IX, p. 194; Borelli, "Introduzione," in *ibid.*, p. xlvi.

[38] ASV, *Senato. Rettori*, F. 11, report of Giovanni Capello and Francesco Corner, December 5, 1637 (attached to letter of April 10, 1638); report of Girolamo Foscarini, July 17, 1643, in *RV*, ed. Tagliferri, vol. XI, pp. 426–427.

city council, for they would thereby command more respect in the community.[39]

Others who worked under Venetian officials whom we know little about included Francesco Vinacese and Pietro Calini, both accountants for the Venetian Camera Ducale. They too dealt with the irregularities of the tax system. Vinacese had served the Venetian state for twenty years when the citizenry's motion for reform began in 1644, and his father had had this position before him.[40]

The professional activities of another segment of the Brescian protesters, notaries who served the Venetian podestà and capitano in Brescia, overlapped with those of certain notaries enrolled in the city council.[41] The notaries working under the podestà, whose duties included recording criminal proceedings, vied with the notaries working in the Maleficio (local tribunal of criminal justice) for the same competencies.[42] The latter were generally members of the city council. The two groups probably came into conflict during the first half of the seventeenth century as the central power attempted to impose greater judicial control over Brescia and the local organs of justice tenaciously defended their autonomy.[43] The same kind of jurisdictional competition also existed between the notaries serving the Venetian capitano in the administration of indirect taxes and the notaries who served in the local tribunal of indirect taxes.[44] Again, the latter were generally members of the city council.

In terms of social origins, our sample of seventy-two aspirants for the Brescian city council shared many attributes with those already in office.[45] Twenty-five (34.7 percent) had surnames that were common

[39] Report of B. Renier, April 12, 1645, in *RV*, ed. Tagliaferri, vol. XI, p. 444. The rectors also pointed out that in Padua the fiscali enjoyed council membership. ASV, *Senato. Rettori*, F. 20, report of B. Renier and G. Venier, October 25, 1644, u.d.

[40] ASB, *Cancelleria Prefettizia Inferiore. Ducali*, Reg. 10, p. 35r.

[41] In 1642 one of the Brescian protesters, Aloisio Benzolo, a notary in the Podestà's Chancellery, refused to cooperate with the public deputies over civil proceedings in the podestà's court. ASCB, *Lettere Pubbliche*, vol. 54, January 9, 1642.

[42] For the competencies of the maleficio and those of the corte pretoria see Povolo, "Aspetti e problemi," pp. 161–162. The notaries who served the Venetian rectors were drawn from the Brescian College of Notaries. The control of membership in this corporation was an internal affair until 1612, when the Venetian Senate ruled that thereafter the rectors would also take part in the selection process. *Parte presa nel consiglio dei Pregadi*, January 12, 1612 *more veneto*, in *Raccolta di privilegi*, p. 58.

[43] See chapter 5.

[44] ASV, *Senato. DRB*, F. 45, letter of Antonio Longo and Domenico Tiepolo, August 20, 1643.

[45] For the social origins of the Brescian councillors I consulted Bettoni-Cazzago, "La nobiltà bresciana," pp. 91–113; Monti della Corte, *Le famiglie del patriziato bresciano*, pp. 83–90; 93–128; ASCB, vols. 1426 1/2 A–C.

to families in the council; eleven of these derived from old noble lineages. The wealth and occupational status of the other forty-seven (65.3 percent) suggest that they were part of the upper crust of the intermediate orders. Of these, only nine were descendants of artisans or merchants; eight had rural origins, but almost all of these last seventeen had left the activities of their fathers or grandfathers to pursue careers in law, medicine, or the notarial corps. This had also been the occupational route of many families in the Brescian city council, who after 1488, abandoned trade and manufacture for one of the professions or the lifestyle of country gentlemen. What we have, then, is a composite group of potentially mobile families.

Legally, however, our sample of seventy-two aspirants fell short of meeting the entry requirements of the Brescian city council. Let us review the requisites for council membership that prevented the protesters from joining the civic nobility. (For a complete list of the city council's entrance requirements in the seventeenth century, see table 11.) First, candidates for the Brescian city council in the seventeenth century had to be *originari* or *benemeriti* or citizens for at least fifty years, with documentation substantiating that their families had paid taxes to the city continuously. Table 12 illustrates that all but seven aspirants met the citizenship requirement: four of these did not enjoy urban citizenship and three fell short of the fifty-year requirement. Sixty-five out of seventy-two (90.3 percent) of our sample of protesters had enjoyed citizenship for more than fifty years. Of these twenty-four were either *originari*, *benemeriti*, or both. However, documenting their status posed a real obstacle: only thirty-five of the sixty-five protesters (48.6 percent of our sample of seventy-two) who claimed to have met the citizenship requirement could substantiate their families' records of taxpaying since the fifteenth century.[46] The removal of the council's provisions of 1488 would reduce the citizenship requirement to thirty years; the elimination of the 1473 revisions of Statute 36 would reduce it to a simple twenty-five years, making it easier for these individuals to document their families' fiscal contributions. They would only have to account for the years between 1619 and 1644. Second, candidates for the municipal council had to be at least thirty years of age. All but one of the aspirants in the sample (98.6 percent) met this requirement. Third, candidates had to be under the civil and criminal jurisdiction of the podestà. I was able to determine that at least two of the protesters,

---

[46] It is possible that these *estimi* were lost or destroyed. For the deficiencies of the prospective council members, BQ, MS. Codici Odorici, No. 105, u.d.; ASCB, vol. 1023a, ff. 161r–168r. In 1544 the Brescian Council admitted new members who lacked one *estimo*. Pasero, "Il dominio veneto," p. 356, n. 3.

Table 11. *The entry requirements of the Brescian Council: (1644)*

Requisite	Year first instituted
Minimum of thirty years of age	Pre-1426
Residence in city the majority of the year and own or rent a domicile	1454
Under the civil and criminal jurisdiction of the podestà	1475
Descendant of *cittadino originario*; family paid taxes with city since 1426[a,b]	
or	
Descendant of *cittadino benemerito*; family paid taxes with city since 1438[a,b]	1488
or	
Record of urban citizenship for 50 years; family paid taxes with city for 50 years[a,c]	
Legitimate birth	1494
Must not have broken civil laws	1494
No debts to the city, including Monti di Pietà	1534
Father not associated with *meccaniche*[a,b]	1546
Grandfather not associated with *meccaniche*[a,b]	1617
Fathers and grandfathers of legitimate birth	1640

Notes: [a]Protesters contest in 1644.

[b] 1644 reform eliminated.

[c] reform substituted with a 25-year residency requirement.

Sources: ASCB, vol. 1322, *fasc.* 18, *Processi di Cittadinanza: Bucelleno* (u.d.); ASV, *Senato. Rettori*, F. 20, "Scritture dei Ecc.mi Rettori di Brescia Mandati Per Occasioni dellj risposta sopra la scrittura dei Signori Ambassiadori di detta città" (unnumbered *fasc.*, n.d.), ff. 29r–46v.

Table 12. *The legal status of citizenship of the Brescian protesters*

I.		Urban	
	a.	*Originario*	12
	b.	*Benemerito*	5
	c.	*Originario* and *benemerito*	7
	d.	Citizen for 50 years or more	41
	e.	Citizen less than 25 years	3
II.		Rural	4
		Total	72

both soldiers, did not qualify, but this requirement was not challenged or discussed in 1644. Fourth, candidates for the city council could not have been associated with the mechanical arts or rural labor for at least three generations. Fifty-five out of seventy-two (76.4 percent) quali-fied; the removal of the 1546 and 1617 provisions would eliminate this obstacle as well. In sum, by eliminating the revisions of 1473, 1488, 1546, and 1617 sixty-two of seventy-two individuals (86.1 percent) would be eligible for the Brescian city council. Approximately ten members of our sample would have been ineligible: seven did not meet the citizenship requirement; one failed to meet the minimum age; and at least two were not under the podestà's jurisdiction.

This socioeconomic and legal profile of a portion of the Brescian protesters aids us in outlining the contours of the movement for reform. To begin with, if we use the admission standards of the Brescian city council employed prior to 1473 and 1488, most of the protesters did not represent a particularly new social force. This is precisely the argument that the advocates for reform were making. However, if we employ the standards prescribed after 1488, and especially after 1546 and 1617, the reform of 1644, from the perspective of the ruling classes, contained more "revolutionary" dimensions: neither Venice nor Brescia recog-nized the intermediate orders as a political force in the sixteenth and seventeenth centuries. What is more, aspirants of rural origins had never been admitted to municipal ruling bodies either in Venice or in Brescia.

This profile also strongly suggests that the protesters were aiming to become a part of the aristocratic structure rather than dismantle it, for their occupations, lifestyles, and economic status closely resembled those of some Brescian city councillors. A case in point is Octaviano Bucelleno q. Antonio, one of the principal leaders of the reform movement, who applied for membership in 1639.[47] The deputati alla civiltà denied membership to Bucelleno, a rentier of considerable social standing, primarily because he lacked records of his family's tax assessments for the period between 1442 and 1517. Though Bucelleno was a *cittadino benemerito,* he could not document his family's tax payments since 1438. Save for the missing *estimi,* the applicant met every other standard of the city council. Bucelleno consulted with a number of Venetian senators about the possibility of a hearing in the Pien Collegio,[48] and in 1643 he succeeded in appealing to the central power in Venice.[49] It appears that Bucelleno enjoyed vital contacts with Venetian representatives, a fact which supports our notion that the protester's social standing was high. The Pien Collegio heard Bucel-

---

[47] ASCB, *Processi di Nobiltà,* 1639–40, vol. 309, ff. 1r–3v.
[48] ASCB, *Lettere Autografe,* vol. 1163, letters of Agostino Luzzago, November 30 and December 2 and 3, 1642.
[49] ASCB, *Provvisioni,* vol. 586, ff. 100r–101r, May 30, 1643.

leno's arguments on April 4, 1643, when he explained that his family had not been on Brescia's tax rolls between 1442 and 1517 because it was exempt from direct taxes by privilege of the Venetian Senate.[50] He argued that the deputati alla civiltà could not deny him membership in the city council since he met the fundamental requisites of urban citizenship. Bucelleno, treating the missing documentation lightly, felt that the Republic should support his candidacy for the Brescian city council. The Brescian councillors organized an energetic defense against Bucelleno, sending representatives to Venice to uphold the authority of the deputati alla civiltà, and they won the case. Bucelleno was denied access to the city council on March 10, just four months before the citizenry's motion for reform was introduced.[51]

During the 1630s and 1640s a number of the protesters, some very close to meeting the standards of the city council, had had experiences similar to that of Bucelleno, though none had had the courage to appeal to the central power. The Clera, for example, were a distinguished family – with honors, privileges, and exemptions since 1452 – who had been denied admission to the city council in 1636. This family led a "noble" lifestyle, and according to the General Council itself there was little doubt that it would have qualified for membership had it met the citizenship requirements established in 1488.[52] The physician Lodovico Cirimbelli is another example of how closely the families applying for membership resembled some of those already in council. Cirimbelli q. Marco Antonio, had all the requisites for office, but was kept out because he failed to meet the citizenship requirement. His family had not resided in the city between 1438 and 1528.[53] In another case,

---

[50] Even exempt families, however, were required to list their property in the urban *estimi*.

[51] ASCB, *Provvisioni*, vol. 587, f. 66r, March 10, 1644.

[52] "Non vi ha dubbio che stando le predette cose se questa famiglia in tempo avesse addimandato gli honori et beneficitij della città sarebbe più giusta stata admessa . . . se non fosse sopravenuta la decisione 1488 Settembre decretato dal Maggior Consiglio della Città 'chiede la porta delli honori . . . a tutti quelli Cittadini, che non sono originarij o benemeriti eccetanti a chi ne fosse in process' la qual parte la sia però apperta la via alla gratia di admetter quelli che pareranno degni d'esser admesse." ASCB, *Provvisioni*, vol. 583, ff. 12v–13v, January 8, 1636. According to Monti della Corte, the Clera were admitted in 1662, *Le famiglie del patriziato bresciano*, pp. 125–126.

[53] ASCB, *Provvisioni*, vol. 589, ff. 4r–4v; 5r–7v, January 7, 1648. Perhaps the council's decision in this case was uncertain, for Cirimbelli *had* passed the vote of the deputati alla civiltà and there had been more members in favor of his admission than against. His son would manage to enter the Council in 1660, on the condition that "cum declaratione quod filij et descendentes numquam admittantur nisi purgata mecanica," ASCB, *Provvisioni*, vol. 595, f. 2r, January 7, 1660.

Aurelio and Marc Antonio Polini q. Giovanni Battista, descendants from a mercantile family who had shed all association with commerce and obtained university degrees, were rejected because of the rule against *meccanici*. In 1644 Paolo Monza, a rentier whose fifteenth-century ancestors were textile merchants,[54] and Andrea Conter, who had made his riches in the linen industry, were both refused council membership. Conter was a very wealthy member of the Università dei Mercanti in Brescia, who owned sixty linen looms on the Riviera of Lake Garda and exported linen valued at 40,000 ducats annually. Although he enjoyed agricultural income from his lands in Mazzano, Milzano, and Cigole, he was tainted with *meccanica*.[55] The Arrighini brothers, custodians of an arms factory in Brescia, were also judged unacceptable for membership in 1644 for the same reason.[56] Aurelio and Lodovico Giorgi q. Lodovico were perhaps the least acceptable of all the applicants mentioned thus far. They were refused membership in 1634 because their ancestors were millers and peasants and some of their relatives still labored in the countryside. The tax records reveal that Aurelio and Lodovico's grandfather had risen to economic prosperity in the sixteenth century. He had purchased large quantities of cultivable land in Nigolera, where the family was said to live a "noble lifestyle." Members of the Giorgi family had served on the local council of Castenedolo for fifty or sixty years. Through the acquisition of wealth, especially landed wealth, and service in a local council, families such as the Giorgi hoped to take the prominence they enjoyed in the rural communities to the city of Brescia, where they sought a place in the council. In 1634 Aurelio and Lodovico initiated procedures to be considered for membership. Their *Processi di cittadinanza* contain testimonies that both they and their ancestors lived noble lifestyles. They did not work with their hands; the family carried a certain noble decorum in the public eye. This criterion nonetheless failed to win the approval of the special committee of public deputies assigned to review the case. Giovanni Paolo Luzzago, Giovanni Battista Averoldo, and Benettino Calino, the Deputati alla Civiltà, rejected the application. The testimonies in the Giorgi application reflect the circumstances upon which many ambitious citizens based their applications for the council: their acquisition of wealth, especially landed wealth; their ability to live

---

[54] ASB, *PE* 1641, B. 12, No. 402. Rejected during a move for reform of the council's entrance requirements in 1644, Monza was one of the protesters who, on an individual basis, was finally given council membership in 1650. ASCB, *Provvisioni*, vol. 590, f. 6r, January 12, 1650.

[55] ASB, *PE* 1641, B. 10, No. 261; Pasero, "Introduzione," *Il catastico Da Lezze*, p. 74.

[56] Pasero, "Introduzione," *Il catastico Da Lezze*, p. 87.

a "noble" lifestyle as rentiers; and their service on a local council or in a minor office in the city.

Relying not only on the favors of the Venetian state, but also on their long reign of exclusive power, the Brescian ruling class buttressed itself with both council provisions and the standards of *vivendi more nobilium*, distancing itself from the intermediate orders. Missing *estimi* that substantiated the family's history of fiscal contributions with the city, a distant association with commerce, manufacture, or agriculture, an interrupted residency in the city were all grounds for refusal. The Clera, the Cirimbelli, the Polini, the Monza, the Conter, and the Giorgi would join Octaviano Bucelleno, the protester who in 1644 would initiate the motion to repeal the 1473 version of Statute 36 and the council's provisions of 1488, 1546, and 1617.[57]

A third observation to be made is the absence of the lower orders from this protest group. The aspirants for council membership, uninterested in any deep social and political transformations, did not stir up the *popolo* to support their reform program. Nor is there any evidence that the *popolo* was particularly interested in a reform at the top. With this we begin to see the conservative dimensions of what local chroniclers called a "revolution" in the Venetian state: it was in essence a last-ditch attempt on the part of Brescia's intermediate orders to become a part of the municipal ruling class. The group proposing change would fall back on distant, legalistic precedents to justify its program of reform.

THE REFORMED COUNCIL

On September 3, 1644 the protesters won their case.[58] For a start, the Senate ordered the rectors to reinstate the original statutes. Thenceforward seventy-two citizens were to be elected from the General Council each year. This would constitute a second council, offsetting that of the public deputies. In addition, the Senate insisted that the rectors be included in all convocations of the Brescian Council. The modifications were designed to achieve a balance of power both within the local governing organs and with the central representatives. Second, the Senate instructed the Venetian rectors in Brescia to reinstate the admission standards that were applied prior to 1473 (see appendix). Amidst the strong protests of the Brescian city councillors, Venetian representatives issued a proclamation inviting the citizenry who met the

---

[57] ASCB, vol. 1322, *fasc.* 18, u.d.; BQ, MS. D:I. 7, f. 87.
[58] ASCB, *Provvisioni*, vol. 587, f. 75r, September 8, 1644.

qualifications for council membership to apply. Bucelleno, Gagliardi, Vinacese, and others began to comply, but certain members of the city council lined up outside the doors of the city chancellery, discouraging applicants with threats of violence. Venetian representatives soon interceded so that the application process could continue.[59] The Brescian upper classes, however, were notoriously violent and no doubt continued to intimidate applicants and their families, a fact that may well explain why the council aspirants subsequently behaved rather timidly.[60] The rectors assigned Buzzone and Gagliardi, two of the strongest advocates of reform, the task of reviewing the fiscal documents of the new applicants to the council.[61] By October the Venetian rectors had selected the new candidates, and the council prepared to convene. The council membership had nearly doubled, making the convention hall in Brescia too small to accommodate the new members. At this point the protesters' program began to fall apart. The old councillors objected to relocating the meeting hall. The new men, according to Lodovico Baitelli (who wrote "The Revolution of the Discontented"), failed to express any views of their own. Baitelli's history of the protest, however, must be read with reservation, as it clearly defends the Brescian councillors. A letter from the public deputies to Agostino Luzzago, the Brescian Nunzio in Venice, contradicts Baitelli, disclosing that the protesters *were* planning to send a statement to the capital city.[62] In the end, the reformed council convened in the same hall, the old councillors seated and the new entrants standing in deference. The council then resumed its duties, proceeding to choose the civic leadership. Nominations were pro forma: the executive membership did not change. The newly appointed councillors failed to make their presence felt.

The old councillors began to campaign for a reversal of the Senate's decision. The public deputies met in private, and drew up a list of their grievances. They would argue that the innovations were an infringement of their basic rights as loyal subjects. At the same time they elected a delegation to journey to Venice and persuade the Senate to revoke its decision. The six Brescian delegates represented some of the most important families in Brescia: Lodovico Baitelli, Camillo Martinengo-

59 ASV, *Senato. Rettori*, F. 20, report of B. Renier and G. Venier, September 27, 1644, u.d.; BQ, MS. D.L.7., ff. 24–25.
60 See Mazzoldi, "Gli ultimi secoli," pp. 63; 64, n. 3.
61 Baitelli described the two fiscali and the podestà as "The Triumvirate," and "unitissimi." BQ, MS. D:I. 7, ff. 29–30; 33; 57; 63; 188.
62 ASCB, *Lettere Pubbliche*, vol. 56, letter from the public deputies to Agostino Luzzago, December 31, 1644.

Cesaresco, Ottavio Calino, Cesare Martinengo, Giovanni Antonio Fenarolo, and Vincenzo Calino.[63] Unfortunately, there is no surviving evidence indicating what, if anything, the new councillors did to block this proposal. Thus at the end of December 1644 six delegates, drawn from the old guard, took lodgings in Venice and initiated negotiations with Venetian senators.

When an official embassy was sent to Venice by one of its subject cities, special forms of protocol had to be observed. First, a formal request was sent to the central government, asking permission to send a group of "orators," as they were called in the seventeenth century, to the capital. The purpose of the delegation was to discuss the issues at stake both in public and in private, with statesmen who were receptive to the Brescian ruling body's arguments. Here individual contacts could be invaluable. One of the Brescian delegates, Lodovico Baitelli, was instrumental in championing the interests of the city council. Venetian stability can perhaps be traced to precisely the kind of relations Baitelli was able to forge with Venetian senators. A distinguished authority on jurisprudence in the Venetian state, Baitelli had frequently served as a consultant for the central government, and Venetian statesmen deeply respected him.[64] Baitelli and the other Brescian delegates made careful preparations before the Senate hearing, visiting nearly the entire governing body on an individual basis. They gave particular attention to the Savi[65] and to the future podestà of Brescia, as well as to the more influential members of the Senate. In all they spoke with seventy magistrates. They called the Venetian statesmen who were sympathetic to their cause *padroni*, suggesting that the local councillors made use of a political patronage system to win their way with the central government. In addition, Baitelli maintained close contact with the Venetian secretaries, whom he referred to as his "dear friends." Later he would send monetary remuneration to these public officials who, he stated, had played an instrumental role in winning the cause of the Brescian ruling class.[66]

Throughout these negotiations it became increasingly apparent that the Venetian Senate was not commanded by unanimous decision. Certain segments of the Venetian ruling class, in particular the Doge,

[63] "Diario Pluda," November 14, 1644, in *Le cronache bresciane*, ed. Guerrini, vol. II, p. 387.

[64] See G. Benzoni's profile of Lodovico Baitelli in *Dizionario bibliografico degli Italiani*, Istituto della Enciclopedia Italiana Fondata da Giovanni Treccani (Rome: Istituto Polgrafico dello stato, 1963), vol. V, pp. 305–306.

[65] Savi may be translated as "Chief Ministers." On their functions see Lane, *Venice*, pp. 254; 257; 428.

[66] BQ, MS. D.L.7, ff. 71–90; 105.

Francesco Erizzo; the Rectors, Bernardino Renier and Girolamo Venier; and Andrea Da Lezze, wished to intervene in Brescian municipal government and neutralize the local oligarchy's power. Others, however, were receptive to Baitelli's skillful defense of local governing practices.[67] Some senators may have feared the alienation of important leaders in the subject city; such action might leave a dangerous weak spot on the western border of the state. Of broader significance, the challenge to aristocratic closure in one Terraferma city would set a serious precedent, perhaps encouraging the discontented elements in other subject cities to rebel against the exclusivity of their local ruling bodies. This could create havoc. Moreover, Venice had traditionally depended upon the mainland municipal elites to govern its subject cities. Thus it was important to maintain a good working rapport with these local power holders. It was one matter to intervene and correct administrative abuse; quite another to challenge the exclusive status and power of these important ruling elites. The situation required careful negotiations and compromise rather than abrasive action.

Much like other early modern states that were attempting to deal with local authorities, Venice faced a difficult decision.[68] If the *Serenissima* sided with the Brescian oligarchy, it would have to continue to cope with the inefficient system of public administration that reduced state revenues. If instead the *Serenissima* sided with the Brescian protesters, it risked a strong aristocratic reaction. In the long run, the second option would undermine the aristocratic concept of state to which the Venetians had traditionally adhered. To allow any political change, such as that proposed in 1644, implied dissolving the entire municipal and state framework, which would have been unthinkable for Venetian patricians. The Venetians opted to compromise with the local ruling class. In April 1645, six months after Venice had instituted the reformed government, the Senate revoked its decision. The Brescian city council would remain an exclusive aristocratic institution. However, maladministration caused by the narrowing basis of municipal power was another matter, which the *Serenissima* did not tolerate. The Ducale of 1645 was careful to prohibit abusive administrative practices and to delineate the boundaries of the public deputies' auth-

---

[67] BQ, MS. D.L.7, ff. 80–82; 84.

[68] Venetian intervention in Terraferma affairs was not always willfully planned by the central government. At times the *Serenissima* exercised authority with reluctance, as a result of pressure from its subjects. See, for example, John Law's study of relations between Verona and her *contado* in the fifteenth century over the conferment of citizenship to *contadini*. Law, "*Super differentiis agitatis*," p. 32.

ority. Briefly, it specified that any modifications in the city statutes had to have the approval of the Venetian Senate. Moreover, councillors could not undertake more than one public appointment at a time. Further, the public deputies should perform the duties prescribed in the city statutes, could not call deliberations, could only discuss city business in public places, could not consult with someone outside their own group unless a Venetian representative was present, and could not make expenditures other than the ones authorized in the city statutes without the approval of the General Council.[69] Venice had astutely used the reform program of the ambitious Brescian protesters in 1644 and 1645 as a lever to arrest the constriction of municipal power and to ensure that the governing practices outlined in the Brescian city statutes were followed.

No doubt the Brescian delegates concluded a pact with members of the Senate, for immediately after their victory the Brescian city council donated 50,000 ducats, as a token of its appreciation to the Senate.[70] For the Venetians, financial expediency was probably an important priority. In addition to correcting the abuses in government in this important subject city, members of the Senate, in their own way, had won a financial victory.

What of the Brescian protesters? The new councillors were ousted from the city council – without much objection. Denied Venetian support, their demands for reform quickly subsided. As if dismissal from the city council were not humiliation enough, the Brescian protesters were also made to contribute to the donation that had won the Brescian ruling class's cause, for the latter fulfilled their obligation to Venice by levying another of the detestable *taglie* of 5 percent on the taxable assets of urban residents.

SIGNIFICANCE OF THE PROTEST MOVEMENT

What we have in the Venetian state in 1644 and 1645 is not a revolution, but a failed reform of conservative dimensions. The protesters seem to have lacked both the self-confidence and the cohesion as a group to implement their program successfully. Even more importantly, Venice had forced them into a position of inertia by sustaining the aristocratic order. The Republic was careful not to tread

---

69 ASV, *Senato. Rettori*, F. 20, *Ducale*, April 7, 1645, u.d.
70 "Diario Pluda," April 29 and May 17, in *Le cronache bresciane*, ed. Guerrini, vol. 2, pp. 390–391. Several Venetian Senators sent letters of congratulations to the Brescian Council. ASCB, *Lettere Autografe*, B. 1164, letters of May 2, 5–9, 12, 1645.

indiscriminately on the prerogatives of municipal council members;[71] instead it intervened cautiously and selectively in their affairs, when the political or fiscal priorities of state demanded it. Without the support of the state, the intermediate orders remained impotent.

In spite of the inherent tensions that resulted from favoring the municipal ruling class over the local populace, Venice was spared any traces of upheaval in Brescia in 1644 and 1645. Although conditions were tense, there was no hint of uprising: simply an attempted reform of the Brescian Council. This case thus illumines how the Republic of Venice maintained its widely acclaimed reputation in the seventeenth century as a preserver of peace, harmony, and political continuity. Initially, the Venetians outwardly exhibited a general concern for the public welfare of their subjects. The Senate attempted in July 1644 to check the abusive administrative practices of the Brescian oligarchy when it sensed that tensions in the city had reached breaking point. Temporarily, at least, the Venetians established a rapport with the protesters, acknowledged their complaints, and seemed willing to impose social and political reform. This strategy undoubtedly served as a safety valve to release some of the protesters' mounting hostility. Still further, this tactic put Venice at an advantage in dealing with the Brescian oligarchy. The Venetians very cleverly played one group against the other. In addition, the professional ties between members of the Venetian ruling class and Brescian councillors appear to have fostered some degree of political stability. This subject merits wider study throughout the Venetian dominions. Baitelli's familiarity with members of the Venetian Senate and with the Venetian secretaries, for example, strongly suggests that the Republic availed itself of informal social and political networks in order to maintain open communication with the provincial ruling class. Moreover, Venetian negotiations with Baitelli and the Brescian delegation contained a measure of flexibility, the measure needed to contain local resistance to the intervention of the state. The Venetians were disposed to bargain and to compromise. Finally, a careful examination of council membership after 1645 reveals that some protesters found their way into the city council shortly after the attempted reform; still others entered in the following decades.

---

[71] In 1547 Belluno witnessed a reform movement analogous to the one in Brescia in 1644. The *popolari* complained of maladministration in local government and pressured Venice to open the city council to their ranks. In this case the Venetian rectors supported the nobles in power, and Venice opted to allow the local nobility to decide whether to admit the *popolari* or not. Vendramini, *Tensioni politiche*, pp. 139–148. In 1582 in Orzinuovi a movement to reform administration and enlarge the local council was quieted by the Council of Ten, which decided to preserve the status quo. Lanaro Sartori, "Introduzione storica," *RV*, ed. Tagliaferri, vol. XIII, p. xxxv.

While Venetian patricians and Brescian councillors alike had refused in 1645 to bow to the collective campaign of the Brescian protesters, in the end there was room for negotiation and compromise on a one-to-one basis. On this point there are some similarities between the Brescian case and those of Jesi and Siena. In the last two cities, aristocratic closure was never fully realized. There were groups from the intermediate ranks who would have liked to participate in urban political life. As groups they did not succeed, yet there was the possibility that individuals on a one-to-one basis could be coopted into the civic nobility. The same possibility existed in Belluno and Cremona. Some aristocratic regimes, thus, kept a channel of mobility open in order to prevent the conflict that stems from strict exclusion.[72] Finally, the Venetians knew when to bend and thus avoid violent conflict. Through moderation – and manipulation – the *Serenissima* was able to contain the conflict in Brescia in 1644 and 1645. For yet another century and a half the aristocratic order that characterized the Venetian territorial state would endure.

[72] See Mozzarelli, "Stato, patriziato," pp. 466; 492–494.

CHAPTER 8

CONCLUSION

BRESCIA AND THE WESTERN EUROPEAN FRAMEWORK

The Brescian case sheds light on developing social, political, and family structures in sixteenth- and seventeenth-century western European cities as a whole. To begin, the narrowing basis of power was a trend that characterized both the rentier elites of France and Italy as well as the variously mixed ruling circles of nobles, merchants, and guildsmen from Strasbourg to Barcelona.[1] The degree of closure varied from place to place as did the degree of consensus over what constituted civic nobility. In rare instances, such as Venice, patricians legally closed their ranks to newcomers. Many other ruling groups, like Brescia, left their doors slightly ajar but in practice shut merchants, craftsmen, and most newcomers out. They preferred instead to uphold an aristocratic ideal representing the fusion of old urban interests with those of the rural nobility. Though in essence the wealth of these aristocratically minded groups was based on land, their political and cultural ideals found expression in the urban arena.[2] Particularly in north and central Italy, citizenship and public office conferred distinct advantages on ruling families that could only be equalled or perhaps surpassed by feudal privilege, for urban centers historically upheld privileged positions *vis à vis* their respective hinterlands. We have seen this to be true for Brescia, and for the municipal elites in the Venetian Terraferma in general, in the way councillors took advantage of their positions to supervise the Monti and hospitals, to design local fiscal and judicial structures, and to

---

[1] · For Barcelona, see J. Amelang, *Honored Citizens of Barcelona: Patrician Culture and Class Relations, 1490–1714* (Princeton: Princeton University Press, 1986), pp. 51–52; and for comparisons with other European cities, pp. 217–221; for the South German cities, see Brady, *Turning Swiss*, p. 13; for Normandy, J. Dewald, *The Formation of a Provincial Nobility. The Magistrates of the Parlement of Rouen, 1499–1610* (Princeton: Princeton University Press, 1980), p. 80.

[2] Cf. the Norman case in Dewald, *Provincial Nobility*, p. 160.

manipulate the system of food provisioning. The municipal councils of the Venetian Terraferma were still important centers of local power in the late sixteenth and seventeenth centuries.

Aristocratically minded groups that were not legally closed invited challenges from outside, as second-rank citizens exerted pressure to enter their privileged circles. The Brescian protest movement of 1644 is a prime example of the kind of pressure that existed in many of the municipalities of the Venetian Terraferma, the Papal States, and Tuscany. Moreover, some of the sixteenth-century Swiss cities, particularly Zurich, also seemed to experience this kind of tension as government became more oligarchic and aristocratic.[3] At the other end of the western European spectrum, ruling groups that were more open enjoyed more stability. Amelang convincingly argues this for Barcelona, where the elite absorbed commoners and conceded political rights to citizens outside its ranks.[4] The amalgamation of old nobles with new in Barcelona fostered the political unity that would preserve the authority of the ruling class. Amelang draws parallels between Barcelona and some of the Dutch and South German cities, where the guilds still had a voice in politics.[5] Apart from outside pressures to break into privileged governing circles, thinly based oligarchies, such as the ones in Brescia, Genoa, and Cremona, were troubled with internal fissures resulting from the ever-narrowing bases of power. The result was a fluid system of alliances. Brescia is exemplary. The city council was not homogeneous; rather it was composed of small groups that held common interests. The stratification of wealth and power among the various families in the council, which became more pronounced in the late sixteenth and seventeenth centuries, created tensions within the governing class as a whole.

A second development in Brescia, the increasing importance of lawyers and notaries in the sixteenth- and seventeenth-century council, is also characteristic of western European urban elites. This trend was a reflection of the growing importance of professionals in European politics and society, particularly as the bureaucratic structures of the state developed more mature forms. In Brescia, nobles of rural origins as well as members of old citizen families became lawyers and judges. Thus, as in France, law gave families that had had very diverse backgrounds in the medieval period common interests and to some

---

[3] D. Jensen, *Reformation Europe* (Lexington, MA: D. C. Heath, 1981), pp. 79–80.
[4] Amelang, *Honored Citizens*, pp. 217–221.
[5] *Ibid.*, pp. 220–221. For Flanders and Brabant, see H. G. Koenigsberger and G. L. Mosse, *Europe in the Sixteenth Century* (London: Longmans, 1968) p. 262; for Strasbourg and Ulm, see Brady, *Turning Swiss*, p. 13.

degree a common identity in the sixteenth and seventeenth centuries. For example, in Normandy Dewald finds that the *noblesse de robe* grew out of aristocratic society. Robe and sword were not antithetical castes; rather they were a cohesive landed elite.[6] In Brescia as well families with diverse backgrounds blended into a judicial elite.

The third characteristic trend regards the behavior of families linked to power structures. Once the narrow base of power was in place, the maintenance of elite status over the long term came to occupy a central role in determining the career, patrimonial, and marriage strategies of the sixteenth- and seventeenth-century family. Moreover, as the fundamental unit of social organization in an oligarchic regime, the family played a key part in constructing the social and political arrangements that guaranteed the interests of power holders. As such it played a prime role in shaping the inner workings of the regional state. Brescia again is exemplary. Effective government in this area of the Venetian dominion required more than tightening the fiscal and judicial apparatus; it involved penetration of the social arrangements and kinship networks forged by the families in the Brescian ruling class. These arrangements were not static but fluid, and statesmen had to tailor their governing methods to changing circumstances. Moreover, effective statecraft required monitoring relations among the subject city's important families. Those relations often hinged on family interests.

STATE DEVELOPMENT AND LOCAL PARTICULARISM

Much like other European state builders, both princes and republics on the Italian peninsula attempted to check local powers while at the same time reinforcing central structures. Many of the Italian regional states of the sixteenth to eighteenth centuries undertook significant reforms in the realms of justice, the fisc, and defense.[7] Cozzi's work on the systems of justice in Venice, Milan, Sicily, and Naples illuminates areas of progress towards centralization.[8] Italian princes (among them the Spanish Viceroys, Cosimo I, and perhaps most significantly, Emanuele Filiberto of Savoy) played a growing role in the mediation of disputes among their subjects.[9] Vigo and Sella's works on the fisc in the

---

[6] Dewald, *Provincial Nobility*, pp. 15; 88; 102; 110; 309.
[7] Fasano Guarini, "Stati," p. 628. For Florence, see Litchfield, *Emergence of a Bureaucracy*, pp. 6–8.
[8] Cozzi's contributions are reviewed in: Fasano Guarini, "Introduzione," *Potere e società negli stati regionali italiani del '500 e '600*, p. 24.
[9] *Ibid.*

Milanese state also illumine areas of progress: in Spanish Lombardy the sovereign attempted to distribute taxes more evenly by eliminating the privileges associated with status.[10]

Any assessment of state development *vis à vis* local particularism, however, must differentiate between the intentions and ambitions of one state over those of another. Florentine princes, historians tell us, had markedly different objectives than the Venetian ruling class. Fasano Guarini has concluded that the Medici's centralizing ambitions changed the functions and competencies of the urban oligarchies of the Florentine state.[11] The Medici gained more control over local governments than did either Venice or the Papal States, gradually undercutting urban autonomy, reinforcing state magistracies and standardizing laws. The Florentine state was more compact; the institutional network was relatively more organic than either the Venetian, Milanese, or Papal States.[12] There was an attempt to distribute taxes more equitably; to regulate the incomes of subject communities; and to control the alienation of commons.[13] The extension of central control came through old, community organizations, upon which new Florentine institutions were superimposed.[14] Though there is no consensus among historians over the Medici's success, the intention appears to have been to place the ruling classes of the Florentine state under central administrative control.[15]

In contrast to Florence, Venetian policy was programmed to achieve neither centralization nor unification. Local particularism, especially the power of urban aristocracies, prevailed throughout the regional state. Agnadello was a turning point in Venetian relations with the mainland.[16] The Republic focused on repairing the breach that had resulted in a temporary loss of her mainland possessions. Yet the state apparatus was not dramatically changed, nor were the Venetian government's

---

[10] Vigo, "Origini," vol. II, pp. 765–775; D. Sella, "Sotto il dominio della Spagna," in *Il Ducato di Milano del 1535 al 1796*, vol. XI of *Storia d'Italia*, ed. G. Galasso (Turin: UTET, 1984) p. 59.

[11] E. Fasano Guarini, "Principe ed oligarchie nella Toscana del '500." *Forme e tecniche del potere nella città (secoli XIV–XVII)*. Annali della Facoltà di Scienze Politiche, in *Materia e Storia* 4(1979–1980): 115–116. Brown finds that the patriciates of dominion towns like Pescia were tied to Medici patronage. Brown, *Pescia*, pp. 178–186.

[12] *Ibid.*, p. 123.

[13] E. Fasano Guarini, "Potere centrale e comunità soggette nel granducato di Cosimo I," *RSI* 89 (1977): 532–537.

[14] *Ibid.*, p. 512.

[15] *Ibid.*, pp. 530–531; see also F. Diaz, *Il Granducato di Toscana. I Medici*, vol. XIII of *Storia d'Italia*, ed. G. Galasso (Turin: UTET, 1976), pp. 103–105.

[16] See Knapton, "Il Territorio vicentino," pp. 47–51.

relations with the urban aristocracies.[17] The systems of justice[18] and the fisc[19] were strengthened, particularly in the late sixteenth and seventeenth centuries, and the number of central institutions grew. There was, however, not absolute consensus within the Venetian ruling class over political action. For example, there were jurisdictional conflicts between the rectors and appeals tribunals in Venice, such as the state lawyers (Avogadori), and between the rectors and the state inquisitors. Further, Venetian capacity to intervene in local affairs was still limited. And we must take a geopolitical approach to studying those limitations. Venetian relations with Brescia or the Friuli, both peripheral areas, were different from those with Padua or the Trevigiano, where Venetians themselves owned extensive properties. Venice tended to be more lenient with the border areas, which were not only in strategic locations but also well endowed with fiefs holding favorable jurisdictions. Finally, it is important to underline that the municipalities claimed ample powers, and that the rectors acted largely as mediators. Each city retained its own municipal statutes and designed its own fiscal and judicial procedures. Without executive structures in the provinces, Venice *collaborated* with municipal institutions. Though Venice dealt more directly with rural institutions over the sixteenth and seventeenth centuries, the municipalities continued to maintain privileged positions.

In the Brescian case, supervision of the Monti di Pietà and the city's hospitals; and design of the *estimo*, of the system of food provisioning, and of other local structures gave councillors ample latitude to protect their own interests. It did not, however, necessarily make their authority absolute. They had to defend challenges and criticisms before Venetian statesmen in the capital city, and before Venetian rectors and other state representatives in Brescia. Further, they had to develop effective methods of negotiation. The Brescian representative in Venice, or nunzio, was a keystone figure in this process. His familiarity with the viewpoints of Venetian statesmen and of lawyers representing other corps within the province, and his observations of Venetian

---

[17] Fasano Guarini, "Introduzione," pp. 23–24.

[18] G. Cozzi, "Ambiente veneziano, ambiente veneto," in *L'uomo e il suo ambiente*, ed. S. Rosso-Mazzinghi (Florence: Sansoni, 1973), pp. 93–146; G. Cozzi, "Authority and the Law in Renaissance Venice," in J. R. Hale, ed., *Renaissance Venice* (London: Faber and Faber, 1973), pp. 293–345; G. Cozzi, "Considerazioni sull'amministrazione della giustizia nella Repubblica di Venezia (sec. XV–XVI)," in *Florence and Venice: Comparisons and Relations* (Florence: La Nuova Italia, 1980), vol. II, pp. 101–133; Cozzi, "La politica del diritto," in *Stato società e giustizia*, ed. Cozzi, vol. I, pp. 17–152.

[19] Knapton, "Il fisco," pp. 15–57; Knapton, "L'organizzazione fiscale," pp. 377–418; Knapton, "Il Territorio vicentino," pp. 33–105.

treatment of other mainland cities, provided city councillors with a basis for planning arguments and strategies before the state. Overall, Venice was careful to respect urban statutes and aristocratic rule, but privileges could also be forgotten and oligarchic abuse that threatened order and stability was ill tolerated. Two examples come to mind: Venetian efforts to redress some of the fiscal inequalities of the Brescian Territorio over the sixteenth and seventeenth centuries and to use the Territorio as a mediator between the capital city and the rural population; and Venetian action in the protest movement of 1644, a reminder to city councillors that the state expected them to live up to their fiscal responsibilities and to keep city finances in working order.

Despite their differing interests, Venetian statesmen and Brescian councillors appear to have made an effort to be cooperative. Ultimately Venice guaranteed the aristocratic order in Brescia and generously delegated power to local councillors. Both parties made efforts to work out their contrasts through negotiation and to find some meeting ground. In the realm of justice, there were, in Cozzi's terms, two legal systems, with local jurists defending local structures and secular traditions on the one hand and Venetian statesmen trying to work with local structures while at the same time meeting the changing needs of the state on the other. In the realm of local government, it appears that both Venetian statesmen and Brescian councillors shared common interests; above all, to maintain order and stability. Thus it is insufficient to examine simply how Venice attempted to monitor the governing practices of Brescian council members, for similar efforts came from within the local ruling class as well. Perhaps the fisc was the most prolific terrain for contrasts between state and periphery, as financial necessity pressed the Venetians to assert more sovereignty. The Republic made efforts to penetrate and check the activities of local bureaucratic organs and to find some meeting ground with local power holders. In a peripheral area such as Brescia, where the families of prominence had enjoyed secular domination, the state during the ancien régime could not realistically hope to do more.

APPENDIX 1

THE FAMILIES INSCRIBED IN THE BRESCIAN COUNCIL: 1588 TO 1650

1.	Alberti	32.	Buratti
2.	Aleni	33.	Caballi
3.	Alventi	34.	Cagnola
4.	Appiani	35.	Calini
5.	Ardesi	36.	Calzavelia
6.	Armanni	37.	Campana
7.	Arrici	38.	Capitani
8.	de Aste	39.	Caprioli
9.	Averoldi	40.	Caravati
10.	Avogadro	41.	Carenzone
11.	Avoltori	42.	Carrara
12.	Baitelli	43.	Carravati
13.	Barbera	44.	Castelli
14.	Barbisone	45.	Cataneo
15.	Bargnani	46.	Cazzaghi
16.	Bazardi	47.	Cazzamali
17.	Belacatti	48.	Cegula
18.	Belasi	49.	Ceruti
19.	Bergognini	50.	Cesarenus
20.	Bettoncelli	51.	Chizzola
21.	Bianchi	52.	Cinalia
22.	Bocati	53.	Coccalio
23.	Bocca	54.	Cocchi
24.	Bona	55.	Comotta
25.	Bonati	56.	Confalonieri
26.	Borgondi	57.	Conforti
27.	Bornati	58.	Coradelli
28.	Briggia	59.	Corte
29.	Brognoli	60.	Covi
30.	Brunelli	61.	Crotti
31.	Buarni	62.	Ducchi

63.	Durante	108.	Lolli
64.	Emigli	109.	Longhena
65.	Fabio	110.	Loni
66.	Faite	111.	Lupatini
67.	Fasana	112.	Luzzaghi
68.	Fausti	113.	Maggi
69.	Faustini	114.	Malveti
70.	Fe	115.	Manerba
71.	Federici	116.	de Mantua
72.	Federici de Curte	117.	Marchetti
73.	Fenaroli	118.	Marende
74.	Feroldi	119.	Marini
75.	Fide	120.	Martinengo
76.	Fisonei	121.	Masperoni
77.	Fobelli	122.	Mauri
78.	Foresti	123.	Mazzole
79.	Gabbiani	124.	Mazzuchelli
80.	Gadaldi	125.	Medici
81.	Gaetani	126.	Mercanda
82.	Gafurri	127.	Merlini
83.	Galli	128.	Monte
84.	Gambara	129.	Montini
85.	Ganassoni	130.	Moresco
86.	Gandini	131.	de Morris Gambara
87.	Garbelli	132.	Nassini
88.	Gavandi	133.	Nazari
89.	Gavardi	134.	Nuolina
90.	Gavattari	135.	Ochi
91.	Gervasi	136.	Odasi
92.	Ghidella	137.	Offlaga
93.	Girelli	138.	Oldofredi
94.	Glerola	139.	Olmo
95.	Gobbini	140.	Oriani
96.	Gorni	141.	Padua
97.	Goti	142.	Pagnani
98.	Grati	143.	Paitoni
99.	Grilli	144.	Palazzi
100.	Guarnari	145.	Papiae
101.	Guerrini	146.	Paratici
102.	de Humeltati	147.	Parenti
103.	Lana	148.	Parpagni
104.	Lantana	149.	Passirani
105.	de Laude	150.	Patusi
106.	Leni	151.	Pedrocchi
107.	Lodetti	152.	Pedroche

153.	Pedroche de Peronis	187.	Scaramutie
154.	Penne	188.	Schilini
155.	San Peregrini	189.	de Scopulis
156.	Peroni·	190.	Senna
157.	Pesente	191.	Seriati
158.	Pezzani	192.	Serina
159.	Pischerie	193.	Sicci
160.	Pischerini	194.	Soncini
161.	Placentini	195.	Stella
162.	Pontecarale	196.	Suardi
163.	Pontevici	197.	Suraga
164.	Pontoli	198.	Tairdini
165.	Ponzoni	199.	Tarelli
166.	Porcellaga	200.	Terzi
167.	Prandoni	201.	Thomasi
168.	Prati	202.	Tiberi
169.	Provagli	203.	Trivella
170.	Pulusella	204.	Trussi
171.	Ripe	205.	Tuzzani
172.	Roberti	206.	Ugeri
173.	Rodengo	207.	Ugoni
174.	Ronzoni	208.	Urcei
175.	Rosa	209.	Ustiani
176.	Rossa	210.	Valtorta
177.	Rovati	211.	Vineltati
178.	Saiani	212.	Violini
179.	Sala	213.	Zamara
180.	Salodi	214.	Zanatta
181.	San Gervasi	215.	Zanetti
182.	Savaldi	216.	Zaniboni
183.	Savalli	217.	Zanucha
184.	Savoldi	218.	Zerbini
185.	Scalvini	219.	Zola
186.	Scanzi	220.	Zoni

APPENDIX 2

A NOTE ON TAXATION

Direct taxation

Individuals as well as corporate entities were required to list their assets and debts. Four deputies from the city council then evaluated the declaration and a tax rate was assigned. Each tax household received a five-digit numerical coefficient in *denari, terzi, sesti, centenari,* and *decime.* In 1641 one *denaro d'estimo* was equivalent to 9,120 *lire planet;* a *terzo* was equal to a third of this sum; a *sesto* to a sixth; a *centenaro* to a ninth; and a *decime* to a tenth. According to the regulations for 1641, a tax rate of 3 percent was applied to the household's total assets (ASV, *Provveditori da terra da Mar,* F. 272, Letter of the deputati all'estimo, May 1, 1647), but the evaluations were deliberately kept low. Each digit corresponded to a specific sum of money, or at times a quantity of grain, to be forwarded to the Camera Ducale to pay for the various direct taxes, e.g., *sussidi, taglie,* etc. (ASB, *Cancelleria Prefettizia Superiore,* B. 61, No. 1., *Estimo: Provvedimenti, Transazioni [città, clero, Territorio di Brescia] 1531–1795.* I would like to thank Professor Bernardo Scalia for this citation.) The register of coefficients assigned to each tax household for 1641 is stored in the Archivio Storico Comunale di Brescia, in vol. 188, "Estimo della Sola Città." The actual tax declarations are in Brescia, Archivio di Stato, *Estimo* (1641), filed according to city districts.

Glossary of direct taxes (based on the *estimo*)

1. *gravezze:* taxes based on immovables and credit. They included:
   a. *gente d'arme:* instituted in 1517 to cover expenses for cavalry.
   b. *ordine di banca,* or, *alloggi di cavalleria:* tax to maintain the militia.
   c. *sussidio:* instituted in 1529 as an extraordinary tax in wartime; it became an ordinary tax. In the seventeenth century the Terraferma provided Venice 100,000 ducats. The Bresciano's share of this was 25,000 ducats.

    d.   *dadia delle lanze*, or, *colta ducale:* for the provinces beyond the Mincio. A tax used to support soldiers.

2.   *taglia* or *taglione:* extraordinary taxes, often in war time.

Glossary of indirect taxes

1.   *dazi:* taxes on foodstuffs and manufactures, or on imports and exports. Among them:
    a.   *gabella:* salt tax.
    b.   *balzello:* extraordinary tax.
    c.   *dogana:* customs tax.
    d.   *pedaggio:* transit tax.
    e.   *macina:* tax on grinding of grain.

Source. F. Besta, *Bilanci generali della Repubblica di Venezia* (Venice: Grafico Vicentini, 1912), pp. clv; clxx–clxxi; clxxvi; clxxvii–clxxviii; clxxx.

BIBLIOGRAPHY

ARCHIVAL COLLECTIONS

Archivio Storico Comunale di Brescia

Actum Deputatorum
Indice Pavone
Lettere Autografe
Lettere Pubbliche
Polizze d'Estimo
Processi di Nobiltà
Provvisioni
Vol. 188, "Estimo della sola città." (1641)
Vols. 1426 1/2 A–C, "Estimo di ciascun nobile e geneologia antica."

Archivio di Stato di Brescia

Fondo Avogadro
Archivio Territoriale ex Veneto
Cancelleria Pretoria. Ducali
Cancelleria Prefettizia Inferiore. Ducali
Cancelleria Prefettizia Superiore
Hospedale Maggiore. Atti di Eredità e Processi: Famiglie Lana, Giovanni Antonio;
    Maggi, Lodovico; Ugone, Carlo.
Polizze d'Estimo 1641, Buste 1–13

Archivio di Stato di Venezia

Avogaria di Comun. Penale
Avogaria di Comun. Processi per Nobiltà
Collegio V (Secreta). Relazioni
Consiglio dei Dieci. Lettere dai Rettori di Brescia ai Capi
Consiglio dei Dieci. Parti Comuni
Provveditori da Terra e da Mar

Senato. Archivio Proprio dei Rettori di Brescia
Senato. Dispacci dei Rettori di Brescia
Senato. Rettori
Senato. Terra

MANUSCRIPTS

BMCV, *Archivio Donà delle Rose*, No. 17. Donà, Leonardo. "Scritture della sua Podestaria a Brescia (1579)"

BMCV, *Archivio Donà delle Rose*, No. 160, untitled

BMCV, Codice Cicogna 2525, No. 33. "Estimo di Brescia e suo Territorio," u.d.

BNMV, MS. It VII 1155 = (7453). Report of Giovanni Battista Cattanio to Piero Contarini, Capitano of Brescia, ff. 167r–190r; report of Michele Scavelli di Ascani, ff. 111r–127v; "Registro di lettere communemente scritte in publico dagli Ecc.mi Sig.i Rettori di Brescia, coad. al foro prefittizio sotto l.Eccmo Venier, Capitano e Zorzi (1645–1646)." ff. 284r–364v

BQ, MS. Codice di Rosa, No. 79, f. 175. Untitled Catalogue of the Brescian Protestors, 1644

BQ, MS. Codici Odorici, No. 105 = O.VI.28. "Istoria delli sediziosi e Malcontenti contro lo stato dell'Ill.ma Città di Brescia con la confermazione delli Privilegi, usi, statuti, e consuetudini della medesima città, 1644." ff. 1r–7v = "Rotolo delli sediziosi"

BQ, MS. F. II. 11, ff. 80r–85r, Averoldo, Lorenzo. "Rappresentanza fatta l'anno 1619 al principe dagli ambasciatori della città. Averoldi, Baitelli e Ugoni"

BQ, MS. D. I. 7, Baitelli, Lodovico. "Istoria della rivoluzione dei malcontenti sediziosi contro la nobiltà e Consiglio di Brescia-l'anno 1644"

BQ, MS. F. II. 11, ff. 92r–100r, Baitelli, Lodovico. "Supplica della città fatta l'anno 1648 per sollievo di gravezze"

BQ, MS. Fe 9m 3a, ff. 143–284, "Elenco delle famiglie nobili di Brescia iscritto nel Gran Consiglio fino al 1796." ff. 143–284

BQSV, MS. Classe IV, Cod. LXV. Baitelli, Lodovico. "Historia del moto della plebe di Brescia per l'ingresso del Maggiore Consiglio, 1644–1645"

CONTEMPORARY WORKS

Botero, G. *Delle relationi universali di Giovanni Botero.* Vicenza: Giorgio Angelieri, 1596

Coronelli, V. *Corso geografico universale.* Venice, 1689

Cozzando, L. *Libreria bresciana.* Brescia: Rizzardi, 1685

Faino, B. *Arbore gentilizio historico della nobile e antica famiglia Luzzago.* Brescia: Rizzardi, 1671

Lanteri, G. *Della economica.* Venice: Vincenzo Valgrisi, 1560

Leggi criminali del Serenissimo Dominio Veneto in un solo volume raccolte e per pubblico decreto restampate. Venice: Antonio Pinelli, 1751

Parti e terminazioni prese in vari consigli della Repubblica in materiale criminali. Venice: Stampatori ducali vari, Sec. XVI–XVIII

Podavinii, D. *De nobilitate Brixiae.* Brescia: Apud Vincentium Sabbium, 1587

Raccolta di privilegi, ducali, giudizi, terminazioni, e decreti pubblici sopra varie materie giurisdizionali, civili, criminali, ed economiche concernenti la città di Brescia. Brescia: Tip. G. B. Bossino, 1732

Rossi, O. *Elogi historici di bresciani illustri. Teatro di Ottavio Rossi.* Brescia: Bartolomeo Fontana, 1620

Savonarola, R. *Universus Terrarum Orbi Scriptorum, Calamo Delineatus.* Patavii: ex typographia olim Frambotti, 1713

Statuti civili della magnifica città di Brescia. Volgarizzati. Brescia: Pietro Vescovo, 1776

Statuta civitatis Brixiae. Brescia: Turlinus, 1557

Statuta magnificae civitatis Brixiae cum reformatione novissima anni 1621. Brescia: Joannis Mariae Ricciardi, 1722

SECONDARY WORKS

Alberti, A. and Cessi, R. *La politica mineraria della Repubblica Veneta.* Rome: Provveditori generali dello stato, 1927

Almagià, R. *Le regioni d'Italia.* Turin: UTET, 1960

Amelang, J. *Honored Citizens of Barcelona: Patrician Culture and Class Relations, 1490–1714.* Princeton: Princeton University Press, 1986

Aspetti e cause della decadenza economica veneziana nel secolo XVII. Venice–Rome: Istituto per la Collaborazione Culturale, 1961

Aymard, M. "Pour une histoire des élites dans l'Italie moderne." In *La famiglia e la vita quotidiana in Europa dal '400 al '600.* Rome: Istituto Poligrafico e Zecca dello Stato, 1986, pp. 207–219

Baker, G. R. F. "Nobiltà in declino: il caso di Siena sotto i Medici e gli Asburgo-Lorena." *RSI* 84 (1972): 584–616

Barbagli, M. *Sotto lo stesso tetto. Mutamenti della famiglia in Italia dal XV al XX secolo.* Bologna: Il Mulino, 1984

Barbieri, G. "Il trattatello 'Della economia' di G. Lanteri, letterato e architetto bresciano del secolo XVI." *Rassegna degli Archivi di Stato* 21 (1961): 35–46

Barni, G. "Mutamenti di ideali sociali dal secolo XVI al secolo XVIII: giuristi, nobiltà e mercatura." *Rivista Internazionale di Filosofia del Diritto* 34(1957): 766–787

Basaglia, E. "Aspetti della giustizia penale nel '700: una critica alla concessione dell'impunità agli uccisori dei banditi." *Atti del Istituto Veneto di Scienze, Lettere ed Arti* 142 (1979–80): 1–16

"Il controllo della criminalità nella Repubblica di Venezia. Il secolo XVI: un momento di passaggio." In *Atti del Convegno Venezia e la terraferma attraverso le relazioni dei rettori.* Edited by A. Tagliaferri. Milan: Giuffrè, 1981, pp. 65–78

Beloch, K. J. "Bevölkerungsgeschichte der Republik Venedig." *Jahrbuchern fur National Ökonomie und Statistik.* Jena: G. Fischer, 1899, pp. 1–49

Bevölkerungsgeschichte Italiens. 3 vols., vol. III: *Die Bevölkerung der Republik Venedig, des Herzogtums Mailand, Piemonts, Genuas, Corsicas und Sardiniens.* Berlin and Leipzig: De Gruyter, 1961

Beltrami, D. *La penetrazione economica dei veneziani in Terraferma. Forze di lavoro e proprietà fondiaria nelle campagne venete dei secoli XVII e XVIII.* Venice–Rome: Istituto per la Collaborazione Culturale, 1961

Saggio di storia dell'agricoltura nella Repubblica di Venezia durante l'età moderna. Venice–Rome: Istituto per la Collaborazione Culturale, 1955

Storia della popolazione di Venezia dalle fine del secolo XVI alla caduta della Repubblica. Padua: A. Milani, 1954

Benzoni, G. "Lodovico Baitelli." In *Dizionario biografico degli Italiani.* Istituto della Enciclopedia Italiana Fondata da Giovanni Treccani. Vol. V. Rome: Istituto Polgrafico dello stato, 1963, pp. 305–306

Berengo, M. "Africo Clemente, agronomo padovano del Cinquecento." In *Miscellanea Augusto Campana.* Edited by R. Avesani, G. Billanovich, M. Ferrari, and G. Pozzi. Padua: Editrice Antenore, 1981, pp. 27–69

"Il Cinquecento." In *La storiografia italiana negli ultimi vent'anni.* 2 vols., vol. I. Milan: Marzorati, 1970, pp. 483–518

Nobili e mercanti nella Lucca del '500. Turin: Giulio Einaudi (Toso), 1965

"Patriziato e nobiltà: il caso veronese." *RSI* 87 (1975): 493–517

"A proposito di proprietà fondiaria." *RSI* 82 (1970): 121–147

La società veneta alla fine del Settecento. Florence: G. C. Sansoni, 1956

Besta, F., ed. *Bilanci generali della Repubblica di Venezia.* 2nd series. Vol. I, Tomo I. Venice: Grafico Vicentini, 1912, pp. xxxxv–ccxxiii

Bettoni-Cazzago, F. "La nobiltà bresciana." In *Brixia.* Brescia: F. Apollonio, 1882, pp. 91–113

Storia di Brescia narrata al popolo. Brescia: F. Apollonio, 1909

Bonfiglio Dosio, G. "La condizione giuridica del civis e le concessioni di cittadinanza negli statuti bresciani del XIII e XIV secolo." *Atti dell'Istituto Veneto di Scienze, Lettere ed Arti. Classe di scienze morali, lettere ed arti* 137 (1978–1979): 523–532.

Bonomi, G. *Il Castello di Cavernago e I Conti Martinengo Colleoni.* Bergamo: Stabilimento Fratelli Bolis, 1884

Borelli, G. "Aspetti e forme della ricchezza negli enti ecclesiastici e monastici di Verona tra secoli XVI e XVIII." In *Chiese e monasteri a Verona.* Edited by G. Borelli. Verona: Banca Popolare di Verona, 1980, pp. 124–165

"Un caso di crisi urbana nel secolo della decadenza italiana." In *La pittura a Verona tra Sei e Settecento.* Edited by L. Magagnato. Vicenza: Neri Pozza, 1978, pp. 247–263

ed. *Chiese e monasteri a Verona.* Verona: Banca Popolare di Verona, 1980

"Introduzione." *Podestaria e capitanato di Verona.* Vol. IX of *RV.* Edited by A. Tagliaferri. Milan: Giuffrè, 1977, pp. xxxvii–li

"Patriziato della dominante e patriziati della Terraferma." *Atti del convegno Venezia e la Terraferma.* Edited by A. Tagliaferri. Milan: Giuffrè, 1981, 79–95

Un patriziato della Terraferma veneta tra XVII e XVIII secolo. Ricerche sulla nobiltà veronese. Milan: Giuffrè, 1974

"Il problema dei patrizi urbani in Italia nell'età moderna." *Economia e Storia* 1 (1978): 123–129

Borelli, G., P. Lanaro, and F. Vecchiato, eds. *Il sistema fiscale veneto. Problemi e aspetti, XV–XVIII secolo.* Verona: Libreria Universitario Editrice, 1982

Bosisio, A. "Il comune." In *Storia di Brescia.* Edited by G. Treccani degli Alfieri. Vol. I. Brescia: Morcelliana, 1961, pp. 561–710

Brady, T. *Turning Swiss: Cities and Empire, 1450–1550.* Cambridge: Cambridge University Press, 1985

Braudel, F. *The Mediterranean and the Mediterranean World in the Age of Philip II.* Trans. Sian Reynolds. New York: Harper & Row, 1972

Brizzi, G. P. *La formazione della classe dirigente nel Sei-Settecento. I seminaria nobilium nell'Italia centro-settentrionale.* Bologna: Il Mulino, 1976

Brown, J. *In the Shadow of Florence. Provincial Society in Renaissance Pescia.* New York and Oxford: Oxford University Press, 1982

Cappelli, A. *Cronología, cronografía e calendario perpetuo.* 4th edn. Milan: Ulríco Hoeplí, 1978

Capretti, F. "Una controversia fra la città e il clero di Brescia nel secolo XVII." *Brixia Sacra* 3 (1912): 3–19

"L'interdetto di Paolo V a Brescia." *Brixia Sacra* 6 (1915): 224–239

Mezzo secolo di vita vissuta a Brescia nel Seicento (1600–1649). Brescia: Scuola Tipografica Opera Pavoniana, 1934

Caro Lopez, C. "La formazione del ceto dirigente a Cividale di Belluno." *Archivio Storico di Belluno, Feltre e Cadore* 221 (1977): 174–183; 222–223 (1978): 45–50; 224 (1978): 81–88; 225 (1978): 134–147

Carozzi, C. "Brescia." In *Storia d'Italia.* Vol. VI: *Atlante.* Turin: Einaudi, 1976, pp. 363–366

Cattini, M. "L'agricoltura nella piana bresciana al tempo del Gallo: strutture fondiarie, forme di conduzione e techniche colturali." In *Agostino Gallo nella cultura del Cinquecento.* Edited by M. Pegrari. Brescia: Tipografia Artigiana, 1988, pp. 25–43

Cessi, R. *Storia della Repubblica di Venezia.* Reprint edition. Florence: Giunti Martello, 1981

Chabod, F. *Lo stato di Milano nell'Impero di Carlo V.* Milan: Tuminelli, 1934

"Stipendi nominali e busta paga effettiva dei funzionari milanesi alla fine del Cinquecento." In *Miscellanea in onore di Robert Cessi.* Vol. II. Rome, 1958, pp. 187–361

"Usi ed abusi nello Stato di Milano a mezzo il '500." In *Potere e società negli*

stati regionali italiani del '500 e '600. Edited by E. Fasano Guarini. Bologna:
Il Mulino, 1978, pp. 99–131
"Y a-t-il un Etat de la Renaissance?" In F. Chabod. *Scritti sul Rinascimento.*
Turin: Einaudi, 1967
Chittolini, G. "Alcune considerazioni sulla storia politico-istituzionale del
tardo medioevo: alle origini degli 'stati regionali.'" *Annali dell'Istituto
Storico Italo-germanico in Trento* 2 (1976): 401–419
"I capitoli di dedizione delle communità lombarde a Francesco Sforza.
Motivi di contrasto fra città e contado." *Felix olim Lombardia. Studi di
storia padana dedicati dagli allievi a Giuseppe Martini.* Milan: Facoltà di
Lettere e Filosofia dell'Università, 1978, pp. 673–698
ed. *La crisi degli ordinamenti comunali e le origini dello stato del Rinascimento.*
Bologna: Il Mulino, 1979
"La crisi delle libertà comunali e le origini dello stato territoriale." *RSI* 82
(1970): 99–120
La formazione dello stato regionale e le istituzioni del contado. Secoli XIV–XV.
Turin: Giulio Einaudi, 1979
"Le terre separate nel Ducato di Milano in età Sforzesca." In *Milano nell'età
di Ludovico il Moro. Atti del convegno internazionale 28 febbraio-4 marzo 1983.*
2 vols., vol. I. Milan: Biblioteca Trivulziana del Comune di Milano,
1983, pp. 115–128
Chojnacki, S. "Dowries and Kinsmen in Early Renaissance Venice." *Journal of
Interdisciplinary History* 4 (1975): 41–70
"Patrician Women in Early Renaissance Venice." *Studies in the Renaissance*
21 (1974): 176–203
Cipolla, C.M. "The Economic Decline of Italy." In *Crisis and Change in the
Venetian Economy.* Edited by B. Pullan. London: Methuen and Co. Ltd.,
1968, pp. 127–145
Storia economica dell'Europa pre-industriale. Bologna: Il Mulino, 1974
ed. *Storia economica d'Europa.* 6 vols. Turin: UTET, 1979–1980
Collana di bibliografie geografiche delle regioni italiane. Vol. XIII: *Lombardia.*
Consiglio Nazionale delle Ricerche. Comitato per le scienze storiche,
filologiche e filosofiche. Naples: La Buona Stampa, 1969
Corazzol, G. "Una fallita riforma del Consiglio di Feltre nel '500." *Rivista
Bellunese* 3 (1975): 287–299
Fitti e livelli a Grano. Un aspetto del credito rurale nel Veneto del '500. Milan:
Franco Angeli, 1980
Livelli stipulati a Venezia nel 1591. Pisa: Giardini editori, 1986
Cortelazzo, M., and P. Zolli. *Dizionario etimologico della lingua italiana.* 4 vols.
Bologna: Zanichelli, 1979
Cozzi, G. "Ambiente veneziano, ambiente veneto." In *L'uomo e il suo ambiente.*
Edited by S. Rosso-Mazzinghi. Florence: Sansoni, 1973, pp. 93–146
"Ambiente veneziano, ambiente veneto. Governanti e governati di qua dal
Mincio nei secoli XV–XVIII." In *Storia della cultura veneta.* Vol. IV/II: *Il
Seicento.* Vicenza: Neri Pozza, 1984, pp. 495–539

"Authority and the Law in Renaissance Venice." In *Renaissance Venice*. Edited by J. R. Hale. London: Faber and Faber, 1973, pp. 293–345

"Considerazioni sull'amministrazione della giustizia nella Repubblica di Venezia (sec. XV–XVI)." In *Florence and Venice: Comparisons and Relations*. 2 vols., Vol. II. Florence: La Nuova Italia, 1979–1980, pp. 101–133

Il doge Nicolò Contarini: Ricerche sul patriziato veneziano agli inizi del Seicento. Venice and Rome: Istituto per la Collaborazione Culturale, 1958

"La politica del diritto nella Repubblica di Venezia." In *Stato, società e giustizia*. Edited by G. Cozzi. Vol. I. Rome: Jouvence, 1981, pp. 15–152

Repubblica di Venezia e stati italiani. Politica e giustizia dal secolo XVI al secolo XVIII. Turin: Giulio Einaudi, 1982

ed. *Stato, società e giustizia nella repubblica veneta (secoli XV–XVIII)*. 2 vols. Rome: Jouvence, 1981 and 1985

Cozzi, G. and M. Knapton. *Storia della repubblica di Venezia. Dalla guerra di Chioggia alla riconquista della terraferma*. Turin: UTET, 1986

Cracco, G. and Knapton, M. eds. *Dentro lo "stado italico." Venezia e la Terraferma fra Quattro e Seicento*. Trent: Gruppo Culturale Civis, 1984

Da Lezze, G. *Il catastico bresciano di Giovanni Da Lezze (1609–10)*. Edited by C. Pasero. 3 vols. Brescia: F. Apollonio, 1969

Dal Pane, L. "La politica annonaria di Venezia." *Giornale degli economisti e annali di economia*, N.S. 5(1946): 331–353

Da Mosto, A. *L'Archivio di Stato di Venezia, indice generale storico descrittivo ed analitico*. 2 vols. Rome: Biblioteca d'Arte Editrice, 1937

Davidson, Nicolas. "Northern Italy in the 1590s." In *The European Crisis of the 1590s*. Edited by P. Clark. London and Boston: G. Allen and Unwin, 1985, pp. 157–176

Davis, J. C. *The Decline of the Venetian Nobility as a Ruling Class*. Baltimore: The John Hopkins University Press, 1962

A Venetian Family and Its Fortune, 1500–1900. Philadelphia: American Philosophical Society, 1975

Davis, N. Z. "Ghosts, Kin, and Progeny: Some Features of Family Life in Early Modern France." *Daedalus* 106 (1977): 87–114

De Maddalena, A. "I bilanci dal 1600 al 1647 di una azienda fondiaria lombarda." *Rivista Internazionale di Scienze Economiche e Commerciali* 2 (1955): 510–525; 671–698

"Contributo alla storia dell'agricoltura della 'bassa' lombarda. Appunti sulla 'possessione' di Belgiojoso (secoli XVI–XVIII)." *Archivio Storico Lombardo*. 8th series 8 (1958): 165–183

"L'Europa rurale (1500–1750)." In *Storia economica di Europa*. Edited by C. Cipolla. Turin: UTET, 1979, pp. 209–285

"Il mondo rurale italiano nel Cinque e nel Seicento." *RSI* 76 (1964): 349–426

Prezzi e aspetti di mercato in Milano durante il secolo XVI. Milan: Malfasi, 1950

Del Torre, G. *Venezia e la terraferma dopo la guerra di Cambrai. Fiscalità e amministrazione, (1515–1530)*. Milan: Franco Angeli, 1986

Dewald, J. *The Formation of a Provincial Nobility. The Magistrates of the Parlement of Rouen, 1499–1610*. Princeton: Princeton University Press, 1980

Diaz, F. *Il Granducato di Toscana. I Medici*. Vol. XIII of *Storia d'Italia*. Edited by G. Galasso. Turin: UTET, 1976

Donati, C. *L'idea di nobiltà in Italia. Secoli XIV–XVIII*. Rome–Bari: Laterza, 1988

"Scipione Maffei e la scienza chiamata cavaleresca. Saggio sull'ideologia nobiliare al principio del '700." *RSI* 90 (1978): 30–71

Ercole, F. "L'istituto dotale nella pratica e nella legislazione statuaria dell'Italia superiore." *Rivista Italiana per le Scienze Giuridiche* 45 (1909): 191–302; 46 (1910): 167–257

Fasano Guarini, E. "Introduzione." *Potere e società negli stati regionali italiani del '500 e '600*. Edited by E. Fasano Guarini. Bologna: Il Mulino, 1978, pp. 7–47

"Potere centrale e comunità soggette nel granducato di Cosimo I." *RSI* 89 (1977): 490–538

ed. *Potere e società negli stati regionali italiani del '500 e '600*. Bologna: Il Mulino, 1978

"Principe ed oligarchie nella Toscana del '500." *Forme e techniche del potere nella città (secoli XIV–XVII)*. Annali della Facoltà di Scienze Politiche. In *Materia e Storia* 4 (1979–80): 105–126

"Gli stati dell'Italia centro-settentrionale tra Quattro e Cinquecento: continuità e trasformazioni." *Società e Storia* 21 (1983): 617–640

Fasolo, G. "Il nunzio permanente di Vicenza a Venezia nel secolo XVI." *Archivio Veneto* 17 (1935): 90–178

Ferraro, J. "Feudal-Patrician Investments in the Bresciano and the Politics of the *Estimo*, 1426–1641." *Studi Veneziani*, N.S. 7 (1983): 31–57

"Oligarchs, Protesters, and the Republic of Venice: The 'Revolution of the Discontents' in Brescia, 1644–1645." *Journal of Modern History* 60 (1988): 627–653

"Proprietà terriera e potere nello Stato veneto: la nobiltà bresciana del '400–'500." In *Dentro lo "stado italico."* Edited by G. Cracco and M. Knapton. Trent: Gruppo Culturale Civis, 1984, pp. 159–182

Ferro, M. *Dizionario del diritto comune e veneto*. Second edition. 2 vols. Venice: Andrea Santini e Figlio, 1845–1847

Frigo, D. "Governo della casa, nobiltà e 'republica': l''economica' in Italia tra Cinque e Seicento." *Governo della casa, governo della città*. Edited by M. Bianchini, D. Frigo, and C. Mozzarelli. *Cheiron* 4 (1985): 75–94

Gaibi, A. "Le armi da fuoco." In *Storia di Brescia*. Edited by G. Treccani degli Alfieri. Vol. III. Brescia: Morcelliana, 1964, pp. 819–884

Goldthwaite, R. "The Florentine Palace as Domestic Architecture." *American Historical Review* 72 (1972): 977–1,012

Grendi, E. "Capitazioni e nobiltà genovese in età moderna." *Quaderni Storici* 8 (1974): 403–444

Grubb, J.S. "Alla ricerca delle prerogative locali: la cittadinanza a Vicenza, 1404–1509." In *Dentro lo "stado italico."* Edited by G. Cracco and M. Knapton. Trent: Gruppo Culturale Civis, 1984, pp. 17–31

Firstborn of Venice. Vicenza in the Early Renaissance State. Baltimore and London: The Johns Hopkins University Press, 1988

"Patriciate and Estimo in the Vicentine Quattrocento." In *Il sistema fiscale veneto.* Edited by G. Borelli, P. Lanaro, and F. Vecchiato. Verona: Libreria Universitario Editrice, 1982, pp. 147–173

"When Myths Lose Power: Four Decades of Venetian Historiography." *Journal of Modern History* 58 (1986): 43–94

Guerrini, P. "Un codice bresciano di privilegi nobiliari." *RA* 25 (1927): 454–460

"Il consiglio generale di Brescia e il governo civile e militare della sua provincia nel Seicento." *RA* 24 (1926): 257–267

"Il Conte Curzio Martinengo-Palatino." *Brixia* 3 (1916): 1–2

"I Conti di Bona di Brescia." *RA* 27 (1929): 227–229

"I Conti di Martinengo e il feudo di Urago d'Oglio." *Brixia Sacra* 15 (1924): 52–96

ed. *Le cronache bresciane inedite dei secoli XV–XIX.* 4 vols. Brescia: Istituto artigianale, 1922–1930

"Famiglie nobili bresciane, Soncino o de Soncino." *RA* 32 (1934): 485–490; 546–554

"Il 'libro d'oro' nella nobiltà bresciana nel '500." *RA* 17 (1919): 196–201; 231–237; 272–276; 319–322

"I Luzzago." *RA* 28 (1930): 198–205; 297–304; 341–348

"Il moto della borghesia bresciana contro la nobiltà nel 1644 ed una satira inedita." *RA* 25 (1927): 175–178

"La nobile famiglia Bornati di Brescia." *RA* 22 (1924): 281–287; 337–340

Il nobile collegio dei giudici di Brescia e la sua matricola dal 1342 al 1796." *RA* 24 (1926): 485–493

La nobiltà bresciana nel periodo delle signorie e la famiglia Cavaleri. Brescia: F. Apollonio, 1942

"Per la storia dei Conti Gambara di Brescia." *RA* 23 (1925): 307–314; 370–374; 398–404

Una celebre famiglia lombarda. I Conti di Martinengo. Studi e ricerche genealogiche. Brescia: Geroldi, 1929

"Gli Ugoni di Brescia." *RA* 18 (1920): 127–132; 299–302; 324–327; 371–377; 19 (1921): 63–69; 137–143; 183–188

Gullino, G. "Considerazioni sull'evoluzione del sistema fiscale veneto tra il XVI e il XVIII secolo." In *Il sistema fiscale veneto.* Edited by G. Borelli, P. Lanaro, and F. Vecchiato. Verona: Libreria Universitario Editrice, 1982, pp. 59–91

"Nobili di terraferma e patrizi veneziani di fronte al sistema fiscale della campagna, nell'ultimo secolo della Repubblica." In *Atti del convegno Venezia e la terraferma attraverso le relationi dei rettori*. Edited by A. Tagliaferri. Milan: Giuffrè, 1981, pp. 203–225

I Pisani Dal Banco e Moretta. Rome: Istituto Storico Italiano per l'Età Moderna e Contemporanea, 1984

Hale, J. R., ed. *Renaissance Venice*. London: Faber and Faber, 1973

Hay, D. and J. Law. *Italy in the Age of the Renaissance, 1380–1530*. London: Longmans, 1989

Hughs, D. O. "From Brideprice to Dowry." *Journal of Family History* 3 (1979): 262–296

Jensen, D. *Reformation Europe*. Lexington, MA: D. C. Heath, 1981

Jones, P. "Economia e società nell'Italia medioevale: la leggenda della borghesia." In *Storia d'Italia. Annali I. Dal feudalesimo al capitalismo*. Turin: Giulio Einaudi, 1978, pp. 187–372

Kent, F. *Household and Lineage in Renaissance Florence: The Family Life of the Capponi, Ginori, and Rucellai*. Princeton, NJ: Princeton University Press, 1977

Kirshner, J. "Between Nature and Culture: An Opinion of Baldus of Perugia on Venetian Citizenship as Second Nature." *The Journal of Medieval and Renaissance Studies* 9 (1979): 179–208

"*Civitas sibi faciat civem*: Bartolus of Sassoferrato's Doctrine on the Making of a Citizen." *Speculum* 48 (1973): 694–713

Kirshner, J. and A. Molho. "The Dowry Fund and the Marriage Market in Early *Quattrocento* Florence." *The Journal of Modern History* 50 (1978): 403–438

Knapton, M. "Cenni sulle strutture fiscali nel Bresciano nella prima metà del Settecento." In *La società bresciana e l'opera di Giacomo Ceruti*. Edited by M. Pegrari. Brescia: Comune di Brescia, Tipografia Mario Squassina, 1987, pp. 53–104

"Il fisco nello stato veneziano di Terraferma tra '300 e '500. La politica delle entrate." In *Il sistema fiscale veneto*. Edited by G. Borelli, P. Lanaro, and F. Vecchiato. Verona: Libreria Universitario Editrice, 1982, pp. 15–57

"L'organizzazione fiscale di base nello stato veneziano: estimi e obblighi fiscali a Lisiera fra '500 e '600." In *Lisiera. Immagini, documenti e problemi per la storia e cultura di una communità veneta. Strutture, congiunture, episodi*. Edited by C. Povolo. Vicenza: Parrocchia di Lisiera, 1981, pp. 377–418

"I rapporti fiscali tra Venezia e la terraferma: il caso padovano nel secondo '400." *Archivio Veneto* 117(1981): 5–65

"Il Territorio vicentino nello stato veneto del '500 e primo '600: nuovi equilibri politici e fiscali." *Dentro lo "stado italico."* Edited by G. Cracco and M. Knapton. Trent: Gruppo Culturale Civis, 1984, pp. 33–115

Koenigsberger, H. G. and G. L. Mosse. *Europe in the Sixteenth Century*. London: Longmans, 1968

Lanaro Sartori, P. "L'attività di prestito dei Monti di Pietà in Terraferma veneta: legalità e illeciti tra Quattrocento e primo Seicento." *Studi Storici Luigi Simeoni* 33 (1983): 161–189

"L'esenzione fiscale a Verona nel '400 e nel '500. Un momento di scontro tra ceto dirigente e ceti subalterni." In *Il sistema fiscale veneto.* Edited by G. Borelli, P. Lanaro, and F. Vecchiato. Verona: Libreria Universitario Editrice, 1982, pp. 189–215

"Gli scrittori veneti d'agraria del Cinquecento e del primo Seicento tra realtà e utopia." In *Atti del Convegno Venezia e la Terraferma.* Edited by A. Tagliaferri. Udine: Del Bianco, 1984, pp. 261–310

"Introduzione storica." *Podestaria e capitanato di Crema, provveditorato di Orzinuovi, provveditorato di Asola.* Vol. XIII of *RV.* Edited by A. Tagliaferri. Milan: Giuffrè, 1979, pp. xv–lii

"Il mondo contadino nel '500: ceti e famiglie nelle campagne veronesi." In *Uomini e civiltà agraria in territorio veronese dall'alto medioevo al secolo XX.* Edited by G. Borelli. 2 vols., vol. I. Verona: Grafiche Fiorini, 1982, pp. 309–344

Lane, F. *Andrea Barbarigo. Merchant of Venice, 1418–1449.* Baltimore: The Johns Hopkins University Press, 1944

Venice and History. The Collected Papers of Frederick C. Lane. Baltimore: The Johns Hopkins University Press, 1966

Venice. A Maritime Republic. Baltimore: The Johns Hopkins University Press, 1973; Italian translation: *Storia di Venezia.* Turin: Giulio Einaudi, 1978

Law, J. "*Super differentiis agitatis Venetiis inter districtuales et civitatem:* Venezia, Verona e il contado nel '400." *Archivio Veneto,* 5th series 116 (1981): 5–32.

"Venice and the 'Closing' of the Veronese Constitution in 1405." *Studi Veneziani,* N.S. 1 (1977): 69–103

Lechi, F. *Le dimore bresciane in cinque secoli di storia.* 8 vols. Brescia: Edizioni di storia bresciana, 1973–1989

Litchfield, R. Burr. *Emergence of a Bureaucracy. The Florentine Patricians, 1530–1790.* Princeton: Princeton University Press, 1986

"Ufficiali e uffici a Firenze sotto il granducato mediceo." In *Potere e società negli stati regionali italiani del '500 e '600.* Edited by E. Fasano Guarini. Bologna: Il Mulino, 1978, pp. 133–151

Macadam, A. *Blue Guide. Northern Italy From the Alps to Rome.* Eighth Edition. London: A. & C. Black; reprint edition. New York: W. W. Norton, 1985, pp. 198–204

Malanima, P. "Città e campagne nell'economia Lombarda del Seicento. Qualche considerazione." *Società e Storia* 16(1982): 351–365

Mallett, M. E. and J. R. Hale. *The Military Organization of the Renaissance State.* London and New York: Cambridge University Press, 1984

Manaresi, C. "I nobili della Bresciana descritti nel Codice Malatestiano 42 di Fano." *CAB* 129 (1930): 271–421

Maranini, G. *La costituzione di Venezia*. Reprint edition. 2 vols. Florence: La Nuova Italia, 1974

Maresca, G. "La nobiltà bresciana." *RA* 30 (1932): 221–229

Marrara, D. *Riseduti e nobiltà. Profilo storico-istitutionale di un'oligarchia toscana nei secoli XVI–XVIII*. Pisa: Pacini. Biblioteca del Bollettino storico Pisano, 1976

Martines, L. *The Social World of the Florentine Humanists, 1390–1460*. Princeton, NJ: Princeton University Press, 1963

Martini, A. *Manuale di metrologia ossia misure, pesi e monete*. Turin: Ermanno Loescher, 1883

Mazzoldi, L. "Un aspetto singolare della devozione di Brescia alla Serenissima." *CAB* 165(1966): 261–281

"L'economia dei secoli XVII e XVIII." *Storia di Brescia*. Edited by G. Treccani degli Alfieri. vol. III. Brescia: Morcelliana, 1963, pp. 127–145

"Gli ultimi secoli del dominio veneto." *Storia di Brescia*. Edited by G. Treccani degli Alfieri. vol. III. Brescia: Morcelliana, 1963, pp. 3–124

Meli, E. "Liutai e organari." In *Storia di Brescia*. Edited by G. Treccani degli Alfieri. Vol. III. Brescia: Morcelliana, 1964, pp. 894–908

Menniti Ippolito, A. "La dedizione di Brescia a Milano (1421) e a Venezia (1427): Città suddite e distretto nello stato regionale." In *Stato, società e giustizia nella Repubblica veneta (secoli xv–xviii)*. Edited by G. Cozzi. Vol. II. Rome: Jouvence, 1985, pp. 49–54

Molesti, R. "Il problema del commercio dei grani nell'economia veneta del '700." *Studi Economici e Sociali* 7 (1972): 165–174

Molinelli, R. *Un'oligarchia locale nell'età moderna*. Urbino: Argalia, 1976

Molmenti, P. *I banditi della Repubblica veneta*. Florence: R. Bemporad and Figlio, 1898

Monti della Corte, A. *Le famiglie del patriziato bresciano*. Brescia: Geroldi, 1960

Fonti araldiche e blasoniche bresciane. Il registro veneto dei nobili detti rurali od agresti estimati nel territorio bresciano tra il 1426 e il 1498. Brescia: Geroldi, 1962

"Il registro veneto dei nobili estimati nel territorio bresciano tra il 1426 e il 1498." *CAB* 159 (1960): 165–274

Mozzarelli, C. "Il sistema patrizio." *Patriziati e aristocrazie nobiliari*. Edited by C. Mozzarelli and P. Schiera. Trent: Libera Università degli Studi di Trento, 1978, pp. 52–77

"Stato, patriziato e organizzazione della società nell'Italia moderna." *Annali dell'Istituto Storico Italo-germanico in Trento* 2 (1976): 421–512

"Strutture sociali e formazioni statuali a Milano e Napoli tra '500 e '700." *Società e Storia* 3 (1978): 431–463

Odorici, F. *Storie bresciane*. 11 vols. Brescia: Pietro di Lor Gilberti, 1853–1859

Ornaghi, L. "'Crisi' del centro statale e 'disseminazione' di centri politici. Note su un indice di trasformazione dello Stato moderno." *Quaderni sardi di storia* 4 (July 1983–June 1984): 43–55

Panazza, G. "Il volto storico di Brescia fino al secolo XIX." *Storia di Brescia.* Edited by G. Treccani degli Alfieri. Vol. III. Brescia: Morcelliana, 1964, pp. 1,059–1,148

Parzani, D. "Il territorio di Brescia intorno alla metà del Quattrocento." *Studi Bresciani* 12 (1983): 49–75

Pasero, C. "Dati statistici e notizie intorno al movimento della popolazione bresciana durante il dominio veneto (1426–1797)." *Archivio Storico Lombardo* 9 (1961)1: 71–97

"Il dominio veneto fino all'incendio della loggia (1426–1575)." *Storia di Brescia.* Edited by G. Treccani degli Alfieri. Vol. II. Brescia: Morcelliana, 1963, pp. 3–396

Francia, Spagna, Impero a Brescia, 1509–1516. Brescia: Geroldi, 1958

"Introduzione." Da Lezze. *Il catastico bresciano di Giovanni Da Lezze 1609–10.* Vol. I, pp. 7–90

"Notizie sul sacro monte delle biade di Brescia e sugli istituti di beneficenza bresciani durante il secolo XVI." *Atti e memorie del III congresso storico lombardo.* Milan: Giuffrè, 1939, pp. 381–406

La participazione bresciana alla guerra di Cipro e Lepanto. Brescia: Geroldi, 1954

Pegrari, M., ed. *Agostino Gallo nella cultura del Cinquecento.* Brescia: Tipografia Artigiana, 1988

"L'anima e la tasca. Etica economica e bisogni reali nelle attività del Monte di Pietà e del Monte Nuovo nei secoli XV–XVII." *Piazza della Loggia. Una secolare vicenda al centro della storia urbana e civile di Brescia.* Edited by I. Gianfranceschi. Brescia: Grafico edizioni, 1986, pp. 203–229

"Il bisogno e l'abbondanza. Considerazioni preliminari sulla società bresciana tra XVII e XVIII secolo." In *La società bresciana e l'opera di Giacomo Ceruti.* Edited by M. Pegrari. Brescia: Comune di Brescia, Tipografia Mario Squassina, 1987, pp. 137–161

"I giochi del potere. Presenza e incidenza del patriziato nella società bresciana del Cinquecento." *Arte, economia, cultura e religione nella Brescia del XVI secolo.* Edited by M. Pegrari. Brescia: Società Editrice Vannini, 1988, pp. 219–237

"L'immagine e la realtà. Attività di credito e vicende dei Monti di Pietà bresciani (secoli XV–XIX)". In *Per il quinto centenario del Monte di Pietà di Brescia (1489–1989).* Edited by D. Montanari. Brescia: Officina grafica artigiane Travagliato, 1989

Peroni, V. *Biblioteca bresciana.* 3 vols. Bologna: Forni Editore, 1818

Pertile, A. *Storia del diritto Italiano dalla caduta dell'Impero Romano alla codificazione.* 6 vols. Padua: Tipografico alla minerva dei Fratelli Salmin, 1873–1887

Pino Branca, A. "Il comune di Padova sotto la Dominante nel secolo XV (rapporti amministrativi e finanziari)." *Atti dell'Istituto Veneto* 93 (1933–1934): 325–390; 879–940; 1,249–1,323

Politi, G. *Aristocrazia e potere politico nella Cremona di Filippo II.* Milan: Sugar Co., 1976

"I dubbi dello sviluppo. Rilevanza e ruolo del mondo rurale in alcune opere recenti (secoli XV e XVII)." *Società e Storia* 16(1982): 367–389

Porqueddu, C. "Le origini delle istituzioni 'provinciali' nel principato di Pavia." In *Annali di Storia Pavese* 2–3 (1980): 9–36

Povolo, C. "Aspetti e problemi dell'amministrazione della giustizia penale nella Repubblica di Venezia. Secoli XVI–XVII." In *Stato, società e giustizia nella Repubblica veneta (secoli xv–xviii)*. Edited by G. Cozzi. Vol. I. Rome: Jouvence, 1981, pp. 153–258

"Crimine e giustizia a Vicenza. Secoli XVI–XVII. Fonti e problematiche per l'approfondimento di una ricerca sui rapporti politico-giudiziari tra Venezia e la Terraferma." In *Atti del convegno Venezia e la Terraferma.* Edited by A. Tagliaferri. Milan: Giuffrè, 1981, pp. 411–432

"L'evoluzione demografica di un centro urbano del Garda in età moderna: Salò." In *Un lago, una civiltà: il Garda.* Verona: Banca Popolare di Verona, 1983, pp. 235–291

ed. *Lisiera. Immagini, documenti e problemi per la storia e cultura di una comunità veneta. Strutture, congiunture, episodi.* Lisiera: Parocchia, 1981

"Processo contro Paolo Orgiano e altri." *SS* 29 (1988): 321–360

Pullan, B., ed. *Crisis and Change in the Venetian Economy.* London: Methuen and Co. Ltd., 1968

"The Occupations and Investments of the Venetian Nobility in the Middle and Late Sixteenth Century." In *Renaissance Venice.* Edited by J. R. Hale. London: Faber and Faber, 1973, pp. 379–408

Rich and Poor in Renaissance Venice. The Social Foundations of a Catholic State. Oxford: Basil Blackwell, 1971

"Service to the Venetian State: Aspects of Myth and Reality in the Early Seventeenth Century." *Studi Seicenteschi* 5 (1964): 95–148

"Wage-Earners and the Venetian Economy, 1550–1630." In *Crisis and Change in the Venetian Economy.* Edited by B. Pullan. London: Methuen and Co. Ltd, 1968, pp. 146–174

Rapp, R. *Industry and Economic Decline in Seventeenth Century Venice.* Cambridge, MA: Harvard University Press, 1976

Romani, M. "Prestigio, potere e ricchezza nella Brescia di Agostino Gallo (Prime indagini)." In *Agostino Gallo nella cultura del Cinquecento.* Edited by M. Pegrari. Brescia: Tipografia Artigiana, 1988, pp. 109–138

Romano, R. "La storia economica. Dal secolo XIV al Settecento." *Storia d'Italia.* 6 vols., vol. II. Turin: Giulio Einaudi, 1974, pp. 1,813–1,931

"Tra XVI e XVII secolo. Una crisi economica, 1619–1622." *RSI* 74 (1962): 480–531

Tra due crisi: l'Italia del Rinascimento. Turin: Giulio Einaudi, 1971

Rossini, A. "Il territorio bresciano dopo la riconquista del 1516." *Studi Bresciani* 12 (1983): 77–96

Rosso–Mazzinghi, S. ed. *L'uomo e il suo ambiente.* Florence: Sansoni, 1973

Saibene, C. "La Padania." In *I paesaggi umani.* Touring Club Italiano. Milan: Touring Club Italiano, 1977, pp. 52–73

Scalia, B. "Le dinamiche della struttura del Territorio bresciano durante il XVI secolo." *Arte, economia, cultura.* Edited by M. Pegrari, pp. 239–253

"Note sull'agricoltura bresciana nei secoli XV–XVI–XVII attraverso gli estimi." In *Atti del convegno su Camillo Tarello e la storia dell'agricoltura bresciana al tempo della Repubblica veneta.* Brescia: Geroldi, 1979, pp. 123–131

Sella, D. "Crisis and Transformation in Venetian Trade." In *Crisis and Change in the Venetian Economy.* Edited by B. Pullan. London: Methuen and Co. Ltd, 1968, pp. 88–105

L'economia lombarda durante la dominazione spagnola. Bologna: Il Mulino, 1982

"Le industrie europee (1500–1700)." In *Storia economica d'Europa.* Edited by C. Cipolla. Turin: UTET, 1979–80

"The Rise and Fall of the Venetian Woolen Industry." In *Crisis and Change in the Venetian Economy.* Edited by B. Pullan. London: Methuen and Co. Ltd, 1968, pp. 106–126

"Sotto il dominio della Spagna." In *Il Ducato di Milano del 1535 al 1796.* Vol. XI of *Storia d'Italia.* Edited by G. Galasso. Turin: UTET, 1984, pp. 3–148

Sismondi, J-C. *Storia delle repubbliche italiane dei secolo di mezzo.* Capolago: Tipografia E. Libreria Elvetica, 1844–1846

Smith, A. "Il successo sociale e culturale di una famiglia veronese del '500." In *Dentro lo "stado italico."* Edited by G. Cracco and M. Knapton. Trent: Gruppo Culturale Civis, 1984, pp. 139–157

Spreti, V. ed. *Enciclopedia storico-nobiliare italiana.* 6 vols. Milan: Unione Tipografia di Milano, 1931–1941

Stella, A. "La proprietà ecclesiastica nella Repubblica di Venezia dal secolo XV al XVII." *Nuova Rivista Storica* 42 (1958): 50–77

Stone, L. *The Family, Sex and Marriage in England, 1500–1800,* abridged edition. New York: Harper Torchbooks, 1979

Stumpo, E. "I ceti dirigenti in Italia nell'età moderna. Due modelli diversi: nobiltà piemontese e patriziato toscano." In *I ceti dirigenti in Italia in età moderna e contemporanea.* Edited by A. Tagliaferri. Udine: Del Bianco, 1984, pp. 151–197

Tagliaferri, A. ed. *Atti del convegno Venezia e la terraferma attraverso le relazioni dei rettori.* Milan: Giuffrè, 1981

ed. *I ceti dirigenti in Italia in età moderna e contemporanea.* Udine: Del Bianco, 1984

L'economia veronese secondo gli estimi dal 1409 al 1635. Milan: Giuffrè, 1966

"Introduzione." *Podestaria e capitanato di Brescia.* Vol. XI of *RV.* Edited by A. Tagliaferri. Milan: Giuffrè, 1978, pp. xv–xlix

"Introduzione." *Podestaria e capitanato di Vicenza.* Vol. VII of *RV.* Edited by A. Tagliaferri. Milan: Giuffrè, 1976, pp. xv–xxxiv

Per una storia sociale della Repubblica veneta: la rivolta di Arzignano del 1655.
Udine: Del Bianco, 1978

ed. *Relazioni dei rettori veneti in Terraferma (RV).* 14 vols. Milan: Giuffrè, 1973–1979

Touring Club Italiano. *Annuario generale dei comuni e delle frazioni d'Italia.*
Milan: Garzante Editore, 1980–1985

Treccani degli Alfieri, G. ed. *Storia di Brescia.* 4 vols. Brescia: Morcelliana, 1961–1964

Tucci, U. "L'industria del ferro nel settecento. La Val Trompia." In *Ricerche storiche ed economiche in memoria di Corrado Barbagallo.* Edited by L. de Rosa. 2 vols., vol. II. Naples: Edizioni scientifiche italiane, 1970, pp. 419–462

Turri, E. "La fascia prealpina." In *I paesaggi umani.* Edited by the Touring Club Italiano. Milan: Touring Club Italiano, 1977, pp. 36–51

Ulvioni, P. *Il gran castigo di Dio. Carestia ed epidemie a Venezia e nella Terraferma, 1628–1632.* Milan: Franco Angeli, 1989

Varanini, G. M. *Il distretto veronese nel Quattrocento: vicariati del comune di Verona e vicariati privati.* Verona: Fiorini, 1980

"Note sui consigli civici veronese (secoli XIV–XV). In margine ad uno studio di J. E. Law." *Archivio Veneto,* 5th series 112(1979): 5–32

Vecchiato, F. "Il mondo contadino nel Seicento." In *Uomini e civiltà agraria in territorio veronese dall'alto medioevo al secolo XX.* Edited by G. Borelli. Vol. I. Verona: Grafiche Fiorini, 1982, pp. 372–375

Vendramini, F. *Le comunità rurali bellunesi. Secoli XV–XVI.* Belluno: Tarantola, Librario Editore, 1979

Tensioni politiche nella società bellunese della prima metà del '500. Belluno: Tarantola, 1974

Ventura, A. "Aspetti storico economici della villa veneta." *Bollettino del Centro Internazionale di Studi di Architettura Andrea Palladio* 11 (1969): 65–77

"Considerazioni sull'agricoltura veneta e sulla accumulazione originaria del capitale nei secoli XVI e XVII." *SS* 9 (1968): 674–722

"Il dominio di Venezia nel Quattrocento." In *Florence and Venice: Comparisons and Relations.* 2 vols., vol. I. Florence: La Nuova Italia, 1979, pp. 167–190

"Introduzione." In *Dentro lo "stado italico."* Edited by G. Cracco and M. Knapton. Trent: Gruppo Culturale Civis, 1984, pp. 5–15

Nobiltà e popolo nella società veneta del '400 e '500. Bari: Laterza, 1964

Vezzoli, G. "L'oreficeria dei secoli XVII e XVIII." In *Storia di Brescia.* Edited by G. Treccani degli Alfieri. Vol. III. Brescia: Morcelliana, 1964, pp. 762–776

Vigo, G. "Alle origini dello stato moderno: fiscalità e classi sociali nella Lombardia di Filippo II." In *Studi in Memoria di Mario Abrate.* 2 vols., vol. II. Turin: Università di Torino, 1986, pp. 765–775

Fisco e società nella Lombardia del Cinquecento. Bologna: Il Mulino, 1979

"Solidarietà e conflitti sociali nella Lombardia Spagnola." In *I ceti dirigenti in Italia in età moderna e contemporanea*. Edited by A. Tagliaferri. Udine: Del Bianco, 1984, pp. 247–258

Vismara, G. "Il patriziato milanese nel Cinque-Seicento." In *Potere e società negli stati regionali italiani del '500 e '600*. Edited by E. Fasano Guarini. Bologna: Il Mulino, 1978, pp. 7–47

Von Schullern-Schrattenhofen, E. "Cenni sulla nobile famiglia Maggi di Brescia." *RA* 26 (1928): 241–249

"La nobile famiglia bresciana Calini di Calino." *RA* 25 (1927): 243–257

"La nobile famiglia Caprioli di Brescia." *RA* 26 (1928): 3–8

Waquet, J. *Le Grande-Duché de Toscane sous les Derniers Médicis*. Rome: Ecole Française de Rome, 1990

Woolf, S. J. "The Problem of Representation in the Post-Renaissance Venetian State." In *Liber Memorialis Antonio Era. Studies presented to the International Commission for the History of Representative and Parliamentary Institutions*. Vol. XXVI. New York: Unesco, 1961 and 1963, pp. 67–82

"Venice and the Terraferma: Problems of the Change from Commercial to Landed Activities." In *Crisis and Change in the Venetian Economy*. Edited by B. Pullan. London: Methuen and Co., 1968, pp. 175–203

Zalin, G. "Il mercato granario di Desenzano." *Il Lago di Garda: Storia di una comunità lacunale*. Salò: Ateneo di Salò, 1969, pp. 117–145

"Il mercato granario in Desenzano nei secoli XVI e XVII. Problemi alimentari e politica annonaria nel territorio benacense." In *Atti del convegno su Camillo Tarello e la storia dell'agricoltura bresciana al tempo della Repubblica veneta*. Brescia: Geroldi, 1980, pp. 33–76

"La politica annonaria veneta tra conservazione e libertà (1744–1797)." *Economia e Storia* 2 (1972): 207–229

Zamperetti, S. "Aspetti e problemi delle comunità del Territorio Vicentino durante il XVI secolo nell'ambito dei rapporti città-contado nello stato regionale veneto." In *Lisiera. Immagini, documenti e problemi per la storia e cultura di una communità veneta*. Edited by C. Povolo. Vicenza: Parrocchia di Lisiera, 1981, pp. 503–532

"I 'sinedri dolosi'. La formazione e lo sviluppo dei corpi territorali nello stato regionale veneto tra '500 e '600." *RSI* 99 (1987): 269–320

"Per una storia delle istituzioni rurali nella terraferma veneta: il contado vicentino nei secoli XVI e XVII." In *Stato, società e giustizia nella repubblica veneta (secoli XV–XVIII)*. Edited by G. Cozzi. Vol. II. Rome: Jouvence, 1985, pp. 61–131

"Quadrare il cerchio. Note sulle vicende politiche e sociali a Vicenza negli ultimi decenni del '500." In *I ceti dirigenti in Italia in età moderna e contemporanea*. Edited by A. Tagliaferri. Udine: Del Bianco, 1984, pp. 95–111

Zanelli, A. "Aggravi della città di Brescia dell'anno 1630." *Archivio Storico Lombardo* 61 (1929): 308–316

Delle condizioni interne di Brescia dal 1426 al 1644 e del moto della borghesia contro la nobiltà nel 1644. Brescia: Tipografia Editrice, 1898

"Le condizioni economiche di Brescia nei primi anni del Seicento. A proposito di due recenti pubblicazioni." *Archivio Storico Lombardo,* N.S. 15 (1937): 242–254

"La devozione di Brescia a Venezia e il principio della sua decadenza economica nel secolo XVI." *Archivio Storico Lombardo* 39(1912): 23–100

"L'istruzione pubblica in Brescia nei secoli XVII e XVIII." *CAB* (1896): 23–53

"Una petizione di Brescia al Senato veneto sulle gravezze imposte alla città ed al Territorio." *Archivio Storico Lombardo* 61 (1929): 298–322

Zanetti, D. "Università e classi sociali nella Lombardia Spagnola." In *I ceti dirigenti in Italia in età moderna e contemporanea.* Edited by A. Tagliaferri. Udine: Del Bianco, 1984, pp. 229–246

Zenobi, B. G. *Ceti e potere nella Marca pontificia. Formazione e organizzazione della piccola nobiltà fra '500 e '700.* Bologna: Il Mulino, 1976

Zulian, G. "Privilegi e privilegiati a Brescia al principio del '600." *CAB* 137 (1935): 69–137

INDEX

abbate, 81, 168; *see also* public deputies
Adige River, 15
Agnadello, 18, 197, 225
agriculture, 125, 186; fertility of the plains,
168; grain production, 29; income from,
34–35, 121, 136; as investment, 185;
subsistence crisis in, 30; of the valleys, 168;
see also food provisioning, grain
provisioning
Amelang, James, 118, 223
ancien régime, 4, 73, 181, 227
annexation: Venetian, 13, 51; *see also* city
listings
annona, 87, 172; *see also* food provisioning
Annual Council, 58
antiquity: of family, 96, 99; and political
preeminence, 95
anziano, 21, 22n13, 54, 168
architecture: of Brescia, 22–23; domestic,
103–104
aristocratization, 2–4, 7–9; of Brescian
Council, 52, 59, 62–69
arms industry, 22, 41–45, 61; Venetian
protection of, 42
arti meccaniche, 69, 186, 207
artisans: exclusion from Brescian Council, 62
arti vili, 61–62, 65
Asiago: annexation of, 13
Asola, 28, 187–188
Auditori, 17
Austria: protection against, 15
Averoldi, Lorenzo, 37–38, 41–43
Averoldi family, 84–85, 94, 95; control of
Monte Nuovo, 159
Avogadori, 17, 226
Avogadro family, 24, 54, 56, 67, 89, 114, 141,
174, 182
avvocati, 81, 97; *see also* public deputies
avvocati fiscali, 66, 183–184

Badoer, Piero, 186

Baitelli, Lodovico, 38, 41, 197n1, 206,
216–217
Baitelli family, 84, 86, 94, 96, 99, 115, 117
banishment, 146–147, 153n72; for
embezzlement, 163
Barbarossa, Frederick (Holy Roman
Emperor), 51
Barbisone family, 96, 115, 163
Belluno: annexation of, 13; council of, 69;
reform movement in, 220n71, 221
benemeriti, 54, 56, 59–60, 70, 114, 206, 210,
212; exemptions from taxes, 182; *see also*
citizenship
Berengo, Marino, 3, 4–5, 7, 155
Bergamo, 24; annexation of, 13; grain
provisioning in, 167; wool industry, 39
birth rate, 118
Bocca family, 54
Bona family, 54, 79
borders: of the Bresciano, 24; Venetian
government of, 187n151, 226; of Venetian
state, 18, 191–192
Borelli, Giorgio, 7, 194
Borgondi family, 54
Bornati family, 79
Botero, Giovanni, 28
bravi, 146, 147, 153–154
Brescia: annexation by Venice, 13, 51, 56, 95;
civic nobility of, 60–61; debts of, 162–163,
201–202; distribution of population, 32;
economy in, 202n18; financial crisis in,
200; fortification of, 24; grain provisioning
in, 166–178; as Lombard duchy, 51; maps
of, 20–21; population of, 30–35; rectors in,
15; urban quarters, 19, 34
Brescian Book of Gold, 78
Brescian Council, 51; biannual reforms,
73–75, 77–78, 116–117; citizenship
requirement, 57n26, 58–60; closure of, 198;
composition of, 52–53; consolidation of
power, 58; economic partnerships in, 129;